20 Million New Jobs by 2020

JOBENOMICS™

A PLAN FOR AMERICA

CHUCK VOLLMER

NEWSWIRE PUBLISHING
Imprint of MORGAN JAMES PUBLISHING • NEW YORK

20 Million New Jobs by 2020

A PLAN FOR AMERICA

by **CHUCK VOLLMER**

© 2010 Chuck Vollmer. All rights reserved.

ISBN 978-0-98461-700-5 (paperback)
Library of Congress Control Number: 2010931848

Published by:

NEWSWIRE PUBLISHING
an imprint of Morgan James Publishing
1225 Franklin Ave. Ste 325
Garden City, NY 11530-1693
Toll Free 800-485-4943
www.MorganJamesPublishing.com

Author Photo by
Jim Goodridge

Interior Design by:
Bonnie Bushman
bbushman@bresnan.net

In an effort to support local communities, raise awareness and funds, Morgan James Publishing donates one percent of all book sales for the life of each book to Habitat for Humanity.
Get involved today, visit **www.HelpHabitatForHumanity.org**.

DEDICATION

This book is dedicated to my Lord and my family.

This book is also dedicated to those who selflessly innovate, create, and employ. America abounds with such people, whose concern for others trumps devotion to self.

TABLE OF CONTENTS

LIST OF FIGURES

GLOSSARY OF KEY ABBREVIATIONS, ENTITIES AND TERMS

$B	Billion dollars (10^9 or $1,000,000,000)
$K	Thousand dollars (10^3 or $1,000)
$M	Million dollars (10^6 or $1,000,000)
$T	Trillion dollars (10^{12} or $1,000,000,000,000)
L-	L-shaped recovery assumes that the economy may not recover due to fiscal flaws. Declining L-shaped recovery is a variation that postulates that economic shocks and international crises will inhibit recovery. Square root is a third derivation that theorizes that the economy bottoms, rises, then levels out.
V/U-	V-shaped recovery assumes that after the economy bottoms, it will rebound. U-shaped recovery is a derivation of the V where the economy dwells at the bottom before it recovers.
W-	W-shaped recovery is when the economy rebounds, recovers, bottoms, then recovers again. The Great Depression and 1980s Recessions experienced W-shaped recoveries.
AMT	Alternative Minimum Tax is an alternative set of rules for calculating an income tax
ARRA	American Recovery and Reinvestment Act of 2009 (Obama's $787B stimulus package)
BEA	Bureau of Economic Analysis (a division within the DoC)
BLS	Bureau of Labor Statistics (US government labor fact-finding agency, part of DoL)
BoA	Bank of America (a major TARP recipient and service holder of 20% of US mortgages)
CBO	Congressional Budget Office (Congressional economic and budget analysts)

CDS	Credit Default Swap (a derivative based on insuring against defaults by creditors, a primary factor in the 2008-2009 economic crisis)
CMS	Centers for Medicare & Medicaid Services
Chapter 9	A section of the US Bankruptcy Code that allows a municipality to file for protection from its creditors if it meets certain eligibility criteria
CIA	Central Intelligence Agency (independent US agency for national security intelligence)
Derivative	An exotic financial instrument that is derived from an underlying asset, like a mortgage
DHS	Department of Homeland Security (US executive branch department)
DoC	Department of Commerce (US executive branch department)
DoD	Department of Defense (US executive branch department)
DoE	Department of Energy (US executive branch department)
DoL or USDL	Department of Labor (US executive branch department)
Dow	Dow Jones Industrial Average, DJIA (the world's leading indices of the 30 most powerful US industries)
EU	European Union, an economic and political union of 27 member nations
Eurozone	An economic and monetary union of 16 EU nations that use the euro as legal tender
Fannie Mae	Federal National Mortgage Association (a US GSE, one of the largest buyers of US home mortgages. Freddie Mac was created to ensure Fannie Mae would not have a monopoly)
FDIC	Federal Deposit Insurance Corporation (bank deposit insurer, an independent agency)
Fed	Federal Reserve System (the US central banking system, an independent entity within the federal government)
FEMA	Federal Emergency Management Agency (Division of DHS)
FHA	Federal Housing Administration (government insurance agency for minority and low-income families who could not afford minimum down payments required by private banks)
FHFA	Federal Housing Finance Agency (US government agency that oversees Fannie Mae, Freddie Mac, the 12 Federal Home Loan Banks, and other vital housing agencies)

FHLB	Federal Home Loan Banks (12 federal regional banks that lend to local banks for housing, infrastructure and economic development projects)
FICA	Federal Insurance Contributions Act payroll tax for both employers and employees, to fund Social Security and Medicare
Freddie Mac	Federal Home Loan Mortgage Corporation (a US GSE, one of the largest buyers of US home mortgages)
GAO	Government Accounting Office (investigating arm of Congress)
GDP	Gross Domestic Product (sum of all goods and services produced in the US by Americans)
GNP	Gross National Product (sum of all goods and services produced in the US)
Ginnie Mae	Government National Mortgage Association (a government owned company created to help make affordable housing a reality for low- and moderate-income households)
GoJ	Government of Japan
GSE	Government-Sponsored Enterprise (a group of financial services corporations created by Congress to enhance credit to the agricultural, home finance and education sectors)
HHS	Health and Human Services (US executive branch department)
IMF	International Monetary Fund (organization of 186 countries focused on monetary issues)
IRS	Internal Revenue Service
Jobenomics	The economics of jobs, wealth and revenue creation.
Jobenomics	This book
MBS	Mortgage Backed Security (a derivative based on the value of underlying mortgages, a primary factor in the 2008 sub-prime mortgage crisis)
NAICS	North American Industry Classification System, the standard used by Federal statistical agencies in classifying business establishments
NYSE	New York Stock Exchange
OECD	Organisation for Economic Co-Operation and Development (an international organization of 30 developed countries committed to democracy and the global market economy)
OPEC	Organization of the Petroleum Exporting Countries (comprised mainly of Arab Gulf region countries, Nigeria, Angola, and Venezuela)

Outlays	The amount spent, as opposed to received, by government
OMB	Office of Management and Budget (White House's financial group)
Private debt	Debt held by the private sector, mainly residential and commercial real estate debt, and consumer debt, including credit cards, automotive loans and student loans
Public debt	National debt owed by the US government to US and foreign lenders
Quants	Quantitative analysts who use mathematical risk management models to predict risk
Receipts	The amount collected by government from taxpayers (mainly individuals, corporations, and excise taxes)
REO	Real-estate owned (residential or commercial real estate mortgages owned by a bank or service organization in lieu of foreclosure or in foreclosure)
S&P 500	Index of Standard & Poor's top 500 US publically traded stocks (a bellwether indicator of the health of the US economy)
Stimulus II	The $787B ARRA, also known as the Obama stimulus program (Note: Stimulus I was the original Bush stimulus program)
SIGTARP	Special Inspector General TARP
TARP	Troubled Asset Relief Program (US $699B program created to purchase toxic financial assets, such as mortgage backed securities [MBS] and credit default swaps [CDS])
Treasury	Department of the Treasury (US executive branch department)
USDL	US Department of Labor (DoL)
VAT	Value Added Tax, a form of indirect sales tax paid on products and services at each stage of production or distribution (often referred to as a national sales tax)

OVERVIEW

Executive Summary. *Jobenomics deals with the economics of job, wealth and revenue creation—the substance of which powers the US economy, sustains the American way of life, and secures US national sovereignty.* Jobenomics, *the book, focuses on the employed and jobs creation—the segment of our society that represents America's economic engine. Today, this engine has stalled. The decade of the 2000s lost one million American jobs, whereas the previous three decades averaged approximately 20 million new jobs per decade. If the next decade, the 2010s, generates only marginal jobs growth, the US economy could collapse under the weight of US debt and obligations. The US has several hundred trillions of dollars worth of debt, which it will not be able to pay if its workforce does not grow. In addition to debt, government overhead continues to explode. Out of a total population of 309 million Americans, there are 178 million non-workers, 35 million government employees and contractors, and 96 million in the private sector workforce. This equates to 1 government worker for every 3 workers in the private sector, which decreased by 13% over the last decade. In the non-worker group, there are approximately 300 million payments of welfare, from Social Security to food stamps. Too few are supporting too many. Consequently, the jobenomics team is launching a national* **20 by 20** *campaign to create 20 million new US private sector jobs by 2020.* **20 by 20** *includes initiatives for government, large business, small and self-employed businesses, foreign investment in US businesses, and major emerging technology initiatives. Through jobenomics, Americans will have common cause and resources to create jobs in order to build a more prosperous future.*

Our Challenge. The official unemployment rate is currently 10%, which is largely a subjective statistic that is driving our country in the wrong direction from an economic and policy perspective. From a *Jobenomics* viewpoint, the non-working/working rate is actually closer to 200%. Today, not including civilian contractors who work directly for the government, there are 106 million US private sector workers out of a total US population of 309 million, thereby generating a non-working/working rate of 192%. If the 10 million civilian government contractors (i.e., those who depend on taxpayer dollars for a living) were subtracted from the 106 million, the rate would be 222%.

Said in another way, 96 million private sector workers are charged with producing sufficient wealth and tax revenue to support 213 million non-employed and government employees. While government employees and retirees pay taxes, government salaries and entitlements, such as Social Security and Medicare, offset their net contribution to the tax base.

These 96 million workers are under considerable economic pressure that may be approaching the breaking point, due to growing familial obligations, government overhead, unemployment, underemployment, entitlement programs and welfare expenditures. In addition, this cadre of private sector workers is diminishing rapidly. Over the last decade, their ranks have shrunk by 13%. If this trend continues, there will not be enough workers to support overhead costs, as well as generating a tax base for government operations.

Several hundred million citizens take advantage of some form of government handout, including Social Security, Medicare, Medicaid, unemployment compensation, housing compensation, food stamps, and dozens of other programs. An aging population, lower fertility rates, anti-immigration and anti-business policies are adding additional pressure to the private sector workforce, which is obligated to pay for hundreds of trillions of dollars worth of US debt and financial obligations. The breaking point may already have been reached, as shown in Figure 1.

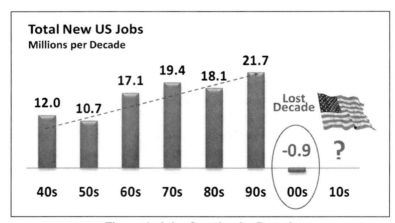

Figure 1: Jobs Creation by Decade

After sixty years of growth in America, jobs creation stopped. The American economic engine lost almost a million private sector jobs in the last decade, compared to gains of nearly 20 million new jobs in each recent decade. Some would say that the lost decade of the 2000s was an anomaly, and that the US economy will naturally right itself over time. *Jobenomics* takes the position that the American economic engine stalled because we turned away from business and self-sufficiency. The possibility of a jobless recovery and chronic US unemployment is disturbingly real. Even optimistic forecasts by our President do not see normal employment rates returning until 2016.

To get our economic engine running again, at a minimum, America needs to create a minimum of 20 million new private sector jobs by 2020 (*20 by 20*). That means that the US economy needs to generate an average of 167,000 new private sector jobs each month. The 1990s generated 181,000 new jobs per month. Adjusted for the differences in total population (228M versus 309M), the 1980s generated an average of 204,000 jobs per month. In the first four months of 2010, not including government hiring, an average of only 39,000 private sector jobs were generated. In May 2010, the economy gained a net 431,000 jobs, largely due to the hiring of 411,000 temporary Census workers. Private employment increased by only 41,000, much less than the 180,000 forecasted. Government hiring may fix the unemployment numbers, but it will eventually harm the economy. Government needs to promote and incentivize the *20 by 20* goal of creating 20 million new private sector jobs.

Our challenge is not with our workforce. Our problem is one of leadership.

The Problem. America is undergoing a stealth employment crisis—yes, employment rather than unemployment, which also is in crisis. Of the two crises, the employment crisis is far more important to resolve.

US private sector employment is collapsing at a greater rate than most people realize. Of the 96 million, 83% are employed with service-providing industries, and 17% are in goods-producing industries (manufacturing 11%, construction 5%, and 1% mining/logging).

The US used to be the greatest manufacturing country on earth. As a percentage of the total population, the total private sector workforce declined 13% in the last decade alone. As a percentage of the total population, US manufacturing has declined 55% in the last three decades. During the 2008-2009 Great Recession, manufacturing lost 5.6 million of the total 8.4 million job losses. Today, less than 4% of all Americans are engaged in manufacturing. These trends cannot continue if the US wants to recover economically and return to prosperity.

From a *Jobenomics* perspective, America needs to begin by changing its negative attitude towards business. At best, Americans have become ambivalent towards business. Business is taken for granted. It is often looked upon as a necessary evil, as opposed to an honorable pursuit. Anti-business sentiment is pervasive with its epicenter emanating from Washington. Anti-business sentiment causes big businesses to be cautious, limit hiring, close operations, and outsource overseas. Anti-business sentiment encourages small business to go out of business, limit hiring, and defer from starting new enterprises. Equally important, anti-business sentiment discourages business investment which is needed to start new businesses and grow existing businesses.

There is an old adage that states there are three ways to make money: (1) by your own hands, (2) by someone else's hands, and (3) by making money-on-money. Over the last three decades, making money-on-money became the first choice of Americans from Wall Street, to Main Street, and even to Washington. Wall Street over-leveraged exotic financial instruments. Main Street over-extended itself by buying oversized homes, investing in the stock markets and 401Ks, and maxing out credit. Washington not only let this happen, but jumped in and became the largest trader of mortgage-backed securities on the global secondary market.

By turning to speculating and investing, America neglected producing and manufacturing. As a result, over the last three decades, America deteriorated from the greatest creditor nation in the world, to the largest debtor nation in the world.

The recent economic crisis serves as a wake-up call. Unfortunately, Americans are turning to government, rather than business, for rescue. Government emphasis is overwhelmingly on the unemployed. To make matters more precarious, anti-business government policies will hasten further decline in private sector employment.

Too few pay for too many. Not counting government and government contract employees, 96 million are employed in the civilian workforce. This workforce is financially responsible for 213 million people who depend on familial, government or retirement income. Historically, families took care of families, but times have changed. Nuclear families no longer represent the dominant American household. Public assistance now often fills the gap.

Our economic engine is struggling to pay for an aging population and the swelling ranks of the unemployed and underemployed. In 2009, the total mandatory (entitlement programs) spending was $2.112 trillion, which exceeded the total collected federal tax revenue of $2.105 trillion. To pay the rest of the bills, like national security, the federal government had to spend $1.5 trillion that it did not have. By 2020, the national debt is projected to be over $20 trillion, but it could go much higher in a slow-growth recovery. In 2010, 48 of 50 states were approaching insolvency. Projections for 2011 and 2012 are not much better, with 46 out of 50 states facing an average budget shortfall of 16.9%. Municipalities and cities are not much better fiscally. Many are considering Chapter 9 bankruptcy.

Public assistance and public service have grown to unsustainable numbers.

- 51 million people receive Social Security payments.
- 45 million are Medicare beneficiaries.
- 59 million receive some form of Medicaid.
- 37 million fall below the poverty level.
- 35 million receive food stamps monthly.
- 35 million work for the government (22 million civilians, 10 million government contractors including postal and census workers, and 3 million in the armed forces).
- 32 million, who did not have health insurance, will be covered in 2010 via the new healthcare reform program.
- 26 million are unemployed (not including 72 million who are off the employment grid).

These numbers equate to several hundred million citizens who annually take some form of federal government payment. State and local governments pay for tens of millions more, like teachers and police, who provide essential services.

Of the 26 million total unemployed, 15 million are "officially" unemployed, and 9 million of these citizens have been unemployed longer than 15 weeks. The number of very long-term unemployed (26 weeks+) almost doubled from 3.7 million in April 2009, to 6.7 million in April 2019. The possibility of chronic US unemployment is disturbingly real.

Several hundred trillion dollars' worth of debt and long-term obligations may soon exceed our ability to pay. Recent US federal government bailouts, stimuli and incentive programs cost over $11 trillion. The US national debt is $13 trillion and is projected to exceed $20 trillion by 2020, with interest payments in the $1 trillion range. Mortgage and consumer debt is $16.5 trillion. Long-term Social Security and Medicare obligations are approximately $100 trillion, but will be bankrupt well before this obligated amount is reached. Corporate and government exposure to exotic financial instruments (derivatives) may be as high as $182 trillion, but nobody knows for sure.

These numbers are so large that they seem surreal. However, they are very real. All these figures were obtained from recent official sources, and are well documented in the following chapters.

The world's richest and wisest man once said that a borrower becomes the lender's slave. He also said that a prudent man sees danger and takes refuge, but the simple keep going and suffer for it. These words are as true today as they were during King Solomon's reign. The tyranny of hundreds of trillions of dollars of debt has altered America's future.

The fact that America has gone from the largest creditor nation to the largest debtor nation over the last three decades is a sobering statistic that reflects how much we have changed. Unfortunately, most people are not aware of the magnitude of our debt and its consequences for future generations. While most people are familiar with the miracle of compound interest (where money makes money on money), few grasp the anathema of compound debt (debt that begets more debt). Albert Einstein considered the principle of compound interest one of the most powerful forces in the universe. He would consider the anathema of compound debt to be equally true.

US federal policymakers have largely turned a blind eye to addressing debt, deficits, spending and job creation issues. This must change. America's future depends on it. US national sovereignty now depends on economic security as much as it does on national security threats from enemies foreign and domestic.

The Solution. The only meaningful way to fix the American economy involves the economics of jobs and revenue creation—jobenomics.

In order to achieve economic security, America needs to create the number of jobs that we did in the 1970s, 1980s and 1990s. The US economy cannot afford another decade of negative jobs growth, as occurred in the 2000s. 20 million new private sector jobs are needed by 2020 (*20 by 20*). Jobenomics is essential to achieve the goal of *20 by 20* in order to preserve our way of life and the American dream.

20 million is the minimum number, since it will provide the number of new jobs required for new workers entering the work force (approximately 16 million) and about half the workers (4 million) who lost their jobs during the Great Recession. 20 million new jobs will produce the tax revenue to keep America's economic engine running. Creating hundreds of thousands of new jobs is not enough. 167,000 new private sector jobs per month are needed to achieve the *20 by 20* goal.

Jobenomics advances the idea of a national **20 by 20** campaign. American innovation, ingenuity and entrepreneurship are the keys to a prosperous future where everyone who wants to work can find a job. 20 million jobs by 2020 is a realistic goal, if American leaders get behind the concept and generate public support for such a campaign. This book outlines a potential structure for such a campaign, as well as a framework for developing an austerity plan in the event that unwanted or unanticipated crises interfere with the jobs creation process.

Americans will respond to a vision, but not to rhetoric. **20 by 20** bumper stickers or lapel pins will not get the job done. Political leaders will have to prioritize their time and efforts on jobs creation with the same unity and intensity that they did averting financial collapse. More importantly, business champions will need to emerge from the private sector to create the next generation of jobs that are applicable to changing demographics, technology and economies.

Creation of enduring, value-added jobs is paramount to a sustained recovery and future prosperity. Spending precious resources on one-time, part-time, and make-work opportunities may reduce suffering, but will not generate the types of professions and careers that are the hallmark of a productive society.

20 by 20 Category	New Jobs (M)
Government	0
Small Business	3
Self-Employed	4
Large Business-Multinational	2
Large & Medium Sized Businesses-Domestic	3
International Corporations and Investors	3
Energy Technology Revolution (ETR) Initiative	5
	20

Figure 2: 20 by 20 Categories

In order to achieve **20 by 20**, policymakers, opinion-leaders and business executives need to divide **20 by 20** into discrete categories, as shown in Figure 2.

- The **20 by 20** goal for government is zero job growth. The US economy has three sectors: government, service-providing industries, and goods-producing industries. The goods-producing sector provides the substantive base of the US economic pyramid. Substantive means being essential, having considerable value and having independent existence. Service-providing industries build upon goods-producing industries. Government exists only because goods-producing and service-providing industries provide the means for the government to function. Considering state budget crises, this goal should be relatively easy, since the bulk of government jobs are in state and local governments. If the federal government imposed a no-growth policy, the total tax burden of government jobs could be reduced.

- The **20 by 20** goal for small, emerging and self-employed is 7 million. This sector is currently under-exploited. With government hiring incentives, low cost loans, tax deductions, and other support, this sector should flourish. The top initiatives in this important category are: incentivizing women-owned businesses, establishing community-based business incubators, developing a national direct-care program, REO private equity/property management initiative, and encouraging business ministries.

Women-owned businesses. From a *Jobenomics* perspective, women are perhaps the greatest untapped asset in America, and should be a key element of the **20 by 20** campaign.

The 2010s is likely to be the decade of women-owned business for the following reasons: (1) the Great Recession has encouraged many women to join the workforce, due to necessity or desire, (2) there are more women in the labor pool, as well as college-educated women who are entering the workforce, (3) male-dominated industries, like construction, are not likely to return to normal until the end of the decade, (4) social norms are changing, allowing greater participation of women in business, (5) many of the future services-related jobs, like elder-care, are likely to dominated by women, (6) women-owned businesses emphasize small, rather than large, businesses that are more likely to grow in the next decade, and (7) most importantly, the rate of employment growth and revenue of women-owned businesses has outpaced the economy and male-dominated businesses for the last three decades.

Today, there are approximately 10 million women-owned businesses that employ 23 million direct and indirect employees, or 22% of the US private sector civilian workforce. 9 million women-owned firms are self-employed businesses without employees. If each women-owned business hires one additional person this decade, 10 million new jobs would be produced. This would equate to 10 million direct jobs—half the **20 by 20** goal. The jobenomics effort intends to help create the conditions that will motivate and incentivize growth of women-owned firms.

Community-based business incubators. Every community in America should have a business incubator that pursues B2B, B2C and B2G opportunities. The focal point of a B2B (business-to-business) incubator is to link emerging businesses with the financial resources of banks, investment funds, private equity funds, and high net-worth individuals. The focus of a B2C (business-to-consumer) incubator is to connect business directly to consumers via the internet, call-centers and telecommuting. The prime focus of a B2G (business-to-government) incubator is to garnish proactive government support for business development and growth.

The biggest contribution that community-based business incubators could facilitate is connecting small business to hospitable investors. Today, venture capital comes at a very high price. Properly structured, community-based business incubators would help reduce startup risk, and subsequently could help reduce the cost of capital, as well as limiting the degree of control that an initial investor has over the emerging business. In addition, community-based business incubators could bundle a number of emerging businesses into a portfolio, and use collective bargaining power to attract capital from venture-capitalists, as well as other traditional and non-traditional sources, such as the day-traders in penny stocks.

Since community-based business incubators' organizations would provide due diligence and validation services, investors might be attracted to their portfolios in significant quantities, especially if the business incubator provided news wire, advertizing, outreach and underwriting services to reduce risk and maximize return.

Community-based business incubators can be structured as either for-profit or not-for-profit entities. The not-for-profit entities could be used for charitable and other tax deductible businesses. The for-profit entities would be used for pure-play commercial pursuits. States and municipalities should consider bonds as a source of startup capital. These bonds could be sold with a guaranteed rate of return to socially-conscious citizens, who believe that jobs creation is a solid investment for their future, as well as the future of their community. State pension funds may be attracted to such an opportunity, which provides a good rate of return, plus potential job opportunities for their pensioners and families.

The jobenomics strategic plan includes community-based business incubators. If the jobenomics concept creates a sufficient groundswell of supporters in the public and private sector, the next logical step is to create a bridging mechanism to link emerging businesses with investment capital at the local level via jobenomics certified and supported business incubators.

Direct-care. In-home and community direct-care positions are projected to increase by several million new jobs, due to an aging population, and the need for in-home or community-assisted living services, as well as in-home child-care services. Today, direct-care jobs are primarily funded through public funds. A national direct-care initiative, designed around a domestic au pair arrangement, could be largely paid by the elderly who need some assistance to retire at home or working families who can't afford child care. Young to middle-aged Americans could be employed to provide direct-care, either on a full-time or part-time basis.

The principal role for government (federal, state and/or local) would be to set up the direct-care program, help train potential caregivers, and provide proper oversight and quality control. Even if an elder-care initiative generated only several hundred thousand jobs, it would help several hundred thousand elderly, and people with disabilities, to live independently and with dignity. An elder-care initiative also would help the families of the elderly, who are often faced with the difficult choice of leaving work to care for an elderly parent, or finding an expensive nursing home. An at-home or community child-care program would be especially valuable to part-time workers who want to supplement their income, or build skills to enter the workforce at a later time.

REO private equity/property management initiative. Due to the glut of homes on the market, banks are repossessing and holding homes at an alarming rate in lieu of foreclosure. These bank-owned properties are called REOs, which stands for real-estate owned. If residential real estate prices continue to fall or the US economy falters, banks may be forced to dump these REOs at bargain prices to speculators. Rather than letting speculators profit, the *Jobenomics* perspective is to create an opportunity for small business.

Real estate and property management communities are comprised of mostly small businesses. If the REOs could be converted into rental properties that are managed by local property management firms, a win-win situation could ensue. First, by converting distressed homes into rentals, the residential real estate market would be more stabilized by renters, rather than leaving the homes vacant until they are eventually sold. Second, home values could be stabilized since property aesthetics would be maintained. Third, shelter would be provided to those who need it. Since the number of rental properties would increase, the price of renting is likely to come down. Fourth, current government energy efficiency incentives would help the construction industry upgrade homes to current energy efficiency standards. A fifth possibility could entail ways for current homeowners to convert in-place to renters. Since the US government is having trouble converting mortgages, it might try converting owners to renters. This would keep families in their homes, and give them an opportunity to repurchase the property in the future.

The place to start a pilot program would be in a city with high foreclosure rates and/or a high percentage of underwater mortgages, such as Las Vegas or Phoenix. If successful, the program could be expanded across the country. Since the residential real estate market is so large ($T), potentially hundreds of thousands of jobs could be created or maintained. A national effort to upgrade residential real estate to energy efficient and green standards would also help the construction and manufacturing industries, thereby adding potentially hundreds of thousands more jobs to domestic industries. Equally important, stabilization of the housing market would eliminate a major distributive force to our economy.

State and municipal government participation could also be valuable, if they worked with the investment community to create REO Private Equity Funds that could be used to acquire, convert, maintain and upgrade properties to 21st century standards. State and municipal pension funds might be interested, since their investments would be collateralized by property that could be underwritten by government. For example, a $250M fund will be able to acquire approximately 500 properties with the average unit price of $500,000, which is the median single family residence price in 80% of the San Diego metro-area. By buying REOs in bulk from the banks, the REO Private Equity Fund could purchase San Diego homes at a 35% discounted price from current listings, which equates to about 60% off of the peak prices in 2005-06. Bulk acquisition is only half the strategy. The other half deals with 100% leasing and property management. The rentals would provide a stable annual income with reasonable returns on investment.

Business ministries. The largest social network in America is the one that is perhaps the least prepared for a jobless recovery. There are 327,000 American churches with a combined membership of over 161 million, and a leadership team (priests and pastors) of almost 400,000. Unfortunately, churches and parishes are unprepared for the tsunami of unemployment that is already upon us. Business ministries are needed to reach within congregations, as well as outside to local communities. While the US church's primary mission is spiritual, it also provides a wide variety of social safety net services, including food pantries, food kitchens and numerous counseling services. It is not uncommon for churches to send missionaries to foreign countries to engage in community development and educational services. Perhaps it is time to employ these skills at home.

If unemployment worsens, churches may be compelled to engage in response to increasing despondency. Given the statistic that hundreds of millions of Americans accept some form of government handout or entitlement program, the need is great. The soaring U1 long-term unemployment rate also indicates that the challenges of the financially downtrodden are likely to increase in the near future. Several decades ago, the church took a rather hard-line approach to the subject of divorce. Now that the American divorce rate is 50%, almost every church has multiple ministries to care for the victims of broken families. In much the same way that mounting divorce rates compelled churches into action, families broken by unemployment, poverty and financial hopelessness should compel churches to develop some form of business ministry, from focus groups, to business incubators, to micro-financing programs.

These five top small, emerging and self-employed initiatives represent only the tip of the iceberg of potential small business initiatives. The jobenomics process and *20 by 20* campaign will identify and publicize on our social network (www.jobenomics. com) new and exciting initiatives as they are discovered. Our social network will also enable thousands of journalists to write about new and exciting ideas and processes. Jobenomics is also part of the Facebook and Twitter networks.

- Large business' *20 by 20* goal is 5 million. The emphasis for large US multinational corporations is on increasing the US expatriate community offshore, as opposed to reshoring jobs back to the US. American business growth is expected to be robust in emerging countries like China and India, and it is important that millions of US expatriate business persons exploit these growth opportunities. *20 by 20* would attempt to create positions for 2 million US expats to work, teach, and train overseas in order to create viable bi-national business opportunities and goodwill. For US non-multinational business, *20 by 20* would attempt to create 3 million new jobs by reciprocal-trade agreements and having the US federal government play a greater role in promoting domestic businesses. Unlike governors and mayors, who play a very active role in promoting business, federal officials are either anti-business or aloof to business. It is amazing that the US federal government would be willing to invest US national treasure in Iraq, and then stand idle while the Iraqis grant oil contracts to countries that opposed US efforts to free their country from totalitarianism and rebuild their economy. The Great Recession and joblessness serve as a wakeup call that the federal government be proactive in promoting and protecting domestic business interests. American business is just as important a part of the diplomatic equation as political largess.

Agriculture and manufacturing are essential elements of our economy. Without food and the means to produce it, the American economy will eventually implode. Much more attention needs to be placed on the 1% of Americans employed in agriculture and the 4% of Americans employed in manufacturing, who are the bedrock of our society. Today, government emphasis is overwhelmingly on growing government jobs and providing more handouts to the unemployed, as opposed to growing critical industries such as these.

- The US should aggressively attract foreign businesses to the US. *Jobenomics* believes that 3 million new US jobs with international corporations in America is a very reasonable *20 by 20* goal. There are ample opportunities in emerging economies to develop subsidiaries in the US. In the 1980s, the Japanese were motivated to build automotive factories (Toyota, Nissan and Honda) in the southeast US in order to build brand and mitigate growing "Buy American" sentiment, which was directly related to the 1982 recession and high American unemployment. In the 2010s, the Chinese, Indians and Indonesians are likely to adopt a similar strategy, and have financial and manufacturing motives to do so. Establishment of assembly, distribution and warehousing operations in economically depressed areas within the US would provide Americans with jobs. The US government should also encourage foreign investment in US businesses, and provide the incentives to do so. After all, the US still has the largest and most vibrant economy on the planet—an economy worthy of foreign investment. Foreign investment programs, like the EB-5 Immigrant Investor Program, are already in place.

- It is imperative that the US take the lead in the energy technology revolution (ETR) that could produce tens of millions of jobs, like the information technology revolution (ITR) and military technology revolution (MTR) did in the 1990s and post-WWII era, respectively. A *20 by 20* goal of 5 million new jobs across the ETR spectrum (renewable energy, to fossil fuels, to exotic new technological breakthroughs, such as batteries and algal biofuels) is not only achievable by 2020, but the failure to do so means that America relinquished these opportunities to other countries.

Jobenomics promotes the principle of self-sufficiency. Individuals need to be more self-sufficient and take control of their own destiny. They can no longer depend on corporations or government to provide jobs. In 2000, there were 1.3 applicants for every job. In 2010, there are 6 applicants for every job. The Information Age and Globalization allows individuals to form small and self-employed businesses as never before in our history. Spooked by stock market volatility, investors are increasingly looking for opportunity with emerging businesses and enterprises. In addition to individuals, *Jobenomics* advocates private sector self-sufficiency and independence from excessive government intervention. The US government needs to reduce its involvement in the US private sector, while increasing its involvement in promotion and protection of the US private sector in the global marketplace.

Jobenomics also promotes the principle of sustainability. Recent US government stimulus programs have been oriented towards big business, state and local government support, and welfare programs. For example, the $787 billion American Recovery and Reinvestment Act of 2009 (ARRA, known as the Obama Stimulus Program) stimulated the economy via purchases by the federal government, payments to state and local governments, one-time payments to individuals and retirees, two-year tax cuts to low and middle income people, and extension of the first-time homebuyer credit. While these programs were worthwhile, they did not focus on sustainable jobs that would endure over time. Providing teachers with one or two more semesters of work was humanitarian, but did not solve the underlying problem of dwindling tax revenues. Providing business the means to flourish will create enduring jobs that produce both wealth and tax revenue on a lasting basis. There is a big difference between providing work and creating enduring jobs. The metaphor of giving a person a fish, as opposed to teaching a person to fish, applies. Make-work and welfare programs are tantamount to giving a person a fish. Enabling innovators and private sector businesses helps people learn how to fish.

Jobenomics anticipates three recovery scenarios (V, W, L)—each with profound implications on job, wealth and revenue creation. A V-shaped recovery is a positive recovery scenario where an economy rebounds after a shock. Eight out of the nine last US recessions resulted in a V-shaped recovery. Our current nascent recovery is V-shaped. A W-shaped recovery, or double dip recession, would be bad for America. Americans experienced a double dip recession during the Carter Era, and a double dip depression during the Great Depression. Today, there are a number of storms on the horizon that could thrust the fragile US economy back into recession. This should not come as a great surprise. Over the last three decades, the American financial system produced a crisis every three to five years. If a series of crises occur simultaneously, an L-shaped recovery could bring the US economy to its knees, or to the brink of collapse as occurred in 2008. *Jobenomics* examines all three scenarios in detail without making a specific prediction on which scenario will transpire. Job creation is important in all three.

Jobenomics advocates economic awareness and understanding. Americans are told their financial system has become so complex, so interconnected, and so global that it is almost impossible to understand. While this may be true, the underlying fundamentals and general relationships are not esoteric. One does not have to understand the complexity of exotic financial instruments to know that they can be dangerous when used for personal gain, or as instruments of national policy. This book incorporates over 150 figures to enhance comprehension. Over 250 footnotes cite source documents and websites, so readers can easily research subject areas and reach their own conclusions.

Jobenomics does not endorse any political party, movement or faction. However, jobenomics does promote job, wealth and revenue creation as a cause célèbre that will attract extensive public attention and debate, and will be a catalyst for a national *20 by 20* campaign to achieve success. The jobenomics team has developed a social network (www.Jobenomics.com) that will help facilitate success, generate public support, and perhaps become a political "third rail."

Jobenomics, this book, is organized into five sections.

- **Employment versus Unemployment**—the cause célèbre.
- **Tyranny of Trillion$: Debtor Nation**—the financial Sword of Damocles.
- **Recovery Scenarios**—the future V-, W-, or L-shaped recovery scenarios.
- **Challenges, Issues and Indicators**—the potential storms on the horizon.
- **The Way Ahead: Job Creation**—the way back to prosperity and economic security.

The first four sections are about the issues facing America, and are consequently data intensive in order to provide an empirical view relatively free of hyperbole. The last section presents *Jobenomics* recommendations for solving these issues.

Since this book captures data at the point of time when the book is published, www.Jobenomics.com will publish updates as new data becomes available and as major events occur. Updated chapters can be downloaded. Our intention is make *Jobenomics*, the book, a living resource document. As America reinvents itself, new *20 by 20* initiatives will evolve and be posted on the jobenomics social network. Innovative ideas need to be shared.

In conclusion, job, wealth and revenue creation is the top priority for America. The tyranny of hundreds of trillions of dollars of debt and obligations will dramatically change America, if we do not produce our way out of it. In addition, numerous potential international and domestic crises could derail our nascent recovery. *Jobenomics* addresses the issues of debt and potential crises as part of the overall strategy to produce jobs, wealth and revenue, whether in good or austere times. In a V-shaped scenario, jobenomics means a more robust recovery and an early return to prosperity. In W- and L-shaped scenarios, jobenomics may be the difference between a financial crisis and a financial collapse. Job, wealth and revenue creation is an antidote to bad fiscal scenarios.

Chuck Vollmer
8 June 2010
Washington DC

EMPLOYMENT VERSUS UNEMPLOYMENT

Chapter 1:

EMPLOYMENT VERSUS UNEMPLOYMENT

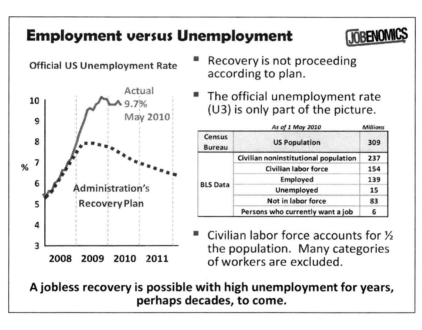

Employment versus Unemployment JOBENOMICS

Official US Unemployment Rate

- Recovery is not proceeding according to plan.

- The official unemployment rate (U3) is only part of the picture.

As of 1 May 2010		Millions
Census Bureau	US Population	309
BLS Data	Civilian noninstitutional population	237
	Civilian labor force	154
	Employed	139
	Unemployed	15
	Not in labor force	83
	Persons who currently want a job	6

- Civilian labor force accounts for ½ the population. Many categories of workers are excluded.

A jobless recovery is possible with high unemployment for years, perhaps decades, to come.

Figure 3: Chapter 1 Summary

Employment, as opposed to unemployment, is the central issue facing future US prosperity. While the unemployed have a higher emotional quotient, the employed provide the staples (wealth and revenue) for individuals, families and government to prosper. Unfortunately, employment is in a stealth crisis that needs to be illuminated and addressed.

Today, America employs 106 million people in the private sector, out of a total population of 309 million. 15 million are officially unemployed. It is the unemployed who get the lion's share of the attention. While caring for the needs of the downtrodden is a moral imperative, facilitating

— 3 —

employment expansion is an economic imperative. Employment expansion also serves the needs of the unemployed. The saying that "the best defense is a good offense" applies. If the ranks of the employed are increased, the numbers of unemployed are likely to decrease significantly as new job opportunities are created, especially if these jobs are added to the base of the socio-economic pyramid, which is most represented by small businesses in the private sector. Increasing government jobs or make-work jobs will not help, since these actions will eventually add to the tax burden of the private sector employed.

As this chapter will address, the official unemployment numbers and rates are subjective statistics that are mostly misunderstood, and frequently misused, by policymakers, opinion-leaders, economists and investors alike. America should focus on the job, wealth and revenue producing elements of our society, at least as much as the unfortunate or dependent elements of society. It is imprudent for government officials to use unemployment statistics as the driving-force in policymaking. By focusing primarily on unemployment statistics, policymakers are trying to steer the ship of state by watching its wake. Unemployment is a symptom caused by the lack of viable employment opportunities, or a lack of willingness to work.

In order for the US to prosper, the focus has to be on those employed in the overall private sector, whose rolls have decreased about 13% in the last decade as a percentage of population. Private sector industry has two components: goods-producing industries and service-providing industries. Of the two, the goods-producing industries secure the base of the US economic pyramid, since they produce tangible goods.

Manufacturing is the primary element of the goods-producing industry. It has been the bulwark of Americana since the industrial revolution. However, this is no longer true. Private sector manufacturing has decreased 55% in the last three decades as a percentage of population, and has decreased from 1/4 to 1/8 of the US economy. Over the same time period, American consumption of foreign manufactured products has increased from 1/10 to 1/3.

Can the US exist without manufacturing? Yes, but America will be subject, to a much greater extent, to the will of foreigners, like the Chinese. Consequently, employment erosion is not only an economic issue, but political and security issues as well.

The key to prosperity depends on creating new jobs. America needs to increase its workforce from 106 million to 126 million by 2020. 20 million new private sector jobs by 2020 is an achievable goal, which is the central subject of jobenomics—the economics of job, wealth and revenue creation.

Something has gone terribly wrong. For the first time since the Great Depression, the US economy lost a million jobs in the private sector over the last decade.

After sixty years of economic growth in America, jobs creation has stopped. It seems that both public and private sector Americans have been so lulled by decades of prosperity that they are lackadaisical about US jobs creation. The economic crisis serves as a wake-up call. Policymakers and opinion-leaders are beginning to talk, but little of significance has been done. Rhetoric is good. Finger-pointing is not productive. Foresight is preferable to hindsight. Action is paramount.

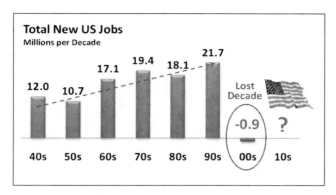

Figure 4: No New Private Sector Jobs in the Last Decade[1]

Figure 4 shows a sobering and terrible story—America experienced a lost decade in the 2000s from an employment perspective. If the economy repeats this performance in the 2010s, the American economy could be seriously damaged or even collapse.

The American economic engine lost almost a million private sector jobs in the last decade, compared to gains of approximately 20 million new jobs in recent decades. Some would assert that the 2000s started with a recession, ended with an economic crisis, and the worst of the storm has passed. Optimists believe that the employment picture will naturally improve as our economic recovery progresses. Others would point out that the 1970s and 1980s each experienced two recessions and continued to create jobs. They would also argue that the US employment crisis could worsen, due to international competition, domestic business malaise, chronic unemployment, and failed government policies. What was lost will be hard to regain in a sluggish economy and less competitive workforce. Many of the 8.4 million jobs lost during the Great Recession (2008-2009) will simply not return as industry has downsized because of international competition, a flagging economy, chronic unemployment, and US anti-business sentiment.

Nobody really knows what the future portends. Everyone is wondering what can be done to start the jobs engine again.

The key to jobs creation begins with understanding the US work force. To start, let's look at the differences between the 1990s and the 2000s—the lost decade. Figure 5 shows the month-by-month difference in jobs growth and losses as recorded by the US Department of Labor (BLS) over the last two decades.

---

1   US Department of Labor, Bureau of Labor Statistics, Payroll Employment, Historical Data, Net Change, Employment, Hours, and Earnings from the Current Employment Statistics survey (National), 8 March 2010, http://data.bls.gov/

| 1990s 21.7 Jobs Growth (Millions) | | | | | | | | | | | |
Jan	Feb	Mar	Apr	May	Jun	Jul	Aug	Sep	Oct	Nov	Dec
1990 342	245	215	40	149	17	-42	-208	-82	-161	-144	-60
1991 -119	-306	-160	-211	-128	87	-47	15	35	12	-58	23
1992 49	-66	50	158	126	60	71	141	35	177	140	211
1993 310	242	-51	309	265	173	295	161	241	277	261	308
1994 268	201	462	353	331	315	363	300	354	207	423	274
1995 321	209	222	162	-16	231	79	271	245	147	148	131
1996 -19	434	263	161	323	278	232	196	220	243	296	167
1997 230	301	312	291	256	253	283	-18	508	339	303	299
1998 270	189	144	277	401	212	119	352	218	193	284	342
1999 121	410	106	376	213	266	291	192	202	408	294	294

| 2000s 0.94 Jobs Lost (Millions) | | | | | | | | | | | |
Jan	Feb	Mar	Apr	May	Jun	Jul	Aug	Sep	Oct	Nov	Dec
2000 249	121	472	286	225	163	-46	3	122	-11	231	138
2001 -16	61	-30	-281	-44	-128	-125	-160	-244	-325	-292	-178
2002 -132	-147	-24	-85	-7	45	-97	-16	-55	126	8	-156
2003 83	-158	-212	-49	-6	-2	25	-42	103	203	18	124
2004 150	43	338	250	310	81	47	121	160	351	64	132
2005 136	240	142	360	169	246	369	195	63	84	334	158
2006 262	326	304	174	31	69	232	141	100	43	201	177
2007 194	104	239	92	149	55	-20	-71	52	86	128	70
2008 -10	-50	-33	-149	-231	-193	-210	-334	-458	-554	-728	-673
2009 -779	-726	-212	-753	-528	-387	-515	-346	-212	-225	-224	64	-109

US Department of Labor, Bureau of Labor Statistics, Payroll Employment - Monthly Changes (Thousands)

Key **Loss** Gain

Figure 5: Employment Growth per Decade [2]

The decade of the 1990s had 17 down-months where employment decreased, and 103 months where employment grew, for an upward percentage total of 86%. The average monthly employment gain (jobs creation) was 180,000 new jobs. Total jobs growth over the entire decade of the 1990s was 21.7 million jobs.

The decade of the 2000s had 51 down-months where employment decreased, and 69 months where employment grew, for an upward percentage total of 57%. The average monthly employment loss was 8,000 jobs. Total job loss over the entire decade of the 2000s was 944,000 jobs.

Regardless of the reasons for the decline in the 2000s, the US economy cannot afford another decade of negative, or slightly positive, jobs growth. Too few are carrying the financial load for too many. In addition, our national debt and annual spending deficits are just too high. Debt and deficits will increase the tax bite on the decreasing few who pay taxes. Jobs creation is essential.

A minimum of 20 million new private sector jobs is needed by 2020. The US produced this number of jobs in each of the previous three decades, and can do it again. 20 million is a minimum number, since it will provide jobs for the 16 million new workers entering the work force this decade, and about half the workers (4 million) who lost their jobs during the Great Recession. This means that American business must produce an average of 167,000 jobs for every month (120) in this decade. The 1990s generated 181,000 new jobs per month. Adjusted for the differences in total population (228M versus 309M), the 1980s generated an average of 204,000 jobs per month. According to the prestigious ADP National Employment Report[3], in the first four months of 2010, an average of only 39,000 private sector jobs were generated (not including government hiring of census workers). Since the BLS includes government hires, their

2   US Department of Labor, Bureau of Labor Statistics, Payroll Employment, Historical Data, Net Change, Employment, Hours, and Earnings from the Current Employment Statistics survey (National), 23 April 2010, http://www.bls.gov/

3   ADP National Employment Report, May 2010 National Employment Report, 3 June 2010, http://www.adpemploymentreport.com/pdf/FINAL_Report_May_10.pdf

numbers are higher. According to the Department of Labor[4], in May 2010, total non-farm payroll employment grew by 431,000, including 411,000 temporary employees hired to work for Census 2010. Private employment increased by only 41,000, much less than the 180,000 forecasted and a far cry from the numbers needed for economy recovery. As addressed throughout this book, employment emphasis must be on the private sector, rather than government, in order to achieve a viable economic recovery.

Understanding the Statistical Picture. It is important to know how the US government generates employment and unemployment statistics, and how these statistics are used, or misused. Most people are familiar with the widely publicized "official unemployment rate" statistic that measures failure. Does it seem odd that we don't have an "official employment rate" statistic that measures the health of the labor force?

The US Department of Labor's Bureau of Labor Statistics (BLS) labor force survey and statistical process provides information about the key elements of the US labor force. Overall the BLS labor force survey and statistical process is an excellent feat of social engineering. Given its importance in today's economic crisis and nascent recovery, its statistical data needs to be interpreted correctly and include all facets of the US workforce.

BLS data is gathered from two primary surveys.

- The Current Employment Statistics (CES)[5] program surveys about 140,000 businesses and government agencies, representing approximately 410,000 individual worksites, in order to provide detailed industry data on employment, hours, and earnings of workers on nonfarm payrolls. Approximately 40% of the establishments surveyed include small businesses. The CES excludes from the labor force persons under 16 years of age, proprietors, self-employed, volunteer workers, farm workers, domestic workers, part-time employees, retired, homemakers, persons confined to institutions such as nursing homes and prisons, persons on active duty in the Armed Forces, those who have no job and are not looking for a job, and those going to school.

- The Current Population Survey (CPS)[6/7] is a monthly survey of 50,000 households conducted by the Bureau of Census for the Bureau of Labor Statistics. The CPS is the primary source of information on the labor force characteristics of the US population. It provides a comprehensive body of data on the labor force, employment, unemployment, persons not in the labor force, hours of work, earnings, and other demographic and labor force characteristics.

The BLS' Current Population Survey (CPS) and Current Employment Statistics (CES) survey take samples of the workforce to build data bases. These data bases go back as much as 50 years. As such, the emphasis 50 years ago was the post-agricultural industrial sector. While

4   Bureau of Labor Statistics, Employment Situation Summary, May 2010, http://www.bls.gov/news.release/empsit.nr0.htm
5   US Department of Labor, Bureau of Labor Statistics, Labor Force Statistics from the Current Population Survey, http://www.bls.gov/ces/
6   US Census Bureau, Current Population Survey (CPS), http://www.census.gov/cps/
7   US Department of Labor, Bureau of Labor Statistics, Labor Force Statistics from the Current Population Survey, http://www.bls.gov/cps/

the CPS and CES have evolved significantly, they are still rooted in the past. For example, the self-employed are not considered a major factor in today's economy, which has become a post-industrial information-based society. To be fair to the BLS and the Census Bureau, they have a number of other data bases that emphasize the employment side of the picture, rather than just the unemployment picture. Unfortunately, policymakers and opinion-leaders tend to stick with indicators, like the "official" U3 rate, that tell only part of the story. Economic recovery will depend more on jobs created, as opposed to jobs lost.

Category	Alternative measures of labor underutilization	Percent (%)
U1	Persons unemployed 15 weeks or longer, as a percent of the civilian labor force	5.8
U2	Job losers and persons who completed temporary jobs, as a percent of the civilian labor force	6
U3	Total unemployed, as a percent of the civilian labor force (official unemployment rate)	9.7
U4	Total unemployed plus discouraged workers, as a percent of the civilian labor force plus discouraged workers	10.3
U5	Total unemployed, plus discouraged workers, plus all other marginally attached workers, as a percent of the civilian labor force plus all marginally attached workers	11
U6	Total unemployed, plus all marginally attached workers, plus total employed part time for economic reasons, as a percent of the civilian labor force plus all marginally attached workers	16.6

Source: US Department of Labor, Bureau of Labor Statistics (June 2010)

Figure 6: Bureau of Labor Statistics' Labor Underutilization Rates[8]

Six alternative measures of labor underutilization are issued on a monthly basis from the CPS. These six labor categories provide visibility into the US unemployment picture. As of May 2010, the unemployment picture is shown in Figure 6.

U3 rate. Other than stock market data and the weather, the "official" US unemployment rate number (technically known as U3) is perhaps the most widely reported number in the media today. The U3 number (Figure 7) drives public policy and private spending.

Currently, 15 million, of a civilian labor force of 154 million Americans, are officially out of work. This equates to a 9.7% U3 rate, as of May 2010. The U3 rate has grown exponentially since the start of the economic crisis, and is at the highest rate since the 1982 recession, which peaked at 10.8%.

U3 rates for major groups are: adult men (10.8%), adult women (8.4%), teenagers above age sixteen (26.4%), whites (8.7%), blacks (16.5%), Hispanics (12.6%) and Asians (7.3%).

---

8   US Department of Labor, Bureau of Labor Statistics, Alternative measures of labor underutilization, Table A-15, 7 June 2010, http://www.bls.gov/news.release/empsit.t15.htm

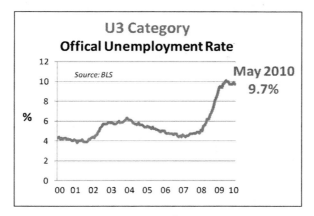

Figure 7: Highest U3 Rate since 1982 [9]

U6 rate. The U6 category calculates total unemployed. In May 2010, the U6 rate was 16.6%. 16.6% of 154 million in the civilian labor force is 25.6 million unemployed, which is significantly higher than the official U3 rate. Recent U6 rates are the highest since the BLS started the U6 category in 1994 (Figure 8).

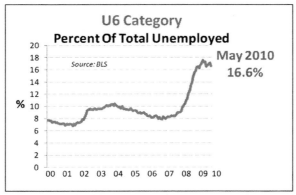

Figure 8: Highest U6 Rate since the BLS Started U6 Category in 1994 [10]

U6 is the sum of U3 (official unemployment rate), plus discouraged workers (U4), plus marginally attached workers (U5), plus total employed part-time for economic reasons. Marginally attached workers are individuals who currently are neither working nor looking for work, but indicate that they want and are available for a job and have looked for work sometime in the recent past. Discouraged workers, a subset of the marginally attached, have given a job-market related reason for not currently looking for a job. Persons employed part time for economic

---

9   Ibid
10   Ibid

reasons are those who want and are available for full-time work, but have had to settle for a part-time schedule.

The U6 rate may be more indicative than the U3 for economic health and recovery perspectives, and should be utilized more by media, opinion-leaders, and policymakers. Marginally attached and discouraged workers make up a large percentage (7.2% or 11 million) of the civilian work-force.

Additional consideration should be given to adding welfare recipients and workers who have permanently given up on job seeking. Perhaps, a new U7 rate would be beneficial to highlight the complete unemployment picture.

A comprehensive unemployment picture is needed to truly understand the future demands on the welfare and unemployment insurance picture. By 2011, 40 states' unemployment funds are projected to be broke, due to the fact that they were unprepared for the current unemployment tsunami.

U1 rate. The long-term unemployment rate (U1) is defined as the percentage of the civilian work force unemployed longer than 15 weeks.

The U1 data does not include a number of important long-term unemployment groups, so the real long-term unemployment rate is significantly higher than the official U1 rate. According to the BLS[11], these groups include:

- Self-employed workers, unpaid family workers, workers in certain not-for-profit organizations, and several other small (primarily seasonal) worker categories.

- Unemployed workers who have exhausted their unemployment insurance benefits, not yet earned benefit rights, or do not file for benefits.

- Disqualified workers whose unemployment is considered to have resulted from their own actions rather than from economic conditions (i.e., discharged workers).

In addition, there are millions of people who are either not-in-the-labor-force or off-the-grid from an accounting perspective. There are a total of 72 million "off-the-grid" people as calculated by this book. This number was determined by the difference between the total US population of 309 million and the BLS' civilian noninstitutional population of 237 million, which includes the civilian labor force (154 million) and the "not in the labor force" (83 million) categories. These numbers will be discussed in greater detail, later in this chapter.

---

11   Bureau of Labor Statistics, Frequently Asked Questions, What do the unemployment insurance (UI) figures measure?, 7 June 2010, http://www.bls.gov/cps/faq.htm#Ques2

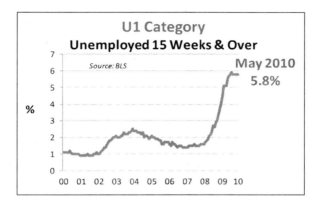

Figure 9: Highest U1 Rate since the Great Depression[12]

Currently, the official U1 rate is 5.8%, or about 9.0 million people, which is the highest rate since the Great Depression (Figure 9).

The number of very long-term unemployed (26 weeks+) has almost doubled from 3.7 million in April 2009, to 6.7 million in April 2010[13]. The possibility of chronic US unemployment is disturbingly real.

The U1 statistic is the most worrisome rate of all BLS labor force underutilization rates. It is the <u>hardcore</u> unemployment rate. Long-term unemployment causes workers to lose skills and confidence. When they tire of looking, welfare is their main option. This is why it is very important to stimulate small business. Small businesses are the mostly likely employers for the long-term unemployed. Many of the millions of workers who were laid off by large companies during the Great Recession of 2008-2009 will remain unemployed even if the overall job market improves. Downsizing, increased productivity, outsourcing and international competition are some of the reasons why these jobs will never return. Unemployment benefits cannot help revive worker skills for jobs that no longer exist.

The U1 statistic is also important from a "nanny state" perspective. Nanny state is a pejorative term used in the sense that the state has to provide for the welfare of the long-term unemployed as a nanny would protect a child. While the vast majority would prefer a job over welfare, there comes a time when an individual becomes so disillusioned, or so accustomed to not working, that the unemployed worker becomes dependent on handouts. As evidenced in depressed areas of major cities, many of these individuals eventually turn to crime or drugs. The downward spiral of hardcore unemployment becomes increasingly expensive from a social-services perspective.

The U1 rate is directly related to the spiraling cost of unemployment benefits. Payments for unemployment benefits in 2009 were more than 2½ times the amount paid in 2008. For Fiscal 2010,

12   US Department of Labor, Bureau of Labor Statistics, Alternative measures of labor underutilization, Table A-15, 7 June 2010, http://www.bls.gov/news.release/empsit.t15.htm
13   US Department of Labor, Bureau of Labor Statistics, Unemployed persons by duration of unemployment, Table A-12, 2 7 May 2010, http://www.bls.gov/news.release/empsit.t12.htm

the cost of unemployment compensation is estimated to exceed $140B, compared to $43 billion in 2008. This includes $60B worth of deficits incurred by the states that no longer can make payments to the unemployed. Congress is considering $100B additional funding to cover core state costs, and provide additional help to the long-term unemployed beyond the core 26-week unemployment insurance package. Also expiring are the COBRA and TANF programs. COBRA (Consolidated Omnibus Budget Reconciliation Act) subsidizes 65% of healthcare insurance to laid-off workers who were formerly covered by employers. TANF (Temporary Assistance for Needy Families) provides temporary assistance until people are reemployed. Potential federal unemployment compensation is likely to reach $250B by the beginning of the government fiscal year 2011.

Chronic Unemployment. Over 11 million Americans get unemployment compensation, with over half receiving payments for more than 26 weeks (6 months). In some high unemployment areas, federal government actions have extended the compensation period to 99 weeks, or almost 2 years. Although a few states require worker contributions, the vast majority of unemployment compensation is funded largely through employer taxes, which puts additional stress on the jobs creation community.

Not including Social Security and Medicare, it is estimated that one out of every three Americans (100 million) currently receive some form of safety net benefit related to long-term unemployment. These safety net programs include unemployment compensation, food stamps, Medicaid, housing assistance, cash programs and other programs for the unemployed, like free cell phones, retraining incentives and educational benefits. The total amount is approaching $500B per year. If long-term unemployment is as chronic as the data suggests, unemployment benefits may evolve from temporary supplemental programs to more permanent entitlements.

In March 2010, a single US Senator (Bunning, R-KY) tried to tie increased unemployment compensation spending to budget cuts in other areas. The outcry from the public was deafening on how he could be so callous to challenge these benefits. Even members of the Senator's own fiscally conservative party did not come to the Senator's aid. The lesson learned by all Washington politicians was that unemployment compensation is such an emotional issue that it might as well be considered an entitlement.

According to the BLS, the number of long-term unemployed over 26 weeks has almost doubled from 3.7 million in April 2009 to 6.7 million in April 2010. The median duration also increased from 11.7 weeks to 21.6 weeks in the same time period, as shown in Figure 10. If this trend continues, it will become a major budget breaker.

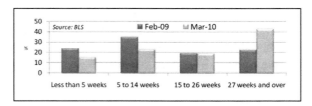

Figure 10: Unemployed Persons by Duration of Unemployment

The people trapped in long-term unemployment are in peril. Quite often the effects are chronic. Many have exhausted unemployment benefits and savings, borrowed from friends and family, sold precious valuables, gone bankrupt, as well as other maladies. Extending social benefits provides no solution without creation of enduring jobs. Today, there are few jobs to be had.

	Jan	Feb	Mar	Apr	May	Jun	Jul	Aug	Sep	Oct	Nov	Dec
2001	1.3	1.3	1.3	1.3	1.3	1.5	1.6	1.6	1.6	1.9	2.1	2.1
2002	2.4	2.5	2.4	2.4	2.2	2.6	2.5	2.4	2.3	2.1	2.2	2.6
2003	2.6	2.7	2.8	2.6	2.7	2.9	2.9	2.7	2.7	2.5	2.5	2.4
2004	2.6	2.5	2.5	2.2	2.1	2.5	2.2	2.1	2.0	1.9	2.2	1.9
2005	2.2	2.2	2.0	1.8	1.9	1.9	1.9	1.8	1.7	1.6	1.6	1.6
2006	1.8	1.8	1.6	1.5	1.4	1.7	1.8	1.6	1.4	1.3	1.4	1.4
2007	1.7	1.6	1.4	1.4	1.4	1.5	1.7	1.5	1.5	1.6	1.5	1.7
2008	2.0	1.9	1.9	1.8	2.0	2.3	2.4	2.6	2.8	2.8	3.1	3.6
2009	4.7	4.8	5.2	5.4	5.6	6.0	6.5	6.1	5.5	5.7	5.9	5.8
2010	5.7	6.0	5.8				Source: BLS JOLTS/Unemployment Reports					

Key 1.0-3.9 4.0-4.9 5.0-5.9 6.0+

Figure 11: One Job per Every Six Applicants[14]

Figure 11 shows the evolution from a low of 1.3 to a high of 6.5 applicants for every job over the last decade. If a 5-fold increase for every job is not bad enough, it is much worse for unskilled workers, who often have to wait literally days in line for an opportunity even to apply for a job. Unless more jobs are created, more and more workers will make the journey from employment, to underemployment, to unemployment, to long-term unemployment, to the obscurity of some nameless entity off-the-grid.

The Size of the US Civilian Work Force. As the old saying goes, the devil is in the details, and this is no exception, regarding US labor force statistics that only account for 50% of the citizens in the US.

	As of 1 May 2010	Millions	
Census Bureau	US Population	309	72M "Off the Grid"
BLS Data	Civilian noninstitutional population	237	
	Civilian labor force	154	
	Employed	139	
	Unemployed	15	9.7% U3 Rate
	Not in the labor force	83	
	Persons who currently want a job	6	

Figure 12: US Population & Labor Force

As shown in Figure 12, the US Census Bureau[15] reports that the total US population is 309 million. The BLS[16] estimates that 237 million are in the civilian noninstitutional population, ages 16 and older, which is the universe for labor force data, from the Census Bureau. This leaves 72 million people off-the-grid from a *Jobenomics* point of view. Furthermore, the BLS reports that there are 83 million "not in the labor force." According to the BLS[17], "not in the labor force includes the

---

14   Bureau of Labor Statistics, Labor Force Statistics from the Current Population Survey, Unemployment Level, Historical Data (http://www.bls.gov/cps/), and Job Openings and Labor Turnover Survey (JOLTS), Latest Job Openings Level, Historical Data (http://www.bls.gov/jlt/), 14 May 2010
15   US Census Bureau, US & World Population Clock, 1 May 2010, http://www.census.gov/main/www/popclock.html
16   Bureau of Labor Statistics, Employment Situation, Household Data, Table A-1, Employment status of the civilian population by sex and age, 1 May 2010, http://www.bls.gov/news.release/empsit.t01.htm
17   Bureau of Labor Statistics, Labor Force Statistics from the Current Population Survey , Frequently Asked Questions, Who is not in the labor force?, and How large is the US labor force?, http://www.bls.gov/cps/faq.

retired, those who have no job and are not looking for one, those going to school (above 16 years of age), and those who have family responsibilities that keep them out of the labor force."

Consequently, according to the BLS, only 154 million citizens, or 50%, are actually in the civilian labor force. Even if one believes that the 83 million "not in the labor force" are truly out of the work force, it does not account for the 72 million that are off-the-grid. The reason that this is important is that many of these citizens in the off-the-grid and "not in the labor force" categories represent a large pool of workers that may eventually want to enter or reenter the labor force.

One of the major areas of off-the-grid personnel includes agriculture, forestry and fishing. The BLS considers these areas as very difficult to quantify and not necessarily worthy of quantification, since "employment in agriculture, forestry, and fishing is projected to have little or no change"[18] in the future. According to the BLS, "most establishments in agriculture, forestry, and fishing are very small. Nearly 78 percent employ fewer than 10 workers. Overall, this industry sector is also unusual in that self-employed and unpaid family workers account for such a high proportion of its workforce."[19] In 2008, agriculture, forestry, and fishing employed a total of 1.3 million wage and salary workers plus an additional 850,600 self-employed and unpaid family workers for a total 2.1 million people, or less than 1% of our population.

Unfortunately for decision-makers, the vast majority of BLS statistics are classified as non-farm statistics. Agricultural employment statistics are also hard to find at the US Department of Agriculture. The USDA's Economic Research Service's data sets stopped updating Farm and Farm-Related Employment in 2002. According the USDA ERS, "these data will no longer be updated or maintained because some of the necessary underlying data are no longer available to ERS."[20] The Secretary of Agriculture makes no mention of overall agriculture or farm employment in his annual Performance and Accountability report.[21]

If the US were truly serious about employment, it would have better understanding of rural America that represents approximately 25% of our population and 95% of our land mass. Instead, policymakers focus on the official U3 unemployment rate that is based on half of our population, and make policy and economic decisions from statistics largely derived from non-farm, non-self-employed, non-military, places of employment.

Of the 154 million in the civilian labor force, the BLS reports that 139 million (90.1%) are reported as employed, and 15 million (9.9%, the BLS U3 rate) are "officially" unemployed. By measuring the "officially unemployed" as a subset of 154 million, versus a much larger number, the official unemployment rate is rather subjective. Given the emphasis that policymakers place on the official U3 unemployment rate, this could lead to poor economic policy decisions.

Leaving ¼ of the US population off-the-grid gives Americans a sense of economic well-being that may not be warranted. For example, as shown in Figure 12, the BLS reports that

---

htm#Ques5

18   Bureau of Labor Statistics, Career Guide to Industries, 2010-11 Edition, Agriculture, Forestry, and Fishing, 7 May 2010, http://www.bls.gov/oco/cg/cgs001.htm

19   Ibid

20   US Department of Agriculture, Economic Research Service, Data Sets, 8 May 2010, http://www.ers.usda.gov/Data/FarmandRelatedEmployment/

21   US Department of Agriculture, 2009 Performance and Accountability Report, 13 November 2009, http://www.ocfo.usda.gov/usdarpt/pdf/FINAL%202k9_USDA_Combined_PAR_11.25.09vF8.pdf

there are only 6 million "persons who currently want a job." The true number is significantly higher. The U6 alone is 26 million, not counting the 72 million unaccounted-for people off-the-grid. When families, pensions, unemployment benefits, and other safety-net programs run out of money, these people will need work or welfare. Said in another way, if the current "official" unemployment rate of 10% is considered dangerous, what would a "realistic" unemployment rate of 17% to 25% do to the economy?

If trillions of dollars of stimuli fail to bring the "official" unemployment rate of 10% down, political heads will roll as the American populous becomes increasingly frustrated. Chronic unemployment rates at 10% or higher would also induce decreased consumption, higher welfare costs, greater mortgage defaults, less investment and greater strain on financial institutions and our nascent economic recovery.

This large number of unaccounted-for poses a big dilemma for policymakers, whose careers increasingly rise and fall on unemployment numbers. If a large percentage of the people who are off-the-grid desire to come back on the grid, the unemployment rates could grow with a growing employment picture. This happened in March 2010, when 130,000 new jobs were added to the workforce after two years of down months. Policymakers expected the unemployment rate to go down, but it remained the same. It happened again in April 2010, when 290,000 new jobs were added to the workforce, and the unemployment rate went up from 9.7% to 9.9%.

The bottom line is that it is time for the US government to get off the slippery slope of gauging success on a rather subjective official unemployment rate that is a backwards-looking statistic. It is time to develop an official employment rate that currently does not exist. The data for this new rate is available and is shown in Figure 13.

Total Private Sector Employment
(Goods-Producing and Services-Providing Industries, Not Including Farm in Millions)

	Jan	Feb	Mar	Apr	May	Jun	Jul	Aug	Sep	Oct	Nov	Dec
2000	108.3	108.5	109.4	110.3	110.9	112.1	112.0	112.1	111.9	112.0	112.2	112.1
2001	109.7	109.9	110.4	110.7	111.4	112.0	111.6	111.6	110.8	110.5	110.1	109.8
2002	107.3	107.4	107.8	108.4	109.1	109.9	109.6	109.6	109.2	109.3	109.3	109.0
2003	106.7	106.7	107.1	107.8	108.6	109.3	109.1	109.2	108.9	109.2	109.2	109.1
2004	106.9	107.1	108.0	109.1	110.1	111.0	110.9	110.9	110.6	111.0	111.1	111.0
2005	108.7	109.1	109.9	111.1	111.9	113.0	113.0	113.2	112.8	113.1	113.5	113.4
2006	111.2	111.7	112.6	113.5	114.3	115.2	115.1	115.3	114.9	115.1	115.3	115.3
2007	113.0	113.2	114.0	114.8	115.7	116.6	116.4	116.4	116.0	116.1	116.3	116.1
2008	113.6	113.6	114.1	114.6	115.2	115.7	115.4	115.2	114.3	114.0	113.2	112.3
2009	109.1	108.4	108.2	108.3	108.7	109.0	108.7	108.5	108.0	108.0	108.0	107.6
2010	105.3	105.3	**106.1**	107.2(P)	107.8(P)					P: preliminary		

Total Government Civilian Employment

	Jan	Feb	Mar	Apr	May	Jun	Jul	Aug	Sep	Oct	Nov	Dec
2000	20.5	20.9	21.1	21.2	21.5	20.9	19.7	19.6	20.5	21.0	21.2	21.2
2001	20.8	21.2	21.3	21.4	21.4	21.1	20.0	20.0	21.1	21.6	21.7	21.7
2002	21.3	21.7	21.8	21.8	21.9	21.5	20.4	20.4	21.4	21.9	22.0	22.0
2003	21.5	21.9	22.0	22.0	22.0	21.6	20.4	20.4	21.3	21.9	22.0	21.9
2004	21.4	21.8	22.0	22.0	22.0	21.5	20.4	20.5	21.5	22.0	22.2	22.1
2005	21.6	22.0	22.1	22.2	22.2	21.7	20.7	20.7	21.7	22.2	22.3	22.2
2006	21.7	22.2	22.3	22.3	22.3	21.9	20.8	20.8	21.9	22.4	22.6	22.5
2007	22.0	22.4	22.6	22.6	22.6	22.2	21.0	21.1	22.1	22.7	22.8	22.7
2008	22.3	22.7	22.8	22.8	22.9	22.5	21.3	21.4	22.4	22.9	23.1	22.9
2009	22.5	22.9	23.0	23.1	23.0	22.6	21.3	21.3	22.3	22.9	23.0	22.8
2010	22.4	22.8	**22.9**	23.0(P)	23.4(P)					P: preliminary		

Source: BLS (Not Seasonally Adjusted Data)

Figure 13: US Employment by Sector [22]

As shown in Figure 13, there are 106.0 million employed in the US private sector, and 22.9 million government employees. The 106 million includes approximately 10 million federal

---

22   US Department of Labor, Bureau of Labor Statistics, Table B-1, Employees on nonfarm payrolls by industry sector and selected industry detail, 1 May 2010, http://www.bls.gov/webapps/legacy/cesbtab1.htm

government contractors, such as defense contractors, postal and census workers, and grantees[23], so the true number is closer to 96 million. However, for simplicity, *Jobenomics* will use the BLS's reference number of 106 million for statistical purposes.

106 million is an important number, since this is the number of private sector workers who don't use taxpayer dollars to pay their salaries. Consequently, if one wanted to generate an "official employment rate," it could be easily achieved by dividing the private sector workforce by the total population. Today, this rate would be 34.3% (106 million/309 million). 34.3% is a more realistic measure of employment health than the 10% unemployment rate number.

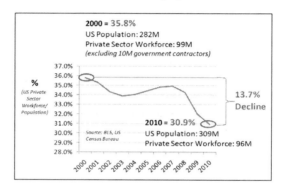

Figure 14: Private Sector Workforce Decline in Last Decade[24]

If we look at what happened to our "official employment rate" over the last decade, we would see a 13% decline (39.4-34.3/39.4) in the private sector workforce, as shown in Figure 14. This graph is particularly enlightening. While the Great Recession of 2008-2009 is responsible for much of this decline, a significant decline happened during the boom years in the early part of the decade. This should not be a surprise, since Americans shifted emphasis from business to making-money-on-money.

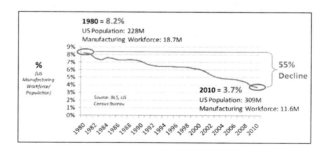

Figure 15: US Manufacturing Decline as Percentage of Population[25]

23 New York University, Robert F. Wagner Graduate School, by Paul C. Light, August 2006, http://wagner.nyu.edu/performance/files/True_Size.pdf
24 US Department of Labor, Bureau of Labor Statistics, Table B-1, Employees on nonfarm payrolls by industry sector and selected industry detail, 1 May 2010, http://www.bls.gov/webapps/legacy/cesbtab1.htm, and US Census Bureau 2010 Statistical Abstract, http://www.census.gov/prod/2009pubs/10statab/pop.pdf
25 US Department of Labor, Bureau of Labor Statistics, Table B-1, Employees on nonfarm payrolls by industry sector and selected industry detail, 1 May 2010, http://www.bls.gov/webapps/legacy/cesbtab1.htm, and US Census

As mentioned earlier, over the last three decades, manufacturing has shrunk from being a dominant economic factor to a relatively minor player in the overall civilian work force. This is depicted in Figure 15, which uses our hypothetical "official employment rate" methodology as related to manufacturing. As shown in Figure 15, the health of manufacturing sector is clearly dire with a 55% decline.

The Administration has a unique opportunity with the 2010 Census to shape a new reporting system that will provide policymakers and citizens with a better employment and jobs creation picture. With more than 1 million people involved in data collection and analysis, the 2010 Census will be the most comprehensive in history. Not only will the Census provide a temporary lowering of the unemployment rate, it will provide the Administration an opportunity to launch a major jobs creation initiative based on more up-to-date employment and demographic data.

Not Going According To Plan. The official U3 unemployment rate is not following the Administration's employment recovery plan. The Administration predicted that unemployment would peak at a little over 8%. It peaked at 10% and stubbornly stays around that level (Figure 16). The U3 came down a little in May 2010 as the federal government added 411,000 part-time workers to the Census rolls. As discussed in the V-shaped recovery chapter, even the most optimistic forecasters now predict that U3 rates might not return to normal until 2015.

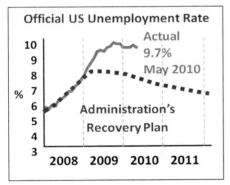

Figure 16: Not Going as Planned

The Washington community's focus is on financial institutions, big corporations and welfare recipients, as opposed to small business, entrepreneurs and innovators. The Administration and Congress are now seeking funds for jobs creation and holding jobs summits. While this is laudable, the amount of funds and attention given to jobs creation is quite meager compared to other priorities.

Jobs creation is largely the responsibility of the private sector. However, Washington has a major role to play. Washington sets the tone for the country. The tone has been largely anti-business and lackadaisical towards jobs creation.

Government has a huge role to play in motivating, strategic planning, national-level initiatives, goal-setting, reporting, awareness, research and development, regulation, and taxation. Most importantly, the US can lighten the bureaucratic load on business—especially small business and the self-employed, who are under-accounted in labor force statistics.

Government jobs creation activities do not require massive amounts of money. After spending $11.6T on bailouts and stimuli, there is not much of an appetite for going deeper in debt, even if more money were available. The largess is largely gone. On the other hand, government has significant sources of funds already embedded in the federal budget. These funds include procurement, R&D, grants, and various operations and maintenance funds. Government funding should only be used for national initiatives with high pay-off potential.

Major US Industry Sectors (Non farm)

Goods Producing	Service Providing	Government
Mining and logging Forestry Oil/Gas/Minerals/Coal	**Trade, transportation and utilities** Wholesale/Retail/Utilities Transportation and Warehousing	**Federal Civilian** US Government Postal
Construction Building (Residential/Nonresidential) Heavy Construction/Civil Engineering	**Information** Publishing Motion Picture and Recording	
Manufacturing - Durable Goods Wood/Minerals/Metals Machinery Computer and Electronics Transportation/Motor vehicles Furniture	Telecommunications/Broadcasting Data Processing/Internet **Financial** Finance and Insurance Real Estate and Leasing	**State** State Government Education
Manufacturing - Non Durable Goods Food/Beverages/Tobacco Textile/Leather/Apparel Paper/Printing Petroleum/Chemicals/Plastics	**Professional and Business Services** **Education and Health Services** **Other** Leisure and Hospitality Repair/Maintenance/Personal services Membership/Association Organizations	**Local** Local Government Education

Source: Bureau of Labor Statistics

Figure 17: Major Industry Employment Sectors

When making decisions on employment and jobs creation, it is essential to start with where the jobs are. According to the BLS[26], the three major US industry categories are goods-producing, service-providing, and government. Within these categories, the major US non-farm industry sectors are shown in Figure 17. Approximately 130 million Americans are employed in these sectors. Today, 112.7 million service-providing industry workers outnumber 18.3 million goods-producing industry workers by over 600%[27].

US Employment Losses By Category
(All Employees Millions)

Year	Goods Producing	Service Providing	Government	Total
Nov-07	22.1	116.0	22.3	**160.4**
Nov-09	18.3	112.7	22.5	**153.5**
	-17%	-3%	1%	-4%

Source: Bureau of Labor Statistics

Figure 18: Employment Losses November 2007 - November 2009[28]

Service-providing industries weathered the Great Recession far better than goods-producing industries. From November 2007 to November 2009, the government work force increased 1%, service-providing industries decreased 3% and goods-producing industries plummeted by 17% (Figure 18).

---

26 US Department of Labor, Bureau of Labor Statistics, Databases, Table B-1, Employees on nonfarm payrolls by industry sector and selected industry detail (seasonally adjusted), 5 December 2009, http://www.bls.gov/webapps/legacy/cesbtab1.htm
27 Ibid
28 Ibid

US Goods-Producing Employment
(All Employees Thousands)

Year	Mining/ Logging	Construc- tion	Manu- facturing	Total
Nov-07	737	7,555	13,780	**22,072**
Nov-09	698	5,960	11,648	**18,306**
	-5%	**-21%**	**-15%**	**-17%**

Source: Bureau of Labor Statistics

Figure 19: Goods-Producing Industry Employment Losses[29]

Construction, manufacturing and mining/logging industries lead the decline in the goods-producing industry sector (Figure 19). About half of recent goods-producing industry lay-offs are due to the residential housing crisis. Given the vast number of foreclosures, the residential real estate market will be in a state of glut for the foreseeable future, and the construction industry may lie idle for quite some time. The same is true for the commercial real estate market.

Government recovery efforts should shift to the service-providing sector that employs 90 million Americans, or 70% of the civilian labor force. It is logical that the government should focus where the biggest employment numbers can be generated. Small business is the biggest portion in the services sector and is the most distressed—especially in the retail and wholesale services sector that employs 20 million.

According to the Department of Labor[30], from 2008 to 2018, service-providing industries are projected to generate almost all of the new jobs. Those with education will prosper. Additionally, the Labor Department forecasts that the top 30 occupations with the largest employment growth overwhelmingly favor healthcare and education services types of jobs. This is to be expected with an aging population and massive healthcare government initiatives. Most of these positions favor traditional female-gender jobs, which have outpaced male jobs, which are predominant in the decaying manufacturing and construction industries.

The Chairman of the Federal Reserve System is dubious about jobs growth. On 7 December 2009, Chairman Bernanke stated the following:[31]

"Though we have begun to see some improvement in economic activity, we still have some way to go before we can be assured that the recovery will be self-sustaining. Also at issue is whether the recovery will be strong enough to create the large number of jobs that will be needed to materially bring down the unemployment rate."

---

29   Ibid
30   Department of Labor, Bureau of Labor Statistics, Databases, Employment Projections – 2008 to 2018, 10 December 2009, http://www.bls.gov/news.release/pdf/ecopro.pdf
31   Federal Reserve, Testimony and Speeches, Speech: Chairman Ben S. Bernanke At the Economic Club of Washington D.C., Washington D.C., 7 December 2009, http://www.federalreserve.gov/newsevents/speech/bernanke20091207a.htm

Since the recession began, the Fed has invested about $6T into banks and big businesses. Considering this historic level of stimuli and bailouts, banks and big businesses should improve. If they don't, the Fed's expenditure of over 2 ½ times America's annual tax revenue would have been a catastrophic mistake. By mentioning "self-sustaining," Bernanke appears to be concerned about how banks, big businesses and the overall economy will fair when stimuli end.

When President Roosevelt withdrew stimuli in the first half of the Great Depression, a nascent recovery ended and America reentered depression. While conditions are vastly different, then and now, Bernanke clearly indicates that jobs creation is paramount. By jobs, he means enduring, high value jobs, not shovel-ready jobs, or make-work jobs, or subsidies to people looking for jobs. As long as banks do not lend, big businesses do not hire, and jobs remain elusive for the 25 million Americans who are unemployed or underemployed, or discouraged workers, America will not recover. A jobless recovery is no recovery.

As evidenced in Europe, long-term unemployment leaves a country's underlying jobless rate permanently higher. The longer people are out of work, the quicker they lose skills, and become discouraged and harder to re-employ.

The stimulus packages were a necessary first step to stabilize the financial industry and a few major iconic manufacturing firms. Now, America needs to shore up the base of the US jobs pyramid (small business), while simultaneously launching national jobs creation initiatives.

American Recovery and Reinvestment Act of 2009 (ARRA). ARRA[32] was enacted by the 111th Congress on 6 January 2009 and is commonly referred to as "the Stimulus Act," "Stimulus II" or the "Obama Stimulus." $787B was allocated to ARRA. ARRA is different from the Troubled Asset Relief Program (TARP), also known as the Emergency Economic Stabilization Act of 2008, or "Bailout Bill" which was enacted 1 October 2008 and allocated $699B.

The introduction to the ARRA Act (HR1) specifically states its objectives:

"An Act: Making supplemental appropriations for job preservation and creation, infrastructure investment, energy efficiency and science, assistance to the unemployed, and State and local fiscal stabilization, for the fiscal year ending September 30, 2009, and for other purposes."

The American Recovery and Reinvestment Act of 2009 created a $787B economic stimulus program. Of the $787B, $288B (37%) is for tax benefits, $275B (35%) is for contracts/grants/loans and $224B (28%) is for entitlements or welfare programs.

As of 1 April 2010, $304B, or 39%, of ARRA funds have been paid out. The most recent financial summary can be found on www.recovery.gov, the official ARRA website. This website was created to foster greater accountability and transparency in the use of funds made available in ARRA. It is an excellent website that provides significant transparency. Due to its transparency, it has also caused controversy, which is a shame, since this is the type of information that Americans need to make informed decisions.

---

32   HR1, The American Recovery and Reinvestment Act of 2009 (ARRA), 6 January 2009, http://frwebgate.access. gpo.gov/cgi-bin/getdoc.cgi?dbname=111_cong_bills&docid=f:h1enr.pdf

The ARRA focus clearly is on government-related social welfare programs and private sector shovel-ready projects. While these are admirable commitments and achievements, ARRA falls short in providing enduring jobs that lead to the creation of more jobs. In addition, as evidenced by Vice President Biden's report, ARRA's emphasis was on short-term jobs as opposed to long-term jobs creation. To be fair, when ARRA was enacted in January 2009, the unemployment rate was 7.6%, up from 5.6% six months earlier.

The states are also using ARRA funding largely for social programs. Nevada is a good example. The BLS[33] ranks Nevada's unemployment rate as one of the worst in the country. At 12.3%, Nevada ranks as 47th. Only the District of Columbia, South Carolina, Rhode Island and Michigan rank worse.

Nevada's Senator Harry Reid, the Act's sponsor, was able to get approximately $1.5B of direct ARRA earmarks for his state, in addition to being able to compete for the overall largess of the remaining portion of the $787B. $1.5B equates to about $500 per Nevada citizen, which is not an unreasonable sum in today's legislative environment. Most of Nevada's earmarks were for social programs in education (37%) and Medicaid (33%). The majority of the funding was in the form of grants. A detailed breakout of funds is listed in Senator Reid's ARRA Resource Guide.[34]

There is a big difference between providing work and creating enduring jobs. The metaphor of giving a person a fish, as opposed to teaching a person to fish, applies. Make-work and welfare programs are tantamount to giving a person a fish. Enabling innovators and small businesses, in the private sector, helps people learn how to fish.

According to the Congressional Budget Office, the ARRA produced about 1 to 4 million jobs. Figure 20 is a chart shown by the CBO Deputy Director to the US Lieutenant Governors Association, and the quote is from a CBO study on the estimated impact of the ARRA on employment and economic output.

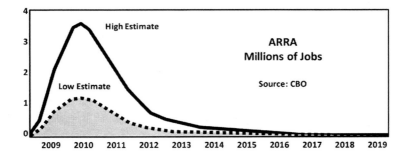

Figure 20: Effect of ARRA on Employment (CBO)[35]

33 Department of Labor, Bureau of Labor Statistics, Local Area Unemployment Statistics: Unemployment Rates for States, November 2009, http://www.bls.gov/web/laumstrk.htm
34 US Senator Harry Reid, ARRA Resource Guide, March 2009, http://reid.senate.gov/issues/upload/reid_arra_guide.pdf
35 Congressional Budget Office, Presentation to the National Lieutenant Governors Association Economic Growth and Employment in the Short Term, Page 7, by Robert A. Sunshine, Deputy Director, 17 March 2010, http://www.

"In sum, CBO estimates that in the fourth quarter of calendar year 2009, ARRA's policies:

- Raised real GDP by between 1.5 percent and 3.5 percent,
- Lowered the unemployment rate by between 0.5 percentage points and 1.1 percentage points,
- Increased the number of people employed by between 1.0 million and 2.1 million, and
- Increased the number of full-time-equivalent jobs by 1.4 million to 3.0 million compared with what those amounts would have been otherwise.

The effects of ARRA on output and employment are expected to increase further in calendar year 2010 but then diminish in 2011 and fade away by the end of 2012."[36]

In May 2010, the CBO[37] updated its figures for the first quarter of 2010 and stated that the ARRA "increased the number of people employed by between 1.2 million and 2.8 million, and increased the number of full-time-equivalent jobs by 1.8 million to 4.1 million compared with what those amounts would have been otherwise." The report also listed the types of activity that the ARRA invested in. These activities include purchases by the federal government, payments to state and local governments, one-time payments to individuals and retirees, two-year tax cuts to low and middle income people, and extension of the first-time homebuyer credit. While these are all worthwhile investments, they tend to be on the welfare side of the equation, rather than producing enduring, value-added jobs.

The number of ARRA-generated jobs estimated by the CBO is higher than the Administration's figures. This is both good and bad. The good news is that more short-term jobs were generated, which increased GDP. The bad news is that this was just temporary, and the effects will evaporate by 2012. The question that remains is, will unemployment go up by 0.7% to 1.5%[38], and will the GDP go down 1.7% to 4.2%[39] after the ARRA stimulus effect is over? Since the vast majority of the stimulus funded temporary jobs and welfare, these negative effects will be felt in 2011 or 2012. The answer is likely yes. This kind of stimuli often gives the economy a sugar-high, but crashes down after the sugar effect wears off. Hopefully, the economy will recover sufficiently to mitigate any downward effects. If the economy falters, or falls back into recession, these numbers will have a compounding effect.

While the ARRA favors the welfare side of the spectrum, historically high unemployment rates and mounting debt are forcing opinion-leaders and decision-makers to pay more attention to the jobs creation side of the equation. There are essentially four levels in the jobs creation equation:

1. Welfare
2. Make-work labor

---

cbo.gov/ftpdocs/113xx/doc11353/3-17-10-NLGA.pdf

36   CBO, Estimated Impact Of The American Recovery And Reinvestment Act On Employment And Economic Output, Oct. 2009 Through Dec. 2009, Page 8, February 2010, http://www.cbo.gov/ftpdocs/110xx/doc11044/02-23-ARRA.pdf

37   CBO, Estimated Impact of the American Recovery and Reinvestment Act on Employment and Economic Output from January 2010 Through March 2010, May 2010, http://www.cbo.gov/ftpdocs/115xx/doc11525/05-25-ARRA.pdf

38   Ibid

39   Ibid

3. Productive labor that directly contributes to a national need
4. Occupations and sectors that beget more jobs

An affluent nation can afford all four categories. A poorer nation cannot. Investing in jobs and individuals that beget jobs makes sense while we have time and resources. At our current spending rate, debt levels may soon become prohibitive.

The issue is enduring, value-added jobs that are sustainable. The US government cannot create sustainable jobs. Fixing bridges, filling potholes, hiring teachers for a semester provide jobs, but these are not sustainable jobs. Once the stimuli end, the jobs are gone. $8000 housing credits and Cash for Clunkers provide a spike that rapidly dissipates when the program ends. While there is merit in jolting the economy or infusing massive amounts of capital to avoid a potential collapse, it does not produce jobs that endure. The government can create temporary jobs, but these will not produce a sustainable economic recovery. What America needs is a policy that rewards states for shrinking welfare and unemployment caseloads, instead of increasing them. States and municipalities should get bonuses (grants, etc.) tied to successful efforts in getting people back to meaningful work.

The major points for Section 1: Employment versus Unemployment (Chapter 1) include:

- America is undergoing a stealth employment crisis.

- America needs to focus on employment, as much or more, than unemployment.

- Unemployment:

  o 2000s lost 1 million jobs, versus 1990s gain of 22 million jobs.

  o Policymaker emphasis on official U3 unemployment rate may not be prudent.

  o Long-term U1 rate is the most serious rate, due to the loss of worker skills and dependency on government welfare.

  o In 2000, there were 1.3 applicants for every job. In 2010, there are 6 applicants for every job.

- Employment:

  o 106 million are in the private sector workforce out of a US population of 309 million. Subtracting government contractors and postal workers, the number is 96 million, which is becoming too small a base to support the tax, welfare and familial overhead.

  o The private sector workforce decreased 13% in the last decade. The manufacturing sector has declined 55% in the last three decades.

  o 23 million are government employees.

  o 83 million are not in the labor force, and another 72 million are off-the-grid.

  o The massive influx of stimulus money has only generated 1-2 million jobs.

- If these trends continue throughout the next decade, the American economic system could be severely damaged or even collapse.

Figure 21: Section 1: Employment versus Unemployment Major Points

TYRANNY OF TRILLION$: DEBTOR NATION

Chapter 2:
AWASH IN DEBT

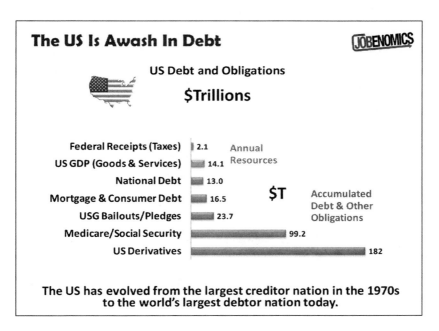

Figure 22: Chapter 2 Summary

The United States is awash in debt. In the last thirty years, America has evolved from the largest creditor nation to the largest debtor nation in history. The *Awash in Debt* chart, shown in Figure 22, presents a macro-economic picture of the US debt and obligation landscape.

Before we explore trillions of dollars worth of total US debt and obligations, it is prudent to understand what a trillion dollars is.

A trillion dollars is a huge amount of money. It is so huge that it is difficult to comprehend. But yet, politicians and opinion-leaders use the term trillions as if it were commonplace. A trillion dollars is not commonplace. The tyranny of hundreds of trillions of dollars of debt and obligations has the power to completely change the course and future of our nation.

A trillion is a million million. 1,000,000 is commonplace. 1,000,000 times 1,000,000 is 1,000,000,000,000. A trillion (T) has twelve zeros. A billion (B) has nine. A million (M) has six. A thousand (K) has three. The symbols T, B, M and K are important, since they will be used throughout the remainder of this book. $T means a trillion dollars. A billion dollars is $B. A million is $M and a thousand is $K. $10Ts refers to tens of trillions of dollars, and $100Ts means hundreds of trillions of dollars.

In order to elucidate $T, several examples make the point.

- Spending $1,000 per minute since the time of Jesus Christ equals a trillion dollars ($T). This calculation is straightforward: 2,000 years x 365 days/year x 24 hours/day x 60 minutes/hour x $1,000 = $1,051,200,000,000 or simply $T.

- End-to-end, a trillion $1 bills is 95 million miles or 4,000 times around the earth or slightly more than the distance between the earth and the sun. This calculation is also straightforward: 1 trillion x ½ foot (the length of a dollar bill) = 500 billion feet. 500B feet divided by 5,280 feet/mile is 94,697,000 miles.

$T may sound simple, but the ramifications are quite profound. 310 million Americans live in the $K-world, or the world of thousands of dollars. 2.6 million Americans (less than 1%) are millionaires. Only 360 Americans are billionaires. None are trillionaires. So when you hear about a $T healthcare system, or $T national security budget, or a $12T national debt, or $85T Medicare obligation, realize that these numbers have profound implications on each American and their future generations.

The simplicity of using the term or symbol $T belies the harshness, severity, or tyranny of the oppressive nature of the hundreds of trillions of dollar worth of debt and obligations that Americans have accumulated.

Federal annual tax receipts were $2.5T in 2008 and have decreased to $2.1T in 2009. State tax revenues (not shown) are approximately $750B annually.

The US GDP is approximately $14.1T annually. GDP is the value of all goods and services produced in America by Americans in a given year.

National (public) debt is currently $13.0T and is projected to rise to over $20T by 2020. The annual interest payment in 2009 was $187B and is projected to grow to $916B by 2020.

Private debt totals $16.5T. Residential real estate debt is $10.5T. Commercial real estate debt is $3.5T. Consumer debt is $2.5T.

The sum total of recent US government stimuli, bailouts, buyouts and incentives was reported to Congress by a senior government official (Special Inspector General of the US government's Troubled Asset Relief Program, SIGTARP) to be as high as $23.7T, but $11.6T appears to be a more verifiable estimate.

The long-range estimates for US entitlement programs are $13.6T for Social Security and $85.6T for Medicare. Since Medicare reserves will be depleted by 2017, it is likely that this number will be much lower.

The US portion of $680T in worldwide derivatives (exotic financial instruments) peaked around $182T. $182T is a highly speculative estimate since derivatives were never regulated or reported by official sources. On the other hand, the devastating collapse of the sub-prime, mortgage-backed securities (a derivative) market almost caused the US financial system to collapse.

Each of these areas is explained, examined and documented in Chapters 3 through 8 of this book. All government-related data was extracted directly from recent US government statistical data bases, including the US Treasury, White House Office of Management and Budget, Congressional Budget Office, Bureau of Labor Statistics, Bureau of Economic Analysis, General Accounting Office, Federal Reserve, Social Security and Medicare Boards of Trustees' reports, and the Federal Deposit Insurance Corporation. Other data, like derivatives and bailout data, were gleaned from reliable sources like *The Wall Street Journal, Bloomberg News* and various economic policy institutes in Washington. Data sources and URLs (website links) are cited in the footnotes.

As one examines this data, one question immediately comes to mind. That question is, who's to blame? Wall Street? Washington? Main Street? The answer is all the above. We all chose to move from a nation of manufacturing and services to a nation of speculators and investors. Wall Street promoted this. Washington supported this. And Main Street jumped on the bandwagon.

Washington turned a blind eye to oversight and regulation while it enjoyed the bounty of increased tax revenues on prosperity. Washington even created the first mortgage-backed securities, and is the largest trader of these types of derivatives in the world. Not to be outdone, Wall Street devised even more exotic financial instruments to leverage underlying assets like homes, commodities, and even credit. Main Street became investors and speculators as well by reducing savings to near zero, buying homes that they could not afford, investing heavily in stocks, and maxing out credit cards.

Americans are victims of prosperity. It changed us. It changed our culture from one of producers to speculators. We adopted a culture and philosophy that emphasized short-term tenets and quick gains. These tenets included:

- Be speculators and investors
- Wealth is the highest good
- Save not, risk a lot
- Plan short-term, not long-term
- Ownership is a right, not a privilege
- Pursue free markets and trade
- Limit regulation and transparency
- Leverage as much as possible
- Credit is better than cash
- Profiteering is not stealing

The ride was great while it lasted. Is the ride over? Maybe, and maybe not. Will it return? Probably not in the near-term. A stable recovery may take a decade, or longer. Some predict never.

The roaring '90s will go the way of the roaring '20s into history. Like the aftermath of the '20s, Americans can rebuild prosperity—one that most likely will be leaner, simpler and perhaps more prosperous in a different sort of way. This assumes that we make an accurate assessment on where we are and plot a new course, starting with the creation of millions of new high-value, enduring jobs. Creating jobs in a potential jobless recovery will not be easy. It will take understanding, foresight, motivation, goal-setting, bipartisanship, consensus and consistency.

The first step to understanding is awareness. Americans need to be painfully aware of the amount of debt that has been accumulated and the consequences of this debt.

The combined total of all debt and obligation categories exceeds hundreds of trillions of dollars, which is unparalleled in the history of America, as well as the world. No nation has ever accumulated this amount of debt. Few nations, on a percentage basis, survive this amount of debt. But the US is not like other nations. We are unique for multiple reasons. However, pride does go before a fall. When facing danger, sober judgment and humility are honorable attributes. Pessimism can be a virtue if it identifies a problem and offers a solution. Our nation does not need optimists as much as it needs pragmatists.

So what does this danger mean for the immediate future? Collapse? No. Change? Yes.

Barring new crises, America's inertia, innovation and abundant wealth should sustain us for the foreseeable future. The ongoing economic crisis has weakened America, but the US is still very resilient. We can handle one emergency at a time, but are much less capable of handling multiple or compound emergencies.

Americans have reason to be concerned about a stable recovery. Massive debt combined with a paralyzed political system is reason enough. In the near-term, we will be less prosperous and less secure than we are accustomed to being. Uncomfortable is the new normal.

In the near-term, the economy is too fragile to undergo massive debt reduction efforts. In addition, there is not enough political will to cut spending. Other than massively increasing taxes, the only other option is to create tens of millions of new, high-value jobs. 20 million new private sector jobs by 2020 is an achievable goal. With the exception of this last decade, where we lost jobs, the previous six decades produced this level of new jobs. If this decade does not produce this level of new jobs, our debt will either collapse the economy or lead to a period of super-inflation.

Chapter 3:

NATIONAL (PUBLIC) DEBT

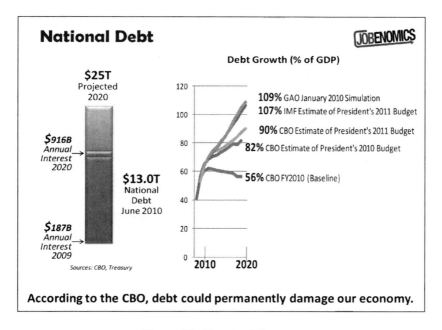

National Debt   JOBENOMICS

Debt Growth (% of GDP)

$25T
Projected
2020

$916B
Annual
Interest
2020

$13.0T
National
Debt
June 2010

$187B
Annual
Interest
2009

Sources: CBO, Treasury

120

100

80

60

40

20

0

109% GAO January 2010 Simulation
107% IMF Estimate of President's 2011 Budget

90% CBO Estimate of President's 2011 Budget
82% CBO Estimate of President's 2010 Budget

56% CBO FY2010 (Baseline)

2010   **2020**

According to the CBO, debt could permanently damage our economy.

Figure 23: Chapter 3 Summary

In dollar terms, US national debt is by far the largest in the world. According to the US Treasury[40], the US National Debt is $13T. National debt is also known as government or public debt as opposed to private debt (mortgages, loans, credit cards, etc.) which adds another $16.5T to US indebtedness.

National debt is presented by the US Treasury as "Debt Held by the Public" and "Intragovernmental Holdings." Debt Held by the Public includes all debt instruments issued by the US Treasury (T-Bills, T-Notes, T-Bonds) that are held by institutions outside the United States

---

40 Treasury Direct, "The Debt to the Penny and Who Holds It", 4 January 2010 and 1 June 2010, http://www. treasurydirect.gov/NP/BPDLogin?application=np

Government, both foreign and domestic. Intragovernmental holdings include funds such as the Social Security Trust Fund.

At the start of 2010, our national debt was $12.3T.

Date	Debt Held by the Public	Intragovernmental Holdings	Total Public Debt Outstanding
01/04/2010	7,803,905,887,172.98	4,486,332,271,084.15	12,290,238,158,257.13

By 1 June 2010, our national debt was $13.0T.

Current	Debt Held by the Public	Intragovernmental Holdings	Total Public Debt Outstanding
06/01/2010	8,572,779,158,729.50	4,478,047,302,157.47	13,050,826,460,886.97

In four months, our national debt increased $761B.

Figure 24: US Treasury's National Debt Clock

US national debt is growing at incredible rates. The debt is increasing at such alarming rates that this book cannot be rewritten fast enough to lock down a stable number. For example, Figure 24 is extracted from the US Treasury website called Treasury Direct which shows the "Debt to the Penny and Who Holds It." On 4 January 2010, the national debt was $12.29T. On 1 June 2010, the national debt was $13.01T—an increase of $761B in 4 months.

	Actual	President's 2011 Budget ($B)										
	2009	2010	2011	2012	2013	2014	2015	2016	2017	2018	2019	2020
Debt Held by the Public	7,545	9,298	10,498	11,472	12,326	13,139	13,988	14,833	15,686	16,535	17,502	18,573
Net Interest	187	188	250	340	434	516	586	652	716	779	844	912

	Actual	CBO Estimate of President's 2011 Budget ($B)										
	2009	2010	2011	2012	2013	2014	2015	2016	2017	2018	2019	2020
Debt Held by the Public	7,545	9,221	10,512	11,579	12,467	13,329	14,256	15,297	16,396	17,553	18,870	20,294
Net Interest	187	209	244	298	365	440	520	596	675	755	834	916

Figure 25: Debt Held by the Public & Net Interest

Both the White House and the US Congress provide budget projections. The Office of Management and Budget (OMB) is the White House budget office, and the bipartisan Congressional Budget Office (CBO) provides financial analysis for Congress. Figure 25 shows the President/OMB's and CBO's budget projections for "Debt Held by the Public." The White House projects Debt Held by the Public at $18.6T by 2020[41], the Congress at $20.3T by 2020[42]. If the intragovernmental holdings projections remain at the current $4.5T level (an optimistic assumption) the total national debt would be approximately **$25T by 2020.**

---

41   The White House, Office of Management and Budget (OMB), Budget of the United States Government, Fiscal Year 2011, http://www.whitehouse.gov/omb/budget/Overview/
42   Congress Of The United States, Congressional Budget Office (CBO), An Analysis of the President's Budgetary Proposals for Fiscal Year 2011, March 2010, http://www.cbo.gov/ftpdocs/112xx/doc11280/03-24-apb.pdf

Figure 25 also shows the President/OMB's and CBO's budget projections for "Net Interest," which is the amount of annual interest payments that the US government has to pay to holders of Treasury securities. By 2020, US annual interest payments are projected at $912B (OMB), and $916B (CBO), almost five times higher than the $187B paid in 2007.

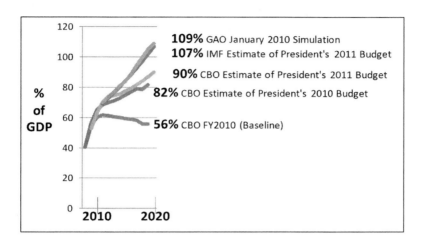

Figure 26: National Debt Growth (% of GDP) between FY2010 and FY2020

In percentage terms, in 2007, the US national debt ranked 61st out of 126 nations[43] with a debt to GDP ratio at 37.5%. GDP is an annual measure of a nation's economic performance, measuring the market value of all goods and services produced within the borders of that country within a given year. Figure 26 shows how much our debt has skyrocketed, from a low of 37.5% to a high estimate of 109%.

In June 2009, a CBO analysis[44] of President Obama's 2010 Budgetary Proposals stated:

"In 2010, the deficit would measure 9.9 percent of GDP, or $1.4 trillion, CBO estimates. The cumulative deficit over the 2010–2019 period would equal $9.1 trillion (5.2 percent of GDP), more than double the cumulative deficit projected under the current-law assumptions embodied in CBO's March baseline. As a result, debt held by the public would rise from 57 percent of GDP in 2009 to **82 percent of GDP by 2019**." (Emphasis added)

In March 2010, a CBO analysis[45] of President Obama's 2011 Budgetary Proposals stated:

"If the President's proposals were enacted, the federal government would record deficits of $1.5 trillion in 2010 and $1.3 trillion in 2011. Those deficits would amount

43   Central Intelligence Agency, The World Factbook, "Country Comparison: Public Debt," 29 November 2009, https://www.cia.gov/library/publications/the-world-factbook/rankorder/2186rank.html#top
44   CBO, "An Analysis of the President's Budgetary Proposals for Fiscal Year 2010," June 2009, http://www.cbo.gov/ftpdocs/102xx/doc10296/06-16-AnalysisPresBudget_forWeb.pdf
45   CBO, "An Analysis of the President's Budgetary Proposals for Fiscal Year 2011", March 2010, http://www.cbo.gov/ftpdocs/112xx/doc11280/03-24-apb.pdf

to 10.3 percent and 8.9 percent of gross domestic product (GDP), respectively....
Under the President's budget, debt held by the public would grow from $7.5 trillion
(53 percent of GDP) at the end of 2009 to $20.3 trillion **(90 percent of GDP) at the
end of 2020.**" (*Emphasis added*)

Within the period from June 2009 to March 2010, the CBO increased national debt
estimates, as a percent of GDP, on President Obama's 2010 and 2011 budgets from a 2010
baseline estimate of 56% to 90%.

Most international organizations believe that the White House/OMB and CBO estimates
are understated. For example, the International Monetary Fund (IMF) estimates that US national
debt will be 107% of US GDP by 2020. The US Government Accountability Office (GAO)
appears to be in agreement with the international community. The GAO is an independent,
nonpartisan, "congressional watchdog" agency that works for Congress and investigates how the
federal government spends taxpayer dollars.

GAO's Long-term Fiscal Outlook[46] is sobering with stark recommendations. As shown in
Figure 27, the GAO's 2020 "Debt Held by the Public" forecast is projected at 109% of US GDP
using its Alternative Fiscal Policy Simulation.

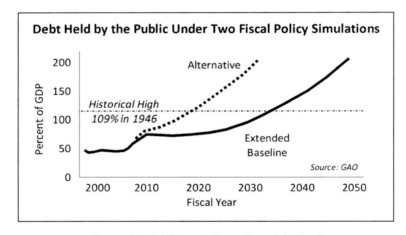

Figure 27: GAO Long-Term Fiscal Outlook

The GAO runs two simulations. "Baseline Extended" follows the CBO's January 2010
baseline estimates for the first 10 years and then holds revenue and spending, other than large
entitlement programs, constant as a share of gross domestic product (GDP). The "Alternative"
simulation is based on historical trends and policy preferences. The historical high for US public
debt was 109% of GDP in 1946, due to the huge fiscal demands of WWII. Under the Alternative
simulation, by 2020, the GAO predicts that the US could quickly pass through this historical

46   GAO, United States Government Accountability Office, The Federal Government's Long-Term Fiscal Outlook
January 2010 Update, http://www.gao.gov/special.pubs/longterm/fed/

high on the way to 200% of GDP around year 2030. The GAO's 2020 prediction is happening 10 years sooner than their simulation showed just 2 years ago.

The GAO's warning[47] is worth quoting:

"GAO's simulations lead to an overarching conclusion: current fiscal policy is unsustainable over the long term. Absent reform of federal retirement and health programs for the elderly—including Social Security, Medicare, and Medicaid—federal budgetary flexibility will become increasingly constrained. Assuming no changes to projected benefits or revenues, spending on these entitlements will drive increasingly large, persistent, and ultimately unsustainable federal deficits and debt as the baby boom generation retires.

Further, there are risks that the federal government's fiscal position could be affected in the future by other factors. The economic recession and the federal government's unprecedented actions intended to stabilize the financial markets and to promote economic recovery have significantly affected the federal government's fiscal condition in recent years, but the ultimate cost of these actions and their impact on the budget will not be known for some time.

Ultimately, addressing the challenges of the future will require looking at the entire range of federal activities. All types of federal spending—that is, for both discretionary and entitlement programs—and tax expenditures will need to be re-examined."

To make matters potentially worse, the GAO, IMF, CBO, and OMB all assume a robust recovery with yearly increases in US GDP. For example, both the President's and CBO's forecasts project robust GDP growth to 6% by 2013. These forecasts also include about $300B annual revenue due to new tax revenue. If the economy stalls for some reason, these assumptions will not be valid. Even more austerely, if the US were to experience a major economic crisis, like a second residential real estate crisis (Chapter 14), or an international crisis, like an Israeli attack on Iranian nuclear sites, the national debt could grow from its projections of $25T in 2020 to a number much higher.

---

47   GAO, United States Government Accountability Office, The Federal Government's Long-Term Fiscal Outlook January 2010 Update, http://www.gao.gov/special.pubs/longterm/fed/

Chapter 4:
PRIVATE (MORTGAGE & CONSUMER) DEBT

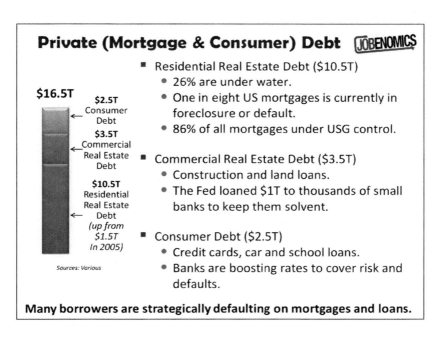

Private (Mortgage & Consumer) Debt JOBENOMICS

$16.5T

$2.5T
←Consumer Debt

$3.5T
←Commercial Real Estate Debt

$10.5T
Residential Real Estate
← Debt
(up from $1.5T In 2005)

Sources: Various

- Residential Real Estate Debt ($10.5T)
  - 26% are under water.
  - One in eight US mortgages is currently in foreclosure or default.
  - 86% of all mortgages under USG control.

- Commercial Real Estate Debt ($3.5T)
  - Construction and land loans.
  - The Fed loaned $1T to thousands of small banks to keep them solvent.

- Consumer Debt ($2.5T)
  - Credit cards, car and school loans.
  - Banks are boosting rates to cover risk and defaults.

Many borrowers are strategically defaulting on mortgages and loans.

Figure 28: Chapter 4 Summary

Private debt (mortgages, loans, credit cards, etc.) is about $16.5T. Residential real estate accounts for the majority of this debt, for a total of $10.5T. Commercial real estate debt is $3.5T and consumer debt $2.5T.

The combined effects of unemployment, a real estate crisis, the recession, low savings, and over-extended lifestyles, have placed great strains on banks and other lending institutions in all three categories.

After an extraordinary infusion of liquidity by the federal government, banks and lending institutions are making money again (along with big bonuses for executives) with relatively few bankruptcies. Unfortunately, most of this money is not reaching the people who need loans to stay in their homes, maintain or start businesses, complete construction projects, go to college, buy automobiles, or pay off personal debts. Gone are the days of no income/assets loans. Due to joblessness, misfortune and/or the recession, many of these consumers are significantly less credit worthy.

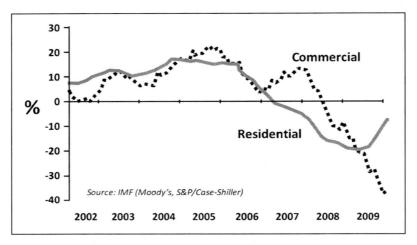

Figure 29: US Real Estate Performance (% Change 2002-2009)[48]

As shown in Figure 29, US real estate performance has been catastrophic. There has been a slight upturn in the residential real estate market. However, the outlook continues to be very bleak. Most experts believe that residential housing values will not return anytime soon. Some areas of the sun-belt, where housing values exploded during the boom years, may not recover in our lifetime.

The commercial real estate sector continues to decline. Over supply, high vacancy rates and a depressed economy could create a perfect storm for this sector. Credit losses arising from commercial real estate are expected to increase in the near future, which is a concern for communities and for banks holding commercial real estate loans.

One bright spot is that investment is beginning to flow into Real Estate Investment Trusts (REITs) which indicates that investors may think that the commercial real estate market has bottomed. Also, as fears of inflation grow, real estate becomes more attractive.

On the other hand, government officials like Treasury Secretary Timothy Geithner, Chairwoman of the TARP Congressional Oversight Panel Elizabeth Warren, and Federal Deposit Insurance Corporation Chief Sheila Bair stated on national television[49] that almost half of all commercial mortgages could be underwater by the end of 2010, posing a very serious (but

48   International Monetary Fund, Global Financial Stability Report, 26 January 2010, http://www.imf.org/external/pubs/ft/fmu/eng/2010/01/index.htm
49   CBS News Business, Commercial Real Estate Eyed as Looming Trouble Spot, 31 March 2010, http://www.cbsnews.com/8301-503983_162-20001478-503983.html

manageable) problem for the economy over the next three years, and the primary force behind small and regional bank failures.

According to the Board of Governors of the Federal Reserve, the total amount of US mortgages (residential, commercial and farm) exceeds $14.4T[50], as of the end of 2009. As shown in Figure 30, the majority of mortgage debt is held by US government federal and related agencies. A large portion of these mortgages will be written off by the government and major financial institutions in the next few years, which will add significant strain on the economy and the nascent recovery.

Figure 30: US Mortgage Debt Holders, December 2009

Residential Real Estate. Residential real estate debt is currently $10.5T and is expected to go higher due to underwater mortgages, foreclosures, and a potential second real estate mortgage crisis.

The 2008 real estate crisis was largely due to the sub-prime mortgage crisis and related mortgage-backed securities (derivatives) which were the catalysts for the Great Recession. Ongoing challenges include underwater mortgages and foreclosures, which are at historic highs. Some real estate areas of the US are so perilous that the economy of the state is threatened. Arizona's growth in the last decade was fueled by booming real estate. Now Arizona has one of the highest foreclosure rates in the nation, and its economy is crashing. One out of two homes in Phoenix is underwater or in foreclosure. The State of Arizona's massive budget deficit is the second largest in the nation (California, which represents the world's fifth largest economy, is first), and is projected to be $3B in 2010.

Many analysts fear that a second residential real estate crisis looms. The principal components of this looming crisis consist of (1) increasing number of foreclosures, (2) rising percentage of underwater mortgages, (3) increasingly seriously delinquent mortgage payment rates, (4) resetting ARM and ALT-A mortgages, (5) problems associated with second mortgages, and (6) potential for a wave of strategic defaults by frustrated homeowners. These factors will be discussed in detail in Chapter 14.

---

50   Board of Governors of the Federal Reserve, Economic Research & Data, Mortgage Debt Outstanding, 24 December 2009, http://www.federalreserve.gov/econresdata/releases/mortoutstand/current.htm

The US government is taking unprecedented steps to mitigate a second crisis. However, unemployment, devalued home prices and market psychology pose significant challenges. The US government (especially the Fed, Treasury, GSEs and numerous housing agencies) is applying trillions (not billions) of dollars to forestall a potential second real estate crisis. While there have been successes, the homeowner rescue effort is slow going. Due to more stringent lending rules, a depressed economy and home values, and unemployment, there are fewer people who qualify for home loans regardless of assistance.

While many believe that all these government homeowner recovery efforts are necessary, many others feel that the mounting national debt and unforeseen consequences of government meddling may pose a greater threat to recovery. Others believe that government efforts are misguided, since the bulk of the government's housing efforts focus on last year's problem of cleaning up toxic mortgages and mortgage-backed securities as opposed to today's growing unemployment problem.

Commercial Real Estate. The commercial real estate market includes offices, shopping malls, hotels, apartments, etc. Commercial property values in the US have plummeted 36% since their peak in 2007. The overall commercial real estate market is now valued at about $6.7T[51].

Commercial real estate outstanding debt is estimated at $3.5T and is in trouble[52]. Of this $3.5T, about 50% is held by banks/thrifts, 25% in commercial mortgage-backed securities and exotic financial instruments held by investment institutions, and 25% by other investors. As of mid 2009, about 9% of commercial real estate loans in bank portfolios were considered delinquent, almost double the level of a year earlier. More than 16% of all construction and development loans were considered delinquent. Construction and development loans are the biggest problem for many banks, due to depressed values and low occupancy rates.

In January 2010, the owners of one of the largest apartment complexes (Stuyvesant Town and Peter Cooper Village) in Manhattan strategically defaulted on their commercial real estate holdings by simply turning over the keys to the lenders and walking away. Three years ago, lenders invested $5.4B into these complexes. Today, their investment is worth less than $1.9B. A large percentage of the original investment capital came from California pension funds, including the California State Teachers' Retirement System (CalSTRS), the largest US teachers' retirement fund with a membership of 833,000, and the California Public Employees' Retirement System (CalPERS) that manages retirement benefits for more than 1.6 million California public employees, retirees, and their families. Their investments are now worth about zero. This is not all that was lost. It is estimated that $18B worth of derivatives were wrapped around these properties that defaulted. Much of this will be lost as well. Numerous pension funds and municipalities are heavily invested in these derivatives.

---

51   Wall Street Journal, "Commercial Loans Failing at Rapid Pace," 21 July 2009, http://online.wsj.com/article/SB124804759792663783.html
52   Board of Governors of the Federal Reserve System, Jon D. Greenlee, Federal Reserve Associate Director, Division of Banking Supervision and Regulation, "Residential and commercial real estate," Testimony before the Subcommittee on Domestic Policy, Committee on Oversight and Government Reform, U.S. House of Representatives, 2 November 2009, http://www.federalreserve.gov/newsevents/testimony/greenlee20091102a.htm

Unlike residential mortgages, which are largely held by the top 10 banks and mostly guaranteed by the US government, commercial real estate mortgages are held by thousands of mid- and small-sized regional and local banks. This makes it a more difficult challenge for the US government to stabilize.

Also, unlike residential mortgages, there was little predatory lending to commercial real estate borrowers, who are much more financially sophisticated than someone buying their first home or car. This fact makes a potential commercial real estate crisis even more troubling, since it points to a structural flaw.

By some worst-case estimates, 55% of commercial real estate mortgages that will come due before 2014 will be underwater. This would be enough to cause another mortgage crisis. US Treasury Secretary, Timothy Geithner, disputes these worst-case scenarios. Secretary Geithner says that current commercial real estate challenges will not set off a new banking crisis[53]. To make his point, Geithner points to an improved GDP rate, bank stabilization efforts, and increased private demand and investment.

Consumer Debt. Consumer debt is currently $2.5T and consists of mainly credit card debt, automobile and school (college) loans. Consumer debt may be one of the bright spots in the US recovery effort. Prior to the recession, people were maxing out credit cards often on extravagant or unrestrained lifestyles. Savings rates plummeted to zero. Slogans like, "just do it" ruled. The recession changed people's attitudes. Saving rates are up. Consumer spending is down. Even though the average American has six credit cards, they are used less.

Unfortunately, there are many citizens so financially stressed that credit cards become short-term solutions. The consequence is often personal bankruptcy. "Bankruptcy filings continue to climb as consumers look to shelter themselves from the effects of rising unemployment rates and housing debt," said American Bankruptcy Institute Executive Director Samuel Gerdano.[54] Consumer bankruptcy filings increased 41% in September 2009 over September 2008.

According to the Federal Reserve[55], the total amount of consumer credit is $2.4T as of February 2010. Outstanding consumer debt fell at a 5.5% annual rate. Revolving credit decreased at an annual rate of 13%, and nonrevolving credit decreased at an annual rate of 1.5%. Revolving credit (like credit cards) is a type of credit that does not have a fixed number of payments, in contrast to installments in nonrevolving credit. Of the $2.4T, $0.86T is revolving (36%) and $1.59T is nonrevolving (auto loans, student loans and other personal loans).

Decreased consumer spending is being felt heavily in the retail business. Decreased retail means a weaker economy and increased unemployment. Even though student loans are

53   Bloomberg News, Secretary Geithner's remarks to the Economic Club of Chicago, "Geithner Says Commercial Real Estate Woes Won't Spark Crisis," www.bloomberg.com/apps/news?pid=20601087&sid=aGGKUQhUZqaQ, 29 October 2009
54   American Bankruptcy Institute, "Consumer Bankruptcy Filings Surge Past One Million During First Nine Months of 2009," 2 October 2009, www.abiworld.org/AM/Template.cfm?Section=Home&TEMPLATE=/CM/ContentDisplay. cfm&CONTENTID=58852
55   Federal Reserve Statistical Release, "Consumer Credit," 7 April 2010, http://www.federalreserve.gov/releases/g19/Current/

increasingly hard to obtain, education, especially technical and vocational training, is doing very well, largely due to the fact that the unemployed and under-employed have more time and increased motivation for retraining.

Chapter 5:

USG BAILOUTS, PLEDGES AND OBLIGATIONS

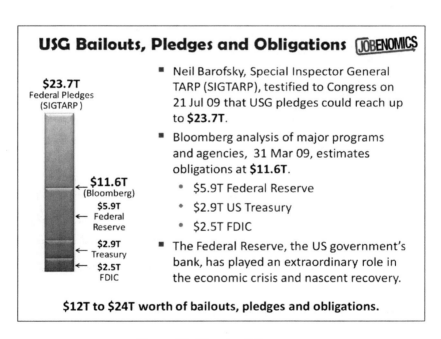

USG Bailouts, Pledges and Obligations JOBENOMICS

$23.7T
Federal Pledges
(SIGTARP)

$11.6T
(Bloomberg)

$5.9T
← Federal
Reserve

$2.9T
← Treasury

$2.5T
← FDIC

- Neil Barofsky, Special Inspector General TARP (SIGTARP), testified to Congress on 21 Jul 09 that USG pledges could reach up to **$23.7T**.

- Bloomberg analysis of major programs and agencies, 31 Mar 09, estimates obligations at **$11.6T**.
  - $5.9T Federal Reserve
  - $2.9T US Treasury
  - $2.5T FDIC

- The Federal Reserve, the US government's bank, has played an extraordinary role in the economic crisis and nascent recovery.

$12T to $24T worth of bailouts, pledges and obligations.

Figure 31: Chapter 5 Summary

Due to extensive media coverage, most Americans are aware of the $787B Obama stimulus package and the $700B Troubled Asset Relief Program (TARP). These two programs represent only the tip of the iceberg. Total US government bailouts, buyouts, pledges and other recovery obligations could total as much as $23.7T. Exact information is hard to obtain. There are two sources, SIGTARP testimony and a Bloomberg analysis, that shed light on what's happening.

SIGTARP Testimony. Neil Barofsky, Special Inspector General TARP (SIGTARP), testified to the US House Committee on Oversight and Government Reform on 21 July 2009. He stated that US government pledges could reach up to $23.7 trillion[56].

SIGTARP is responsible for management, transparency, oversight, and enforcement of TARP ($700B) and TARP-related ($2.4T to $2.9T) spending. Figure 32 shows the data that Barofsky presented to Congress (amounts are in $B):

Program	Brief Description or Participant	Total Projected Funding at Risk ($B)	Projected TARP Funding ($B)
Capital Purchase Program ("CPP")	Investments in 649 banks to date; 8 institutions total $134 billion; received $70.1 billion in capital repayments	$218	$218
Automotive Industry Financing Program ("AIFP")	GM, Chrysler, GMAC, Chrysler Financial; received $130.8 million in loan repayments (Chrysler Financial)	79.3	79.3
Auto Supplier Support Program ("ASSP")	Government-backed protection for auto parts suppliers	5	5
Auto Warranty Commitment Program ("AWCP")	Government-backed protection for warranties of cars sold during the GM and Chrysler bankruptcy restructuring periods	0.6	0.6
Unlocking Credit for Small Businesses ("UCSB")	Purchase of securities backed by SBA loans	15	15
Systemically Significant Failing Institutions ("SSFI")	AIG investment	69.8	69.8
Targeted Investment Program ("TIP")	Citigroup, Bank of America investments	40	40
Asset Guarantee Program ("AGP")	Citigroup, ring-fence asset guarantee	301	5
Term Asset-Backed Securities Loan Facility ("TALF")	FRBNY non-recourse loans for purchase of asset-backed securities	1,000	80
Making Home Affordable ("MHA") Program	Modification of mortgage loans	75	50
Public-Private Investment Program ("PPIP")	Disposition of legacy assets; Legacy Loans Program, Legacy Securities Program (expansion of TALF)	500-1000	75
Capital Assistance Program ("CAP")	Capital to qualified financial institutions; includes stress test	TBD	TBD
New Programs, or Funds Remaining for Existing Programs	Potential additional funding related to CAP; other programs	131.4	131.4
Total		$2,365 – $2,865	$769

as of 6/30/2009

Figure 32: Total Potential Funds Subject To SIGTARP Oversight

TARP-related spending of $2.4T to $2.9T (indicated in Figure 32) is about 10% of the total $23.7T spending. Mr. Barofsky provided no other information to back up the claim that US government pledges could exceed $23T. However, this was enough to make headlines around the world.

The October 2009, SIGTARP Quarterly Report to Congress provides valuable insight into at least 10% of the overall recovery process. The entire report is posted on the web.[57] The degree

---

56   Neil Barofsky, Special Inspector General TARP, Testimony to the US Congress' House Committee On Oversight And Government Reform, 21 July 2009, www.house.gov/apps/list/hearing/financialsvcs_dem/barofsky_testimony.pdf
57   SIGTARP, Quarterly Report to Congress, 21 October 2009, http://www.sigtarp.gov/reports/congress/2009/October2009_Quarterly_Report_to_Congress.pdf

of transparency regarding bailouts, buyouts, stimuli, pledges and obligations that SIGTARP provides to the American people is enlightening.

The transparency dilemma is an issue that concerns SIGTARP. As stated in the Executive Summary of the report,

> "On the cost side of the ledger, although it will take many years to assess all of the costs associated with TARP, financial and otherwise, this report begins to categorize them. It is useful to analyze any Governmental intervention in the market like TARP against three distinct types of cost: the financial cost to the taxpayers; the "moral hazard" damage to market incentives created by Government intervention; and a cost that has received scant attention thus far — the impact on Government credibility due to the failure to explain what is being done with billions of taxpayer dollars transparently and forthrightly."

A paragraph on the accomplishments and challenges ahead in the SIGTARP report's Executive Summary is also insightful,

> "…it appears that the dramatic steps taken by the U.S. Department of the Treasury and other agencies through TARP and related programs played a significant role in bringing the system back from the brink of collapse. On the other hand, the risk of foreclosure continues to affect too many Americans, unemployment continues its rise, and the stresses on the commercial real estate market threaten to increase the pressure on banks and small businesses alike yet again."

In other words, we are making good strides towards recovery, but there are many challenges yet to be resolved.

The report goes on to say,

> "Market behavior is bound to be impacted by the massive infusions of Government capital into the very institutions that caused the crisis; by the modifications of mortgages for homeowners who may have borrowed irresponsibly; and by the provision of cheap, non-recourse loans to incentivize the purchase of the same volatile and over-valued asset-backed securities that were a major cause of the current crisis. The firms that were "too big to fail" last October are in many cases bigger still, many as a result of Government-supported and -sponsored mergers and acquisitions; the inherently conflicted rating agencies that failed to warn of the risks leading up to the financial crisis are still just as conflicted; and the recent rebound in big bank stock prices risks removing the urgency of dealing with the system's fundamental problems. Absent meaningful regulatory reform, TARP runs the risk of merely re-animating markets that had collapsed under the weight of reckless behavior."

The January 2010, SIGTARP Quarterly Report to Congress[58] states that the overall focus "has begun to shift" from bailing out banks, to mitigating foreclosures, lending to small businesses and dealing with the asset-backed securities markets. TARP will be winding down by October 2010, and redeploying approximately $150M of the remaining funds, plus $170M of TARP repayments, to these new focus areas.

The good news about TARP is that the US financial system is more stable, but the bad news is that the fundamental problems in the financial system have yet to be addressed. Quoting directly from the report,

"…even if TARP saved our financial system from driving off a cliff back in 2008, absent meaningful reform, we are still driving on the same winding mountain road, but this time in a faster car."

Bloomberg Analysis. A Bloomberg analysis[59], written in September 2009, estimates the overall US government recovery spending at $11.6T. The following data (Figure 33) was provided.

Grand Total ($B)	**$11,563.65**		
Federal Reserve	**$5,870.65**	**US Treasury**	**$2,909.50**
Primary Credit Discount	110.74	TARP	700.00
Secondary Credit	1.00	Tax Break for Banks	29.00
Primary dealer and others	147.00	Stimulus Package (Bush)	168.00
ABCP Liquidity	145.89	Stimulus II (Obama)	787.00
AIG Credit	60.00	Treasury Exchange Stabilization	50.00
Net Portfolio Commercial Paper Funding	1,200.00	Student Loan Purchases	60.00
Maiden Lane (Bear Stearns assets)	29.50	Citigroup Bailout Treasury	5.00
Maiden Lane II (AIG assets)	22.50	Bank of America Bailout Treasury	7.50
Maiden Lane III (AIG assets)	30.00	Support for Fannie/Freddie	400.00
Term Securities Lending	75.00	Line of Credit for FDIC	500.00
Term Auction Facility	375.00	Treasury Commitment to TALF	100.00
Securities lending overnight	10.42	Treasury Commitment to PPIP	100.00
Term Asset-Backed Loan Facility (TALF)	1,000.00	Cash for Clunkers	3.00
Currency Swaps/Other Assets	606.00	**FDIC**	**$2,477.50**
GSE Debt Purchases	200.00	Public-Private Investment (PPIP)	1,000.00
GSE Mortgage-Backed Securities	1,250.00	FDIC Liquidity Guarantees	1,400.00
Citigroup Bailout Fed Portion	220.40	Guaranteeing GE Debt	65.00
Bank of America Bailout	87.20	Citigroup Bailout FDIC Share	10.00
Commitment to Buy Treasuries	300.00	Bank of America Bailout FDIC Share	2.50
		HUD	**$306.00**
		Hope for Homeowners (FHA)	300.00
		Neighborhood Stabilization (FHA)	6.00

**Figure 33: Bloomberg Analysis of
Federal Government Recovery Commitments**

The data in Figure 33 provides a snapshot in time regarding the different agencies and programs. The big players in the recovery effort are the US Federal Reserve System at $5.9T,

---

58   SIGTARP, Quarterly Report to Congress, 30 January 2010, http://www.sigtarp.gov/reports/congress/2010/January2010_Quarterly_Report_to_Congress.pdf
59   Bloomberg.com, Fed's Strategy Reduces U.S. Bailout to $11.6 Trillion (Update2), 5 September 2009, http://www.bloomberg.com/apps/news?pid=newsarchive&sid=ahys015DzWXc

the US Treasury at $2.9T, the Federal Deposit Insurance Corporation at $2.5T, and the US Department of Housing and Urban Development at $0.3T.

The TARP and Obama Stimulus programs are highlighted to remake the point that they represent only the tip of the iceberg. The highly-touted and highly-visible Cash for Clunkers Program is also highlighted. At $3B, the Cash for Clunkers Program is only 1/10th of 1% of the total Treasury obligation ($3B/$2.9T=0.001) and 3/100th of 1% of the overall total ($3B/$11.6T=0.0003). The percentages are so small, compared to a tremendous amount of hype, that it makes one wonder about the credibility of government. Notwithstanding, Americans were so starved for good news about the economy and their beloved automobile industry (an icon of American culture and pride), that the marketing blitz was justified.

The US Federal Reserve System. The US Federal Reserve System[60], also known as the Federal Reserve, or simply the Fed, is the central banking system of the United States. The Fed is both the US government's bank and the bankers' bank. As an independent institution, the Federal Reserve System has the authority to act on its own without prior approval from Congress or the President. The Fed was created by Congress to be self-financed and is not subject to the congressional budgetary process. In this way, the Fed is considered to be "independent within government."

The Federal Reserve System has a number of layers. The top layer is the 7-member Board of Governors, who are appointed by the President and confirmed by the US Senate. Ben Bernanke is the current Chairman of the Board. The second layer is comprised of 12 regional Federal Reserve Bank districts, each with a board of nine directors, 3 of whom are appointed by the Fed's Board of Governors and 6 are elected by commercial banks in the district. The third layer consists of approximately 4,900 member banks that are private institutions (mainly national and state-chartered banks). Each member bank is required to subscribe to non-tradable stock in its regional Federal Reserve Bank, entitling them to receive a 6% annual dividend. While not officially part of the Fed, the Federal Deposit Insurance Corporation (FDIC) is a sister institution with 9,500 members. The FDIC-insured lending institutions comprise the vast majority of all bank deposits in the US. A very small number of small banks are neither an FDIC nor a Fed member bank.

The primary responsibility of the Fed is the formulation of monetary and credit policy in pursuit of maximum employment, stable prices, moderate long-term interest rates, and economic growth. The Fed supervises and regulates banking institutions to ensure banking safety and to protect consumers. The Fed also plays a major role in operating the nation's payments system.

The Federal Reserve System, through its twelve Reserve Banks, performs many services for the US government including (1) servicing accounts that enable financial operations of various departments/agencies/quasi-government enterprises, (2) servicing deposit accounts for federal unemployment taxes, individual income taxes withheld by payroll deduction, corporate income taxes, and certain federal excise taxes, (3) issuing and redemption of public debt instruments like Treasury securities, savings bonds and mortgage-backed securities, and (4) providing other banks

---

60   The Federal Reserve, http://www.federalreserve.gov/

services like check processing, wire transfers, automated (electronic) clearing houses, and making Social Security, payroll and vendor payments.

The Federal Reserve's income is derived from interest on Treasury securities, interest on foreign currency investments, fees received for services provided to depository institutions, and interest on loans to depository institutions. Since the Fed is run as a non-profit organization, after paying its expenses, the Federal Reserve turns the rest of its earnings over to the Treasury.

The Fed also handles American money. For example, the paper money in your wallet is a Federal Reserve Note, which is backed by nothing other than the faith and guarantees of the US government. Hence, Federal Reserve Notes are fiat currency, that is declared (by fiat) by the US government to be legal tender. By stamping "Federal Reserve Note" (Figure 34) on each note, the Fed pledges the face value of the money. The Fed collateralizes the face value of their pledges by Treasury securities and mortgage-backed securities on the Fed's balance sheet.

Figure 34: Federal Reserve Note

The currency is actually printed by the Bureau of Engraving and Printing, sold to the Fed for the cost of printing (a few cents), circulated by the Fed to its member banks, and disseminated into the communities serviced by the twelve Reserve Banks.

The total amount of currency and securities that the Fed handles is huge. According to the Federal Reserve's statistical release[61], as of 11 February 2010, the Fed had $1T in Federal Reserve notes outstanding, $3T in marketable securities (Treasuries and GSE mortgage-backed securities), $2.3T worth of funds that depository institutions hold on deposit at the Federal Reserve to satisfy reserve requirements, and $2.3T worth of total assets on their balance sheet.

While running the nation's payments system is important, the Fed's primary responsibility is to formulate and control monetary and credit policies of the US. The Fed normally does this by setting interest rates, controlling the money supply by printing money and trading government securities, and regulating the amount of reserves held by banks.

---

61   Federal Reserve, Monetary Policy, The Federal Reserve's balance sheet , 11 February 2010, http://www. federalreserve.gov/monetarypolicy/bst_fedsbalancesheet.htm

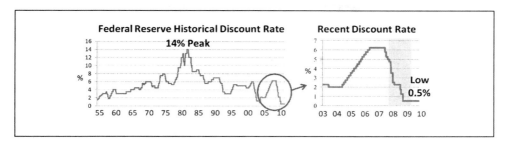

Figure 35: Federal Reserve Discount Rates

Historical Fed discount rates are shown in Figure 35. Over the last five decades, the peak discount rate was a staggering 14% that the Fed used to combat rampant inflation in the 1980s. The lowest discount rate is 0.5% today which was dropped to encourage lending and liquidity due to the Great Recession.

To understand the role that the discount rate plays in the banking system, one must first understand the four layers of interest.

- **Bank rate.** Most consumers are familiar with the interest at their local bank when they apply for a mortgage, auto or other loan. The **bank rate** (currently 5% to 6%) is based on the **prime rate**.

- **Prime rate.** The prime rate (currently 3.25%) is the interest rate offered by banks to their most valued customers. The prime rate is based on the **discount rate**.

- **Discount rate.** The discount rate (currently 0.5%) is the rate that the Fed charges its depository banks and thrifts who need to borrow money from the Fed. The Fed directly sets the discount rate based on the economic/monetary policy it wants to achieve, as well as the underlying rates that banks charge one another, which is called the **federal funds rate**.

- **Federal funds rate.** The federal funds rate (currently 0 to 0.25%) is the rate of interest at which federal funds are traded among banks, pegged by the Federal Reserve through its Open Market Operations.

The Fed's Open Market Operations influence national money supply via the sale of Treasury securities and other financial instruments. 59%, or $7T, of the US national debt is held in Treasury securities.

The Fed is also involved with the sale of $3T worth of mortgage-backed securities that fund US government housing and mortgage agencies and enterprises. To conduct these trades, the Fed deals with an exclusive network of about 20 broker-dealers[62] representing some of the top financial institutions in the world, including Barclays, Citigroup, Credit Suisse, Daiwa, Deutsche Bank, Goldman Sachs, HSBC, JP Morgan, Morgan Stanley, Nomura, RBS and UBS. In many ways, the Fed is the world's largest investment bank dealing in US government tradable securities.

---

62   Federal Reserve Bank of New York, Primary Dealers List, 16 February 2010, http://www.newyorkfed.org/markets/pridealers_current.html

Normally, the Fed stays out of the private sector, but these are not normal times. As a result of the economic crisis, the Fed was compelled to enter the private sector in essentially three ways:

- Printing money to increase liquidity, to increase lending and bailout banks,
- Rescuing too-big-to-fail financial institutions, and
- Buying mortgage-backed securities that are toxic to banks, major financial institutions and insurance companies.

These three actions are shown in Figure 36, which was presented by the President and CEO of the Federal Reserve Bank of St. Louis to a concerned Chinese group of investors (the largest foreign holder of US Treasury securities) in Shanghai, China on 11 January 2010.

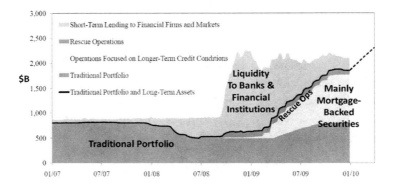

Figure 36: Composition of Federal Reserve Assets [63]

After September 2008, the Fed launched a massive liquidity effort by pouring $Ts in short-term lending into financial firms and markets. A host of new programs was created, including repurchase agreements, term auction credits, commercial paper funding facility, liquidity swaps and various other loans and bailouts. This liquidity effort was designed to be temporary in nature with a minimum risk to inflation. The liquidity effort worked. It saved a number of banks from insolvency without creating inflation. Unfortunately, while banking profits and bonuses have returned, lending has not, due to higher credit standards, less credit worthy opportunities/individuals, and lender timidity.

This liquidity, coupled with near-zero interest rates, has also found its way into the US stock markets, which have rapidly recovered 50% to 70% of their losses during the Great Recession. The infusion of $T of Fed liquidity money and $T of sidelined investor money (money that was removed from the markets due to the panic, and now being reinvested in stocks due to low bank and Treasury interest rates) are creating a financial bubble that could burst like the tech-bubble did a decade ago.

63   James Bullard, President and CEO, Federal Reserve Bank of St. Louis, The First Phase of the U.S. Recovery and Beyond, Shanghai, China, 11 January 2010, http://research.stlouisfed.org/econ/bullard/GIC_ShanghaiJanuary_11_2010.pdf

As a result of the economic crisis, the Fed also launched an aggressive asset purchase program, called quantitative easing. Quantitative easing involves buying securities, which increases the money supply, which promotes increased liquidity and lending. The Fed committed to buying $1.725T in toxic assets by the end of April 2010. The effects of the Fed's asset purchase program can be seen in Figure 36 in the dramatic rise on Fed-held mortgage-backed securities. In essence, the Fed is now carrying the bad debt that formerly resided on the balance sheets of major financial institutions and insurance companies.

So how does the Fed get the money to rescue financial institutions like AIG, Bear Sterns, Citigroup, Bank of America and other institutions? Since the private sector was unable to help these financial corporations, the US government believed that it had to intervene to prevent a meltdown of the entire US financial system. To raise the money, the Fed sold Treasury securities (T-bills, T-notes, and T-bonds) to be used for a bailout. The Treasury securities were auctioned to the public at low interest rates, which attracted a lot of interested lenders who were willing to lend the government money at a median interest rate of near 0%. The Fed, in turn, loaned this money to the institutions at a variable rate around 10%, with the proviso that they could repay when able. The US government also took a percentage of ownership (via warrants and other forms of control) in these companies. Not only did the Fed get money from the sale of the Treasury securities, it positioned itself to make a lot of money due to the spread in interest rates (i.e., 0% and 10%) when the company repaid the loan. Even if these companies do not pay back the loans, the Treasury will still pay back its investors, possibly by printing money, if necessary.

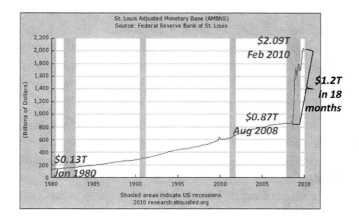

Figure 37: Money in Circulation

As needed, the Fed is able to control the money supply (print and destroy money). In response to the financial crisis, the Fed went into overdrive in printing money to infuse liquidity into the financial system. As shown in the Fed's adjusted monetary base graph[64], Figure 37, the amount

---

64   Federal Reserve Bank of St. Louis, Economic Research, Series: AMBNS, St. Louis Adjusted Monetary Base, 14 February 2009, https://research.stlouisfed.org/fred2/series/AMBNS

of money added to the money supply was unprecedented in US history. Between August 2008 and February 2010 (18 months), over $1.2T worth of new US money entered into circulation.

The US Treasury. The Department of the Treasury is an executive department of the US federal government established to manage government revenue. The Treasury is responsible for promoting economic prosperity and ensuring the US financial security. The Treasury also advises the President on economic issues. The Treasury operates and maintains systems that are critical to the nation's financial infrastructure, such as the production of coin and currency, the disbursement of payments to the American public, revenue collection, and the borrowing of funds necessary to run the federal government.[65]

Second to the Fed, the Treasury has been a major force in mitigating the 2008-2009 Great Recession. Treasury programs, like the TARP and Stimulus II are mandated by Congress and funded by selling of Treasury securities that are added to the national debt.

By committing nearly $3T of taxpayer money, the Treasury provided financial assistance to distressed individuals, banks, corporations and institutions. As a result, it has become one of the largest social welfare organizations in the world.

The Federal Deposit Insurance Corporation. The Federal Deposit Insurance Corporation (FDIC) is an independent agency created by the Congress to maintain stability and public confidence in the nation's financial system by insuring deposits, examining and supervising financial institutions for safety, soundness, consumer protection, and managing receiverships.[66]

The FDIC is not funded by taxpayers. It is funded by premiums that member banks pay for deposit insurance coverage, and from earnings on investments in Treasury securities. FDIC funding normally averages $20B to insure more than $4 trillion of deposits, virtually all the 9,500 banks[67] and thrifts in the US. In 2008, the FDIC temporally increased the individual deposit insurance from $100,000 to $250,000. This increase is scheduled to expire 31 December 2013, but is likely to be extended if economic conditions warrant an extension.

Since the Great Recession began, the FDIC has seized 145 banks, compared with only three in 2007. This includes four of the ten largest failed banks in US history. The FDIC projects that the cost of all failures resulting from the current crisis will reach $100B. Since this amount exceeds projected FDIC reserves, and insurance premiums are not sufficient to cover potential losses, the FDIC Board voted to require member banks to prepay three years' worth of premiums to cover the expected shortfall. If the economic recovery falters and the FDIC reserves are completely depleted, they would likely turn to the Treasury to sell more securities which would add to the national debt. Since all "deposits are backed by the full faith and credit of the United States Government," the US government would not allow a run on banks. It was this concern (run on banks) that prompted the FDIC to raise the standard maximum deposit insurance amount

---

65   US Treasury, "Duties & Functions of the U.S. Department of the Treasury," www.ustreas.gov/education/duties/
66   The Federal Deposit Insurance Corporation, http://www.fdic.gov/about/mission/index.html
67   The Federal Deposit Insurance Corporation, Dynamic Depositor Discipline in U.S. Banks, November 2003, http://www.fdic.gov/bank/analytical/working/wp2003_07/index.html#fig04

(SMDIA) from $100K to $250K. After all, the FDIC is proud of the fact that since its inception in 1934, no depositor has "ever lost a penny of FDIC-insured deposits."[68]

Overall, the FDIC has performed well during the recent financial crisis. One of the major reasons for this success is that FDIC's scope and mission are well and narrowly defined. One of the more successful government programs to stabilize the financial system has been the FDIC's $1.4T Temporary Liquidity Guarantee Program (TLGP) that allowed banks (mainly the too-big-to-fail banks) to issue short-term notes that were backed by the US government. The TLGP helped to defrost credit markets which were frozen early in the 2008 economic crisis.

The FDIC, in conjunction with the Treasury and Fed, is deploying about $1T to the Public-Private Investment Program (PPIP)[69] to repair balance sheets throughout the US financial system and ensure that credit is available to both households and businesses. In other words, the FDIC is buying toxic assets from banks, auctioning these toxic assets to private investors at a discount, and sharing the risk.

While the FDIC has been proactive and largely successful, free-market advocates worry about the amount of US government involvement in the banking system and the unforeseen consequences of government manipulation and risk-sharing.

Repaying the US Government. So now that US banks and financial institutions are returning to profitability, are they paying back the US government? The answer is mostly yes. As of 31 December 2009, Treasury had invested $204.9 billion in 707 institutions, and $121.9 billion had been repaid.[70] The big banks are returning to profitability and paying back taxpayers. Beyond most people's expectation, General Motors repaid their TARP loans early and with interest. In this case, the federal government bailout worked as planned.

However, small banks, mortgage (Fannie/Freddie) institutions, insurance (AIG) and automobile companies like Chrysler are still struggling, and it's likely that many of their debts will never be repaid. The majority of the 700 smaller community banks have not returned bailout money. In fact, the number of delinquent banks has risen from 8% to 12% from November 2009 to February 2010.[71] The Treasury Department could also take a hit from its guarantees on billions of dollars of toxic mortgages and other derivatives (discussed later).

As SIGTARP warned, the US government may have opened Pandora's Box by meddling too deeply in the private sector. While it was necessary to save the financial system yesterday, we don't yet know the effects on tomorrow.

---

68   Federal Deposit Insurance Corporation, FDIC Insurance Coverage Basics, http://www.fdic.gov/deposit/ Deposits/insured/basics.html
69   US Treasury, PIPP Fact Sheet, "Treasury Department Releases Details on the Public Private Partnership Investment Program," 23 March 2009, http://www.ustreas.gov/press/releases/tg65.htm
70   SIGTARP, Quarterly Report to Congress, 30 January 2010, Page 36, http://www.sigtarp.gov/reports/ congress/2010/January2010_Quarterly_Report_to_Congress.pdf
71   Washington Post, Small banks lag in repaying Treasury for bailout funds, by Binyamin Appelbaum and David Cho, 18 March 2010, http://www.washingtonpost.com/wp-dyn/content/article/2010/03/17/AR2010031704046. html?wpisrc=nl_headline

Without new regulation and oversight rules, which are currently being formulated in Congress, the financial industry is rapidly returning to old ways. Executive bonuses are returning to all-time highs, albeit in the form of stock rather than cash. Financial institutions once too-big-to-fail are now really-too-big-to-fail. Now that we have consolidated our major banks into mega-banks, if another economic crisis arrives, our financial system's troubles may be too-big-to-recover.

An important issue yet to be addressed is the issue of power. Within the last year, the Fed, Treasury and FDIC committed $11.6T, which is over four times the annual tax revenues of the US government ($2.5T), and almost equal to all the goods and services (GDP of $14T) that America produces during a year. Moreover, how does the Fed, an "independent" organization, have the ability to deploy almost $6T without prior approval from Congress, the President, or the consent of the American public? In this financial emergency, the money appears to be working as planned. Prior approval may have only provoked endless debate. Nonetheless, these actions have taken the US, and the world, into uncharted territory without established checks and balances.

Chapter 6:
ENTITLEMENT PROGRAMS

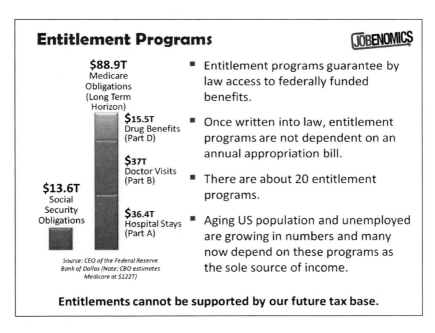

Entitlement Programs

JOBENOMICS

$88.9T Medicare Obligations (Long Term Horizon)

$15.5T Drug Benefits (Part D)

$37T Doctor Visits (Part B)

$13.6T Social Security Obligations

$36.4T Hospital Stays (Part A)

Source: CEO of the Federal Reserve Bank of Dallas (Note: CBO estimates Medicare at $122T)

- Entitlement programs guarantee by law access to federally funded benefits.

- Once written into law, entitlement programs are not dependent on an annual appropriation bill.

- There are about 20 entitlement programs.

- Aging US population and unemployed are growing in numbers and many now depend on these programs as the sole source of income.

Entitlements cannot be supported by our future tax base.

Figure 38: Chapter 6 Summary

US federal budget outlays are grouped into three general budget categories: mandatory spending (entitlements), discretionary spending, and net interest.

- **Mandatory Spending: Entitlement Programs**. Entitlement programs guarantee by law access to federally-funded benefits and include Social Security, Medicare, Medicaid, Income Security (supplemental security income, earned income and child tax credits, foster care and others), Federal Civilian & Military Retirement, Veterans, and Other Programs (subsidies for social services, agriculture, higher education, recovery programs, military and children's healthcare, FDIC deposit insurance, telecom and internet services for the poor, other). Once written into law, entitlement programs are not dependent on an annual appropriation bill.

According to the President's 2011 budget,[72] mandatory entitlement program annual spending is projected to grow 60%, from $2.1T in 2010 to $3.3T by 2020. As a percentage of total outlays, mandatory entitlement program spending is projected to grow slightly from 56% in 2010 to 57% in 2020.

- **Appropriated "Discretionary" Spending: Defense & Other Departments.** Discretionary spending programs require federal government decision-makers to adjust spending, at their discretion via appropriation bills, on each program on an annual basis. Appropriations permit federal agencies to incur obligations and make payments not to exceed their appropriated budget, during the fiscal year which runs from 1 October through 30 September. A continuing resolution is often passed if an appropriations bill has not been signed into law by the end of the fiscal year. The US House and Senate both have 12 appropriations subcommittees: Agriculture; Commerce, Justice, and Science; Defense; Energy and Water Development; Financial Services and General Government; Homeland Security; Interior and Environment; Labor, Health and Human Services, and Education; Legislative Branch; Military Construction and Veterans Affairs; State and Foreign Operations; Transportation and Housing and Urban Development. In 2009, the Department of Defense accounted for 52% of discretionary spending.

  According to the President's 2011 budget, appropriated discretionary spending is projected to grow 14% from $1.4T in 2010 to $1.6T in 2020. As a percentage of total outlays, discretionary spending is projected to decrease from 38% in 2010 to 27% in 2020.

- **Net Interest Payments on the National Debt.** Net interest refers to the money (mandatory spending) that the US federal government pays on interest on the national debt. Since about half of the US national debt is owed to foreigners, nearly 50% of the interest payments leave the US. According to the President's 2011 budget, net interest is projected to grow from $188B in 2010 to $912B by 2020. As a percentage of total outlays, net interest will increase from 5% in 2010 to 16% in 2020.

$B	2010	2011	2012	2013	2014	2015	2016	2017	2018	2019	2020	2010-2020 Growth
Mandatory	2057	2100	2079	2191	2316	2413	2579	2698	2823	3060	3256	58%
Discretionary	1397	1376	1340	1343	1367	1396	1425	1460	1496	1534	1573	13%
Net Interest	188	250	340	434	516	586	652	716	779	844	912	385%

Figure 39: Growth of Mandatory, Discretionary, Net Interest Spending 2010-2020

---

72   Office of Management and Budget, Budget of the United States Government: Fiscal Year 2011, Table S-3, Page 149, March 2010, http://www.gpoaccess.gov/usbudget/fy11/pdf/budget.pdf

Figure 39 shows the growth of the three general budget categories: mandatory spending (entitlements), discretionary spending, and net interest. In essence, $Ts worth of debt will cause Americans to trade national security for net interest payments, which are largely owned by foreign entities, many of whom are adversarial towards the US. Mandatory entitlement programs will continue to grow over the period to over double the size of discretionary spending. If the economy does not grow robustly as projected by the President's budget, discretionary spending could be further reduced, since entitlement programs and net interest are fixed payments.

Entitlement Evolution. US national-level social security was instituted in 1935 by President Franklin Delano Roosevelt largely in response to the Great Depression.

The original social security program covered <u>only</u> industrial workers. As US prosperity grew, so did entitlements. In 1950, farmers, service sector and government workers were added to the rolls. In 1965, Congress enacted the Medicare program, providing medical benefits, as well as adding Medicaid for the poor. In 1972, COLA (cost of living allowance) was introduced. In 1999, payroll deductions were set for Social Security (6.2%) and Medicare (1.45%) with employers contributing matching amounts. In 2010, a national healthcare program was enacted.

The underlying assumption of these enactments was that America was bountiful and that bounty needed to be shared. The enactors did not envision that America would forfeit its position as the world's largest creditor nation and become the world's largest debtor nation.

Over the last 75 years, Social Security/Medicare has morphed from a government funded, worker's reward program to a mandatory social welfare program co-paid by workers and employers. Social Security started out with a pro-jobs mentality and has evolved into a program that often threatens jobs creation. With an aging population in a stagnant economy, employers and taxpayers will bear the entitlement burden. Since aging is a given issue, significant attention needs to be given to growing the economy via the generation of enduring, high-value jobs.

Entitlement Programs. In 2010, the total US mandatory spending is projected at $2.06T,[73] which is roughly equal to all the federal tax revenues received in 2009.

The big three entitlement programs are Social Security, Medicare and Medicaid. In 2008, the Social Security Administration paid benefits to about 55.8 million[74] people, or about 18% of the entire US population or 58% of the US non-government, private sector labor force (96 million). In addition to Social Security, 45 million were Medicare beneficiaries,[75] and 59 million[76] accepted $320B[77] worth of Medicaid payments from federal and state sources.

---

73 The White House, Office of Management and Budget (OMB), Budget of the United States Government, Fiscal Year 2011, http://www.whitehouse.gov/omb/budget/Overview/
74 Social Security Administration, Office of Retirement and Disability Policy, Fast Facts & Figures About Social Security, July 2009, Page 1, http://www.ssa.gov/policy/docs/chartbooks/fast_facts/2009/fast_facts09.pdf
75 The Henry J. Kaiser Family Foundation, statehealthfacts.org, Total Number of Medicare Beneficiaries, 2008, http://www.statehealthfacts.org/comparemaptable.jsp?typ=1&ind=290&cat=6&sub=74&sortc=1&o=a
76 The Henry J. Kaiser Family Foundation, statehealthfacts.org, Total Medicaid Enrollment, FY2006, http://www.statehealthfacts.org/comparemaptable.jsp?typ=1&ind=198&cat=4&sub=52&sortc=1&o=a
77 The Henry J. Kaiser Family Foundation, statehealthfacts.org, Total Medicaid Spending, FY2007, http://www.statehealthfacts.org/comparemaptable.jsp?typ=4&ind=177&cat=4&sub=47&sortc=1&o=a

Other entitlement and benefit programs, from food stamps (35 million monthly[78]), to housing and rent subsidies, to mortgage assistance, to cash and free cell phone programs exceed $150B annually.

According to the 1997 Budget Enforcement Act, these expenditures are funded by permanent appropriations and are considered mandatory, regardless of the number of people eligible for benefits. These entitlement programs have cost of living allowance adjustments (COLA) tied to the Consumer Price Index for Urban Wage Earners and Clerical Workers (CPI-W), which means that payments will automatically increase with inflation. COLAs have been in effect since 1975 and reached a high of 14.3% in 1981. For the first time ever, the COLA was set at 0% for 2010, since there was no increase in the CPI-W from the third quarter of 2008 to the third quarter of 2009. However, President Obama authorized, as part of the American Recovery and Reinvestment Act of 2009, a one-time payment of $250 to nearly 53 million individuals who receive benefits.

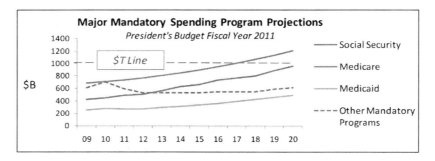

Figure 40: President's 2011 Budget Mandatory Spending Projections

The President's 2011 Budget,[79] as published by the Office of Management and Budget (OMB) which serves the President, is shown in Figure 40 for major entitlement programs.

Entitlement Program	2008 Actual $B	2009 Actual $B	2020 Projected $B	
Social Security	$612	$678	$1,170	
Medicare	456	499	1,038	81%
Medicaid	201	251	458	
Income Security	260	348	283	
Civ & Mil Retirement	129	138	188	
Veterans	45	50	79	
Other	85	325	92	
Total	$1,788	$2,289	$3,308	

Figure 41: CBO Budget and Economic Outlook for Entitlement Programs

78   US Department of Agriculture, Food and Nutrition Service, Supplemental Nutrition Assistance Program (SNAP), 26 April 2010, http://www.fns.usda.gov/snap/
79   Office of Management and Budget, Budget of the United States Government: Fiscal Year 2011, Table S-3, Page 149, March 2010, http://www.gpoaccess.gov/usbudget/fy11/pdf/budget.pdf

The CBO's entitlement program cost estimates generally agree with White House projections. Figure 41 was derived from CBO's The Budget and Economic Outlook, dated August 2009 and January 2010.

In 2008, entitlement spending was $1.79T.[80] In 2009, entitlement spending was $2.29T.[81] In 2020, entitlement spending is projected at $3.3T with Social Security, Medicare and Medicaid 81% of the total. The CBO projects both Social Security and Medicare will exceed $1T per year.

Both the White House and CBO forecast a doubling of Social Security and Medicare over the next decade. Many other analysts believe that these entitlement program spending projections are conservative and could be higher. The numbers could be much higher, considering the economic plight of new retirees and the unemployed. More and more baby boomers are entering retirement solely dependent on Social Security and Medicare, since many have had their retirement accounts (savings, stocks, 401Ks) and home equity wiped out in the recession. In 2007, Social Security provided the majority of retirement income for 64% of the aged[82]—before the Great Recession wiped out many retirement accounts.

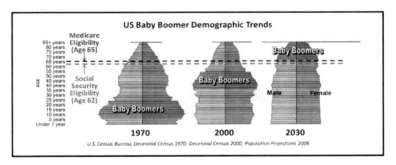

Figure 42: Baby Boomer Demographics

Figure 42 was generated from US Census Bureau[83] demographic data and projections. It depicts the effects of an aging US population. By 2030, everyone who is older than 46 in 2010 will be eligible for Social Security and Medicare. It also shows that the supporting taxpayer base is evolving from a pyramid to a column, which places significantly more financial pressure on a smaller number of people. In 2010, there are about 5 citizens between the ages of 20 and 64 for each person aged 65 and older. By the time most of the baby boomers have retired in 2030, this ratio is projected to have declined to around 3.[84] It is imperative that the 2030 US workforce has good, high-paying jobs in order to support the weight of retirees, who are increasingly dependent

80   CBO, "The Budget and Economic Outlook: An Update," August 2009, http://www.cbo.gov/doc.cfm?index=10521&zzz
81   Congressional Budget Office, The Budget and Economic Outlook: Fiscal Years 2010 to 2020, January 2010, http://www.cbo.gov/ftpdocs/108xx/doc10871/01-26-Outlook.pdf
82   Social Security Administration, Office of Retirement and Disability Policy, Fast Facts & Figures About Social Security, July 2009, Page 1, http://www.ssa.gov/policy/docs/chartbooks/fast_facts/2009/fast_facts09.pdf
83   US Census Bureau, Age Data of the US, Selected Characteristics of Baby Boomers 42 to 60 Years Old in 2006 (PPT), http://www.census.gov/population/www/socdemo/age/general-age.html#bb
84   Ben S. Bernanke, Chairman Federal Reserve System, Speech at the National Commission on Fiscal Responsibility and Reform, Washington, D.C., 27 April 2010, http://www.federalreserve.gov/newsevents/speech/bernanke20100427a.htm

on government entitlement benefits. What is affordable today probably will not be affordable 20 years from now, especially if the US economy plateaus and/or retirees live longer.

The swelling ranks of the unemployed are also dependent on many of the benefits offered by various entitlement programs. The Income Security, Veterans, and Other Programs categories are projected to be relatively flat, but could grow significantly if the US economic recovery struggles to grow. In addition, the proposed US healthcare system will add $1T worth of entitlements over the next decade. This $1T is not included in the CBO or OMB estimates, since the new healthcare legislation was only recently passed.

The General Accounting Office's long-term outlook on entitlement programs is even more foreboding than that of the CBO or OMB.

Under GAO's Simulations Based on the Trustees' Assumptions for Social Security and	Federal Fiscal Gap 2010-2084			
	Fiscal Gap		Change required to	
	Trillions of present value 2009 dollars	Percent of GDP	Percent increase in revenue	Percent decrease in noninterest spending
Baseline Extended	$41.1	4.8%	24.2%	20.0%
Alternative	$76.4	9.0%	50.5%	34.2%

Source: GAO

Figure 43: GAO Entitlement Program Long-Term Projections

As shown in Figure 43, The GAO places the long-term fiscal gap between $41.1T and $76.4T.[85] This is up 20% from simulations done only nine months earlier (March 2009) which predicted the long-term fiscal gap between $33.7T and $62.9T.[86]

According to the GAO, "absent policy actions aimed at reforming the key drivers of our structural deficits—health spending and Social Security—the federal government faces **unsustainable growth in debt**." (Emphasis added)

To correct ominous trends, the GAO says there are two options: raise revenues by 21.5% to 43.6%, or decrease non-interest spending (discretionary and/or mandatory) by 18.0% to 30.9%. Clearly, the US needs to do both. Increasing revenues, via national public/private business initiatives focused on next-generation jobs creation, would be more advantageous and less painful than cutting spending, in an environment characterized by partisanship and ideological gridlock.

The Medicare Trustees agree with this sentiment. The current Board consists of the Secretary of the Treasury, the Secretary of Labor, the Secretary of Health and Human Services, and the Commissioner of Social Security. According to the Trustees, Medicare Part A (Hospital Fund)

---

85   United States Government Accountability Office (GAO), The Federal Government's Long-Term Fiscal Outlook, January 2010 Update, Page 7, http://www.gao.gov/new.items/d10468sp.pdf
86   United States Government Accountability Office (GAO), The Nation's Long-Term Fiscal Outlook, March 2009 Update, Page 9, http://www.gao.gov/new.items/d09405sp.pdf

reserves will be gone by 2017, and Social Security Disability Insurance by 2021.[87] Since Medicare is largely funded by payroll taxes, a languishing economy will empty the Medicare coffers more quickly. When the coffers are empty, benefits will have to be cut, taxes increased, or funds borrowed, thereby increasing the national debt. The proposed new healthcare system could also help drain the coffers since, as currently proposed, the new system will slash $465B from the Medicare budget.

In a letter to the President,[88] the Trustees issued the following warning:

"The financial difficulties facing Social Security and Medicare pose serious challenges. For Social Security, the reform options are relatively well understood but the choices are difficult. Medicare is a bigger challenge. Its cost growth can be contained without sacrificing quality of care only if healthcare cost growth more generally is contained. But despite the difficulties—indeed, because of the difficulties—it is essential that action be taken soon, particularly to control healthcare costs."

Who Pays For Social Security & Medicare? Since 68% of Social Security and Medicare is paid by employers and employees in the form of payroll taxes, these entitlement programs are directly related to business prosperity, employment and competitiveness in a global marketplace.

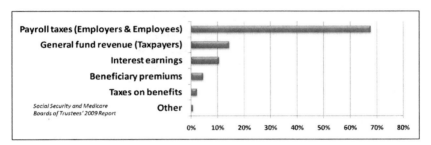

Figure 44: Funding Sources for Social Security and Medicare

Social Security and Medicare funding comes from six sources (Figure 44):

- Payroll taxes (68%)
- General fund revenue (14%)
- Interest earnings (11%)
- Beneficiary premiums (5%)
- Taxes on benefits (2%)
- Other sources (1%)

Payroll taxes are collected from employers and employees, who each pay a tax of 7.65%. A total of 15.3% is collected on each dollar earned via the Federal Insurance Contributions Act (FICA) tax. The self-employed pay combined employer and employee tax rates for a total of 15.3%.

---

87   Status of the Social Security and Medicare Programs, "A Summary Of The 2009 Annual Social Security. And Medicare Trust Fund Reports," Social Security and Medicare Boards of Trustees, May 2009, http://www.ssa.gov/OACT/TRSUM/index.html
88   Ibid

Figure 45 was created from data released by the Boards of Trustees of Social Security and Medicare and their 2009 Annual Report to the President.[89] It shows the overall picture regarding who pays for Social Security and Medicare.

Source *(in $billions)*	Social Security		Medicare		Total	
	Old Age Survivors Insurance	Disability Insurance	Hospital Insurance (Part A)	Supplementary Medical Insurance (Part B & D)		
Payroll taxes (Employers & Employees)	$574.6	$97.6	$198.7	—	$870.9	68%
General fund revenue (Taxpayers)	—	—	$0.7	$184.1	$184.8	14%
Interest earnings	$105.3	$11.0	$15.6	$3.5	$135.4	11%
Beneficiary premiums	—	—	$2.9	$55.2	$58.1	5%
Taxes on benefits	$15.6	$1.3	$11.7	—	$28.6	2%
Other	—	—	$1.2	$7.2	$8.4	1%
Total	$695.5	$109.8	$230.8	$250.0	$1,286.1	100%

Source: Social Security and Medicare Boards of Trustees

Figure 45: Social Security and Medicare Trust Funds

Social Security and Medicare funding is allocated to four separate trust funds. For Social Security, the Old-Age and Survivors Insurance (OASI) Trust Fund pays retirement and survivors benefits, and the Disability Insurance (DI) Trust Fund pays disability benefits. For Medicare, the Hospital Insurance (HI) Trust Fund pays for inpatient hospital and related care (Part A). The Supplementary Medical Insurance (SMI) Trust Fund pays for physician and outpatient services (Part B) and the prescription drug benefit (Part D).

How Large Are Social Security & Medicare Total Unfunded Liabilities? President and CEO[90] of the Federal Reserve Bank of Dallas, Richard Fisher, places the amount of money the Social Security system would need today to cover all unfunded liabilities at **$13.6T,** and the unfunded liability for Medicare at **$85.6T**. Quoting Mr. Fisher,

"The unfunded liability for Medicare A is $34.4 trillion. The unfunded liability of Medicare B is an additional $34 trillion. The shortfall for Medicare D adds another $17.2 trillion. The total…$85.6 trillion….Were I not a taciturn central banker, I would say the mathematics of the **long-term outlook for entitlements, left unchanged, is nothing short of catastrophic.**"[91] (Emphasis added)

The Heritage Foundation,[92] a leading public policy research institute, analysis supports Mr. Fisher's Medicare unfunded liability numbers. The Heritage analysis estimates the cost of the long-term horizon at $88.9T (Figure 46). This estimate was based on the Medicare Trustees'

89   Ibid
90   Federal Reserve Bank of Dallas, Richard W. Fisher, President and CEO of the Federal Reserve Bank of Dallas, "Storms on the Horizon," 28 May 2008, http://www.dallasfed.org/news/speeches/fisher/2008/fs080528.cfm
91   Status of the Social Security and Medicare Programs, "A Summary Of The 2009 Annual Social Security And Medicare Trust Fund Reports," Social Security and Medicare Boards of Trustees, May 2009, http://www.ssa.gov/OACT/TRSUM/index.html
92   The Heritage Foundation, 1 December 2009, http://www.heritage.org/about/

estimates of Medicare's long-term unfunded obligations and general revenue requirements, as reported in the 2009 Report[93] to President Obama from Secretaries Tim Geithner (Treasury), Kathleen Sebelius (HHS) and Hilda Solis (Labor).

Medicare	Part A	Part B	Part D	Total
75-Year	$13.4T	$17.2T	$7.2T	$37.8T
Long-Term Horizon	$36.4T	$37.0T	$15.5T	$88.9T

Source: Boards of Trustees, Federal Hospital Insurance and Federal Supplementary Medical Insurance Trust Fund, "2009 Annual Report", 12 May 09, Tables III.B10, III.C15, III.C23

Figure 46: Medicare's Unfunded Obligations

The ultimate amount of long-term entitlement liabilities is unknown. Nobody really knows because it depends on many assumptions. The CBO chart in Figure 47 makes this point. A casual glance at the graphic reveals an ever-increasing range of possibilities and outcomes. The one thing that is known for certain is that future US generations cannot possibly service this amount of debt. Unless American employment increases significantly (thereby producing increased tax revenue), the US government is rapidly approaching the point in time when it cannot borrow or print money to cover deficit spending. When this time arrives, the US federal government will be faced with disastrous options, including defaulting on obligations to seniors, super-inflation, or economic collapse.

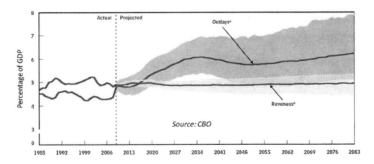

Figure 47: CBO Potential Ranges of Social Security Outlays and Revenues Under the Scheduled Benefits Scenario, 1985 to 2083[94]

Figure 47 shows CBO's range of Social Security outlays and revenues as a percent of GDP, extrapolated to 2083. The dark lines indicate CBO's projections of expected outcomes. Shaded areas indicate an 80% probability. The overall message is that revenues have very little chance of covering the cost of the Social Security program. The CBO reports that if the law remains

---

93   2009 Annual Report of the Boards of Trustees of the Federal Hospital Insurance Trust Fund and the Federal Supplementary Medical Insurance Trust Fund, Transmittal Letter to President Obama from Secretaries Geithner (Treasury), Sebelius (HHS) and Solis (Labor), 12 May 2009, http://www.cms.hhs.gov/ReportsTrustFunds/downloads/tr2009.pdf
94   CBO, "CBO's Long-Term Projections for Social Security: 2009 Update," Page 11, August 2009, http://www.cbo.gov/ftpdocs/104xx/doc10457/08-07-SocialSecurity_Update.pdf

unchanged, 33 years from now (2043), the Social Security Administration will not have the legal authority to pay full benefits.

New US Government Healthcare Insurance Program. No discussion about US entitlement programs would be complete without a discussion about the new US government healthcare insurance program in relation to overall healthcare reform.

National healthcare is not new. According to the Centers for Medicare & Medicaid Services (CMS),[95] the agency responsible for administering the Medicare and Medicaid programs, the first coordinated efforts to establish government health insurance were initiated at the state-level between 1915 and 1920. During World War II, government health insurance services were expanded as employee fringe benefits due to government limitations on wage increases. In 1950, Congress enacted a law to improve access to medical care for needy persons who were receiving public assistance. In 1965, Congress established the Medicare (Title XVIII for the elderly) and Medicaid (Title XIX for the poor) programs as part of the Social Security Act. In 1997, the State Children's Health Insurance Program (SCHIP) was added.

In 2010, US public healthcare spending for Medicare, Medicaid, and SCHIP is over $800B. These programs are managed by CMS. Other publicly-funded healthcare spending is for Department of Defense healthcare for military personnel, the Department of Veterans Affairs healthcare for veterans, state-run healthcare under Workers' Compensation programs, and numerous programs for R&D, public medical facilities, maternal and child health services, school health programs, subsidies for public hospitals and clinics, Native American healthcare services, substance abuse and mental health activities, and medically-related vocational rehabilitation services. To this list, the new national healthcare program was added in March 2010. Officially, two acts, an executive order and a rider were signed:

- The Patient Protection and Affordable Care Act (Public Law 111-148)

    o   Patient Protection and Affordable Care Act's Consistency with Longstanding Restrictions on the Use of Federal Funds for Abortion (Executive Order)[96]

- The Health Care and Education Reconciliation Act of 2010 (Public Law 111-152)

    o   The Student Aid and Fiscal Responsibility Act (rider to PL 111-152)

According to the US Senate,[97]

"Together with the Patient Protection and Affordability Act, the Health Care and Education Reconciliation Act will ensure that all Americans have access to quality, affordable health insurance and put students ahead of private banks."

---

95   Centers for Medicare & Medicaid Services, Department of Health and Human Services, "BRIEF SUMMARIES of MEDICARE & MEDICAID Title XVIII and Title XIX of The Social Security Act as of November 1, 2008", http://www.cms.hhs.gov/MedicareProgramRatesStats/downloads/MedicareMedicaidSummaries2008.pdf
96   The White House, Office of the Press Secretary, Executive Order, Ensuring Enforcement And Implementation Of Abortion Restrictions In The Patient Protection And Affordable Care Act, 24 March 2010, http://www.whitehouse.gov/the-press-office/executive-order-patient-protection-and-affordable-care-acts-consistency-with-longst
97   US Senate, Democratic Policy Committee, http://dpc.senate.gov/healthreformbill/healthbill61.pdf

The major elements of the legislation focused on health insurance and provisioning for the poor, including expanding eligibility, subsidizing premiums, providing business incentives and healthcare exchanges, and prohibiting denial of coverage based on preexisting conditions.

The student aid rider had nothing to do with healthcare. The rider eliminated the $60B private-sector student loan industry and replaced it with a government lending program. According to the legislation, the savings from eliminating the private-sector middleman will go directly into Pell grants for student loans for needy students, community colleges, and historically black colleges and universities, as well as $19B that will be diverted for deficit reduction. Those who oppose the measure argue that it is an unnecessary government takeover that will replace an efficient private-sector loan operation with a more inefficient and politically-motivated bureaucracy. To those on the political right, it was just another example of government intervention in the private sector. To those on the political left, it was a justified action to eliminate the middle man. To *Jobenomics*, it further increases government employment, which is opposite to the direction recommended by this book. Hopefully, more money will get to students, but over the long-haul, the private sector has proven to be more efficient than government. If this were not the case, FedEx or UPS would never have gotten a foothold over the US Postal System.

Now let's get back to the healthcare issue. The US population is 309 million. 260 million are covered by health insurance. 50 million are not. Of the 260 million, 180 million are covered by employers. Of the 50 million, many (the young) do not want it, and others (small businesses, self-employed and part-timers) cannot get it, or cannot afford the higher premiums.

The new healthcare legislation is intended to reduce costs for the covered, and to bring 32 million (out of the uncovered 50 million) under the healthcare umbrella. Unfortunately, the legislation places much more emphasis on the 32 million without insurance, as opposed to the 260 million that have insurance. Additionally, it places significant burdens on business and the wealthy to bear the brunt of the costs associated with covering the uninsured.

The Congressional Budget Office announced they estimate that the Democrats' revised healthcare bill will cost $940 billion over the next 10 years. The bill puts new obligations on business and individuals, requiring for the first time that most Americans carry health insurance, and penalizing companies that don't provide coverage for their workers. From a jobs creation perspective, this will be a disincentive for those who can create jobs, especially small businesses.

According to a Forbes analysis,[98] new healthcare spending would be for the uninsured ($466B), Medicaid expansion for the poor ($434B), and a minor sum for small business tax credits ($40B). The costs would be covered by Medicare budget cuts ($465B), increased taxes on the wealthy ($210B), healthcare and drug company industry fees ($107B), new taxes ($103B), premiums on new long-term care programs ($70B), penalties for those who refused to participate ($65B), and taxes on high-cost healthcare plans ($32B).

---

98   Forbes.com, Who Pays for ObamaCare?, by David Whelan, staff writer at Forbes, 25 March 2010, http://blogs. forbes.com/sciencebiz/2010/03/who-pays-for-obamacare/

The CBO and Joint Committee on taxation estimate that enacting both pieces of legislation would produce a net reduction in federal deficits of $143B over the 2010–2019 time period.[99] Opponents calculate a $500B increase for the following reasons:

- The bill front-loads revenues and back-loads spending,
- Unrealistic transfers from the Medicare budget that will likely be funded from the general account when Medicare reserves are depleted (as early as 2017),
- A number of discretionary spending program increases were not counted,
- The provision for corporations to deposit higher estimated tax payments is unrealistic,
- Savings from eliminating the private-sector student loan program will not materialize with a new government bureaucracy that replaces private sector organizations.

In an op-ed to the Wall Street Journal,[100] US Commerce Secretary Gary Lock argues that the new healthcare legislation is "undeniably pro business and pro jobs." He uses the following points to show that the new comprehensive health-care legislation will significantly benefit business:

- By cutting the number of uninsured (32 million people), insurance companies will be able to reduce premiums to the insured since they will no longer have to cover the hidden costs of emergency room care for the formerly uninsured.
- The law invests $5B in a new reinsurance program for early retirees, between ages 55 and 64, which will allow employers to reduce family premiums as much as $1,200.
- The law contains numerous reforms that will slow the rate of growth for healthcare costs over time, which will benefit business.
- $40B in tax credits for four million small businesses over the next decade to help cover the cost of employee health coverage will be a boon for small businesses.

Hopefully, Secretary Lock's assessment about the new healthcare legislation will come true, but most business owners are skeptical. The Secretary's op-ed was in response to major company writedowns (AT&T $1B, Deere $150M, Caterpillar $100M, 3M $90M, et al.) due solely to the health bill, which has generated waves of corporate losses. There is obviously a conflict between government analysis and corporate accounting. Whether this healthcare bill is good for business or not remains to be proven. On the other hand, healthcare reform is needed, especially for small businesses and the self-employed. If the current healthcare bill becomes a catalyst for meaningful healthcare cost reduction and true reform, then it will be a good thing. If not, it will be an affliction on the public and business. Nobody knows if the new healthcare bill will be a boon or a boondoggle to the economy. Only time will tell.

The Issue of US Healthcare Affordability. The issue of US healthcare affordability is hotly debated. The key issue on healthcare affordability revolves around the fact that US healthcare costs equate to about 1/6 of US GDP. According to CMS,[101] the total national health (public

---

99   Congressional Budget Office Letter from Director Elmendorf to Speaker Pelosi, Estimate of the direct spending and revenue effects of an amendment in the nature of a substitute to H.R. 4872, the Reconciliation Act of 2010, 20 March 2010, http://cbo.gov/ftpdocs/113xx/doc11379/Manager%27sAmendmenttoReconciliationProposal.pdf
100   Gary Lock, US Commerce Secretary, Wall Street Journal Op-Ed, "Don't Believe the Writedown Hype, Taken as a whole, health reform is undeniably pro business and pro jobs", 1 April 2010, http://online.wsj.com/article/SB1000 1424052702304252704575155712878109470.html
101   Centers for Medicare & Medicaid Services Department of Health and Human Services, "Brief Summaries of Medicare & Medicaid Title XVIII and Title XIX of The Social Security Act as of November 1, 2008," http://www.cms.

and private) expenditures are projected to double to reach $4.3T in 2017, up from $2.1T in 2006. Consequently, the pertinent questions are, is this doubling too much, and what are the consequences of $4.3T worth of national healthcare expenditures in 2017? The answer is directly related to how much the US economy grows, as much as it is to cutting rising healthcare costs. If the GDP stays flat (W- and L-shaped recoveries), then it is way too much. If the GDP grows at a 6% rate annually through 2017 (a robust V-shaped recovery), then this level of expenditure is very acceptable. The point is that there are several ways to mitigate the healthcare cost equation: focus on the numerator or focus on the denominator. (For the mathematically challenged, the numerator is the number written above the line in a common fraction, and the denominator is the number below the line.) For example:

- If US GDP remains at the $14T level, $4.3T equates to **31% of US GDP,** which is tantamount to a national crisis.
- If US GDP grows to the $22.6T level, the percentage used by CMS, $4.3T will be only **19% of US GDP**.
- If our GDP grows to $30T, the percentage drops to 14% of US GDP, which is an improvement over 2006 when healthcare was 16%.

Therefore, focusing on jobs creation to increase GDP (the denominator) would help reduce the effects of increased healthcare costs. In other words, make more in order to spend more.

Working on the numerator also works, but it may prove to be harder. Once an entitlement program is enacted, it often takes on a life of its own. Social Security did. Medicare did. Universal healthcare coverage probably will also.

The Patient Protection and Affordable Care Act (Public Law 111-148) and the Health Care and Education Reconciliation Act of 2010 (Public Law 111-152) have just started the healthcare debate in America. There is much left to be done on healthcare reform. The state of the economy will dictate how ongoing healthcare reform is received by the American public.

There are a lot of pro and con arguments about public versus private healthcare. The perspective of *Jobenomics* on the healthcare debate is largely from a view of a debt and jobs perspective, both of which are paramount to providing adequate healthcare. To minimize debt and enhance jobs creation, an ideal healthcare reform package should:

- Avoid layers of bureaucracy.
- Emphasize reducing costs to those who are covered.
- Introduce tort reforms, arbitration and cross-state programs.
- Emphasize high-deductible Medical/Health Savings Accounts (MSA/HSAs).
- Introduce insurance co-ops, especially for small business.
- Increase transparency, oversight and penalties for fraud and corruption.
- Make Americans more accountable for their own healthcare spending.

Cost-cutting, and making small businesses more profitable and attractive places of employment, should be the centerpiece of healthcare reform. Today, the US spends about $2T/year on healthcare. On an individual basis, we spend about twice as much as other nations. If we can reduce these costs by 5% to 25%, it would provide a significant boost to productivity and the economy.

US Culture of Entitlement. In 2011, entitlements and net interest payments will total $2.4T. Total receipts are expected to be $2.6T. Consequently, the US government plans to spend about as much on entitlement programs as it receives. To pay for the rest of government operation, the federal budget forecasts $1T deficit spending each year through the year 2020. If the US economy fails to recover robustly, or if another disruption or economic crisis occurs, deficit spending could be considerably higher.

The US culture of entitlement spending is not sustainable by the American tax base. A robust recovery may be many years coming. Entitlement relief, as opposed to more entitlements, needs a greater role in the public debate–a debate centered on statistics, not emotion. If Americans don't debate now, they certainly will debate later when conditions are worse. Social Security and Medicare Trustees said it best to President Obama:

> "The financial challenges facing Social Security and especially Medicare need to be addressed soon. If action is taken sooner rather than later, more options will be available, with more time to phase in changes and for those affected to plan for changes."[102]

The consequence of waiting is best articulated by one of America's founding fathers, Benjamin Franklin, who said:

> "When the people find that they can vote themselves money, that will herald the end of the republic."

Perhaps a better warning is from President Franklin Delano Roosevelt, the founding father of America's modern entitlement system, who said:

> "Welfare is a narcotic, a subtle destroyer of the human spirit."

---

102 Social Security Online, Status of the Social Security and Medicare Programs, A Summary Of The 2009 Annual Reports, Social Security and Medicare Boards of Trustees, http://www.ssa.gov/OACT/TRSUM/index.html

Chapter 7:

DERIVATIVES: EXOTIC FINANCIAL INSTRUMENTS

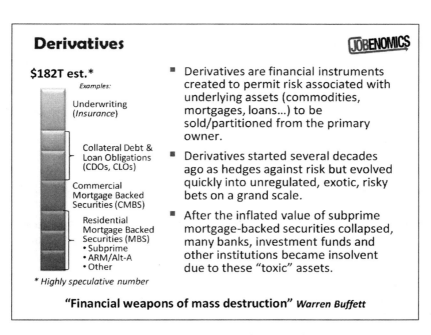

Derivatives

JOBENOMICS

$182T est.*

Examples:

Underwriting
(*Insurance*)

Collateral Debt &
Loan Obligations
(CDOs, CLOs)

Commercial
Mortgage Backed
Securities (CMBS)

Residential
Mortgage Backed
Securities (MBS)
• Subprime
• ARM/Alt-A
• Other

* Highly speculative number

- Derivatives are financial instruments created to permit risk associated with underlying assets (commodities, mortgages, loans...) to be sold/partitioned from the primary owner.

- Derivatives started several decades ago as hedges against risk but evolved quickly into unregulated, exotic, risky bets on a grand scale.

- After the inflated value of subprime mortgage-backed securities collapsed, many banks, investment funds and other institutions became insolvent due to these "toxic" assets.

"Financial weapons of mass destruction" *Warren Buffett*

Figure 48: Chapter 7 Summary

Warren Buffet calls derivatives "time bombs" and "financial weapons of mass destruction."

"We view them (derivatives) as time bombs both for the parties that deal in them and the economic system...In our view...derivatives are financial weapons of mass destruction, carrying dangers that, while now latent, are potentially lethal." Warren Buffett, the Chairman of Berkshire Hathaway, March 2003.

Buffet was right. Exploding derivatives were largely responsible for the Great Recession of 2008-2009, and continuing economic concern. Contrary to popular opinion, derivatives are still very much in play, and little has been done to provide transparency into a very clandestine process.

So why do very few Americans know about derivatives? The answer is that they are esoteric (i.e., known or understood by only a small number of people).

To a Wall Streeter, derivatives are financial instruments created to permit the risk associated with an underlying security to be sold and/or partitioned away from the primary holder of the underlying security. To the Main Streeter, derivatives are complex, exotic financial instruments that are traded in unregulated, secretive environments by a privileged few. To one group of Washingtonians, derivatives are a political nightmare that almost derailed the US economy and remain potential "time bombs" to economic recovery. To another group of Washingtonians, derivatives are a way for the US government housing enterprises to make money and enable national policy, such as providing mortgages to the poor.

It was a US government sponsored enterprise (GSE) that created the first derivatives for the US housing industry in 1983. Today, the US government controls 86% of US home mortgages, and their GSEs make money via fees and guarantees on real estate derivatives, called residential mortgage-backed securities. The US government not only helped create the exotic financial instruments that almost collapsed the US financial system, but it continues to be one of the world's largest (if not the largest) trader of derivates in global secondary markets.

Since most people who read this book are laymen, a layman's explanation will be provided on how derivatives evolved, what role derivatives played in the subprime mortgage crisis, and how derivatives are impacting the American recovery process. While the evolution of derivatives is complex, convoluted and esoteric, it is important that Main Street Americans have a basic understanding regarding the effect $100Ts worth of derivatives had, and will continue to have, on our society. The totality imposed by derivatives is too-big-not-to-understand on a simplified level. The government's role in and use of housing derivates is discussed in more detail in Chapter 14.

When people invest in a derivative, they are placing a "bet" that the value <u>derived</u> from the underlying asset will increase or decrease by a certain amount within a certain period of time. At the time of purchase, this person signs a binding contract to buy or sell an asset at some point in the future, but pay for it in the present at a locked-in price. To make a bet, the investor or trader does not have to own the asset. To make this point clear, a sports analogy might be useful. A bookie does not have to own a football team to make a bet on the outcome of the game. Nor does an advertizing agency, television or radio, all of whom benefit from the underlying asset, in this case the football team. By the time of the Superbowl, more money is made on the side bets and sideshows than the actual game itself. The same is true on derivatives. This is all good for the economy, unless the game is cancelled, like happened during the subprime mortgage crisis.

The most common types of derivatives are futures and options. A futures contract requires the owner to buy or sell the asset on the given date. An options contract gives the owner the option to buy or sell an asset at a set price on or before a given date.

Since derivatives have no value themselves, they depend on the value of another asset, called an underlying asset. Underlying assets include mortgages, equities (stocks), commodities (corn, gold, oil, etc.), loans, bonds, interest rates, exchange rates, indices, a host of other assets, and unusual items like the weather. The weather? A weather derivative acts as a financial instrument that helps to reduce the amount of risk in the event of bad weather. In other words, it is a type of weather insurance policy that is used to protect investors who trade in agriculture and other areas that could be adversely affected by weather. Much in the same way, credit derivatives provide insurance regarding defaults on loans, credit cards, mortgages and like credit products. Investment banks, hedge funds and insurance companies are parties that frequently agree to assume risk associated with credit products.

Derivatives started as hedges against risk in the agricultural sector. Let's describe a hypothetical agricultural transaction. A Kansas farmer needs cash for the upcoming planting season. Before planting in the spring, the farmer sells his unplanted crop to a merchant for a discounted price of \$X. The farmer has hedged his risk against a bad crop and gets the cash he needs. The merchant bets on the future (a futures contract) harvest price. If the price is what the merchant expects, he makes (\$X+). If not, he loses (\$X-) money, depending on the price of corn. Shortly after signing the corn "future" contract, the merchant decides to sell his future to a group of ethanol traders who are betting that the value of corn would be worth a lot more in a gas tank than on a table. They buy an option from the merchant at X++. The merchant partially hedges his bet from cash on the option. Mid-summer, the merchant gets worried about drought conditions in the Midwest, and decides to hedge his bet by buying a weather derivative at X--, to insure his corn bet from a potential crop failure. In this example, the future, option and weather insurance were all derived (a derivative) from the underlying asset of corn. All these transactions occurred before the corn was harvested.

In our example, the farmer and merchant hedged. The insurer underwrote. Continuing the example, bring on the speculators and arbitrageurs. A speculator is someone who bets on the movement of an asset with the intent of making a profit with a minimum investment. A speculator often is a trader or a hedge fund manager. An arbitrageur is one who engages in arbitrage. Arbitrage is the practice of taking advantage of a price differential between two or more markets and making a profit between the differences. An arbitrageur usually works at an investment bank or a brokerage firm. In the corn example, our speculator exploits an opportunity to trade the ethanol future to a global warming group. The speculator also finds a pension fund looking for a high rate of return. At the same time, an arbitrageur sees a price difference on the price of corn on the Chicago Mercantile Exchange and a foreign exchange, and quickly profits on the difference. Four more entities enter the game with derivations on the corn yet to be harvested.

No one acted unethically in these complex corn-derivative transactions. A lot of money was made by numerous people from the merchant, ethanol group, underwriter, trader, global warming group, pension fund, and arbitrageur. Most importantly, the farmer got the money he needed to plant his corn in the first place.

Based on the corn example, derivatives are beneficial as they contributed to wealth generation and contributed to a far more flexible, efficient and resilient financial system.

"These increasingly complex financial instruments (derivatives) have especially contributed, particularly over the past couple of stressful years, to the development of a far more flexible, efficient and resilient financial system than existed just a quarter-century ago." Alan Greenspan, Chairman of the Federal Reserve, 2002

The use of derivatives accelerated to a degree that no one could expect. Total world derivatives reportedly rose to $700T. No one really knows the exact number, since derivatives are unregulated, non-transparent and under-reported. US derivatives grew in 15 years from several trillion to an estimated $182T. At the peak, US derivatives were worth as much as the world's total net wealth.

Derivatives made many billionaires, and uncounted millionaires. Everyone was happy until the subprime mortgage crisis. The subprime mortgage crisis caused the derivative bubble to burst and almost took down the entire US financial establishment in the process. Collateral damage occurred around the world. More importantly, the complex derivate Gordian Knot will take decades to untie, if ever.

The Role of Derivatives in the Subprime Mortgage Crisis. The genesis of the subprime mortgage crisis reaches as far back as WWII. The American dream has always been fulfilled by owning a home, but few could afford one. After WWII, to accommodate millions of returning vets and transition from a wartime to a peacetime economy, homeownership was encouraged. Millions of small, affordable homes were built for the vets with financial aid from the government. As time marched on, homeownership was extended to anyone who needed a home and could afford it with some government help. More government subsidies were granted, and new government agencies formed.

In the last decade, home ownership morphed from a privilege, to a right. Consequently, home mortgages were granted to almost anyone who applied for one. Since everyone had a right, subprime mortgages were made by lenders to people with poor credit ratings or limited credit histories. Risk was guaranteed, or underwritten, by government sponsored enterprises, like Freddie Mac and Fannie Mae. The chief executives of these agencies were incentivized by Congress and HUD to sell, sell and sell more under the auspices that homeownership would give citizens a larger stake in the American dream.

Exotic mortgages (like variable-rate, interest only, extended and negative amortization ARMs) were created to lure borrowers by lowering initial payments to near zero. Mortgage brokers were often paid as much by lenders, as serving the borrowers who paid them for advice. Predatory lenders steered borrowers, who qualified for prime loans, into riskier subprime loans. The lenders then spread the risk to investors by packaging subprime loans into asset-backed securities, and selling these securities on the secondary market with US government backing. European investors were particularly drawn to these high yield-bearing financial instruments, which were underwritten by US government, and given thumbs-up by leading rating agencies. In order to participate in the bonanza, the US government bought massive amounts of subprime securities, which it used to finance government projects without having to approach the taxpayers for money. According to Alan Greenspan,[103] "To purchase these mortgage-backed securities, Fannie and Freddie paid whatever price was necessary to reach their affordable housing goals."

As in the corn example, three entities were involved: the subprime homeowner (the farmer), the bank (the merchant) and the underwriter (the US government). Then came the derivatives and derivative investment banks, speculators/traders/hedge funds and arbitrageurs, plus a few entities including brokers, appraisers and rating agencies.

A new category of derivatives, called CDOs, emerged. Collateralized debt obligations (CDOs) are an unregulated type of asset-backed security and structured credit product. Subsets of CDOs were created for mortgages (CMOs, collateralized mortgage obligations), other type of loans like credit cards (CLOs, collateralized loan obligations) as well as other structured products that were bets on almost any conceivable asset or debt.

The first CDO was created by two Wall Street investment banks for Freddie Mac in 1983. Essentially, the US government, via Freddie Mac, created a legal special purpose entity, that was separate from the government, which could own and trade a set or pool of mortgages. These pools were packed into financial instruments called mortgage-backed securities (MBS) for both residential (RMBS) and commercial (CMBS) real estate.

The subprime mortgage crisis started with the collapse of the residential MBS market, that was sponsored and underwritten primarily by the US government. The subprime mortgage story is an interesting saga of government intervention and Wall Street exploitation. It is a story that continues to unfold. As discussed in Chapter 14 (Potential Second Residential Real Estate Crisis), the rest of the story may soon be known. The ending largely depends on how toxic financial instruments (aka derivatives) are purged from our financial system, and how these financial weapons of mass destruction (according to Warren Buffett) are contained in the future. Before we discuss the ending, let's start with the fundamentals.

In the old days, a homeowner would get a mortgage from a local bank. These banks are now known as commercial banks, which are in the business of taking deposits and making loans, including mortgages to Main Street Americans. Investment banks are banks for qualified investors (the rich). The government has different sets of rules for both. A commercial (local) bank must retain more funds relative to loans than investment banks. This is called leverage. A commercial bank usually has stricter leverage requirements, usually 10:1. For every ten dollars they loan, they must keep one dollar in reserve. Since investment banks are for qualified, or accredited, investors (i.e., the rich), who can afford more risk, they lever out to 20:1. Other financial institutions, like hedge funds, can lever out to 40:1. The US federal government provides a lot of oversight and regulation to commercial banks and insures deposits through the FDIC. Less regulation is provided for investment banks that are overseen by the Securities and Exchange Commission (SEC). Hedge funds are not regulated.

---

103 Testimony of Alan Greenspan, Financial Crisis Inquiry Commission, 7 April 2010, http://fcic.gov/hearings/pdfs/2010-0407-Greenspan.pdf

With the advent of MBS, the mortgage process changed. First, a homeowner would get a mortgage from a local commercial bank. Then the local bank would bundle a group, or pool, of mortgages into an MBS, and sell them to a big investment bank or other financial institution. These big institutions would then market, trade and sell the MBS to other institutions like pension funds, private investors, municipalities, foreign governments, central banks and others. MBS were traded much in the same way as stocks and bonds. These pooled mortgages were then divided in tranches, rated, and sold at different levels of risk. Rating agencies, like Standard & Poors, rated them like many other securities with AAA, AA, and lesser ratings. The lower-rated MBS had more risk, but generated higher returns. Since the US government was the underwriter for most of the mortgages, including the poor quality subprime loans, MBS traded briskly. Because of government backing, poor-quality, high-return MBS were especially attractive. Everyone in the financial sector seemed to want a piece of the action. During the boom years in the early 2000s, MBS and other derivatives, created hundreds of trillions of dollars worth of new wealth based on bets on the bountiful real estate market—the Superbowl of the economy.

New financial instruments (derivatives) were created on top of the MBS. As shown in Figure 49, layers of options, swaps, arbitrages were wrapped around the MBS and their underlying residential real estate asset (the home). Eventually, these layers became worth significantly more than the underlying asset that was "secured" by a subprime borrower, who was financially unstable by his/her very nature. Nobody seemed to worry. After all, Americans had a right to homeownership, the US government was the underwriter, and appreciation on home values seemed to be unlimited.

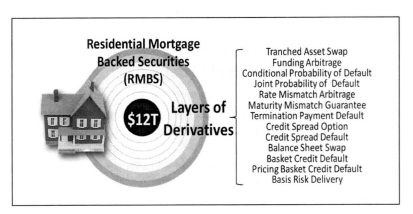

Figure 49: Residential Mortgage-Backed Securities Derivatives

By 2007, everyone was in the game. Government and the media promoted homeownership. More and more poor people entered the market with low-interest, adjustable rate loans, which were quickly approved, often without regard for the applicant's income or ability to pay. Investors lapped up as many MBS and other side-bets as they could afford, and when they ran out of money, they leveraged by borrowing more. Credit rating agencies inflated MBS investment grade ratings, which enabled traders to sell to more risk-averse investors. MBS that should have been rated as junk were upgraded to investment grade securities. The stock market soared. Developers overbuilt homes, townhouses and condos in anticipation of an unending bonanza. Main Street speculators were busily buying and flipping properties. Existing homeowners, flush with unexpected equity on highly appreciating homes, spent lavishly and borrowed on the equity of their home. Second mortgages and home equity lines of credit flourished. Many homeowners spent more income from these second mortgages and lines of credit than they did from their regular jobs. All was good. Then the bubble broke, just like other over-inflated real estate asset bubbles, such as the Japanese real estate bubble collapse in the 1990s. The pin that popped the bubble was the subprime mortgage pin.

The majority of the subprime loans were issued as adjustable rate mortgages to those who could not afford them. When these mortgages reset, many of the homeowners, who were poor in the first place, defaulted on their payments. MBS securities began to lose value. When interest rates began to rise and the housing market started to decline, defaults soared, and investors panicked. The subprime MBS and related outer layers of derivatives began to unravel and collapsed. The financial institutions that widely held any kind of derivative began to fail. Too-big-to-fail banks were rescued. Others were not. Insurance companies, like AIG, were also deemed too-big-to-fail. The value of their underwriting (called credit default swaps) had risen to $66T, or five times the US GDP.

When the housing bubble burst, the stock market, home values and home equity tanked. World capitalization (stocks) dropped $36T, and US household net worth dropped by $20T within the year. Due to extraordinary government efforts and infusion of $10Ts of liquidity into the financial system, Western economies were pulled back from the brink—for the time being.

The Rest Of The Story Is Yet To Unfold. While most people are familiar with the miracle of compound interest (where money makes money on money), few grasp the anathema of compound debt (debt that begets more debt). Several hundred $T of derivatives has created a new business normal. Several hundred trillion of anything usually changes the status quo. The dilemma for America is that the derivatives conundrum is still with us. Mortgage-backed securities and related derivatives are still in play. The rest of the story also includes other asset-backed securities wrapped around commercial real estate, credit cards, and student and auto loans. Mortgage debt has begotten more debt in other venues—a debt that will still take years, or decades, to resolve.

Reform, transparency, oversight and regulation are clearly needed. The US government, in partnership with the financial sector, needs to set a proper course of action and restructuring. Unfortunately, this may be impossible in the near-term for a number of reasons. First, the acrimony against Wall Street is too high in Main Street and Washington to make reasoned judgments. America is in the blame game. It is far easier for Washington to point to Wall Street, as opposed to looking at its own role in the derivatives market. Second, Washington is locked in a "capitalism versus socialism" debate, which preempts any forward movement on how to oversee and regulate the financial industry. Third, few understand the shadowy nature of the derivatives.

For example, AIG is still trying to untie the Gordian Knot of credit default swaps. Government pressure and threats from private citizens are causing professionals who understand the subtleties of derivatives to quit and transfer to other jobs. Lastly, the future impact on the economy of remaining and new derivatives is yet unknown.

As Secretary Geithner aptly stated [104]

"...the debate is not really about financial reform or no reform; about re-regulation or deregulation. It's a debate about ideas, and about the best ways to improve an undeniably flawed system; about the role of government; about the balance between efficiency and stability; about how to protect consumer choice and financial innovation, while constraining predation and fraud; and about getting the incentives right."

Government regulation and oversight reforms are absolutely necessary, but over-regulation will stifle the industry and economic prosperity. The geopolitical financial center has already begun to migrate to Asia and places like Dubai. Too many punitive rules and regulations will hasten this migration. Partly in response to government pressure and media indignation, Halliburton established a co-headquarters in Dubai, where their Chairman and CEO now resides and works. In a global society, multinational corporations will move to where it is most profitable. This is not disloyal. It is business normal. Tighter regulation and taxation in the London financial sector has already caused many investment and financial institutions to move offshore. According to the Mayor of London, Boris Johnson, 9,000 bankers and a number of financial institutions are planning to leave London because of the British government's new tax policy.[105]

Consequently, it is not too hard to imagine a future where the world's financial centers are located in the East, as opposed to the West. It is imperative that we Americans not kill our Golden Goose. Unbridled capitalism proved to be unwise. Unbridled government intervention may prove to be worse.

---

104 Treasury Secretary Timothy F. Geithner, Remarks before the American Enterprise Institute on Financial Reform Washington, D.C., 22 March 2010, http://www.aei.org/docLib/Geithner%20Remarks%2003-22-10.pdf
105 Skynews, Mayor Boris Johnson: 'Bankers Are Fleeing London', by Rob Cole, 15 January 2010, http://news.sky.com/skynews/Home/Business/London-Mayor-Boris-Johnson-Says-Bankers-Are-Leaving-London-Due-To-Tax-As-%20Obama-Reveals-US-Bank-Levy/Article/201001315523528?%20lpos=Business_Third_Politics_Article_Teaser_Region__9&lid=ARTICLE_15523528_London_Mayor_Boris_Johnson_Says_Bankers_Are_%20Leaving_London_Due_To_Tax_As_Obama_Reveals_US_Bank_Levy

Chapter 8:
US RESOURCES

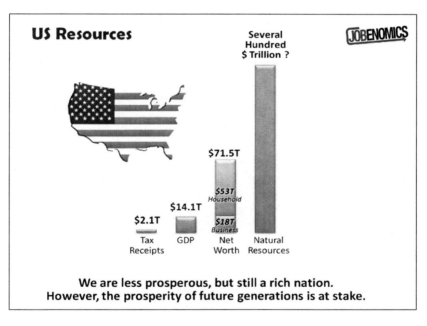

US Resources

Several Hundred $ Trillion ?

JOBENOMICS

$71.5T

$53T
Household

$14.1T

$2.1T

$18T
Business

| Tax Receipts | GDP | Net Worth | Natural Resources |

We are less prosperous, but still a rich nation.
However, the prosperity of future generations is at stake.

Figure 50: Chapter 8 Summary

The ongoing economic crisis has weakened America, but the US is still very resilient, especially considering our net worth and natural resources. The US economy is still the largest in the world.

Annually, the US government collects approximately $2.1T in tax receipts which it spends for national programs and services. Americans produce $14T worth of annual goods and services (GDP). American household and business net worth is $71.5T. Most importantly, the US is a nation with abundant natural resources whose value exceeds hundreds of trillions of dollars. We have ample land for agriculture, ample water supplies, and essential energy and mineral sources to sustain us for the foreseeable future. What's at stake is not our future, but the future for our children.

According to the Federal Reserve, the total US net worth is $71.5T. US household net worth is $53.4T[106] and US business net worth is $18.1T.[107][108] Households represented 75% of the total, and business 25%.

US Net Worth ($T)

	07 QIV	08 QI	08 QII	08 QIII	08 QIV	09 QI	09 QII	09 QIII	09 QIV	10 QI	
Households	64.5	61.6	60.0	56.8	51.4	48.3	50.3	53.0	53.5	54.6	7€
Business	23.2	22.7	22.0	21.8	20.3	18.6	18.0	17.9	17.5	17.5	2⁴
	87.6	84.3	82.0	78.5	71.7	66.9	68.3	70.9	71.0	72.1	
	Peak	-3.4	-5.6	-9.1	-15.9	**-20.7**	-19.3	-16.8	-16.6	**-15.6**	
						Trough				-18%	

Source: Federal Reserve Z.1 Release, Tables B.100/102/103   *Loss from 2007*

Figure 51: US Household & Business Net Worth

As shown in Figure 51, in 2007, just prior to the recession, total US net worth peaked at $87.6T. At the depth of the recession, Americans lost $20T worth of net worth, but rebounded $8T in the next three quarters to only a $12.1T loss.

While an $8T rebound in 2009 is reason to celebrate, one should remember that the stock and housing markets are being stimulated by the infusion of $12T worth of government funds. The true measure of success can only be determined when the stimuli end and the economy operates on its own. Americans will likely know whether the glass is half-full or half-empty by the end of 2010.

When we look at US assets (excluding liabilities) the US financial landscape looks even better. Americans own a lot. Consequently, it is important that we protect these assets for future generations.

---

106 The Federal Reserve, Statistical Release, Flow of Funds Accounts of the United States, B.100 Balance Sheet of Households and Nonprofit Organizations, 11 March 2010, http://www.federalreserve.gov/releases/z1/current/accessible/b100.htm

107 The Federal Reserve, Statistical Release, Flow of Funds Accounts of the United States, B.102 Balance Sheet of Nonfarm Nonfinancial Corporate Business, 11 March 2010, http://www.federalreserve.gov/releases/z1/current/accessible/b102.htm

108 The Federal Reserve, Statistical Release, Flow of Funds Accounts of the United States, B.103 Balance Sheet of Nonfarm Noncorporate Business, 11 March 2010, http://www.federalreserve.gov/releases/z1/current/accessible/b103.htm

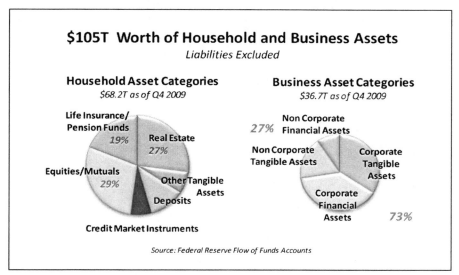

Figure 52: US Household & Business Total Assets

The assets (net worth excluding liabilities) of US households and businesses exceed $105T as of Q4 2009. As shown in Figure 52, household assets are $68.2T as of Q4 2009. The major household asset categories include equities (stocks and mutual funds) for 29%, real estate 27%, and life insurance/pension funds 19%.

A primary reason that the Great Recession hurt individual households is due to the high percentage of stocks and real estate in individual portfolios. Unemployment and derivatives are having a significant impact on the pension fund category. The largest pension fund in the US, California's CalPERS, lost 30% of its value in the last two years.

Business assets are $36.7T as of Q4 2009. Corporations account for 73% of the total and non-incorporated businesses account for 27%. Their assets are about equally split between financial and tangible assets.

The best way to protect these assets is to limit spending and increase employment. Since limiting government spending is hard to do in an economic recovery, employment is our best option. To be meaningful, America needs to generate at least 20 million new private sector jobs this decade.

The major points for Section 2: Tyranny of Trillion$: Debtor Nation (Chapters 2 through 8) include:

- America has hundreds of $T worth of debt and obligations.

- America has hundreds of $T worth of assets and natural resources.

- The best way forward is to mitigate our debt and husband our resources. The US spending/receipts gap must be closed to avoid crushing debt and promote recovery.

- Economic recovery is in progress but we won't really know if it is stable until after US government stimuli end.

- The most important way to ensure a viable recovery is to focus on jobs creation with emphasis on value-added, enduring jobs.

Figure 53: Section 2: Tyranny of Trillion$: Debtor Nation Major Points

RECOVERY SCENARIOS

Chapter 9:
ECONOMIC RECOVERY
SCENARIOS

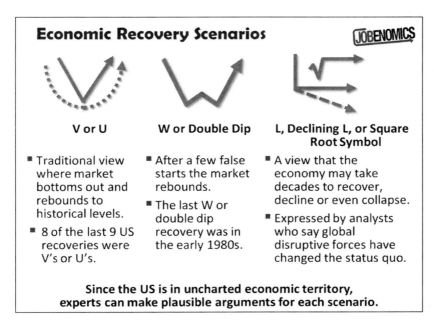

Economic Recovery Scenarios JOBENOMICS

V or U	W or Double Dip	L, Declining L, or Square Root Symbol
▪ Traditional view where market bottoms out and rebounds to historical levels. ▪ 8 of the last 9 US recoveries were V's or U's.	▪ After a few false starts the market rebounds. ▪ The last W or double dip recovery was in the early 1980s.	▪ A view that the economy may take decades to recover, decline or even collapse. ▪ Expressed by analysts who say global disruptive forces have changed the status quo.

**Since the US is in uncharted economic territory,
experts can make plausible arguments for each scenario.**

Figure 54: Chapter 9 Summary

There is much debate among economists and policymakers about the shape of the recovery. Essentially, there are three basic scenarios: V, W and L.

V-Shaped Scenario. The V-shaped scenario is the predominant historical scenario. The premise of a V-shaped recovery is that the market rebounds after hitting bottom, and returns to or exceeds previous highs. The U variant stays at the bottom for a short time before returning to normal. Eight out of the nine recessions that the US has experienced since WWII have been V-shaped recoveries.

Due to rebounding US stock markets (Dow, S&P and NASDAQ), policymakers tout the V as proof that recovery is underway, and that government stimulus packages are working. Economists further argue that the normal business cycles are a series of peaks and troughs. Recessions (troughs) are distinctly shallower, briefer, and less frequent than expansions (peaks). Since the US economy is still the largest and most powerful in the world, Americans should expect a peak greater than before. While the current recession (aka The Great Recession) has been bad, our current economic balance sheet is no worse than it was a decade ago.

Chapter 10 discusses the V-shaped recovery scenario in more detail.

W-Shaped Scenario. The W-shaped scenario happened during the 1975 to 1982 recessionary era. It also happened during the Great Depression. The premise is the market rebounds, then decreases, and rebounds again returning to historic highs. The W is a double V, also known as a double-dip recession. After a false start, optimism returns to the marketplace. Past W-shaped scenarios were largely caused by excessive or inappropriate government policies and intervention. A future double-dip recession could be induced by another domestic financial crisis or an international event.

Chapter 11 discusses the W-shaped recovery scenario in more detail.

L-Shaped Scenario. The L-shaped scenario has not happened in recent US history, but has occurred numerous times in other countries. The L-shaped recovery premise is that the market does not rebound, or takes a significant amount of time before it rebounds. The declining L postulates that the economy erodes, and in extreme cases, collapses. The square root symbol is a third variant, where the recovery dips, recovers slightly (due to stimuli), and then flattens. Economists who believe that the current economic crisis has been caused by flawed economic principles endorse the L. Numerous anti-capitalists also ascribe to this point of view since they believe that the American-era is over, and is in decline. Even V and W advocates acknowledge that multiple crises, or a catastrophic event, could cause an L, or even a declining L, depending on the severity of the crisis or event. Examples include a nuclear event, a massive energy crisis ($500 barrel of oil), a second major real estate crisis, a cyber Pearl Harbor event, and similar disastrous events.

Chapter 12 discusses the L-shaped recovery scenario in more detail.

The Self-Stabilizing Paradigm. Most economists believe that the US economy is a self-stabilizing system. They believe that, like a well crafted boat, the economy of the most powerful nation in the world will eventually upright itself after a turbulent storm.

A small but growing number of economists reject the self-stabilizing paradigm, and predict no near-term recovery for the following reasons:

- The hundreds of $T of public and private sector debt trumps historical precedent. Consequently, the future is unknown, and current economic models may no longer be valid.

- $11.6T worth of US government stimuli was an "all-in" play. As a result, there will be limited resources to combat a second economic crisis.

- The infusion of government stimuli may have covered up fundamental flaws in our economic system that will regenerate after the stimuli end. For example, the toxic nature of derivatives still has not been resolved several years after the economic crisis. In addition, government intervention has increased, rather than decreased, which disincentivizes economic growth in the private sector. Until the flaws in the financial infrastructure are fixed, an enduring economic recovery is not likely.

- Market volatility and investor nervousness can rapidly wipe out months of economic gains. Even minor events can cause wild gyrations in the world equity markets.

- The global economy experienced the first reversal in modern economic history which ushered in a new economic area.

- Financial institutions are returning to old ways, and governments are incapable of implementing needed reform.

- Millions of households are financially ruined by loss of home equity and stocks. Many baby boomers will depend on Social Security and Medicare, increasing the debt burden and making recovery more difficult.

- Unemployment, welfare, entitlements, poverty and conflict will cripple recovery efforts. In addition, many of the Western economics have become so top heavy that their future tax base may no longer support the load. In the US, there is one government worker for every three workers in the private sector, who have to carry the government load, as well as several hundred million citizens who accept some form of government handouts annually.

- The economies of Western nations have become so bloated and uncompetitive that a geo-financial shift to the East may occur sooner than most would expect. Emerging economies in the East will attract more investment capital than declining economies in the West.

Until government stimuli end and markets operate on their own power, it is probably too early to assess if the self-stabilizing paradigm is valid or not. Infusion of massive amounts of US government money created market euphoria that will dissipate after the stimuli are gone.

The View From Outside the US. It is often worthwhile to have an outside perspective on an issue. The International Monetary Fund (IMF) has been quite vocal on the US role in the worldwide financial crisis and their view is worthy of consideration.

The IMF is an organization of 186 countries, working to foster global monetary cooperation, secure financial stability, facilitate international trade, promote high employment and sustainable economic growth, and reduce poverty around the world.[109] Two IMF reports (one during and one after the crisis) articulate the foreign point-of-view.

According to the IMF's April 2009 World Economic Outlook, Crisis and Recovery Report, the IMF was skeptical about the prospects of stable US and Western world recoveries. While they don't specifically mention the terms L-shaped recovery or declining L, their words indicate thus. In addition, they imply that self-stabilizing mechanisms of the Western economies have been marginalized because of excessive financial practices and chronic underlying problems. The following are paraphrased excerpts from the April 2009 report, which was written at the height of the economic crisis:[110]

- The US is the epicenter for the crisis. Falling wealth, tight credit markets, and heightened uncertainty about job security and earnings are reining in private demand. Declining output and employment are causing declines in loan repayments. The damage to bank balance sheets is tightening access to credit, feeding back into private investment and consumption.

- The global economy is in a severe recession inflicted by a massive financial crisis and an acute loss of confidence. Wide-ranging and often unorthodox policy responses have made some progress in stabilizing financial markets, but have not yet restored confidence nor arrested negative feedback between weakening activity and intense financial strains.

- The current outlook is exceptionally uncertain, with risks still weighing on the downside. A key concern is that policies may be insufficient to arrest the negative feedback between deteriorating financial conditions and weakening economies in the face of limited public support for policy actions.

- Core problem areas include corporate and household defaults will increase; fiscal costs of bank rescues will escalate; financial institutions (including life insurance companies and pension funds) will run into serious difficulties; stress in the financial sector will drive greater deleveraging and asset sales, tightening of access to credit, greater uncertainty, higher saving rates, and even more severe and prolonged recessions.

- Past episodes of financial crisis have shown that delays in tackling the underlying problem mean an even more protracted economic downturn and even greater costs, both in terms of taxpayer money and economic activity.

- A key challenge will be to calibrate the pace at which the extraordinary monetary and fiscal stimulus now being provided is withdrawn.

- Compared with previous recessions, the current US recession is already severe. Sharp falls in wealth, restrictions in credit, and the extent of the downturn imply that quick recoveries in private demand are unlikely.

---

109   International Monetary Fund, Homepage, About, http://www.imf.org/external/about.htm
110   International Monetary Fund, World Economic Outlook, Crisis and Recovery, April 2009, http://www.imf.org/external/pubs/ft/weo/2009/01/pdf/text.pdf

Eight months later, the IMF's January 2010 Update[111] to the World Economic Outlook, entitled *"A Policy-Driven, Multispeed Recovery"* is not as severe, but is still very cautious. Highlights of this report include:

- The IMF acknowledges significant improvement in the global economy and credits "extraordinary policy stimulus" by government that has forestalled a second Great Depression. The amount of stimulus funding has been unprecedented.

- Monetary policy has been "highly expansionary" and has generated record low interest rates that have generated tremendous liquidity and profit taking.

- Central bank balance sheets have expanded to unprecedented levels in the US and Europe.

- The IMF predicts that, while recovering, the economies of the West will "remain sluggish by past standards" as opposed to emerging and developing economies that are expected to be "relatively vigorous."

Good Job—Now Where Do We Go From Here? The key question facing the world today is what will happen when the US "extraordinary policy stimulus" is withdrawn? This question provokes additional questions. Will up stay up, or must what goes up come down? What will happen during the next financial crisis which is sure to come? According to Secretary Geithner, the American financial system produced a significant financial crisis every three to five years over the last thirty years.[112]

For all its faults, the US federal government has done an extraordinary job bringing us back from the brink. Now delicate disengagement is needed and, hopefully, the economy will continue to improve under its own power. It is also time for serious bipartisan debate on financial reform and the role of government in preparing for the next crisis. Most importantly, the US must focus on jobs creation—the antidote for W- and L-shaped scenarios.

111 International Monetary Fund, World Economic Outlook, Update, A Policy-Driven, Multispeed Recovery, 26 January 2010, http://www.imf.org/external/pubs/ft/weo/2010/update/01/pdf/0110.pdf
112 US Department of the Treasury, Treasury Secretary Timothy F. Geithner Remarks before the American Enterprise Institute on Financial Reform, 22 March 2010, http://www.treas.gov/press/releases/tg600.htm

Chapter 10:
V-SHAPED RECOVERY
AND JOBS

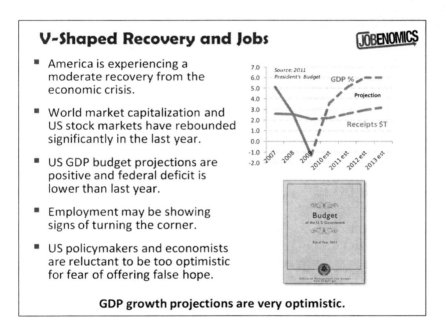

V-Shaped Recovery and Jobs   JOBENOMICS

- America is experiencing a moderate recovery from the economic crisis.

- World market capitalization and US stock markets have rebounded significantly in the last year.

- US GDP budget projections are positive and federal deficit is lower than last year.

- Employment may be showing signs of turning the corner.

- US policymakers and economists are reluctant to be too optimistic for fear of offering false hope.

GDP growth projections are very optimistic.

Figure 55: Chapter 10 Summary

Hooray! The Great Recession is over. There are many signs that a V-shaped economic recovery is underway. These signs include:

- US stock markets are up nearly 50% to 70% from their lows in March 2009.
- World market capitalization is up 73% from its lows in March 2009.
- Big banks are recovering and most are repaying bail-out funds.
- Corporate profits are up.

- GDP is increasing.
- Employment picture is improving.
- The size of annual deficit spending is decreasing.
- No new major conflicts have erupted.
- International community is still investing in the US.

 After two years of struggle, these signs are good news. Considering the fact that the US economy could have collapsed, this is very good news. Not only is this a testimonial to the strength of the American economy, but to the officials who took bold and unprecedented actions to save the economy. This is why *Time Magazine* chose Ben Bernanke, Chairman of the Federal Reserve, its 2008 Man of the Year. The economic crisis was overwhelmingly the most important news item, and *Time Magazine* responded to the sentiment of its readers and a grateful nation.

Perhaps one of the most significant signs of a V-shaped recovery is shown by the "V" in the total market capitalization of all publicly traded companies in the world.

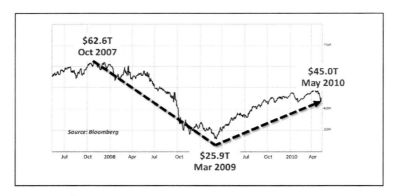

Figure 56: World Market Capitalization [113]

As shown in Figure 56, the total market capitalization (share price times the number of shares outstanding) of all publicly traded companies in the world was $62.6T in October 2007. During the economic crisis the world lost 59% of its net worth, which fell to a low of $25.9T in March 2009. As of 10 May 2010, the total market capitalization of the world's publicly traded companies rose to $45.0T, a net gain of 73%, but still off 28% from its high in 2007.

The three major US stock markets have also rebounded between 50% and 70% from their lows in 2009. As shown in Figure 57, the S&P 500's recovery shows the classic characteristics of a V-shaped recovery. Proponents say that government stimuli are working, a bounce is occurring, there are lots of good stocks, and that the bear market is turning into a bull market.

---

113 Bloomberg.com, World Capitalization WCAUWRLD:IND Exch Mkt Cap USD (Millions), 11 May 2010, http://www.bloomberg.com/apps/cbuilder?ticker1=WCAUWRLD%3AIND

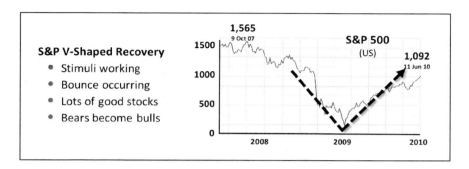

Figure 57: S&P 500 V-Shaped Recovery

The Standard & Poor's S&P 500 is an index of 500 actively traded large-cap stocks. The 500 are a combination of companies that are on the largest US stock exchanges. The S&P 500 is considered a leading indicator for the American economy, since it covers a wide range of companies in several stock exchanges. A V-shaped recovery in the S&P 500 is considered a bellwether sign.

Looking to the future, the President's 2011 Budget assumptions[114] are optimistic and clearly reflect a strong V-shaped recovery scenario (Figure 58).

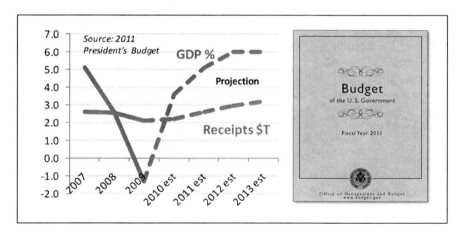

Figure 58: President's 2011 V-Shaped Recovery Projections

After dropping precipitously from 2007 to 2009, the US GDP, in the President's budget assumptions, is projected to rebound rapidly to 6%, which will generate a 52% increase in federal tax revenues from 2010 to 2014. Every American hopes that these assumptions are correct.

---

114 The White House, Office of Management and Budget, Budget of the US Government, Fiscal Year 2011, Economic Assumptions, Table S-13, http://www.whitehouse.gov/omb/budget/Overview/

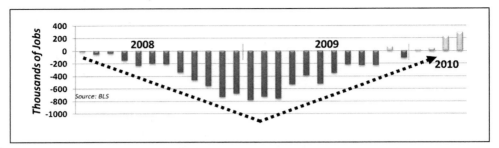

Figure 59: Employment Picture—Turning the Corner?

A strong case that one can make for a V-shaped recovery, as shown in Figure 59, is the employment picture which is beginning to turn the corner from deep lows. After losing 8.4 million jobs in 2008 and 2009, the first four months of 2010 have netted a gain of 573,000 jobs,[115] or 143,000 jobs a month, which is slightly above the replacement rate of 130,000—the rate necessary to supply jobs for new workers entering the labor force. However, most of these jobs were government jobs. According to ADP,[116] a leading employment survey company, only an average of 39,000 private sector jobs was generated during the first four months of 2010.

With all this good news, why are US policymakers and economists reluctant to be too optimistic? One obvious reason is politicians' fear of offering false hope in an election season. Another reason is the fact that we are experiencing only a moderate recovery as opposed to a robust recovery. A moderate recovery means that it could take years before America gets back to normal, which leaves the US financial system more vulnerable to potential economic aftershocks. The most important reason has to do with jobs. If America does not produce approximately 20 million new private sector jobs in the next decade, the V-shaped recovery may flatten into a square root-shaped recovery.

20 million jobs equates to a monthly total of 167,000 new jobs per month for each of the 120 months in this decade. 20 million new jobs is the number required to absorb new workers entering the workforce and reemploy half of those who lost jobs in the Great Recession. 20 million new jobs is also the average number of new jobs created in each of the three previous decades prior to the 2000s that lost 1 million jobs.

Creating an average of 167,000 jobs per month will not be easy after a recession. A look at previous US recessions and depressions provides a glimpse of the magnitude of the jobs creation task before us. By most accounts, the 2008 to 2009 recession/financial crisis is considered somewhere between a recession and a depression. Hence, it has been nicknamed the Great Recession.

---

115 Bureau of Labor Statistics, Change in Total Nonfarm Payroll Employment: Historical Data, 7 May 2010, http:// www.bls.gov/ces/
116 ADP National Employment Report, May 2010 National Employment Report, 3 June 2010, http://www. adpemploymentreport.com/pdf/FINAL_Report_May_10.pdf

A recession is defined as a significant decline in economic activity lasting more than a few months, normally visible in real GDP (more than two quarters), personal income, employment, production, and wholesale-retail sales. Major recent US recessions and durations include:

- 1973-74, Oil crisis and stock market crash, 2 years
- 1980-82, Energy crisis and high inflation, 2 years
- 2001-03, Dot.com crash, 9/11, accounting scandals, 2 years

A depression is defined as a severe recession characterized by extreme unemployment (10%+), restriction of credit and loans, reduced output and investment, numerous bankruptcies, reduced amounts of trade and commerce, highly volatile currency fluctuations and devaluations, and price deflation often followed by super- or hyperinflation. US depressions and durations include:

- 1807-14, Embargos and trade crisis, 7 years
- 1873-96, European stock market crash, 23 years
- 1929-39, US stock market and banking crash, 10 years

Economies tend to recover quickly from recession, but slowly from major financial crisis which damages critical elements of the economic infrastructure. For the US economy to really recover, Americans need to start spending money again. Consumer spending is 70% of our GDP. As long as unemployment continues at double-digit rates, people won't be buying and inventories will remain high. For those still employed, many endure wage and bonus cuts. In addition to the jobs picture, the recession depletes household net worth. Many of these households are occupied by retiring baby boomers, who are aggressively saving as opposed to spending.

By the end of 2010, much of the $11.6T worth of stimuli, bailouts and buyouts by the Fed, Treasury and FDIC will be spent. Unemployment, dollar status, and public/private debt will replace government stimuli as the dominant factors in economic recovery. Unemployment rates above 10% will become a politically acute issue that could undermine investor confidence and consumer spending. The international community is devaluing the dollar, and pushing for a new reserve currency. While a weaker dollar makes our exports stronger, the US still imports more than it exports. If oil imports rise by $50/barrel due to a weaker dollar and increased demand, Americans will spend an additional $219B per year (12 million barrels/day x 365 days/year x $50 = $219B) out of their pockets. This money could have been spent more productively elsewhere. US debt is also affecting economic growth. $29T ($12.9T public, $16.5T private) worth of debt stifles capitalization that is crucial to business growth and expansion. More and more attention is being paid to debt service, which diverts attention from producing the goods and services vital to a V-shaped recovery.

Yes, the country is recovering. No, mission success is not achieved. The duration of the recession was about two years. A stable economic recovery may take as long or longer, perhaps a decade.

A decade? Economic shocks can occur in many ways, including monetary policy fluctuations, asset bubbles, oil shocks, recessions, and financial crises. Each shock produces trauma. However, different shocks produce differing levels of trauma. The 2008 oil shock raised prices at the gas pump to $5/gallon, but this price spike was short lived. Recessions following financial crises take longer than average to recover. Regrettably, the Great Recession was a combination of a financial crisis, asset (housing) bubble, monetary fluctuation, energy crisis, and a recession. Consequently, the Great Recession was a product of an almost perfect storm. Recovery will be longer and weaker than most people expect. Recovery will also be difficult due to loss of US manufacturing competitiveness, and high demand for capital and resources in rapidly growing emerging markets like China.

The 2008-2009 Recession is called "Great" due to its amplitude. The reason for predicting a decade-long recovery period is based on historical precedent and anticipated healing time. It takes more time to heal from a broken bone than it does a common cold. In addition, a broken bone has a higher potential for crippling than does a cold. It takes even longer to heal if the body is in a relatively weak condition. Even the most ardent V-shape economists acknowledge the fragility of the US economy. Compared to the 1982-1983 Recession that produced higher unemployment rates than the 2008-2009 Great Recession, the amplitude of the Great Recession was far worse and will have longer lasting effects.

U3 Rate	Year	Jan	Feb	Mar	Apr	May	Jun	Jul	Aug	Sep	Oct	Nov	Dec	Job Changes	
9.7%	1982	-327	-6	-129	-281	-45	-243	-343	-158	-181	-277	-124	-14	1326.0	1.3M Gained
	1983	225	-78	173	276	277	378	418	-308	###	271	352	356		
7.5%	2008	-10	-50	-33	-149	-231	-193	-210	-334	-458	-554	-728	-673	-8363.0	8.4M Lost
	2009	-779	-726	-753	-528	-387	-515	-346	-212	-225	-224	64	-109		

1982-83 Recession Compared To 2008-09 Recession

Source: Bureau of Labor Statistics

Figure 60: 1982 Recession versus Great Recession Job Losses[117]

Figure 60 compares the job losses in the 1982-1983 Recession to the Great Recession. The two year average unemployment (U3) rates were greater in the 1982-1983 Recession (9.7%) than the Great Recession, which averaged more than two percent lower (7.5%). However, due to amplitude, or severity, of the Great Recession, the numbers of jobs lost were significantly more severe. 8.4 million jobs were lost in the Great Recession, whereas the 1982-1983 Recession ended with a net gain of 1.3 million jobs. As a result, the official unemployment rate is projected to remain high and will not get back to the normal range until the end of the decade at the earliest—even though a V-shaped recovery is anticipated. As shown in Figure 61, the President's 2011 budget assumptions project that unemployment will not return to normal range (in the 5% range) until 2016.

---

117 US Department of Labor, Bureau of Labor Statistics, Databases, Change in Non-Farm Employment (1-Month Net Change), Employment, Hours, and Earnings from the Current Employment Statistics survey (National), 8 March 2010, http://data.bls.gov/PDQ/servlet/SurveyOutputServlet?data_tool=latest_numbers&series_id=CES0000000001&output_view=net_1mth

	Actual		White House Projections										
	2008	2009	2010	2011	2012	2013	2014	2015	2016	2017	2018	2019	2020
U3 Rate	5.8%	9.3%	10.0%	9.2%	8.2%	7.3%	6.5%	5.9%	5.5%	5.3%	5.2%	5.2%	5.2%

Source: OMB   Leveling Out To Normal Range

Figure 61: President's 2011 Budget Unemployment Rate Assumptions[118]

While the 1982-1983 Recession's recovery was quite robust, with 2 million jobs added to the workforce in the last four months of 1983, it took until 1988 for the U3 rate to drop into the 5% range. Consequently, even if the US economy recovers in 2010, it may take 5 years for U3 rates to improve to the point where Americans are comfortable again.

For reasons explained in Chapter 1 (US Employment), a robust V-shaped recovery might even make the official unemployment rate go up, which would be tragic from a market psychology point of view. The US saw this phenomenon in April 2010, where 290,000 new jobs were added to the workforce after two years of down months. With this good news, Americans expected the unemployment rate to go down. It didn't. It did the opposite, and increased from 9.7% to 9.9% as more people were energized to reenter the workforce. With 26 million unemployed (U6 rate) and 72 million people off the work grid, this phenomenon may be commonplace as unemployment compensation and welfare benefits run out, and savings are depleted.

So if you are an ardent V-shaped recovery advocate, don't expect the unemployment picture to get better soon. With half the US population officially considered outside the workforce, there are a number of factors that could continue to keep the unemployment rate at 10%. If the US labor force does not increase substantially, the economy simply will not recover. 96 million people in the private sector workforce cannot support 35 million people who work for the government, and the 178 million people who do not work, due to age, infirmity, retirement, family obligations, lack of skills, or unwillingness. V-shaped recovery advocates should be the most ardent advocates for *20 by 20*. It is much easier to produce 20 million new private sector jobs by 2020 during a V-shaped recovery when people are optimistic and investors are less risk averse. 20 million new private sector jobs would increase the workforce base and lighten the overhead burden. 116 million private sector workers would have a much easier job supporting 35 million government salaries and 158 million non-workforce citizens. Balancing the load is a key tenet of Jobenomics. America needs to focus on employment, rather than unemployment, as the main indicator for economic recovery.

---

118 The White House, Office of Management and Budget, Budget of the US Government, Fiscal Year 2011, Economic Assumptions, Table S-13, http://www.whitehouse.gov/omb/budget/Overview/

Chapter 11:
W-SHAPED RECOVERIES AND JOBLESSNESS

W-Shaped Recoveries And Joblessness JOBENOMICS

- The Great Depression had a W-shaped recovery and high unemployment that lasted a decade.
  - Peak unemployment reached 23%.
  - Joblessness increased, decreased, and increased again when the US relapsed into depression. Joblessness finally decreased as the US geared up for entry into WWII.

- The '70s –'80s Recessionary Era had a W-shaped recovery and high unemployment that lasted a decade.
  - Peak unemployment reached 10.8%.
  - Joblessness peaked in 1975 at 10%, decreased, and peaked again in 1982 when the US relapsed into recession. Joblessness finally decreased as the US geared up for the telecom and internet booms.

While the conditions during the '30s and '80s were much different from today, W-shaped recoveries and joblessness serve as vivid examples.

Figure 62: Chapter 11 Summary

Non V-shape theorists say, "whoa, slow down, the recession ain't over yet". This view is espoused by a very diverse group, from naysayers to very credible economists. In the very credible category, the National Bureau of Economic Research (NBER), the non-profit group that makes the official pronouncements on business cycle dates, says that the recession is not over yet.

Regarding the end of the Great Recession, which officially began in December 2007, NBER[119] stated that, as of April 2010,

> "Although most indicators have turned up, the committee decided that the determination of the trough date on the basis of current data would be premature. Many indicators are quite preliminary at this time and will be revised in coming months. The committee acts only on the basis of actual indicators and does not rely on forecasts in making its determination of the dates of peaks and troughs in economic activity. The committee did review data relating to the date of the peak, previously determined to have occurred in December 2007, marking the onset of the recent recession."

In other words, in the sage words of Yogi Berra, "It ain't over 'til it's over."

The NBER committee consists of seven respected economists, like Ben Bernanke and Christina Romer (Chairwoman of the White House Council of Economic Advisors). Their decision not to declare the end of the Great Recession reflected a concern that the economy may succumb to a double-dip recession despite the recent advances in the economy. Their decision was far from unanimous, but it was significant enough for the NBER committee members to take a very cautious and unusual position.

While the US is currently undergoing a nascent recovery, a number of potential near-term downside forces could stifle recovery and send the US economy back into a double-dip (W) recession, or according to the NBER decision, deeper into the current recession. The primary downside, or destructive, forces include:

- The threat of chronically high US unemployment.
- A potential second real estate crisis due to foreclosures, underwater mortgages, serious delinquencies and strategic defaults.
- An economic crisis caused by insolvent states and municipalities.
- Economic meltdown of the eurozone caused by the spread of the Greek contagion.
- Investor malaise or panic caused by withdrawal from $11.6T worth of US stimuli, changes in US monetary policy (e.g., raising interest rates), and liquidation of mortgage-backed and other securities off the Federal Reserve balance sheets.
- The unknown degree of impairment and stability in the global financial system due to the economic crisis, debt, and continued use of exotic financial instruments.
- Collateral damage from international incidents, such as a conflict with Iran or a Korean conflict.
- Unknown effects of major policy changes and government interventions.
- Unknown-unknown events of the magnitude of 9/11.

The US has experienced two W-shaped recoveries. The first W happened during the 1930s in the Great Depression. The second occurred from 1974 to 1985, when back-to-back triple recessions dominated the US economic landscape. Both Ws lasted approximately a decade, and

---

119 Business Cycle Dating Committee of the National Bureau of Economic Research, NBER Committee Confers: No Trough Announced, 12 April 2010, http://www.nber.org/cycles/april2010.html

both featured persistent high unemployment. During the Great Depression era, unemployment ranged from 13% to 23% for 10 years in a row. Between 1974 and 1985, unemployment ranged from a low of 5% to a peak of 10.8%.

According to the NBER,[120] a recession begins when the economy reaches a peak of activity and ends when the economy reaches its trough. Between trough and the next peak, the economy is in an expansion. The Great Depression W lasted almost 9 years before a 7 year expansion that peaked at the end of WWII. The 1974–1985 Era was actually a "double W" that lasted 9 years until an 8 year expansion ensued. The actual shapes and duration are depicted in Figure 63.

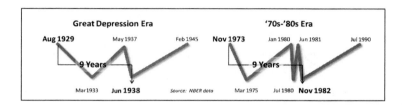

Figure 63: Previous Ws

Great Depression Era. While the baseline conditions during the Great Depression were significantly different from today, the severity and length of joblessness during the 1930s continues to serve as a vivid example (Figure 64).

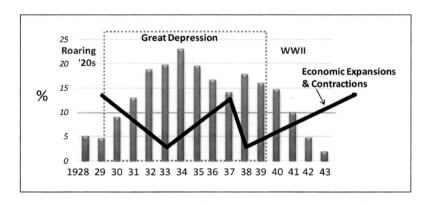

Figure 64: Great Depression Era "W" and Joblessness

The history of the Great Depression's bout with joblessness is pertinent today, inasmuch as politicians react to suffering the same today as yesteryear. The response to joblessness in the 1930s consisted of the infusion of massive economic stimuli and monetary manipulation, a spate of new social programs (Social Security, FDIC, and numerous New Deal welfare programs), increased taxation on the wealthy and the implementation of the Individual Income Tax, and the creation

---

120 The National Bureau of Economic Research, US Business Cycle Expansions and Contractions, http://www.nber.org/cycles/cyclesmain.html#

of a huge national debt that reached 109% of GNP. A timeline of major events from 1928 to 1945 is provided:

- 1928. The Roaring '20s are in full swing. Average prices of stocks rise 40%. Unemployment rate is 5%, but major disparities between rich and poor exist. Hoover elected President.

- 1929. Economic expansion peaks in August. Recession begins. Stock market crashes on October 24 (Black Tuesday). Banks fail. Unemployment rate is 4.6%.

- 1930. Federal Reserve cuts the prime interest rate from 6 to 3.5%. The Smoot-Hawley Tariff puts 40% tariffs on imports. GNP falls 9.4%. Major banks fail. Unemployment rate climbs to 8.9%.

- 1931. GNP falls another 8.5%. Unemployment rises to 13.0%.

- 1932. GNP falls a record 13.4%. Unemployment rises to 18.8%. Industrial stocks down 80%. 40% of all banks failed. International trade down 67%. Glass-Steagall Act creates FDIC and increases power of the Federal Reserve. Top tax rate is raised from 25% to 63%. President Roosevelt (FDR) elected and Democrats win control of Congress. FDR moves the dollar off the gold standard to allow greater monetary intervention and manipulation.

- 1933. Third banking panic. FDR closes banks to stop a depositor run. Attempted plot to overthrow FDR foiled. Unemployment rises to 19.8%. FDR creates New Deal for relief, reform and recovery. Numerous new agencies formed. Massive transfer of wealth from rich to the poor. Farm prices down by 50%. Federal Reserve cuts the prime interest rate to 1.75%.

- 1934. More FDR New Deal programs. Unemployment peaks at 23%. GNP increases 7.7%. Recovery is announced. Federal Reserve cuts the prime interest rate to 1%.

- 1935. More FDR New Deal programs. Social Security formed. Wealth Tax Act passes increasing taxes on the rich, estates and inheritance. Small business tax rate decreased to 12%. Supreme Court declares the National Recovery Administration unconstitutional limiting FDR's power to regulate employee wages and hours. FDR reelected. Unemployment falls to 19.5%. Recovery continues due to stimulus.

- 1936. More FDR New Deal programs. Rural Electrification Act passed starting major infrastructure projects. Congress overrides FDR veto on veterans' bonuses. Top tax rate increased to 79%. Recovery continues. GNP grows a record 14.1%. Unemployment falls to 16.6%.

- 1937. **Recovery stalls. Economy succumbs to second depression**. More FDR New Deal programs. Supreme Court declares the National Labor Relations Board unconstitutional and FDR unsuccessfully tries to reorganize the Court (FDR's infamous court packing scheme).

- 1938. GNP falls 4.5 percent due to recession. First minimum wage law enacted. Democrats lose 71 Congressional seats during November elections. Unemployment rises to 17.8%.

- 1939. WWII starts in Europe with Hitler's invasion of Poland. FDR borrows and spends significantly to build up Armed Forces and defense manufacturing. Congress opposes entry into WWII. Depression ends. Unemployment drops to 16%.

- 1940. War buildup continues. Military draft started. SEC power increased to supervise investment companies and advisors. Unemployment drops to 14.6%.

- 1941. Pearl Harbor attacked. America enters WWII, first against Japan, then Germany. Unemployment drops to 9.9%.

- 1942. Unemployment drops to 4.7%.

- 1943. Unemployment drops to 1.9%.

- 1944: Individual Income Tax Act passed, raises the maximum rate to 94%. Unemployment drops to 1.2%.

- 1945. WWII ends. US emerges an economic superpower with 50% of world GNP (due to destruction and economic collapse in Europe and Asia). National debt 109% of GNP. Unemployment rises to 1.9% and continues to rise to 5.9% by 1950.

	Great Depression 1929-1939	Great Recession 2008-2009
Stock Market	-85%	-50%
Capital investments	-97%	Credit/loans/investments hard to get
Bank failures	-40%	<1% (government support working)
Unemployment rate	-23%	-10% official (17.3% total)
Jobs lost	-13 million	-7.2 million (population twice the size)
US GDP slide	-32%	-4%
Real estate	-53% farms	-31% (national home prices from '06 peak)
Deflation rate	-10%	- 1%
Top tax rate raised	25% to 63% (94% by 1944)	35% (39% projected)

Figure 65: Great Depression & Great Recession Comparison

The timeline in Figure 65 shows a number of similarities and differences between the Great Depression and the recent Great Recession.

Some of the major similarities between then and now include the excesses of the Roaring '20s compared to the roaring '90s (rapid credit expansion, financial innovation and high levels of leverage), massive government spending to stimulate the economy and transfer wealth, a Democrat-controlled White House and Congress, infrastructure jobs programs and increased welfare spending, new entitlement programs, and liquidity and funding problems.

Differences include a different era (industrial versus agricultural), a conservative judiciary, the number of bank failures, better banking and depositor protection, the degree of international trade protectionism, the military and defense industry buildup and the effects of a massive military jobs program, the emergence of the US with 50% of world's GDP as opposed to 25% today, and the emergence of new economic superpowers (ala China) as opposed to the US being the sole superpower.

From a percentage perspective, the Great Depression of 1929-1939 was significantly more economically stressful than the Great Recession of 2008-2009. The world economy was stronger in 2008 than in 1929, and policymakers acted more swiftly to keep the initial crisis from deepening. Hopefully, this will continue to be true in 2018 when a decade by decade comparison can be made. Until then, it is important that the US implement financial reforms in relation to the Great Recession as was implemented after the Great Depression.

At the top of the 2010 priority list is determining the proper role of government in the private sector, oversight of financial institutions that are now too-big-to-fail, and regulating the use and transparency of exotic financial instruments (derivatives). Not only do Americans need greater protection from the excesses and greed in the financial marketplace, but we need a counter-balance to better stem government meddling, intervention and manipulation of the marketplace. Unlike the Great Depression that was mainly caused by Wall Street, the Great Recession was largely caused by US government intervention in the housing markets, and the US government's creation, manipulation and trading of mortgage-backed securities.

'70s-'80s Recessionary Era. The 1973-75 Recession (commonly called the '70s Recession) put an end to the post-WWII economic boom. The primary causes for the '70s Recession were war (Vietnam), energy (1973 Oil Crisis) and competition from newly industrialized countries (such as Asian steel manufacturers). Unemployment rose steadily, peaking at 9% several months after the recession ended.

The 1980-82 Double Recession (commonly called the Early '80s Recession) was comprised of two recessions. The first began in January 1980 and lasted 7 months. Unemployment rose to 7.5%. The second started in June 1981 and lasted until November 1982. The most common reasons given for this recession were unemployment, aggressive monetary policy in response to high inflation, and the 1979 energy shock. In response to high inflation, the Federal Reserve slowed the rate of money growth and significantly raised interest rates. The prime interest rate peaked at 21.5%, the highest rate in modern US history. Unemployment peaked at 10.8%, also the highest rate in recent US history.

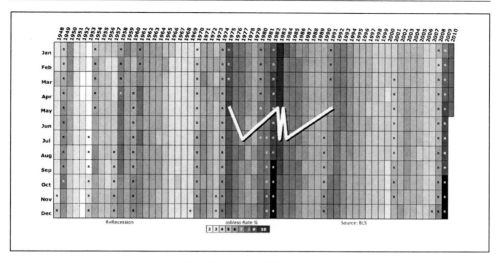

Figure 66: '70s-'80s Era "W" And Joblessness

The timeline,[121] recessionary months, unemployment rates and the W-shaped recovery are depicted in Figure 66. Starting in 1973, US joblessness was a major problem for two decades, ending in the early 1990s with the advent of the information technology revolution that generated millions of new jobs and spurred economic growth.

Similarities between then and now include high unemployment, massive involvement of the Federal Reserve, energy shocks, prolonged foreign conflicts (the Cold War), and increased competition from emerging economies.

Differences include: deflation versus inflation, and the availability and use of exotic financial instruments like derivatives.

Issues for 2010. The driving issue for both the Great Depression and '70s-'80s Recessionary Era became joblessness. The same is true today. While issues like financial reform and government intervention are key issues, they are secondary to the greater issue of getting people back to work, so they can take care of their families and generate tax revenues for our government to work. We need to focus on a national jobs creation campaign that will generate approximately 20 million new, value-added, private sector jobs by 2020.

121 Wall Street Journal, US Unemployment: A Historical View, November 2009, http://online.wsj.com/public/resources/documents/JOBSHISTORY09.html

Chapter 12:

DECLINING L-SHAPED RECOVERY FORCES AND FACTORS

Declining L Forces And Factors

- **Current Declining L economies:**
  - Japan
  - Greece

- **Potential disruptive events/crises:**
  - Economic
    - ✓ Second real estate crisis
    - ✓ Prolonged inflation/deflation
    - ✓ Energy crisis/disruption
  - Military
    - ✓ Mideast nuclear event
    - ✓ Major terrorist attack
  - Non-Man Made
    - ✓ Major natural disaster(s)
    - ✓ Pandemics
  - Unknown-unknowns

Major disruptive forces could collapse economies.

Figure 67: Chapter 12 Summary

Of all the variations of the L-shaped recovery scenario, the declining L is the worst because it indicates economic decline or collapse. There are several pertinent declining L national examples that include:

- Japan, which is slowly deteriorating due to the lingering effects of an asset bubble burst and ineffective government intervention.

- Greece, which is experiencing a national debt crisis as well as potentially defaulting on its sovereign debt and other obligations.
- Both Japan and Greece are useful case studies, since what's happening in these countries could transpire in the US.

There are plausible threats that could induce a declining L scenario in the US that include:

- A wide range of known and unknown-unknown disruptive forces and factors.
- The near-term military threats to US economic well-being posed by a conflict with Iran.

Following the burst of the US housing bubble and the resulting economic crisis, the US government pursued a path very similar to the Government of Japan (GoJ) after the burst of the Japanese asset bubble in 1990. Both bursts led to a period of deflation. The Japan deflationary period has lasted twenty years. The US deflationary period lasted one year. Most analysts predict an inflationary future for America. A growing few see the future as deflationary (see Chapter 16). If deflationary, then the Japanese case study becomes even more relevant.

The Hellenic Republic (Greece) represents one of the 27 members of the European Union (EU). It is also a member of the inglorious PIGS group, which includes Portugal, Italy, Greece and Spain. All of the PIGS are financially distressed countries that are putting tremendous financial pressure on the EU and its common currency, the euro (€). What makes the Greek/PIGS case study pertinent are the parallels between the insolvent member nations of the EU and the insolvent states within the US. If a number of small member states can disrupt the EU (the largest collective economy in the world), what would the economic collapse of a few states do to the US? Equally pertinent is that the EU went "big" using the US bailout playbook. In May 2010, the EU unveiled a financially breathtaking $966B plan to save the eurozone from the Greek/PIGS contagion. As a result, the vanguards of the Western world (US and EU) have placed "all-in" bets to shock their financial systems back into health.

Of all the military threats that can disrupt the US economy, Iran heads the list. Conflict with Iran can disrupt, or even collapse, the US economy via blocking the transit of oil through the Strait of Hormuz, initiating conventional or nuclear warfare in the Gulf region, or conducting large scale terrorist attacks within the US.

Japan Case Study. Most Americans use Great Britain as a model for what the US economy may look like in the future. Japan may be a better model.

In the 1980s, the Japanese experienced a huge economic boom that inflated a tremendous asset bubble similar to the asset bubble that materialized in the US over the last decade. The Japanese asset bubble was so huge that it was rumored at one point that the property value of the greater Tokyo metropolitan area was equal to the property value of the rest of the world.

In December 1989, the Japanese asset bubble burst. Their economy nearly collapsed. Their stock market has yet to recover. Locked in a twenty year deflationary spiral, their economy continues to languish in a declining L-shaped scenario.

As shown in Figure 68, Nikkei 225 has lost 74% of its value. The Nikkei 225 is a stock market index for the Tokyo Stock Exchange. The Nikkei is the most widely quoted index for Japanese stocks, similar to the US Dow Jones Industrial Average.

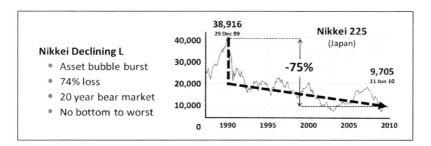

Figure 68: Nikkei Experience

The 1989 Japanese financial crisis not only caused their markets to crash, but ushered in decades of stagnant economic growth. During this period, the fragile Japanese economy rebounded several times, but succumbed again to unforeseen aftershocks, like the Asian economic crisis, the Dot.com crash, and the Great Recession. Consequently, growth in Japan has been slower throughout the 1990s and 2000s than growth in other major industrial nations.

	Jan	Feb	Mar	Apr	May	Jun	Jul	Aug	Sep	Oct	Nov	Dec
2010	-1.29%	-1.10%	-1.09%	-1.19%								
2009	0.00%	-0.10%	-0.30%	-0.10%	-1.08%	-1.76%	-2.25%	-2.24%	-2.24%	-2.53%	-1.87%	-1.68%
2008	0.70%	1.01%	1.20%	0.80%	1.29%	2.00%	2.30%	2.09%	2.09%	1.68%	0.99%	0.40%
2007	0.00%	-0.20%	-0.10%	0.00%	0.00%	-0.20%	0.00%	-0.20%	-0.20%	0.30%	0.60%	0.70%
2006	-0.10%	-0.10%	-0.20%	-0.10%	0.10%	0.50%	0.30%	0.90%	0.60%	0.40%	0.30%	0.30%
2005	0.20%	-0.10%	0.00%	0.10%	0.10%	-0.50%	-0.30%	-0.30%	-0.30%	-0.79%	-0.99%	-0.40%
2004	-0.30%	0.00%	-0.10%	-0.40%	-0.50%	0.00%	-0.10%	-0.20%	0.00%	0.50%	0.80%	0.20%
2003	-0.40%	-0.20%	-0.10%	-0.10%	-0.20%	-0.40%	-0.20%	-0.30%	-0.20%	0.00%	-0.50%	-0.40%
2002	-1.37%	-1.57%	-1.18%	-1.08%	-0.88%	-0.69%	-0.79%	-0.89%	-0.69%	-0.89%	-0.40%	-0.30%
2001	-0.39%	-0.29%	-0.68%	-0.78%	-0.78%	-0.88%	-0.78%	-0.78%	-0.78%	-0.78%	-0.98%	-1.18%
2000	-0.68%	-0.68%	-0.58%	-0.77%	-0.68%	-0.58%	-0.58%	-0.49%	-0.97%	-1.16%	-0.88%	-0.49%
1999	0.19%	-0.10%	-0.39%	-0.10%	-0.39%	-0.29%	-0.10%	0.29%	-0.19%	-0.67%	-1.15%	-1.06%
1998	1.88%	1.98%	2.28%	0.39%	0.48%	0.10%	-0.10%	-0.29%	-0.19%	0.19%	0.78%	0.58%
1997	0.60%	0.60%	0.50%	1.98%	1.98%	2.28%	1.98%	2.18%	2.47%	2.57%	2.18%	1.88%
1996	-0.50%	-0.40%	-0.10%	0.20%	0.20%	0.00%	0.40%	0.20%	0.00%	0.50%	0.50%	0.60%
1995	0.50%	0.20%	-0.30%	-0.20%	-0.10%	0.20%	0.10%	-0.20%	0.10%	-0.69%	-0.69%	-0.40%
1994	1.31%	1.21%	1.31%	0.80%	0.80%	0.50%	-0.20%	0.00%	0.20%	0.79%	1.00%	0.60%
1993	1.23%	1.43%	1.22%	0.91%	0.91%	0.91%	1.93%	1.82%	1.51%	1.31%	1.01%	1.11%
1992	1.77%	1.98%	1.97%	2.37%	2.05%	2.27%	1.65%	1.75%	2.06%	1.02%	0.61%	1.12%
1991	4.00%	3.56%	3.66%	3.41%	3.40%	3.41%	3.52%	3.29%	2.64%	2.71%	3.03%	2.62%
1990	3.24%	3.70%	3.68%	2.74%	2.50%	2.29%	2.29%	2.84%	2.71%	3.01%	3.80%	3.07%

Key: Deflation less than 1% | Normal: 1% to 2.9% | Inflation 3%+

Figure 69: Deflation in Japan [122]

For the most part, Americans have little understanding of how much the life of the average Japanese citizen has changed over the last several decades. On the surface, to visitors, life in Japan

---

122 Rate Inflation, Japan-Historical Inflation Rates, 15 April 2010, http://www.rateinflation.com/inflation-rate/japan-historical-inflation-rate.php?form=jpnir

appears to be like it always has been. Underneath the surface, the Japanese economy has been gradually deteriorating and slowly degrading in quality-of-life for the Japanese people.

To truly understand what's happening in Japan, one has to appreciate a deflationary mentality.

Figure 69 shows Japanese deflation, from the Japanese market crash to the present. Over the last 20 years, 14 years have been deflationary.

Deflation has changed the culture of Japan in several ways. First, the Japanese have become counter-consumers of Japanese goods and services. From a deflationary point-of-view, if the price is going to be lower tomorrow, why buy today? Second, the Japanese have become voracious savers. While saving may be good for a rainy day, it restrained economic growth. It also allowed the Government of Japan (GoJ) to sell long-term government bonds at very low rates, which was used to run up an astronomic national debt on government programs that did not work.

Rather than incentivizing jobs creation from a bottom-up orientation, the GoJ relied on government sponsored programs and big industrial corporations to drive the economy. As small businesses disappeared, along with an aging population, a general deflationary malaise enveloped the country.

Deflation ravaged goods and services. Households withheld spending. Consumption went down. Big ticket goods were not sold. Price wars weeded out weaker companies. The middle class shrunk. Small businesses disappeared. Midsize Japanese companies, unsure how to invest, avoided recapitalization.

Numerous Japanese industrial icons, like Toyota, still dominate the export-oriented economy, but are in trouble competitively. Asset deflation continues to take a toll on Japanese banks. New businesses struggle to get credit, even though the Bank of Japan has held interest rates near zero in an attempt to spur demand. An aging population and low birth rates are depopulating the country, and further weakening demand, consumption and the economy.

The GoJ has struggled with numerous government programs to correct problems with the economy, speculative financial practices, cronyism, entrenched bureaucracies, and deflated real estate. Despite twenty years' worth of efforts, the government has achieved limited change. One thing that has changed is the Japanese national debt, which has soared to 200% of GDP[123]—the highest in the developed world.

Fortunately for the GoJ, 95% of its national debt is held internally by its citizens. As a point of comparison, almost 50% of the US national debt held by the public is owned by foreigners. The reason this is fortunate for the GoJ is that government has far more control over its populace than it does over foreign investors who have a right to dictate policy in regard to their investments. The GoJ is also fortunate that the Japanese people are renowned for their loyalty and devotion to their government. Considering the Nikkei's continual decline and near zero interest rates at banks, bonds were the best investment option. This has allowed the GoJ to reduce Japanese 10-year bond

---

123 International Money Fund, Data and Statistics, World Economic Outlook, October 08, http://www.imf.org/external/pubs/ft/weo/2008/02/weodata

yields from 7% in 1990, to 1.4% today. Unlike citizens of other countries, the Japanese did not cut their losses and reinvest in foreign equities or bonds. With the additional invisible yields supplied by deflation, Japanese bond holders (private citizens, pension funds and corporations) continue to stay the course. Since the GoJ is so dependent on the sale of bonds to finance basic operations, as well as debt, any change in their ability to sell bonds could be disastrous for their economy. A high percentage of Japanese bond holders are elderly Japanese. As they age and deplete their savings, the GoJ may have to look elsewhere in the country for new customers.

Notwithstanding the high percentage of internally-held national debt and GoJ assurances, international credit rating agencies are threatening to lower the country's bond ratings, due to the combination of an aging population, out-of-control debt, declining international competitiveness, and deflation.

Aging. Japan is the grayest country in the world, with one in five of its citizens currently over 65. An elderly population, coupled with low fertility rates, is bad for any economy. Twenty years ago, six workers supported a Japanese retiree. In the near future, the number will be two. A smaller tax base cannot support the level of spending of previous generations. Older populations live off savings rather than investing. At some point, and many feel that this point has passed, the Japanese savings will be depleted to the level where buying bonds is no longer an option for many. In addition, Japanese pension funds are reportedly running out of money with which to buy government bonds. Without the elderly and pension funds to buy government debt, it will be up to the central bank and large corporations to keep the GoJ solvent.

Debt. Japanese national debt-to-GDP ratio is already the highest in the developed world. In 2010, for the first time since WWII, the Japanese government will borrow more money than take in tax revenue (44 trillion yen bond sales, versus 37T yen tax revenue[124]). If the GoJ has a hard time selling its long-term bonds, it will have difficulty servicing debt. In 2010, several $T worth of GoJ bonds are due to roll over, which will set the borrowing bar much higher. Interest payments on debt have reached 35% (compared to 8% for the US) of tax revenue, which has been falling significantly. There is even a possibility that the GoJ could domestically default on bonds.

Competition. Japanese industry is the bright spot on the Japanese economic landscape. It is the economic engine of the country. Large interlocking corporate entities, called keiretsu, are the economic Goliaths of Japan. These keiretsu control the country as much as does the GoJ. In 2010, Japanese corporate profits were the highest on record, albeit from much suppressed lows due to the recession. However, times are changing. Rivals in South Korea and China are usurping Japanese market share in traditional industries. China is on the verge of overtaking Japan as the world's second largest economy. Since Japanese domestic consumption is low and going lower, the country depends on industrial exports to keep GDP growing. However, a high percentage of the Japanese exports are helping to fuel China's growth. Exports of high-tech manufacturing tooling will eventually give China a competitive edge over Japan.

---

124 Ministry of Finance, Speech on Fiscal Policy by Minister of Finance Kan at the 174th Session of the National Diet, 29 January 2010, http://www.mof.go.jp/english/budget/e20100129.htm

Deflation. Japanese bondholders have been buying 10-year bonds for over a decade at yields below 2%. Deflation has provided invisible gains for these bondholders. In an aging society with a high percentage of fixed income families, deflation makes savings go further since their yen buys more. The commonly held view amongst the Japanese is that deflation will continue to hold down or reduce prices until the mid-2010s. This view will continue to reduce consumption and weaken the national economy. Many analysts disagree with this view and are positioning themselves for a potential meltdown when the deflationary spiral hits bottom.

After 50 years of almost unbroken political leadership by the Liberal Democratic Party (LDP), a frustrated Japanese populace had enough, and voted for a big change directed against old thinking and old ways. In 2009, the main opposition party, Democratic Party of Japan (DPJ), took power on a platform that is decidedly anti-status quo and anti-establishment. The following is a quote from the DPJ website.[125]

> "Our View of the Status Quo. Today's Japan is no longer responding to the changing times. This is because bureaucracy-led protectionism and conformity and the structure of collusion have reached a dead end. Before Japan enters an age of fewer children and an aging population in the early 21st century, we must overthrow the *ancien régime* locked in old thinking and vested interests, solve the problems at hand, and create a new, flexible, affluent society which values people's individuality and vitality."

The Great Recession was probably the catalyst that toppled 50 years of LDP rule. In December 2009, the Japanese experienced the largest drop in consumer prices in the last four decades. The DPJ took advantage of the fact that the public was unhappy with the CEO-class and the LDP bureaucrats that supported them. The Japanese people wanted change in a major way. They got it by putting the DPJ into power. After less than a year in power, the DPJ is rocked with funding scandals that have undermined the party and its leadership. The GoJ is now adrift.

On 1 June 2010, Prime Minister Hatoyama announced that he would step down, eight months after taking office. The DPJ's promise of change appears to be short lived. While there were political missteps, such as ministerial scandals and disputes about American bases in Okinawa, *Jobenomics* attributes the Hatoyama's rapid fall from grace to economics. As quoted by Hatoyama, "unfortunately, the politics of the ruling party did not find reflection in the hearts of the people.... It is regrettable that the people were gradually unwilling to listen to us." The Japanese people, like most Americans, want jobenomics—the economics of job, wealth and revenue creation— regardless of what party will provide this to them. Today, national sovereignty depends as much on economic security, as it does national security.

Many believe that Japan has finally reached the point in time where previous financial practices will no longer work. But these soothsayers have been wrong before, as the GoJ skillfully maneuvers its debt-ridden economy. As the GoJ has proven, it is not about the amount of debt, but rather a government's ability to finance the debt. As long as a government can borrow and

---

125 The Democratic Party of Japan, Our Basic Philosophy, dated April 1998, accessed 7 April 2010, http://www.dpj.or.jp/english/about_us/philosophy.html

print money with the approval and support of its citizenry and investors, it will stay afloat. However, in the course of time, hundreds of trillions of yen worth of debt will have its dominion.

Thirty years ago, Japan was viewed as the world's economic powerhouse. Thirty years ago, the US was the world's largest creditor nation. The US and Japan are still the two largest world economies, but the economic crisis has significantly weakened both. Both are debtor nations. The prolonged declining L scenario that reshaped Japan could reshape America as well.

Greek/PIGS Case Study. The global financial community is watching the PIGS, which is a derogatory acronym for Portugal, Italy, Greece and Spain. All of these countries are in financial turmoil. All have serious debt issues and are experiencing declining L-shaped economic scenarios. Moreover, the PIGS are threatening the financial stability of the entire European Union (EU), which is bifurcating into the have (France, Germany, UK) nations that are beginning to show signs of economic growth, and the have-nots (PIGS) that are skating near the edge of financial abyss.

Like any family, financial issues generally bring out the worst in people. This is no exception in the 27-nation European Union where 16 of the nations share the euro as a common currency. Traditional rivalries, like those between Germany and France, as well as Eastern and Western Europe are beginning to intensify as financial difficulties continue to worsen with the PIGS. While the PIGS are in the worst trouble, they are not unique. Thirteen of the 27 EU members face debts equal to more than 60% of their GDP, the limit set by the European Commission. This group includes the UK and France.

Of the four PIGS countries, Greece is teetering closest towards defaulting on their sovereign (national) debts. The Greek national debt is 125% of GDP, and their annual budget deficit is 12.7% of GDP, making it the worst economy in Europe. The good news is that Greece is a small economy representing only 2.5% of Europe's GDP.

There is mounting concern that Greece will be unable to finance a budget deficit, which is more than four times the EU's debt limit, or make payments on its sovereign debt. A Greek default has far-reaching financial and political implications for the EU, which by charter constitutes a single market. If one part of its market is allowed to fail, what does that mean for the viability of the entire market? The term that most economists and policymakers use is "contagion." They are as much concerned about the Greek contagion spreading as the Greek crisis itself.

Increasingly investors fear that the Greek contagion will spread to Portugal, Spain and Italy whose credit ratings are also falling. If this continues, investors will be unwilling to fund these countries regardless of their economic fundamentals. Without the ability to sell bonds or borrow money, these countries will default on their debts and sovereign obligations. Default will put significant pressure on European banks that own securities from these countries. The European Central Bank (the EU equivalent of the US Fed) controls the monetary policy of the 16 eurozone member states. It is also the major source of funding for countries like Greece, and could face major losses on its own loan portfolio if Greek banks fail and the government defaults.

Economists shocked the world in 2009 by predicting that Greece might default on its debt payments and other obligations. Immediately, credit rating agencies began downgrading Greece's debt. One rating agency downgraded the Greeks to junk bond status and forecast that investors may have as low as a 30% chance of recovering their investments if the Greeks default.

This shock rippled through the European Union and the rest of the world's financial community. The value of the European Union's common currency, the euro, immediately started to fall against the US dollar. In addition, the entire European Union's financial system is threatened, since many of the major banks, like the European Central Bank, face major losses if the Greeks default.

As a result of their debt, the Greeks need to borrow money. Since Greece cannot print euros, they have to borrow either by selling bonds or by asking for loans from other countries. Their preference is selling Greek bonds over receiving bailout money from other countries.

In order to sell domestic bonds, the Greek government had to do two things to attract potential investors to buy Greek bonds: dramatically increase the interest rate of their bonds as compared to other nations, and commit to reducing their budget deficit.

The Greeks increased the yield on their benchmark 10-year bonds to double or triple the yield of other EU 10-year bonds. At double and triple the yield of other bonds, the Greeks were able to obtain enough short-term capital to keep the government running for several months. But, they needed to sell more. When they held a bond auction in April 2010, the Greeks were able to auction off only a portion of their bonds. It was apparent that investor confidence was waning.

With limited ability to raise money through bond sales, the Greeks turned to the EU, which responded with a limited amount of bailout money in the form of loans. This bailout money caused a lot of contention within the EU, due to anger at Greek corruption and profligate spending habits. Tension was especially acute between France, which favored more generous bailouts, and Germany, which favored more of a tough-love approach. In the end, a limited amount of loans were provided with a precondition that the Hellenic Republic had to institute strict austerity measures to force some brutal sacrifices in order for the Greeks to put their fiscal house in order.

As part of the austerity measures, Greece had to make good on its commitment to reduce debt from 12.7% to 8.7% of GDP by the end of 2010—a 31% reduction. In order to accomplish this goal, the Hellenic Republic is cutting employees, freezing wages, raising taxes, increasing retirement ages, and curtailing many government services. In addition, the Greek government increased its Value Added Tax (VAT) rate to 23%, as well as increasing excise taxes for fuel, tobacco and alcohol.

This austerity plan has drawn praise from other eurozone finance ministers, who have devised an emergency aid package for financial assistance for the Greeks, in case their domestic reduction and borrowing efforts do not solve the Greek sovereign debt issues.

While the program is popular with some financially-oriented outsiders, Greek citizens are not so happy. Rightfully so, since the austerity measures will likely lead to massive GDP contraction, which will make the life of the average citizen much more difficult. In protest, public sector workers in Greece launched nationwide strikes—some of the largest protests in

Greek history. Transportation workers deserted train stations. Unemployed school teachers staged anti-government demonstrations. Angry youths firebombed a central Athens bank, killing three people, in protest against Greek austerity measures.

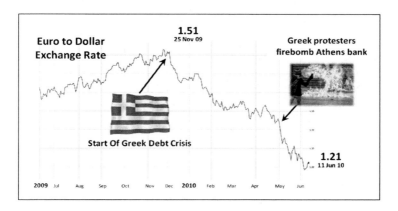

Figure 70: Greek Debt Crisis Devalues the Euro

Greek protests are having a deleterious effect on the euro as shown in Figure 70. In addition, the more violent the protesters become, the lower credit ratings the Greek government and Greek banks receive. Credit rating agencies are closely watching the demonstrations and protests in order to determine whether the Greek government can implement the austerity plans to reduce the need for future foreign aid. At the end of the day, the primary thing that the protests generated was greater scrutiny from the international community on enforcement of Greek austerity measures, in fear that the Greek debt contagion will spread to other countries in the EU.

At the end of April 2010, the EU and IMF agreed to a $145 billion bailout loan that would give the Greeks breathing room until they could regain market confidence. Regrettably for the Greeks, the rescue package may not materialize as promised. A number of countries, like Germany, are experiencing significant pushback from their citizens and are renegotiating their commitment. 90% of the German people object to financing the Greeks. In the middle of May 2010, the EU rolled out a broader bailout and buyout plan to inoculate the entire eurozone from the Greek contagion. The EU plan totaled $996B (€750B) from EU, IMF, European Central Bank, and the US Federal Reserve. The EU contribution includes loans to governments and buying government debt. The IMF pledges up to $332B (€250B) aid to states. The European Central Bank is buying government and corporate debt on the open market, expanding cash reserves of member banks via low interest loans. The US Federal Reserve is providing unlimited short-term loans to European banks.

Many international policymakers and opinion-leaders believe that any IMF (and Fed) involvement with EU signals a key turning point in the EU. It signals that the EU cannot take care of its own, despite its charter as a political and economic union. It also signals that national interests prevail over regional interests, thereby reducing the future viability of the fledgling Union that was established on 1 November 1993. It is also calling into question the future of the euro, the world's second largest reserve currency that entered circulation on 1 January 2002. Some market-watchers predict the end of the eurozone. A few eurozone countries may abandon the euro and return to their previous domestic currencies. At the top of the list is Germany, which is the largest economic powerhouse in the European Union. A German return to the Deutsche Mark would likely be the death knell for the euro. Others argue that the massive EU/IMF/Fed bailout package will weaken the resolve of ailing countries to implement tough austerity programs, or cause countries like Greece and Ireland to retreat from tough austerity programs already implemented.

Jobenomics estimates that the $966B bailout plan will work for a year or two, and will follow the path of the US recovery. If there are no structural flaws in the EU economy, and barring future crises, the EU should recover. On the other hand, if there are structural flaws that are merely covered up by the infusion of $1T worth of liquidity, the eurozone could collapse when this liquidity evaporates. History will judge this current era as the "great Western bet." If the US and EUs bets payoff, they will be deemed wise and propitious. If they don't, Western economies will likely give way to the East, and a new world order.

If an economic crisis envelopes the EU, it will likely spread to the US. In fact it already has. On 6 May 2010, a brief panic about Greece's defaults, along with reticence regarding US economy and a technical glitch, sent the Dow Jones Industrial Average down over 1,000 points or 9%. Had this drop not recovered, it would have been the largest drop in the Dow's history. The opposite also happened. The day after the EU announced the $966B bailout plan, the Dow rose 450 points in day—the largest one day rally in several years.

The US and EU are economically linked. Disturbance in one directly affects the other. While there is natural competition between the EU and the US, they function together as vanguards of democracy, capitalism, freedom and human rights. The EU and US are the also vanguards for the Western way-of-life.

From a geo-political point of view, the West is teetering and the East is expanding. The global economic balance-of-power could shift rather quickly if the West stumbles economically. It is not inconceivable that Beijing or Abu Dhabi could replace New York and London as the financial capitals of the world. As stated in the Abu Dhabi Economic Vision 2030,[126] "Abu Dhabi is not just seeking to develop its economy. The aim is for the Emirate to take its place among the most successful economies of the world by 2030." While Abu Dhabi benchmarks its economy against smaller nations, it has the financial resources of a creditor nation to play a much greater role in the international financial community.

The best course for the US to avoid the challenges facing the EU is to be proactive in cutting spending and reducing debt. Leadership and vision are required. One such EU leader is Brian Cowen.

---

126 The Government of Abu Dhabi, The Abu Dhabi Economic Vision 2030, Leading International Status, Page 10, November 2008, http://gsec.abudhabi.ae/Sites/GSEC/Content/EN/PDF/Publications/economic-vision-2030-executive-summary-mandate2,property=pdf.pdf

Ireland is sometimes included in the PIGS terminology, but the Irish government is proactively and vigorously fighting to discourage the financial community from including them in this demeaning category. Irish Prime Minister, Brian Cowen, is a zealous advocate regarding fiscal constraint and debt reduction. He is cutting public-sector salaries, including his own, and reducing social services to assure foreign investors that Ireland can meet its obligations. So far, his efforts are working and the financial community (especially the rating agencies) is giving the Irish the benefit of the doubt. While the financial community's acronym remains PIGS, as opposed to PIIGS, the Irish public has not been as generous to the Irish government, which has the lowest popularity and approval ratings in recent Irish history.

Most politicians are reactive. Proactively addressing debt issues is risky for any politician. Usually it means political death. It is easier for a politician to criticize than correct. It often takes a crisis or collapse before enough political will can be generated to address a problem. While the US government reacted successfully to avert financial collapse, it has been reticent to proactively address debt reduction and financial reform efforts, like the Irish Prime Minister.

Known and Unknown-Unknown Disruptive Forces and Factors. There are a number of known and unknown-unknown crises and events that could propel the US economy into a prolonged declining L period.

A major crisis, or combination of smaller events, could severely threaten the US economy in a relatively short period of time. The sub-prime mortgage crisis triggered an economic crisis that nearly brought the US financial system to the brink of collapse.

Some of the leading known disruptive declining L forces and factors include:

- Economic
  - o Second real estate crisis (residential or commercial)
  - o Prolonged period of high inflation/deflation
  - o Devalued dollar or new reserve currency
  - o Municipal/state bankruptcies
  - o Energy crisis/disruption

- Military
  - o Mideast nuclear event/domestic dirty bomb
  - o International conflicts/wars/cyber warfare
  - o Major terrorist attack/biological warfare/EMP (electromagnetic pulse) attack

- Non-Man Made
  - o Major natural disaster(s), pandemics
  - o Astronomical/eschatological event

- Unknown-unknowns

The US recovery also could be disrupted by unknown-unknown declining L forces and factors. Unknown-unknowns (unk-unks) have been a part of the US military wargaming community since the early 1980s. Unk-unks acknowledge possibilities that are not conceived at a given point in time. The 9/11 Trade Tower attack was an unk-unk. The Eyjafjallajökull Icelandic volcano was an unk-unk that cost the airline industry three years of profits. The BP oil spill is another unk-unk. The response guide for unk-unks cannot be written, but only nervously anticipated. It is not unusual for lives of individuals, as well as the future of nations, to turn about on an unanticipated or unintended event.

Figure 71: Conflict/Wars a Declining L Catalyst

As shown in Figure 71, of all the military threats facing the US, war with Iran has the most menacing consequences from both security and economic standpoints. North Korea is perhaps the second most menacing threat. Following the alleged sinking of a South Korean warship by a North Korean submarine in March 2010, the North Korean threat is rapidly moving to the forefront in the global stage. On a moment's notice, the North Koreans could conduct a barrage of 11,000 artillery tubes, or a nuclear weapon, to lay waste to Seoul, a capital city of 11 million people and an Asian center of commerce. The failing health of Kim Jong Il, the 69 year old Stalinist dictator of North Korea, only adds to international tensions. Whether it is Iran, Korea, or some unk-unk location, the world is more dangerous today than at the height of the Cold War.

A brief discussion may be worthwhile to show how an event, like war with Iran, could be a catalyst for a declining L scenario.

From a strategic perspective, Iran is the lynchpin in a larger strategic equation that involves both Russia and China, both of which support Iran politically, militarily and economically. If Iran is successful in establishing itself as the dominant regional power in the Middle East, the global geo-political center would shift increasingly from the West to the East.

Iran is provoking a conflict with the West, using American and Israeli occupation in the Middle East as the cause célèbre for an Islamic common cause. However, there are more fundamental reasons motivating the Ayatollahs and the leaders of the Islamic Republic of Iran. These reasons include:

- Political: Supreme Leader Ali Khamenei and President Mahmoud Ahmadinejad repeatedly state that their primary political objective is to revive the crumbling Islamic Revolution. An external enemy helps advance the ultra-conservative position over reformers and youth who want détente with the West.

- Economic: Control of 50% of the world's oil reserves greatly benefits Iran. Increasing economic sanctions will either motivate Iranian leaders towards moderation or encourage their aggressiveness.

- Military: Compared to several hundred thousand members of US forces in neighboring Iraq and Afghanistan, the Islamic Republic has several million combat personnel strategically positioned to attack Western coalition forces. Additionally, they openly state their right to develop a nuclear capability.

- Religious: Messianically-inclined Shia leaders are preparing for the establishment of a global Caliphate, confrontation with Israel and America, and expected near-term return of the Islamic messiah, the Mahdi.

- Historical: Confederacy with Shiite Iraq is a historic opportunity after 1,000 years of domination from Sunni Arabs and Ottoman Turks.

The Iranian leaders have repeatedly stated that war with the West is inevitable. Iran is currently engaged in a war of words. When they achieve nuclear weapons capability, their rhetoric may turn to military action, especially if they feel that they are about to be attacked by Israel and Israel's Western allies.

Military planners foresee three possible engagement scenarios: closing the Strait of Hormuz, military action against Israel, and military action against America either at home (terrorist attack) or abroad.

Strait of Hormuz. Closing the Strait of Hormuz would create a global energy and economic crisis. The Strait of Hormuz is of great strategic importance. It is the only sea route through which oil from Kuwait, Iraq, Iran, Saudi Arabia, Bahrain, Qatar, and the United Arab Emirates, can be transported to the rest of the world. Between 20% and 25% of the world oil supplies transit the narrow Strait of Hormuz.

The strait at its narrowest is 21 miles wide with two 1-mile wide channels for marine traffic separated by a 2-mile wide buffer zone. Iran has conducted several major naval exercises to showcase its capability to close the Strait of Hormuz and Supreme Leader Ali Khamenei has publicly stated that Iran will close the Strait if provoked. If the Strait is closed, the price of oil could quadruple overnight. More importantly, the disruption of the flow of oil would quickly impact the economies of numerous nations, including the US.

Military action against Israel. President Ahmadinejad has stated on numerous occasions that Iran intends to "wipe Israel off the map," "very soon," with a single decisive blow. Preemptive military action against Israel would likely entail a coordinated missile attack, including 40,000 short-range rockets (Katyusha), hundreds of medium-range missiles (Scud) and a few nuclear-tipped theater ballistic missiles (Shehab). Israeli leadership takes these threats seriously and is considering preemptive military action of its own, which could include the use of nuclear weapons. The use of nuclear weapons by either side, or military intervention by the US or Israel to destroy Iranian nuclear development sites, would have major consequences in the global political/economic balance-of-power. It is hard to foresee any outcome that would benefit the US economically or otherwise.

Military action against America at home or abroad. As a result of the 1980-1988 Iran-Iraq War, the longest conventional war in the 20th Century, the Iranian military has maintained the bulk of their 32 divisions and 87 brigades, most of which are stationed on the Iraqi border. Several million Iranian troops, along with Iranian special operation forces (Qods) already in Iraq, could quickly overwhelm the 98,000 US troops in Iraq. Any such action would precipitate a major military response from the US. To counter this response, the Iranians would likely create diversionary or retaliatory attacks within the US.

The types of terrorist actions that they could inflict within the US have been the subject of much conjecture and study. The most serious types of attacks would cause massive loss of life and devastating economic impact. To accomplish an Iranian version of shock and awe, bio-terrorism, dirty bombs, or an offshore EMP explosion would be the most devastating. According to the US Commission to Assess the Threat to the US from Electromagnetic Pulse (EMP),[127]

> "Because of the ubiquitous dependence of US society on the electrical power system, its vulnerability to an EMP attack, coupled with the EMP's particular damage mechanisms, creates the possibility of long-term, catastrophic consequences."

In conclusion, the declining L scenario may not be as farfetched as many of the V-shape advocates expound. As the old fighter pilot adage states, one emergency is usually not a problem, but compounded multiple emergencies are almost always catastrophic. The recent economic crisis serves as a wake-up call to the frailty of the US economic system which is not as robust as it used to be, and to the danger of more exposed disruptions by potential known and unknown-unknown threats.

---

127 US Congress, Report of the Commission to Assess the Threat to the US from Electromagnetic Pulse (EMP) Attack, Critical National Infrastructures, April 2008, http://www.empcommission.org/docs/A2473-EMP_Commission-7MB.pdf

The major points for Section 3: Recovery Scenarios (Chapters 9 through 12) include:

- There are three general recovery scenarios: V, W and L. Each has slight derivations.

- V-Shaped Recovery Scenario

  o The US is currently experiencing a V-shaped economic recovery, as evidenced by a V-shaped employment picture and V-shaped stock market.

  o The Administration has done an excellent job leading the nation away from the financial brink, but it is way too early to state mission success.

- W-Shaped Recovery Scenario

  o W-shaped recoveries are double dip recessions or depressions. The Great Depression was a W, as were the dual recessions in the early 1980s.

  o There is a great deal of concern about how the financial system will react after the extraordinary amount of liquidity that was infused into the economy is eventually withdrawn.

  o There are a number of near-term events (e.g., US housing and/or eurozone crises) that could send the US back into recession.

- L-Shaped Recovery Scenario

  o L-shaped recoveries are no-growth economic recoveries that decay or collapse economies.

  o Japan has been in a 20-year, deflationary declining L scenario. Greece and a number of other financially troubled EU nations are experiencing declining L scenarios. These serve as excellent case studies for the US.

  o The economic system is weakened from the economic crisis, and vulnerable to major events like a war with Iran or a nuclear event in the Middle East.

Figure 72: Section 3: Recovery Scenarios Major Points

CHALLENGES, ISSUES AND INDICATORS

Chapter 13:

CLOSING THE SPENDING/ RECEIPTS GAP

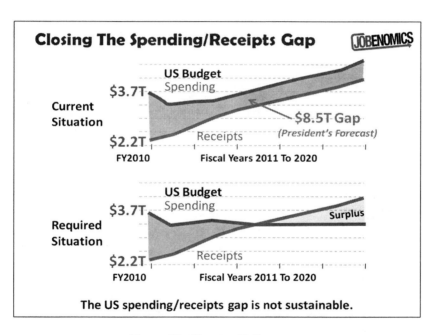

Figure 73: Chapter 13 Summary

The terrorist and economic crises demanded massive amounts of spending by the Bush and Obama Administrations. For the most part, this money was well spent. Looking to the future, America needs to start spending within its means. The US spending/receipts gap is not sustainable. Current spending projections are very risky, especially if the US gets hit with an economic aftershock, a major event, or an unk-unk.

— 123 —

A dual strategy is needed. The first part involves cutting spending. The other involves creating jobs in order to increase revenue. The longer we delay fixing the spending/receipts gap, the quicker the day of reckoning will be upon us.

In order to achieve consensus on strategy, Americans need to understand: (1) the size of the federal spending/receipt gap, (2) the size of the states' spending/receipts gap, and (3) the inevitability of major tax increases until new sources of revenue can be generated.

The Federal Spending/Receipts Gap.

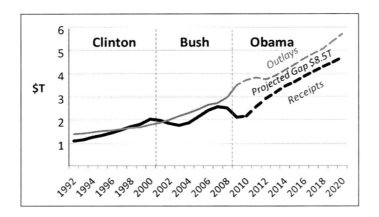

Figure 74: Spending/Receipts Gap during Clinton, Bush and Obama[128]

Figure 74 provides a perspective on the actual and projected spending/receipts gap during the Clinton, Bush and Obama Administrations.

The Clinton Administration provided the Bush Administration with a surplus. The Clinton Administration was fortunate to preside during an era where tens of millions of jobs were created by the information technology revolution. These jobs generated a tax surplus.

The Bush Administration provided the Obama Administration with a deficit. The aftermath of 9/11 was significantly more expensive than the event itself. $T were committed to fighting terrorism abroad (Iraq and Afghanistan) and at home (creation of the Department of Homeland Security). The initiation of the Medicare Part D (prescription) entitlement program also added to the deficit. However, the primary cause of the deficit was speculation in and the leveraging of exotic financial instruments, like mortgage-backed securities, that created a housing asset bubble, which started well before President Bush took office, and ended in an economic crisis that the Obama Administration inherited.

President Obama took office in January 2009. From an economic viewpoint, the following year was historic from a spending/receipts gap perspective. The US federal budget deficit of $1.4T

128 White House Office of Management and Budget, Budget of the United States Government, Fiscal Year 2011, Table S-1, Budget Totals, Page 146, http://www.whitehouse.gov/omb/budget/fy2011/assets/tables.pdf

in FY2009 was the largest spending/receipts gap in modern American history.[129] Spending rose by 18% in 2009, the fastest rate of growth since 1975. Tax receipts tumbled to $2.1T, a 17% decrease from 2008. These two factors caused the federal deficit to triple as a percent of GDP, from 3% to 10%—the highest deficit as a share of GDP since 1945.

From an economic rescue perspective, deficit spending in 2009 was justifiable. Regardless of one's political affiliations or economic inclinations, the Obama Administration performed an exceptional effort in rescuing the economy from entering a second depression. Two individuals are worthy of special mention: Treasury Secretary Tim Geithner and Fed Chairman Ben Bernanke. Their efforts will be the subject of economic and political case studies for years to come.

From a social welfare perspective, deficit spending in 2009 was not as justifiable. To a fiscal conservative, it was reckless. To a social liberal, it was a once in a lifetime opportunity that was justified by both need and the mandate for change in the 2008 elections, that gave the Democratic Party the White House and a super-majority in Congress.

Year 2009 now is in the past, and the future is far more important. The Obama Administration budget forecast continues deficit spending for the 2011 to 2020 time period. They argue that $8.5T deficit spending will be required to clean up the economy as well as to care for the needy.

President's 2011 Budget ($T)

	2011	2012	2013	2014	2015	2016	2017	2018	2019	2020	Total
Revenues	2.57	2.93	3.19	3.46	3.63	3.89	4.09	4.30	4.51	4.71	37.3
Outlays	3.83	3.76	3.92	4.16	4.39	4.67	4.87	5.08	5.42	5.71	45.8
Total Deficit	-1.3	-0.8	-0.7	-0.7	-0.8	-0.8	-0.8	-0.8	-0.9	-1.0	**-8.5**

CBO Estimate of President's 2011 Budget

	2011	2012	2013	2014	2015	2016	2017	2018	2019	2020	Total
Revenues	2.46	2.81	3.09	3.34	3.50	3.69	3.87	4.03	4.21	4.42	35.4
Outlays	3.80	3.72	3.84	4.07	4.30	4.59	4.81	5.03	5.36	5.67	45.2
Total Deficit	-1.3	-0.9	-0.7	-0.7	-0.8	-0.9	-0.9	-1.0	-1.2	-1.3	**-9.8**

Civilian Budget Watchers Analyses*

Total Deficit	*Center for Budget and Policy Studies, Concord Coalition, Peterson-Pew Commission, Brookings Institution, National Academy of Sciences	**-11.0**

Figure 75: Annual Budget Deficit 2011-2020

The CBO[130] calculates the gap at $9.8T (Figure 75). Independent civilian budget watchers, from the Center for Budget and Policy Priorities to the National Academy of Sciences,[131] place

---

129 CBO, Director's Blog, Monthly Budget Review, Federal Budget Deficit Totals $1.4 Trillion in Fiscal Year 2009, November 2009, http://cboblog.cbo.gov/?p=422

130 CBO's Baseline and Estimate of the President's Budget, Table 1, Comparison of Projected Revenues, Outlays, and Deficits in CBO's March 2010 Baseline and CBO's Estimate of the President's Budget, 5 March 2010, http://www.cbo.gov/ftpdocs/100xx/doc10014/Chapter1.5.1.shtml

131 Center for Budget and Policy Priorities, Obama Budget Reduces Deficit By $1.3 Trillion Over Next Decade Compared To Current Policies-But Much More Action Will Be Needed, by Kathy A. Ruffing and James R. Horney, 5 April 2010, http://www.cbpp.org/files/4-5-10bud.pdf

the deficit closer to $11T, largely based on the predictions that additional tax revenues based on rolling back tax exemptions on the middle class, such as the Alternative Minimum Tax (AMT) exemptions, will not materialize.

The $8.5T, $9.8T or $11T deficit forecasts are all based on optimistic V-shaped recovery assumptions discussed in Chapter 10 (V-Shaped Recovery). These assumptions include robust growth in GDP, gradual decline in unemployment, and no major economic aftershocks. In other words, these projections assume tax revenue growth. In addition, these numbers will be added to the $12.6T national debt that already exists.

However, if a W- or L-shaped recovery occurs, the spending/receipt outlook could be catastrophic, as calculated in Figure 76. Figure 76 shows the President's V-shaped recovery projections ($8.5), a W-shaped recovery where the recovery stalls for three years before growing again, and an L-shaped recovery where the tax revenues stay at the 2010 level.

$T	Fiscal Year	Outlays President's 2011 Budget	Tax Receipts		
			V-Shaped Recovery	W-Shaped Recovery	L-Shaped Recovery
Actual	2009	3.5	2.1	2.1	2.1
Projected	2010	3.7	2.2	2.2	2.2
President's 2011 Budget Request	2011	3.8	2.6	2.6	2.2
	2012	3.8	2.9	2.1	2.2
	2013	3.9	3.2	2.3	2.2
	2014	4.2	3.5	2.6	2.2
	2015	4.4	3.6	2.9	2.2
	2016	4.7	3.9	3.2	2.2
	2017	4.9	4.1	3.5	2.2
	2018	5.1	4.3	3.6	2.2
	2019	5.4	4.5	3.9	2.2
	2020	5.7	4.7	4.1	2.2
		45.8	37.3	30.8	21.7
	Deficit		-8.5	-15.0	-24.2
			"V"	"W"	"L"

Figure 76: W- and L-Shaped Recovery Deficits

$15.0T Ten-Year Budget Deficit Assuming A W-Shaped Recovery. An economic shock (like a second housing crisis, nuclear event, EU/Japanese economic meltdown, or a natural disaster of the magnitude of a major California earthquake) could plunge the US back into a recession. Another three year recession would cause the 2011-2020 deficit to swell to $15.0T. This $15.0T is in addition to the $13T of national debt that already exists.

$24.2T Ten-Year Budget Deficit Assuming An L-Shaped Recovery. If multiple crises or major events occurred and created a no-growth, L-shaped scenario, the deficit could be as high as $24.2T. In actuality, this level of deficit would never be reached, because the US government would be forced to cut outlays and raise taxes significantly. However, if the multiple crises were severe enough to generate a declining L-shaped recovery as discussed in Chapter 12, cuts in outlays or increased taxes might not be enough to stem the decline.

The bottom line is that the US is potentially on a very slippery slope economically. Perhaps, now is not the time to be making bets on new social welfare programs. If we are in a betting mood, we should be wagering on jobs creation that would generate new revenue that could be spent on welfare and eliminate poverty.

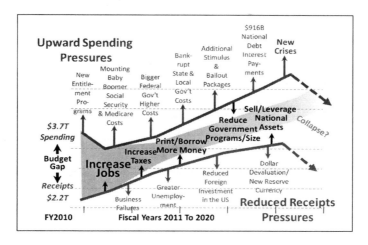

Figure 77: Challenges to Closing the Gap

There are four ways to reduce the spending/receipts gap: (1) cut spending, (2) increase tax revenues via new jobs, (3) increase the tax bite on people already paying taxes, and (4) inflate out of debt.

In President Obama's 2010 State of the Union Address,[132] he promised to cut spending.

"Starting in 2011, we are prepared to freeze government spending for three years. Spending related to our national security, Medicare, Medicaid, and Social Security will not be affected. But all other discretionary government programs will. Like any cash-strapped family, we will work within a budget to invest in what we need and sacrifice what we don't. And if I have to enforce this discipline by veto, I will."

Since the national security, entitlements and interest accounts "will not be affected," the President will freeze government spending on only 14% of the federal budget. National security (23%), entitlements (56%) and interest (7%) accounts equate to the other 86%. Consequently, it is unlikely that the President could achieve any meaningful budget cuts even if Congress would let him.

If an L-shaped scenario occurs, the federal government will be forced to first make major cuts in discretionary accounts over mandatory spending accounts. The national security account is overwhelmingly the largest discretionary account and would be a prime target for cutbacks. Entitlements (Social Security, Medicare, et al.) are mandated by law and hard to cut in a financial crisis. Interest payments have to be paid unless the government chooses to default, which is

---

132 The White House, Office of the Press Secretary, Remarks by the President in State of the Union Address, 27 January 2010, http://www.whitehouse.gov/the-press-office/remarks-president-state-union-address

unlikely. In contrast to cutting entitlements or defaulting on interest payments, axing the Defense Department would be relatively easier to accomplish. Most likely, the federal government would declare a moratorium on recapitalizing the armed forces, withdraw troops from foreign soil, and reorganize the departments of Defense and Homeland Security into a single, leaner organization tailored to a different threat matrix.

How much would a drastic cut in national security help the budget? As calculated hypothetically in Figure 78, the answer is not much. If an L-shaped scenario stalled tax revenue receipts at current levels (i.e., no growth) and the government decided to cut the national security (DoD) account in half starting in FY2014, the resulting savings would only amount to about $2T, leaving a ten-year gap of $22T.

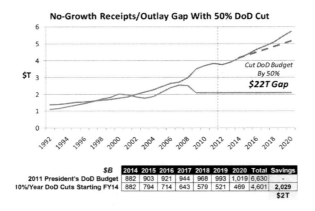

$B	2014	2015	2016	2017	2018	2019	2020	Total	Savings
2011 President's DoD Budget	882	903	921	944	968	993	1,019	6,630	-
10%/Year DoD Cuts Starting FY14	882	794	714	643	579	521	469	4,601	2,029
									$2T

Figure 78: Cutting Defense Will Have Only a Minimum Effect on the Deficit

In regard to inflating out of debt, there is a growing suspicion that the US government has resigned itself to this possibility. Some informed skeptics think that the powers that be (i.e., the President, the Federal Reserve, and the Treasury Department) may harbor a secret wish that inflation actually will happen. Some inflation solves several problems. If residential real estate inflates in value, some upside-down mortgages turn right-side up. Inflated values will help homeowners refinance at better interest rates. Also, inflation allows government to pay back our massive national debt with cheaper dollars. For example, if the inflation rate were 7% per year for 10 years, our national debt would be effectively cut in half. Of course, it would naive to assume that foreign holders of US national debt would stand for this. In fact they are already taking steps, like posturing for a new reserve currency, to prevent this from happening.

So what's the answer? The prudent approach would freeze spending, increase taxes appropriately, and commence a major private sector jobs creation initiative. However, before addressing potential federal government actions, it would be wise to consider the states' spending/receipts gap that could be as virulent to the US federal government as the PIGS crisis is to the EU.

The States' Spending/Receipts Gap. The spending/receipts gap is not sustainable in the vast majority of states, many of which are approaching insolvency.

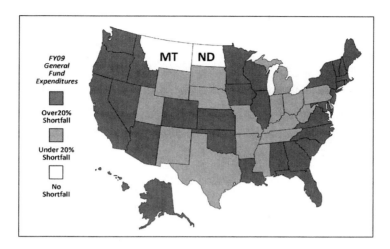

Figure 79: States with Budget Shortfalls

According to an analysis by the Center on Budget and Policy Priorities[133] in FY2009, 48 out of 50 states face budget shortfalls with combined gaps of $600B for fiscal years 2009 through 2012 (Figure 79). The mineral-rich and sparsely populated states of North Dakota and Minnesota are the only two that are fiscally sound. For the 48 other states, unemployment, lower home equity values, reduced consumer spending, and increased demand for essential services are leading many towards insolvency. The rising demand for food stamps, welfare benefits, and Medicaid from millions of unemployed Americans are straining state and local government in ways not experienced since the Great Depression.

According to an updated forecast by the Center on Budget and Policy Priorities,[134] fiscal years 2011 and 2012 do not provide much relief for state budgets (note: the fiscal year begins in July in most states). The Center predicts that 46 of 50 states, a slight improvement over FY2010, with Arkansas and Alaska joining North Dakota and Minnesota in the black, will face FY2011 budget shortfalls of $120B to $180B, or 17% to 27% of budgets of these 46 states. This is only a slight improvement over FY2010 where 48 out of 50 states had a budget deficit of $200B, or 30% of budgets of these 48 states. State budget-closing actions could cost the US economy up to 900,000 public- and private-sector jobs without more federal help. For FY2012, the Center predicts much

133 Center on Budget and Policy Priorities, Recession Continues To Batter State Budgets; State Responses Could Slow Recovery, by Elizabeth McNichol and Nicholas Johnson, 19 November 2009, http://www.cbpp.org/files/9-8-08sfp.pdf, and Center on Budget and Policy Priorities, Slideshow: The State Budget Crisis and the Economy, 48 States Face Budget Shortfalls, http://www.cbpp.org/slideshows/?fa=stateFiscalCrisis
134 Center on Budget and Policy Priorities, Recession Continues To Batter State Budgets; State Responses Could Slow Recovery, by Elizabeth McNichol and Nicholas Johnson, Updated 27 May 2010, http://www.cbpp.org/files/9-8-08sfp.pdf

of the same, assuming that new economic crises are held at bay and the economy continues to recover at its current pace.

According to the National Association of State Budget Officers and the National Governors Association,[135]

"States are currently facing one of the worst, if not the worst, fiscal periods since the Great Depression. Fiscal conditions significantly deteriorated for states during fiscal 2009, with the trend expected to continue through fiscal 2010 and even into 2011 and 2012."

State budget shortfalls between 2009 and 2012 are projected at $297B, not including $135B of federal aid.[136] To cover these shortfalls, state budget cuts are underway (employees, healthcare, elderly/disabled, education, police, corrections and social services), state taxes are being raised (sales, individual, business, excise), and a number of policy and tax reforms are being considered, like taxing internet sales.

While states are slashing budgets, dwindling tax receipts are negating budget-cutting measures. Increased unemployment and business closures mean reduced state income tax revenue. Losses of home equity and economic uncertainty reduce consumer spending, which reduces state sales and excise tax revenue. Individual, sales and excise taxes are the big three revenue generators for states. Unlike the federal government, states cannot print money or go into debt. With the exception of Vermont, all states have balanced budget requirements. With a dwindling tax base, over 30 states have increased the tax bite on the remaining taxpayers, some significantly, with more to come.

A November 2009 Pew Center on the States study[137] ranks the top ten states in fiscal peril as California, Arizona, Rhode Island, Michigan, Oregon, Nevada, Florida, New Jersey, Illinois, and Wisconsin. These states all have different stories, but share common issues, including unbalanced economies, a spending/receipts gap, and paralyzed legislatures with weak political resolve. According to the Pew study:

"These states' budget troubles can have dramatic consequences for their residents: higher taxes, layoffs or furloughs of state workers, longer waits for public services, more crowded classrooms, higher college tuition and less support for the poor or unemployed. But they also pose challenges for the country as a whole. The 10 states account for more than a third of America's population and economic output. And actions taken by state governments to balance their budgets—such as tax increases and drastic spending cuts—can slow down the nation's economic recovery."

The updated February 2010 Pew State of the States study,[138] showed the ARRA funding was,

---

135   National Association of State Budget Officers and the National Governors Association Fiscal Survey of States, December 2009, http://www.nasbo.org/Publications/FiscalSurvey/tabid/65/Default.aspx
136   National Association of State Budget Officers and the National Governors Association Fiscal Survey of States, June 2010, http://www.nasbo.org/LinkClick.aspx?fileticket=gxz234BlUbo%3d&tabid=38
137   The Pew Center on the States, Beyond California: States in Fiscal Peril, November 2009, http://downloads. pewcenteronthestates.org/BeyondCalifornia.pdf
138   The Pew Center on the States, State of the States 2010, How The Recession Might Change States, February 2010, Page 12, http://archive.stateline.org/images/2010_Feb-SOTS/006_10_RI%20State%20of%20the%20States_

"…the biggest transfer of federal funds to states in history….with $135 billion going directly to their bottom lines: $87 billion for Medicaid costs and $48 billion in state stabilization funds, primarily for education."

The study also predicts lasting fundamental changes for the states due to the effects of the economic crisis. Essentially, citizens will have to expect a new normal which has not yet been accepted.

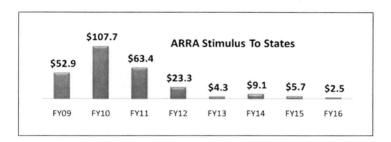

Figure 80: ARRA's Lifeline to the States Is Decreasing

The ARRA lifeline will end as shown in Figure 80. By October 2010, 60% of all the ARRA funding will have been spent. It is extremely unlikely that another recovery package, the size or magnitude of the ARRA, will be forthcoming. The bulk of the remaining 40% is oriented to infrastructure projects like highways, broadband and energy. Consequently, most of the welfare aid and assistance for teachers and other services will no longer be available.

The 2010-2011 school season, which starts in the summer, will likely be the worst school year since the Great Depression. Several hundred thousand layoffs are projected. Districts are closing schools, cutting programs, enlarging classes, trimming transportation, reducing benefits, delaying maintenance, and shortening school days to save money.

Secretary of Education, Arne Duncan, has called for an educational state of emergency, and has petitioned Congress for a $23B aid bill (sponsored by Senator Harkin) to retain teachers, hire new teachers and provide for on-the-job training for educational careers. Duncan estimates that teacher layoffs in 2010 could total from 100,000 to 300,000 unless Congress acts. Sen. Harkin said the cost of the bill doesn't need to be offset by other revenue because it would be considered emergency spending. The Secretary and Senator anticipated little push-back from the opposition. Education and children are emotional issues. The initial push-back was from private school advocates, who argue that federal money is exclusively given to public schools, whose teacher salaries and benefits are way out of line with the private school system. More push-back is happening within moderate Democrats, who are concerned about deficit spending. As of June 2010, the White House has given only lukewarm support for the $23B aid bill as US debt is being to be recognized as the greater issue.

What's happening in Greece could happen in California, Arizona, Illinois, New Jersey or New York, which are all struggling financially.

In April 2010, Standard & Poor's Ratings Services lowered its BBB+ rating on Hellenic Republic (Greece) long-term bonds to BB+ junk bond status. Moody's (A3) and Fitch (BBB-) rating services followed suit, but not to junk bond status. The rating services have California's long-term bond ratings slightly above junk bond status, A-, A- and Baa for S&P, Fitch and Moody's respectively. Junk bond status is the level where many investors will not invest (Figure 81).

Grade	Long Bond Rating Definition	S&P	Moody's	Fitch
	Prime, maximum safety.	AAA, AAA-	Aaa	AAA
Investment grade bonds	High grade, high quality.	AA+, AA, AA-	Aa1, Aa2, Aa3	AA+, AA, AA-
	Upper medium grade quality.	A+, A, A-	A1, A2, A3	A+, A, A-
	Medium grade quality.	BBB+, BBB, BBB-	Baa1, Baa2, Baa3	BBB+, BBB, BBB-
Below investment grade. "Junk bonds"	Speculative.	BB+, BB, BB-	Ba1, Ba2, Ba3	BB+, BB, BB-
	Highly speculative.	B+, B, B-	B1, B2, B3	B+, B, B-
	In poor standing.	CCC+, CCC, CCC-	Caa1, Caa2, Caa3	CCC+, CCC, CCC-
	Extremely speculative.	CCC+, CCC, CCC-	Ca1, Ca2, Ca3	CCC+, CCC, CCC-
	Imminent default or in default.	D	C	DDD, DD, D

Figure 81: Bond Ratings

Even with massive federal help in 2009, California still had to cut the state budget by about 25%, eliminating many essential services. The budget crisis has affected virtually every interaction Californians have with the state. Essential services have been cut several days a month. Public transportation has been reduced. State employees are getting downsized and salaries cut. K-12 classrooms are getting larger. Fewer police are on the street. Public university tuition has doubled. State pension funds are in trouble. California government approval ratings are at single digits for the first time in history.

Region	Peak Month	Peak Price	January 2010 Median	% Chg From Peak
Monterey Region	Aug-07	$798,210	$290,620	-63.6%
High Desert	Apr-06	$334,860	$124,480	-62.8%
Riverside/San Bernardino	Jan-07	$415,160	$173,790	-58.1%
Sacramento	Aug-05	$394,450	$174,830	-55.7%
Palm Springs/Lower Desert	Jun-05	$393,370	$179,760	-54.3%
CALIFORNIA	May-07	$594,530	$287,440	-51.7%
Northern Wine Country	Jan-06	$645,080	$351,360	-45.5%
Los Angeles	Aug-07	$605,300	$332,270	-45.1%
San Francisco Bay Area	May-07	$853,910	$486,190	-43.1%
San Diego	May-06	$622,380	$366,780	-41.1%
Ventura	Aug-06	$710,910	$420,690	-40.8%
San Luis Obispo	Jun-06	$620,540	$367,650	-40.8%
Santa Clara	Apr-07	$868,410	$525,000	-39.5%
Orange County	Apr-07	$747,260	$480,790	-35.7%

Source: California Association of Realtors

Figure 82: California Residential Real Estate Values, January 2010[139]

To make matters worse in California, as of January 2010, the California residential real estate market is still down 51.7% from its May 2007 high (Figure 82). According to the California Association of Realtors resales are projected to continue to decline 3.5% this year. New housing permits have dropped from over 200,000 in 2005 to about 29,000 in 2009, and 2010 does not look any better.

Residential real estate has a tremendous impact on state and local economies. Real estate taxes are the principal source of income for schools and universities. Real estate construction is

---

139 California Association of Realtors, 2010 California Housing Market Update Inland Valleys Association of Realtors, 5 March 2010, http://www.car.org/media/ppt/econppt/03-05-10InlandValleysAORWeb1.ppt

a leading source of employment. Real estate values constitute the leading component on many individuals' retirement portfolios. A 50% loss of home values and an 85% drop in construction will have negative ramifications well into the future for the US' largest state that generates 13% of America's total GDP.

With the exception of Arkansas during the Great Depression, states have never defaulted on state-issued bonds. All 50 states still have investment-grade credit bond ratings—as of April 2010. However, bonds are only part of the states' debt challenge. Hidden debts may prove to be the greater challenge.

Pension funds may be the largest component of a state's hidden debt. States are required to disclose debt on bonds, but not on pension funds. By some estimates, California's debt as a percentage of gross state product (the state equivalent of US GDP) quadruples when pension debt is added to bond obligations.

Unemployment and derivatives are having a significant impact on the pension fund category. The largest pension fund in the US, California's CalPERS lost 30% of its value in the last two years. After losing about $1T in the markets, state and local pension funds are on the horns of a major dilemma: slash retirement benefits, or pursue high-return, high-risk investments like derivatives. Within 10 to 15 years, it is estimated by a number of analyses that state and local governments will have less than half the money they need to pay pension benefits. Depending on employment and market conditions, the time could even be less. Warren Buffett has called pensions "ticking time bombs" that could blow up in government's face due to the fact that retirees are depleting resources faster than investments can replenish the losses from the Great Recession. The high-risk strategies that many states are taking with hedge funds, derivatives, futures and swaps may bankrupt them, if the economy slides back into recession or experiences an L-shaped recovery.

How big is combined state debt? Nobody really knows. However, two economists at Northwestern University and the University of Chicago, put the number above $5T.[140]

The hidden debt of pension funds is likely to increase significantly if the stock markets take a dip. Unlike companies and many individuals who are quietly moving their pension funds out of stocks into safer investments like bonds, states are seeking higher returns to make up and catch up. According to numerous sources, such as a recent New York Times investigative report,[141] pension funds are investing in derivatives, junk bonds and foreign stocks. Risky portfolios increase the probability of lower ratings and investments.

While states are unlikely to default, even with the combined general obligation/bond/pension debt load, many would likely be rated at or below junk bond status if their total amount of debt were made public. In today's bitter partisan environment, replete with negative political attack ads and personal assaults, it is possible for dueling politicians to create investor blowback or give rating agencies ammunition for downgraded ratings. The Greek debacle started when the Prime Minister claimed that his predecessor left him debt three times the known amount. The

---

140 Novy-Marx, Robert and Rauh, Joshua D., Public Pension Promises: How Big are They and What are They Worth? (December 18, 2009). Available at SSRN: http://ssrn.com/abstract=1352608
141 New York Times, Public Pension Funds Are Adding Risk to Raise Returns, by Mary Williams Walsh, 8 March 2010, http://www.nytimes.com/2010/03/09/business/09pension.html?th&emc=th

upcoming US 2010 mid-term election debates have the potential to ignite some serious negative financial consequences for states and municipalities.

Medicaid is a shared federal and state responsibility that many states can no longer afford. The federal government pays part of the cost, but states set many of their program rules and benefits. Now that federal stimulus money is winding to an end, states foresee a much greater challenge in the future. Governor Schwarzenegger rhetorically asked Californians, "Which child should we cut, the poor one or the sick one?"

Because of its size and costs, Medicaid's increasing caseloads produce far more damaging effects on state budgets than other programs. In 2009, more than 3 million people joined Medicaid, pushing enrollment to a record 46.8 million, exacerbating the financial strains on already burdened states and complicating the federal politics of health care. In response, many states are reducing medical services available to Medicaid patients, or payments to doctors, hospitals and other providers of health care.

No state has gone bankrupt and it is unlikely that any will, since the federal government will likely bail them out. However, municipalities (a city, county, town, or public authority) can go bankrupt under Chapter 9 of the bankruptcy code. Under Chapter 9, a municipality can file for protection from its creditors if it meets certain eligibility criteria. A municipality must first get approval from the state legislature and then make a good-faith effort to negotiate with its creditors before filing for bankruptcy. Chapter 9 is widely considered a last resort, and filings under it are more onerous than other parts of bankruptcy code because of the resulting uncertainty for everyone from municipal employees, to bondholders, to credit rating agencies.

Even state capitals are considering Chapter 9 bankruptcy. In Pennsylvania, Harrisburg's City Council is advocating filing for municipal bankruptcy to deal with debt issues. The primary issue facing Harrisburg is $288M worth of debt associated with a failed trash incinerator, which costs the city approximately $70M per year in principal and interest payments that they no longer can afford. Many of the City Council members advocate Chapter 9 bankruptcy over selling public assets, like city-owned parking facilities. A bankruptcy judge in a Chapter 9 case can order reduced payments or entire elimination of the incinerator debt. While this action may be convenient in the short-term, it has significant long-term implications in selling municipal bonds and financing debt.

Due to the Great Recession, many municipalities are having difficulty paying interest on municipal bonds that traditionally are considered low risk. A municipal bond is a bond issued by a city, local government, or its agencies for a multiplicity of purposes. Even the mention of Chapter 9 signals that municipalities may be willing to default on their securities.

California is especially hard hit due to job, home equity, and pension system losses. In San Diego, political leaders recently were pressured to file for Chapter 9 bankruptcy protection as a way to get around benefits packages for public workers. The California pension system, the largest in the US, lost 1/3 of its assets in the recession. In Long Beach, pension obligations make up 10% of the city's budget. In 2008, Vallejo, California, filed for Chapter 9 due to inability to pay pension obligations. In 2009, small cities in Alabama, Illinois and Pennsylvania filed Chapter 9 for various reasons. If the economy does not recover quickly or falls back into recession, the US is likely to see a wave of Chapter 9 filings in larger cities and metropolitan areas.

Many major metropolitan areas are in serious financial trouble. These cities depend on states for revenue and support. Urban areas plagued with high unemployment rates include Detroit, Philadelphia, Chicago, Los Angeles, Youngstown, Orlando, Fresno, El Centro, Flint, Bakersfield, Fort Meyers, Daytona, Portland, Fort Wayne, Hartford, Modesto, Myrtle Beach, Saginaw, Sandusky, Sumter and Yuma. Many of these cities have chronic high unemployment rates. Others are suffering from the effects of the bursting housing bubble and the collapse of the construction market. Chapter 9 bankruptcy in several major cities could cause a domino effect that could derail the national recovery.

At what point does a spending/receipt gap grow so large that it is terminal? The answer may be in Detroit. Detroit is dying. It is a city of approximately 1 million besieged people. It is besieged by joblessness, crime, race issues, educational system failure, housing collapse, and poverty. It has gone from the once proud Motor City to a welfare city. Detroit has the highest unemployment rate of any major US metropolitan area.[142] Detroit is in the top four crime-ridden cities out of 400 US cities.[143] Only 25% of Detroit children graduate from high school. Detroit Mayor, Dave Bing, stated in his first State of the City[144] address that Detroit is "near bankrupt financially, ethically and operationally." His statistics are frightening: 30% unemployment, $325M deficit, 50,000 homes in foreclosure, a culture of corruption, tens of thousands of blighted buildings. Even with these horrendous statistics, Mayor Bing insists that Detroit is not terminal and proposes three priorities for his Administration:[145]

1. Aggressive job and business creation and retention, focused on emerging industries and small business.
2. Fixing the City's business climate and making us more attractive to both existing and new businesses.
3. Preparing our workforce to enter industries and jobs that need workers today and will need more tomorrow.

America prays that Bing and the citizens of Detroit can revive the city. The mayor's priorities are right on. Focusing on business and jobs creation is the only way to work out of the tyranny of debt, poverty, crime and decay. Putting people to work in productive jobs is the key to success. Bing's priorities mirror the *Jobenomics* priorities of job, wealth and revenue creation.

The financial genocide of Detroit needs to be front-and-center on the American agenda. If we can fix Detroit, we can fix an America dilemma that has persisted way too long. Fixing Detroit is the best way to stop the Detroit contagion from taking hold in other major cities across America, as well as providing an optimistic future for 1 million people in this financially besieged city. It will also help the other 9 million citizens of Michigan, and the 67 million people in America's Midwest Region, who have to bear some of the financial and mental costs of a once great city and epicenter for American manufacturing.

---

142 Bureau of Labor Statistics, Metropolitan Area Employment and Unemployment Summary, 7 April 2010, http://www.bls.gov/news.release/metro.nr0.htm
143 Federal Bureau of Investigation, Crime in the United States, Semiannual Uniform Crime Report, 21 December 2009, http://www.fbi.gov/ucr/2009prelimsem/index.html
144 Mayor Dave Bing, State of the City Address to the City Council, City Clerk and all public officials from Detroit, 24 March 2010, http://wchbnewsdetroit.com/detroit/wchb/mayor-dave-bing-gives-state-of-the-city-address-full-text/
145 Ibid

Increasing Taxes to Close the Spending/Receipts Gap. Annual budget deficits will force governments to increase taxes to cover shortfalls. As Ben Franklin would say, "in this world nothing can be said to be certain, except death and taxes"– especially in today's economic environment.

During the Great Depression, a dozen of the wealthiest Americans, who opposed President Roosevelt's New Deal programs and high taxes on the rich, developed a plan to overthrow  the President and install a fascist government. They approached Major General Smedley Butler, a two-time Medal of Honor winner, to lead a coup d'état with an army of 500,000 men. Butler exposed the plot, known as the Business Plot or White House Putsch, to Congress who quietly broke up the conspiracy.

Could such a conspiracy happen today? Probably not. However, movements, like the Tea Party, are growing in popularity. A *New York Times*/CBS News poll states that 18% of Americans consider themselves supporters of the Tea Party movement.[146] The Tea Party's anger is largely directed at Washington's lavish spending and increased taxation policies.

The possibility of increased taxation by all levels of government is a near certainty.

- Federal taxes on businesses and on high and middle income wage earners will increase. It may be necessary to institute a new tax system, like a national sales tax or flat tax.
- Insolvent states will increase or impose new income, real estate and sales taxes.
- Municipal taxes (licensing, registration, utility) will increase as more and more US cities approach Chapter 9 bankruptcy.

Total US Tax Burden by Category: 2008

Category	Tax	Total	%	Federal	State
Federal	Individual income tax	$ 1,059,858,091,000	34.2%	$ 1,059,858,091,000	
Federal	Employment taxes	$ 877,484,111,000	28.3%	$ 877,484,111,000	
Federal	Corporation income tax	$ 300,746,433,000	9.7%	$ 300,746,433,000	
State	Individual income tax	$ 279,097,959,000	9.0%		$ 279,097,959,000
State	Sales tax	$ 240,790,396,000	7.8%		$ 240,790,396,000
State	Excise taxes	$ 117,268,050,000	3.8%		$ 117,268,050,000
State	Other taxes	$ 81,305,848,000	2.6%		$ 81,305,848,000
State	Corporation income tax	$ 50,816,155,000	1.6%		$ 50,816,155,000
Federal	Excise taxes	$ 49,306,378,000	1.6%	$ 49,306,378,000	
Federal	Estate and gift taxes	$ 28,802,193,000	0.9%	$ 28,802,193,000	
State	Property tax	$ 12,508,592,000	0.4%		$ 12,508,592,000
		$ 3,097,984,206,000	100%	$ 2,316,197,206,000	$ 781,787,000,000
		$3T		75%	25%

Figure 83: US Tax Burden (Federal and State Taxes) 2008

The total US tax burden is over $3T, of which $2.32T[147] is federal taxes and $0.75T is state taxes[148] (Figure 83). Municipal taxes (licensing, registration, utility) add even more to the total.

146 *New York Times*, The System Is Broken: More From a Poll of Tea Party Backers, by Megan Thee-Brenan and Marina Stefan, 17 April 2010, http://www.nytimes.com/2010/04/18/us/politics/18tea.html
147 Internal Revenue Service Data Book, 2008, Table 1, Internal Revenue Collections and Refunds, by Type of Tax, http://www.irs.gov/pub/irs-soi/08databk.pdf
148 Federation of Tax Administrators, 2008 State Tax Collections, http://www.taxadmin.org/fta/rate/08taxdis.html

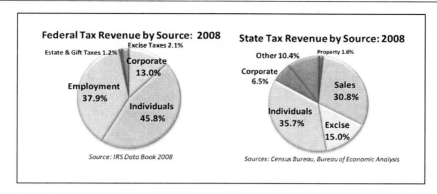

Figure 84: US Tax Revenue By Source (Federal and State Taxes) 2008

In 2008, federal tax revenues came mainly from individual income taxes (45.8% of total federal revenues), employment taxes (37.9%) on Social Security and Medicare Part A, and corporate taxes (13%). In 2008, state tax revenues mainly came from individual income taxes (35.7% of total state revenues), sales taxes (30.8%), and excise taxes (15%) on businesses, motor vehicles, fuel, alcohol and tobacco (Figure 84). Of the combined total, individual income taxes were the highest, with employment taxes second, and tied for third were corporate (12% federal and state) and sales/excise (12% combined).

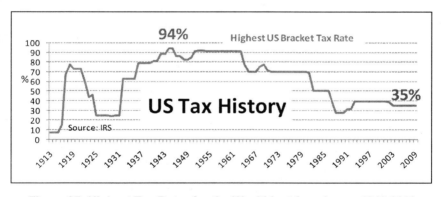

Figure 85: Highest Tax Rates for the Wealthiest Americans, 1913-2009

According to IRS data,[149] the highest tax bracket for the wealthiest Americans reached 94% in 1944 (Figure 85). From 1936 until 1980 the top income tax bracket stayed above the 70% level. Given today's debt crisis and high unemployment, tax rates for the wealthiest Americans could rise significantly from the current level of 35%. Unfortunately, for all US taxpayers, including the rich, the amounts of hidden taxes were much lower in earlier decades than they are today. In other words, the top tax bracket does not have to reach previous levels to have the same bite.

---

149 Internal Revenue Service, SOI Tax Stats, Historical Table 23, U.S. Individual Income Tax: Personal Exemptions, January 2010, http://www.irs.gov/taxstats/article/0,,id=175910,00.html

	Tax Brackets					Capital Gains	Dividends
Current	10%	25%	28%	33%	35%	15%	15%
2011	15%	28%	31%	36%	39.6%	20%	39.6% (Max)

Figure 86: Expiring "Bush" (EGTRRA & JGTRRA) Tax Cuts

So what's on the docket for 2011? The answer is about $300B worth of new tax revenues, or a $300B reduction of disposable personal income, depending on your point of view. This new tax revenue will come from three sources: expiring "Bush" tax cuts, expiring "Obama" ARRA credits, and reduction of AMT limits. The "Bush" tax cuts provided by the Economic Growth and Tax Relief Reconciliation Act of 2001 (EGTRRA) and the Jobs and Growth Tax Relief Reconciliation Act of 2003 (JGTRRA) are scheduled to expire at the end of 2010, when individual rates, capital gains and dividends reset to previous levels as shown in Figure 86. The "Obama" Making Work Pay provision in the American Recovery and Reinvestment Act of 2009 (credit of up to $400 to individuals and $800 to married taxpayers filing joint returns in 2009 and 2010) will also expire in 2010. The temporary relief for many taxpayers caught under the Alternative Minimum Tax (AMT) provision of tax code falls from $46,700 to $33,750 for individuals and $70,950 to $45,000 for couples in 2009 and 2010 respectively.[150]

Everyone knows that the rich bear the biggest tax burden, but most are unaware of the growing gap between taxpayers and tax consumers. Economists at the Tax Foundation[151] estimate the top-earning 40% of families will transfer close to $1T to the bottom-earning 60% in 2012. Families earning less than $86,000 receive more in federal spending than they pay in federal taxes. It is estimated that the bottom 50% of US taxpayers pay no income tax at all. If this trend continues, tax consumers will have unrestrained voting power to transfer wealth from the rich. The other endangered taxpayer species is the employer. In 2008, employment taxes were $877B. This burden is particularly onerous on small businesses.

The Tax Foundation study[152] finds federal income tax rates would have to roughly triple to close the nation's staggering budget deficit in 2010. Quoting the Tax Foundation,

"To close the deficit, federal income tax rates for joint filers which today range from 10 percent to 35 percent would have to be increased to between 27.2 percent and 95.2 percent—a tax hike of unprecedented size."

While 95% seems laughable, perhaps it is not. The GAO puts the number in the 50% range, assuming that a 34% simultaneous decrease in noninterest spending happens. If the taxpayer has to assume the full load, the net increase would equate to 84%.

---

150 CBO, Policies For Increasing Economic Growth And Employment In 2010 And 2011- January 2010, Future Tax Changes Under Current Law, Box 2, Page 6, http://www.cbo.gov/ftpdocs/108xx/doc10803/01-14-Employment.pdf
151 Tax Foundation, Tax Watch, Taxpayers vs. Tax Consumers, Winter 2010, http://www.taxfoundation.org/files/tw-winter2010.pdf
152 Ibid

Federal Fiscal Gap 2010-2084

Under GAO's Simulations Based on the Trustees' Assumptions for Social Security and	Fiscal Gap		Change required to	
	Trillions of present value 2009 dollars	Percent of GDP	Percent increase in revenue	Percent decrease in noninterest spending
Baseline Extended	**$41.1**	**4.8%**	**24.2%**	**20.0%**
Alternative	**$76.4**	**9.0%**	**50.5%**	**34.2%**

Source: GAO

Figure 87: GAO Predicts Huge Tax Increases

The GAO chart[153] depicted in Figure 87 was included in the Trustees Assumptions for Social Security and Medicare. The Trustees include Secretaries Tim Geithner (Treasury), Kathleen Sebelius (HHS) and Hilda Solis (Labor). The highlighted area depicts the change required to close the spending/receipts gap in Social Security and Medicare. It indicates that revenues (taxes) need to be increased 50.5% and noninterest spending decreased by 34.2% on top of current receipts and outlays. According to the Trustees, Medicare Part A reserves will be gone by 2017 and Social Security Disability Insurance by 2021,[154] if not earlier, if the economy recovers slowly.

While the Tax Foundation's and Trustees' numbers are apples-and-oranges comparisons replete with widely varying assumptions, both groups, one from the political right and one from the left, indicate that huge tax rate increases are necessary if budget cutting does not occur and employment does not improve soon.

Without a significant increase in employment-generated revenues, massive tax increases in federal, state, and municipal taxes will have to be enacted. Much of these taxes will be in hidden taxes on various goods and services. In addition, it is highly likely a VAT (value-added tax) will be levied on Americans. A VAT is known by other names including national sales tax, goods and services tax, consumption tax. VATs are common in Europe, where countries like France receive 50% of their revenue from VATs. VATs differ from sales taxes where the tax is added at the time of consumption (sales). A VAT adds a tax at every stage of production, or whenever there is a transaction. In poorer countries with high unemployment, VATs are preferred to other sources of revenue collection. Due to the fact that most Americans do not pay individual income tax, a VAT would reach a greater percentage of the population, much in the same way that FICA does today (more US citizens pay FICA than pay individual income taxes). While the US Senate voted

153 GAO, The Federal Government's Long-Term Fiscal Outlook, January 2010 Update, Page 7, http://www.gao.gov/new.items/d10468sp.pdf
154 Status of the Social Security and Medicare Programs, A Summary Of The 2009 Annual Social Security And Medicare Trust Fund Reports, Social Security and Medicare Boards of Trustees, May 2009, http://www.ssa.gov/OACT/TRSUM/index.html

in April 2010 against the idea of a VAT, many politicians believe that a VAT will eventually be needed to close the US federal spending/receipts gap.

In conclusion, the US spending/receipts gap is not sustainable. The gap must be closed to avoid crippling debt, dollar devaluation and a host of other maladies.

Significant tax increases will have to be implemented if recovery is not imminent. Tax increases will occur at all levels—federal, state and municipal. The federal government has a $1T+ per year spending/receipts gap. 48 out of 50 states are operating in the red. Many municipalities are approaching Chapter 9 bankruptcy. Since budget cutting is often too difficult to do with paralyzed legislatures, in the short term, tax increases are the only other way to cover debts and deficits. In the long-term, jobs creation is the best way to increase revenues.

Increased taxation will have a number of nasty side-effects:

- Inhibits jobs creation.
- Limits economic recovery.
- Decreases economic incentive.
- Contributes to the inflation equation.
- Curtails the impact of stimulus programs.
- Motivates businesses to be more conservative.
- Motivates consumers to spend less and save more.
- Encourages cheating, evasion, hostilities and class warfare.
- Creates a have/have-not society and the erosion of the middle class.

If President Bush #41 could not keep his "read my lips, no new taxes" pledge, it is doubtful that President Obama can keep his no new taxes for the lower and middle class.

Chapter 14:
POTENTIAL SECOND RESIDENTIAL REAL ESTATE CRISIS

Potential Residential Real Estate Crisis JOBENOMICS

- **1st Real Estate Crisis**
  - The 1st real estate crisis was largely due to US government intervention, the sub-prime mortgage crisis, and government-created mortgage-backed securities which were the catalysts for the Great Recession of 2008.
- **2nd Real Estate Crisis**
  - A potential crisis is pending due to:
    - ✓ Increasing number of foreclosures
    - ✓ Rising percentage of underwater mortgages
    - ✓ Increasing seriously delinquent mortgage payment rates
    - ✓ Resetting ARM and ALT-A mortgages
    - ✓ Problems associated with second mortgages and home equity lines of credit
    - ✓ Potential wave of strategic defaults by frustrated homeowners

US government is taking unprecedented steps to mitigate a 2nd crisis.

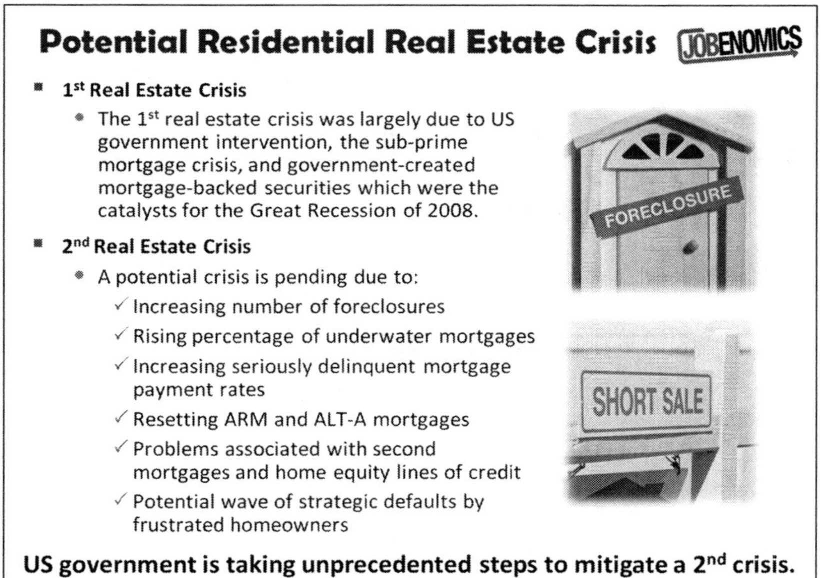

Figure 88: Chapter 14 Summary

The US housing crisis is not over yet. To understand what is happening, one must understand what has happened. Counter to popular opinion, the US government has been and will continue to be the major player in the housing crisis.

The Current Situation. Due to the Great Recession, the new home market and its related construction business collapsed from its peak in 2005 of 1.4 million sales, to a low of 300 thousand in early 2009. The existing (older) home market sales fared better from a peak of 7.3

million to a low of 4.5 million. The ratio of existing home sales to new home sales increased from 5 to 1, to about 10 to 1. The primary reasons that existing homes did better than new homes was due to tight credit for new construction loans and a flood of distressed sales on existing homes. Since builders couldn't compete with the low prices of foreclosed properties, existing home sales stayed elevated relative to new home sales.

Figure 89: Sales of New and Existing Homes[155]

As of Q1 2010, the numbers of existing home sales (5.3 million) and new home sales (410 thousand) are showing some signs of recovery (Figure 89). However, the volatility in the housing market is extremely high with median home prices hitting five year lows of $214,000[156] for new homes and $170,700[157] for existing homes. Foreclosures, short-sales, serious delinquencies, underwater mortgages and strategic defaults are at all-time highs, which makes the current situation precarious from an economic recovery perspective, despite massive US federal government intervention.

The ongoing residential real estate crisis has been likened to a Vietnam War on the US financial system. Almost monthly, the Obama Administration announces another program trying to bring lenders and borrowers to the peace table. Like President Lyndon Johnson during the Vietnam War, President Obama is making bold efforts across the housing spectrum (homeowners, banks, GSE) to avoid a second crisis, but he can't seem to catch a break in a constantly changing war of attrition that had its roots as far back as President Roosevelt. Administration actions include:

155 Modified chart, Making Home Affordable Program Servicer Performance Report Through March 2010, New and Existing Home Sales, Page 3, http://www.makinghomeaffordable.gov/docs/Mar%20MHA%20Public%20 041410%20TO%20CLEAR.PDF
156 US Census Bureau, Median and Average Sales Prices of New Homes Sold in United States, April 2010, http:// www.census.gov/const/uspricemon.pdf
157 National Association of Realtors, Existing-Home Sales and Prices Overview, 22 April 2010, http://www.realtor. org/research/research/ehsdata

- Homeowner actions. Administration homeowner programs that lower interest payments on primary mortgages, resolve problems with secondary mortgages, reduce principal amounts and provide relocation assistance have not met with much success.

- Lender actions. Administration lender programs that bail out financial institutions, remove toxic mortgage-backed securities, and underwrite mortgages have not motivated banks to lend more, or reduce, modify, or write down distressed primary or second mortgages.

- GSE actions. The Administration has also struggled with reorganizing and bailing out its own floundering government housing agencies.

Like the Johnson Administration, the Obama Administration is in so deep in this economic war of attrition that it can't get out quickly without facilitating a disaster. A second mortgage crisis caused by a bank fire sale of REOs (property owned by a lender, due to foreclosure or in lieu of foreclosure) or a wave of strategic defaults (walking away from underwater mortgages) by disenchanted or angry homeowners, could plunge the US economy back into recession.

As of April 2010, the Administration is launching a new fourfold offensive strategy on the foreclosure crisis, which includes increased financial incentives to:

- Distressed homeowners who keep paying on underwater mortgages via reduced payment (principal and interest) amounts or refinancing.
- Banks that cut the principal balance on underwater mortgages.
- Banks that modify second mortgages.
- Banks that conduct short sales in lieu of foreclosing.

The Administration is also planning to help state housing finance agencies in economically hard hit areas (a total of $600M to North Carolina, South Carolina, Ohio, Oregon and Rhode Island), as well as those states that suffered the worst in the housing crisis (a total of $1.5B for California, Nevada, Arizona, Michigan and Florida). The money for these efforts will reportedly come from unexpended TARP funds and interest repayments from financial institutions that have repaid or are in the process of repaying TARP loans. A bright spot for the US Treasury will be the payback of Citigroup's TARP loans that could exceed $8B, the largest profit returned from any firm that accepted bailout funds, and the second-largest stock sale in history.

Perhaps equally important is the commitment by the Administration to relook at the federal government's future role in the housing-finance system, which has become a tar-baby for all involved. Secretary Geithner is calling for a major revamping of the housing-finance system that can no longer exist in its current form. According to Secretary Geithner, the economic crisis "was the result of failures in government policy and oversight, failures in the design and enforcement of rules and regulation."[158]

---

158 US Department of the Treasury, Treasury Secretary Timothy F. Geithner Remarks before the American Enterprise Institute on Financial Reform, 22 March 2010, http://www.treas.gov/press/releases/tg600.htm

Moral Hazard. Contrary to popular opinion, the collapse of the US housing market was caused more by Washington than any other player. Secretary Geithner would probably agree. Volumes have been written about the role of Wall Street in the economic crisis. Very little has been written about Washington's culpability in the housing meltdown.

US government policies and market intervention induced the growth of the US residential real estate bubble and its subsequent collapse. If guilty of nothing else, Washington is guilty of a moral hazard. A moral hazard occurred when the US government insulated borrowers, lenders and speculators from mortgage risks by promoting homeownership, underwriting/insuring mortgages, and trading mortgage-backed securities. The very act of insulation caused the market to behave differently than it normally would have (i.e., a moral hazard).

In 2008, during the Bush Administration, the US government placed key housing institutions under conservatorship. In other countries, conservatorship is called nationalization. Washington prefers the connotation of receivership. Regardless of what connotation one prefers, the US government is now charged with the protection and viability of the housing market. Today, the US government overwhelmingly controls the power and funding mechanisms that are essential to the recovery of the US housing market. Consequently, the future of American residential real estate rests largely on government policies and actions.

Ever since the Great Depression, Washington has intervened and manipulated the residential real estate market. Every US President, Republican or Democrat, conservative or liberal, has endorsed homeownership as an essential part of the American dream. As President Bush stated,[159] "I believe owning something is a part of the American Dream…everybody who wants to own a home has got a shot at doing so." As President Obama said about the home mortgage crisis, "(it is) a crisis which is unraveling homeownership, the middle class, and the American Dream itself."[160]

Over the last eight decades, Washington created a number of government-owned or government-sponsored enterprises (GSEs) to make the American dream of homeownership come true.

- In 1932, Congress created the Federal Home Loan Bank (FHLB) System to provide funding to American financial institutions. 12 regional Federal Home Loan Banks lend to local banks to finance housing, economic development, infrastructure, and jobs. Today, about 80% of US local lending institutions regularly borrow from Federal Home Loan Banks.

- In 1938, Fannie Mae (Federal National Mortgage Association) was created to make mortgages more available to low-income families. Fannie Mae has three businesses: single-family, housing and community development, and capital markets that provide services and products to lenders and partners.

---

159 Remarks By The President (Bush) On Homeownership at the Department of Housing and Urban Development Washington, D.C., 18 June 2002, http://www.hud.gov/news/speeches/presremarks.cfm
160 The White House, Remarks By The President On The Home Mortgage Crisis, Dobson High School, Mesa, Arizona, 18 February 2009, http://www.whitehouse.gov/the_press_office/remarks-by-the-president-on-the-mortgage-crisis/

- In 1968, Ginnie Mae (Government National Mortgage Association) was created to help make affordable housing a reality for millions of low- and moderate-income households by channeling global capital into the nation's housing markets.

- In 1970, Freddie Mac (Federal Home Loan Mortgage Corporation) was created and chartered by Congress to provide liquidity, stability and affordability to the US housing and mortgage markets. Freddie Mac has three business lines: a single family credit guarantee business for home loans, a multi-family business for apartment financing, and an investment portfolio.

- In 2008, the Federal Housing Finance Agency (FHFA) was created as a super-agency. The FHFA[161] domain includes Fannie Mae, Freddie Mac, the 12 Federal Home Loan Banks, the Office of Federal Housing Enterprise Oversight, the Federal Housing Finance Board, and the GSE mission office at Housing and Urban Development. FHFA is empowered to regulate all of the vital components of the US secondary mortgage markets—a market of packaged home loans that are resold as securities to investors. Secondary mortgage buyers (like Fannie and Freddie) were created by the US Government to make it easier for people to get mortgages, because banks would have the option of selling loans and increasing liquidity, rather than being stuck with the mortgages for the full term of the loan. To give the FHFA the power it needed, the FHFA placed the two biggest US secondary mortgage buyers (Fannie and Freddie) under conservatorship. Conservatorship is a term for being nationalized. This action was probably the most sweeping government intervention in US financial history.

Today, the US government, via the FHFA, controls 84% of all US residential mortgages, as well as the vast majority of private lending institutions that service the US housing industry. The combined debt and obligations of FHFA's GSEs is approximately $6T with 34 million loans.

As shown in Figure 90, the performance of these GSE mortgages has been steadily decreasing since the Great Recession. From QIV 2008 to QIV 2009, seriously delinquent payments (60+ days overdue) have increased 54% (from 4.6% to 7.1%) and foreclosures in process have increased 60% (from 2% to 3.2%) of all GSE mortgages. In number terms, 2.4 million loans are seriously delinquent and 1.1 million are in the foreclosure process.

GSE Mortgage Performance	2008 QIV	2009 QI	2009 QII	2009 QIII	2009 QIV
Current and Performing	89.9%	89.8%	88.6%	87.2%	86.4%
Seriously Delinquent	4.6%	4.8%	5.3%	6.2%	7.1%
Foreclosures in Process	2.0%	2.5%	2.9%	3.2%	3.2%

Figure 90: GSE Mortgage Performance[162]

---

161 Federal Housing Finance Agency, 13 November 2009, http://www.fhfa.gov/Default.aspx?Page=4
162 US Treasury, Office of the Comptroller of the Currency and Office of Thrift Supervision, OCC and OTS Mortgage Metrics Report, Fourth Quarter 2009, Table 8. Overall Portfolio Performance, http://www.occ.treas.gov/ftp/release/2010-36a.pdf

Most Americans assume that the FHFA juggernaut operates and funds its commonwealth via taxpayer dollars. This is only partly true. The vast amount of their funding comes through government-created derivatives in partnership with the capital markets. Many of FHFA's enterprises also sell stock, and receive generous cash infusions and bailouts from the Federal Reserve and US Treasury when their funds run short.

Fannie Mae and Freddie Mac are FHFA's major organizations that are charged with keeping the US residential home flotilla from sinking. They are also FHFA's biggest money makers. Fannie and Freddie are the largest buyers of US mortgages. They are deeply involved in pooling mortgages, selling them as mortgage-backed securities to various investors, and guaranteeing the credit risk of their GSE generated mortgage-backed securities from defaulting homeowners.

Both Fannie Mae and Freddie Mac are publically-traded, government-run corporations classified as government sponsored enterprises of the US federal government. Fannie Mae trades on the New York Stock Exchange under the trading symbol (NYSE: FNM) and Freddie Mac (NYSE: FRE). Both GSEs are in the business of making money available for new home purchases, especially to low-income families. The GSEs generate their funds in four ways: (1) interest rate spreads, (2) guaranty fees on credit risks associated with GSE mortgage-backed securities, (3) selling stock to private and government investors, and (4) Federal Reserve and US Treasury cash infusions and bailout money.

The primary way Fannie and Freddie raise funds is #2, guaranty fees on credit risks associated with GSE mortgage-backed securities. According to the Fannie Mae website,[163]

> "Fannie Mae operates in the U.S. secondary mortgage market. Rather than making home loans directly to consumers, we work with mortgage bankers, brokers and other primary mortgage market partners to help ensure they have funds to lend to home buyers at affordable rates. We fund our mortgage investments **primarily by issuing debt securities** in the domestic and international capital markets." (Emphasis added)

The Freddie Mac website essentially says the same,[164]

> "Freddie Mac conducts business in the U.S. secondary mortgage market – meaning we do not originate loans – and **works with a national network of mortgage lending customers**.

> In our Single-Family business, we use mortgage securitization to fund millions of home loans every year. Securitization is a process by which we purchase home loans that lenders originate, put these loans into **mortgage securities** that are sold in global capital markets, and recycle the proceeds back to lenders… What makes the securitization process work? Families paying their mortgages every month. Because once a family moves into their home, their monthly payments of **mortgage principal**

---

163 Fannie Mae, About Us, 10 January 2009, http://www.fanniemae.com/about/index.html;jsessionid=2PHLS0JA VRDEXJ2FQSISFGQ?p=About+Fannie+Mae
164 Freddie Mac, Our Business, 10 January 2009, http://www.freddiemac.com/corporate/company_profile/our_ business/

and interest are transferred ultimately to securities investors. When a family stops making payments—often due to loss of income—Freddie Mac steps in and makes those payments to securities investors. Managing this risk, known as credit risk, is how we generate revenue. Each time we fund a loan, **we collect a credit guarantee fee** from the lender selling us the loan. This fee is intended to protect us in case of loan default.

Through our Multifamily business, we work with a **network of lenders** to finance apartment buildings around the country… In this business line, Freddie Mac finances most of its loan acquisitions by issuing **corporate debt securities**. We generate revenue by producing what is known as net interest income; that is, the difference between the interest payments we collect on the multifamily loans we own and the yields we pay securities investors for investing in our debt. Freddie Mac also funds some multifamily loans through **securitization**. And we invest in certain **commercial mortgage-related securities** that contain multifamily loans as well as Low-Income Housing **Tax Credits**.

The investment portfolio invests in **mortgage-related securities** that are guaranteed by Freddie Mac and other financial institutions. The portfolio also invests in individual loans that are guaranteed by Freddie Mac but not immediately securitized. As a bidder in the market, the investment portfolio helps to make **mortgage-related securities** more liquid and mortgage funding more available… We fund acquisition of mortgage securities by issuing **debt securities**, generating net interest income." (*Emphasis added*)

Ginnie Mae is a government-owned corporation within the Department of Housing and Urban Development. While it does not originate loans or participate in mortgage-backed securities, Ginnie Mae guarantees investors timely payment of principal and interest on government mortgage-backed securities.[165]

"Ginnie Mae does not buy or sell loans or issue mortgage-backed securities (MBS). Therefore, Ginnie Mae's balance sheet doesn't use derivatives to hedge or carry long-term debt. What Ginnie Mae does is guarantee investors the timely payment of principal and interest on **MBS backed by federally insured or guaranteed loans**.…As such, Ginnie Mae works with two groups of businesses: **Issuers of mortgage-backed securities** and **Investors/Sponsors of mortgage-backed securities**". (*Emphasis added*)

In 1983, Freddie Mac commissioned two Wall Street powerhouses (Salomon Brothers and First Boston) to create the first financial derivative based on mortgages. This derivative was called a collateralized mortgage obligation (CMO), which was a financial debt instrument comprised of different types of bonds designed to attract investors from financial institutions, brokerage firms, homebuilders, and banks. Essentially, Freddie Mac used the CMO to pool a number of mortgages, split and package them into various securities, and sell these packaged-securities to investors. For example, as every homeowner knows, mortgages have two primary components: principal and interest. Principal packages are sold to investors interested in home equity. Interest-only packages are sold to speculators interested in making money on money. Freddie Mac also

---

165 Ginnie Mae, About, http://www.ginniemae.gov/about/about.asp?Section=About

got into the insurance business by guaranteeing credit defaults on homeowners who were unable to make principal or interest payments on their home loans.

President Obama was correct when he said, "In the end, the home mortgage crisis, the financial crisis, and this broader economic crisis are all interconnected, and we can't successfully address any one of them without addressing them all."[166] In many ways, US government-created and government-managed mortgage-backed securities are the common thread. US government sponsored enterprises created mortgage-backed securities to generate cash for more mortgages. Due to the fact that these financial instruments were backed by the US government, they quickly spread through the global financial system. Soon thereafter, US government sponsored enterprises began guaranteeing defaults from homeowners who could not afford to make mortgage payments. Government backing and guarantees begat more lending and the creation of additional derivatives based on the underlying government's mortgage-backed security. Washington politicians incentivized CEOs of government sponsored lending institutions to reach out to people with limited ability to pay. Homeownership had become a right, rather than a privilege. Since everyone had a right, down payments were reduced, lending requirements were relaxed, and subsidies were introduced. The real estate bubble grew at exponential rates. Then the sub-prime MBS house-of-cards collapsed. This collapse cascaded a mortgage crisis, a housing crisis, and a US financial downturn that threatened global markets.

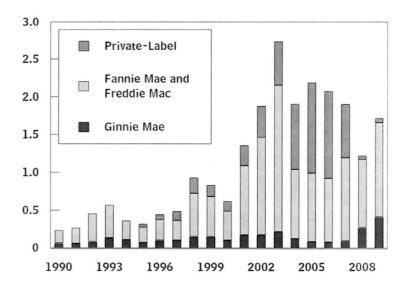

Figure 91: CBO: Issuance of Mortgage-Backed Securities ($T)[167]

---

166 The White House, Remarks By The President On The Home Mortgage Crisis, Dobson High School, Mesa, Arizona, 18 February 2009, http://www.whitehouse.gov/the_press_office/remarks-by-the-president-on-the-mortgage-crisis/

167 Congressional Budget Office, The Budget and Economic Outlook: Fiscal Years 2010 to 2020, Figure 2-4 Issuance of Mortgage-Backed Securities, Page 29, Congressional Budget Office based on data through 2008 from Inside Mortgage Finance, The 2009 Mortgage Market Statistical Annual, vol. 2, The Secondary Market (Bethesda,

Today, the US government is still trying to assuage the toxicity of their mortgage-backed securities. According to the FHFA Acting Director, Edward DeMarco's testimony[168] to the US Senate Banking Committee,

> "With continuing uncertainty regarding economic conditions, employment, house prices, and mortgage delinquency rates, the short-term outlook for the Enterprises remains troubled and likely will require additional draws under the Senior Preferred Stock Purchase Agreements. The Treasury Department and the Federal Reserve have made other, sizeable purchases of **housing GSE securities** to instill confidence in their securities, provide stability to mortgage markets, and lower mortgage rates. Treasury has purchased approximately $192 billion of the **Enterprises' mortgage-backed securities (MBS)**. The Federal Reserve has purchased $831 billion worth of **Enterprise MBS** and $134 billion in debt issued by Fannie Mae, Freddie Mac, and the FHLBanks. This combined support from the federal government exceeds **$1 trillion** and has allowed Fannie Mae and Freddie Mac to continue providing necessary liquidity to the mortgage markets." (*Emphasis added*)

In other words, due to the toxicity of mortgage-backed securities, most of the 14 US GSEs (Fannie, Freddie, FHLBs) are unable to maintain minimum required capital levels and are operating in the red. To give Fannie and Freddie a fighting chance of survival, the US Treasury bought $1B worth of stock (Senior Preferred Stock Purchase Agreements) to "prevent a negative net worth position for either GSE."[169] Fannie and Freddie ran through this money quickly, and obtained an additional $1T worth of stimulus and bailout money from the Treasury and Federal Reserve to keep the GSEs and US housing market afloat. In essence, the toxic mortgage-backed securities have been assumed by the Federal Reserve, with approximately $1.5T MBS on their balance sheet.

Potential Second Residential Real Estate Crisis. Many analysts fear that a second residential real estate crisis looms. The principal components of this looming crisis consist of (1) increasing number of foreclosures, (2) increasing seriously delinquent mortgage payment rates, (3) rising percentage of underwater mortgages, (4) resetting ARM and Alt-A mortgages, (5) problems associated with second mortgages, and (6) potential for a wave of strategic defaults by frustrated homeowners.

- **Foreclosures**. According to the Congressional Oversight Panel in charge of the Troubled Asset Relief Program (TARP),[170] "The United States is now in the third year of a foreclosure crisis unprecedented since the Great Depression, with no end in

---

Md.: Inside Mortgage Finance Publications, 2009), Data for 2009 are estimated, January 2010, http://www.cbo.gov/ftpdocs/108xx/doc10871/01-26-Outlook.pdf

168 Statement of Edward J. DeMarco, Acting Director, Federal Housing Finance Agency before the U.S. Senate Committee on Banking, Housing, and Urban Affairs On "The Future of the Mortgage Market and the Housing Enterprises," 8 October 2009, http://www.fhfa.gov/webfiles/15105/DeMarcoTestimonySBC100809.pdf

169 US Treasury, Frequently Asked Questions: Treasury Senior Preferred Stock Purchase Agreement, HP-1131, 11 September 2008, http://www.treas.gov/press/releases/hp1131.htm

170 The Congressional Oversight Panel's October oversight report, An Assessment of Foreclosure Mitigation Efforts after Six Months, 9 October 2009, http://cop.senate.gov/documents/cop-100909-report.pdf

sight." Foreclosures are currently four times the historical average. One in eight US mortgages is currently in foreclosure or default.

Since the recession began, over 6 million homes entered foreclosure and that number is expected to double to 12 million in the near future. In 2009, approximately 1,500,000 foreclosure actions were initiated and 444,000 were completed. The number would have been much higher without government moratoriums, and newly initiated home retention efforts by the federal government and banks that are saturated with unsalable properties in a down market.

If one added homes in the foreclosure process, and foreclosed homes in bank inventories, the *Wall Street Journal*[171] estimates that it will take nearly 9 years (103 months) to dispose of the backlog (Figure 92).

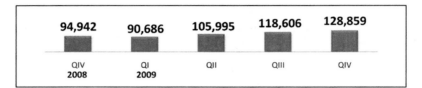

94,942	90,686	105,995	118,606	128,859
QIV 2008	QI 2009	QII	QIII	QIV

Figure 92: Completed Foreclosure Actions[172]

It is estimated that as many as 5 to 7 million properties are eligible for foreclosure but have not yet been repossessed and put up for sale. It takes about a year to complete a foreclosure process and many years to clear the backlog of homes in distressed markets. At some point this shadow wave between the increasing delinquency rate and foreclosures becomes overwhelming for banks that will be forced to repossess the homes. Many economists fear that this wave will break in the latter part of 2010 or early 2011. The severity of this breaking wave depends on (1) the impact of ending US government bank/mortgage stimuli, (2) the unemployment rate, (3) W- or L-shaped economic recovery scenarios, (4) homeowner and market psychology regarding strategic defaults.

Purchase of foreclosures has become more difficult for qualified buyers due to speculators. Speculators have more cash than the average homebuyer, who needs a loan in addition to their cash down payment. In today's economy, most banks prefer a speculator with a 100% cash offer over a prospective homeowner with 20% cash and an 80% mortgage. A new era of land-barons is emerging, except these barons will be 21st Century home-barons, as opposed to the 19th Century land-barons. W- and L-shaped recoveries could exacerbate speculation in safe havens, like residential real estate.

171 *Wall Street Journal* and LPS Applied Analytics, Number of the Week: 103 Months to Clear Housing Inventory, 24 April 2010, http://blogs.wsj.com/economics/2010/04/24/number-of-the-week-103-months-to-clear-housing-inventory/
172 US Treasury, Office of the Comptroller of the Currency and Office of Thrift Supervision, OCC and OTS Mortgage Metrics Report, Fourth Quarter 2009, Table 6. Completed Foreclosures and Other Home Forfeiture Actions, http://www.occ.treas.gov/ftp/release/2010-36a.pdf

Bank-owned or real estate-owned (REO) properties are properties that are acquired by lending institutions as a result of foreclosure, or in lieu of a foreclosure. These REOs will present significant investor interest as the wave of serious delinquencies and defaults generates more and more foreclosures in 2011 and 2012. According to JP Morgan estimates[173] , by the end of 2012, the following metropolitan areas will have significant foreclosures (REOs) as a percent of home sales: Phoenix 39 to 50%, San Diego 24 to 31%, Los Angeles 22 to 28%, Chicago 21 to 28%, Oakland 18 to 23%, San Jose 14 to 18%, and New York 12 to 16%.

The financial industry can tell when the REO bubble is about to burst by looking at the scavengers beginning to circle overhead. Sovereign wealth funds, private equity funds, and hedge funds are putting together hundreds of $B worth of liquidity in order to swoop down and scoop up steeply discounted REOs. When will this happen? Many predict that the REO dam will break in 2011. Since January 2008, the number of days in mortgage default and foreclosure process has risen from 251 days to 438 days in April 2010.[174] In some states, like New York (561 days) and Florida (518 days), the foreclosure process takes as long as 19 months to complete due to volume, the legal process and government intervention.

There is evidence that homeowners are quitting payments on their mortgages earlier in the process, and using the proceeds for other purposes. To many the adage of "eat, drink and be merry for tomorrow we die" applies. To others, they have just resigned themselves to the inevitable and are protecting as much as their remaining savings as possible. Regardless of the reason, the banks have to pick up the load. As a result, REOs, bank-owned real estate, are growing on bank balance sheets. The good news is that bailouts, infusion of government liquidity, and the rise of the stock market has buoyed many bank balance sheets, so they can afford to "rope-a-dope" the REO crisis in hopes of a residential real estate rebound. If the market rebounds, the banks can unload the REOs at a profit. If the real estate market continues to be depressed, or if the economy falters, banks will eventually have to unload their REOs, perhaps at fire sale prices. *Jobenomics* forecasts that is likely to take place in 2011, if a V-shaped recovery does not ensue.

- **Seriously delinquent mortgages.** Serious delinquencies, defined as a borrower who has not made a mortgage payment in three months, and foreclosure rates go hand-in-hand. About seven million US households are behind on their mortgage payments. As of the end of 2009, the number of serious delinquencies had reached an all-time high since delinquency records were started in 1979.

---

173 JP Morgan Chase & Co., Retail Financial Services Presentation, by Charlie Scharf, JP Morgan RFS CEO, Page 34, 25 February 2010, http://files.shareholder.com/downloads/ONE/866755614x0x352810/7bc05ff9-a45b-41f0-acb2-19ae0936811d/RFS_Investor_Day_2010_FINAL_PRINT.pdf
174 New York Times, Owners Stop Paying Mortgages, and Stop Fretting, by David Streitfeld, 31 May 2010, http://www.nytimes.com/2010/06/01/business/01nopay.html?th&emc=th

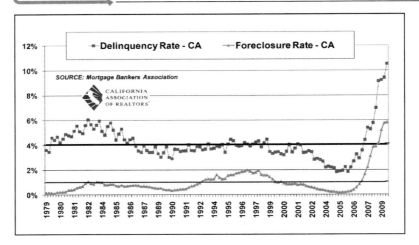

Figure 93: California Delinquency and Foreclosure Rate Profile 1979 to 2009

As shown in Figure 93, delinquencies and foreclosures have increased almost 600% in California[175] over the last two years. According to the Mortgage Bankers Association,[176] the percentage of US mortgages that were more than three months delinquent rose from 1.89% in 2005, to 9.67% by the end of 2009. This tsunami of delinquencies is threatening a new wave of foreclosures in 2010 and 2011 if the economy and employment rates do not improve.

This delinquency wave is a silent, or a shadow wave, since lending institutions are hesitant to foreclose when there are so many unsold, undervalued homes on the market. Many lenders are giving distressed homeowners more time and/or reduced payments to keep them from defaulting on their mortgages. Both the lenders and borrowers are looking to the US government for loan modification assistance, mortgage relief programs, cash incentives, emergency extensions, and mediation assistance.

States that have issued moratoriums to slow down the foreclosure process may have created a greater backlog with more devastating consequences. More foreclosures later will further depress home values.

In the end, success depends on a viable economic recovery and increased employment in value-added jobs. Without these two critical elements, the US government's borrowing and bailout power will eventually be truncated, and the general populace will not be able to afford to buy even highly discounted homes. However, it will be a bonanza for speculators. Those who have cash will be king.

---

175 California Association of Realtors, 2010 California Housing Market Update Inland Valleys Association of Realtors, 5 March 2010, http://www.car.org/media/ppt/econppt/03-05-10InlandValleysAORWeb1.ppt
176 Mortgage Bankers Association, National Delinquency Survey - 2009 4th Quarter, http://www.mbaa.org/ResearchandForecasts/ProductsandSurveys/NationalDelinquencySurvey.htm

- **Underwater mortgages**. About one in four homeowner mortgages is underwater. Due to ARM and Alt-A resets, increasing unemployment, and economic setbacks, underwater homes could increase to one in every two homeowners by 2011. Underwater mortgages are mortgage arrangements that leave the owner with more debt on the property than the current market value. More simply, it is worth less than what is owed, which results in negative equity. Negative equity is having a profound effect on the US recovery effort. Negative equity also portends to be catastrophic to millions of homeowners and retirees who planned on tapping the equity in their homes for retirement income.

  Underwater mortgages are projected to increase significantly. A recent Deutsche Bank AG report[177] predicts that homes that are underwater will increase from 14 million homes currently (26% of all US homes) to 26 million homes (48%) by 2011. Moody's Economy.com agrees with the trend but projects that by 2011, only 18 million homeowners will have negative equity. The Deutsche Bank report further predicts that housing prices will continue to decline by approximately 14% and that "further deterioration will depress consumer spending and boost defaults by borrowers who face unemployment, divorce, disability or other financial challenges."

  Underwater mortgages are often associated with short-sales. A short-sale involves the sale of a house in which the proceeds fall short of what the owner still owes on the mortgage. In a short-sale, a prospective buyer makes an offer to the homeowner selling his or her property. The homeowner then negotiates with the issuing bank to make arrangements for the difference. However, for a large number of the 14 million underwater US homes, there no longer is a bank because their mortgage was bundled and sold as part of mortgage-backed security.

  If the residential mortgage-backed security (RMBS) is owned by an investment bank, and the credit default is underwritten by an insurance company, the process gets complicated. The prospective buyer has to contact the investment bank to see if they can unbundle the mortgage from the RMBS. Unfortunately for the buyer, investment banks are not highly motivated to unbundle the RMBS. Even if the investment bank did unbundle, it has to get permission from the insurance company that is on the hook for the short-sale loss. Most investment banks and insurance companies prefer to avoid short-sales, in case the housing market improves. The bottom line is that many short-sales are just too hard to do, despite US government homeowner recovery efforts.

- **Resetting ARM and Alt-A mortgages**. This crisis involves resetting ARM (adjustable rate mortgages) and Alt-A (Alternative A-paper) mortgages. An ARM is a mortgage where the interest rate is periodically adjusted, based on a variety of indices. An Alt-A mortgage is a mortgage that is considered riskier than A-paper, or prime, and less

---

177 Deutsche Bank, "Drowning in Debt –A Look at Underwater Mortgages," 5 August 2009, www.sacbee.com/static/weblogs/real_estate/Deutsche%20research%20on%20underwater%20mortgages%208-5-09.pdf.

risky than subprime. From a creditworthiness perspective, prime credit scores are usually above 660, Alt-As are between 620 and 659, and sub-prime is below 620.

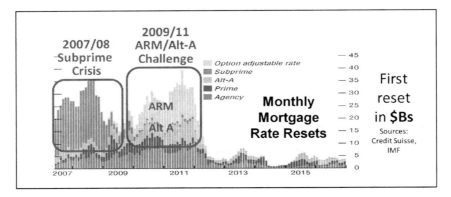

Figure 94: Option ARM/Alt-A Challenge

During the last decade, banks issued Alt-A to many unqualified buyers. During the boom years prior to the recession, many homeowners and speculators opted for ARMs and Alt-A with low interest rates. Now during the recession and high unemployment, these ARMs and Alt-A are resetting. 500,000 ARMs worth $1T are resetting in the next several years. Figure 94, developed by Credit Suisse using IMF data, illustrates the potential second mortgage tsunami.

The US government's massive influx of liquidity to banks and home retention actions has provided ample time and incentive for many ARMs and Alt-A mortgage-holders to convert to conventional mortgages with fixed rates. This is good news. The bad news is that option ARMs and Alt-As are still performing poorly. For example, as shown in Figure 95, Option ARMs perform 1/3 less well than the overall portfolio of GSE mortgages, are 2.5 times more seriously delinquent, and almost 4 times more likely to be in foreclosure.

GSE Mortgage Performance QIV 2009	Current and Performing	Seriously Delinquent	Foreclosures in Process
Overall Portfolio	86.4%	7.1%	3.2%
Option ARMS	66.2%	17.8%	11.9%
		2.5 Times Higher	3.7 Times Higher

Figure 95: Option ARM Performance[178]

- **Second mortgages**. Home-equity loans and home-equity lines of credit, commonly called second mortgages or second-lien loans, are a major impediment to government efforts to mitigate the foreclosure crisis. There is over $1T worth of US second mortgages.

---

178 US Treasury, Office of the Comptroller of the Currency and Office of Thrift Supervision, OCC and OTS Mortgage Metrics Report, Fourth Quarter 2009, Table 11. Performance of Option ARMs, http://www.occ.treas.gov/ftp/release/2010-36a.pdf

In 2009, the federal government launched an effort to lower payments on second mortgages, but due to the complicated web of various stakeholders and lenders, little progress has been accomplished. More importantly, there is growing discord between holders of first and second mortgages, who are often unwilling to agree on common terms on writing down principal or interest rates on distressed borrowers.

Government programs to help distressed borrowers focus on lowering the payments on their primary mortgage, but millions of homeowners took out second and third mortgages that used the home as collateral. Consequently, second-lien loans become a problem since first mortgages usually can't be modified or written down because lien priority dictates that junior loans be erased first. According to SIGTARP, Neil Barofsky, most lenders refuse to reduce or extinguish second liens when modifying primary mortgages.

Approximately 50% of distressed homeowners possess second mortgages which were used for sundry purposes, often to support excessive lifestyles, pay for other distressed loans like credit card bills, or be used like an ATM to get cash, which became known as cash-out refinancing.

During the boom years when home values were skyrocketing, homeowners used home-equity loans as cash-out refinancing. Based on higher reappraised property values and rates, borrowers could refinance homes at low interest rates and pocket the difference. Local governments had little objection to this hedonistic practice due to increased property tax revenue. Cash-out refinancing was especially acute in the sub-prime category, where less creditworthy individuals opted for tantalizingly low ARM teaser rates offered by subprime lenders seeking to expand their revenues on the backs of high-risk borrowers. It was not uncommon for people to make more money on refinancing than they could during their entire work year. It was also a way for people burdened with credit card bills, auto loans, and other needs to cash out. With the exception of a few states, most states and the federal government turned a blind eye to cash-out refinancing and are now suffering the consequences of more expensive government-funded safety net and rescue programs.

In 2009, distressed homes sales reached a peak of 32% share of the real estate market for existing homes. It is predicted that this peak will be exceeded again in late 2010 or 2011, further depressing home values and placing the residential real estate market in peril.

The financial community is studying the possibility of a mini-crisis at the end of 2010 regarding potential write downs of second mortgages. The four biggest US banks (Bank of America, Citigroup, JPMorgan and Wells Fargo) hold 42% of the outstanding $1.1T second mortgages.[179] Due to the historic amounts of liquidity injected into the banking system during the Great Recession, bank profits skyrocketed

179 Bloomberg & Amherst Securities Group LP, Bank Profits Dimmed by Prospect of Home-Equity Losses (Update3), 12 April 2010, http://www.bloomberg.com/apps/news?pid=newsarchive&sid=aYyC7r7E8N3M

to industry wide peaks in mid 2009. Now this liquidity is being withdrawn at the same time that a potential mortgage crisis is beginning to unfold. Writedowns of second mortgages could pose a problem for these banks if coupled with a wave of strategic defaults on the prime mortgages.

- **Strategic defaults**. A second real estate tsunami could be triggered by waves of strategic defaults. A strategic default is when a homeowner simply walks away from a home, giving the keys to the lender.

Strategic defaults could generate a nasty domino effect. Distressed homeowners transfer distress to lenders, who will distress underwriters who are obligated to cover defaults. Too-big-to-fail underwriters, like AIG, would likely turn again to US government-sponsored enterprises, like Fannie and Freddie, for more assistance. To cover GSE costs, the US government would either distress taxpayers via higher taxes, or sell more Treasuries that would add to the national debt. The domino effect would likely touch foreign governments that are invested heavily in Treasury securities, and investors who own derivatives on trillions of dollars' worth of residential mortgage-backed securities.

To date, most underwater US homeowners are dutifully paying their mortgages. Most are struggling to hold on to the American dream of owning a home even if they could save thousands of dollars by walking away from their monthly mortgage payments and renting for a much lower cost. Some are doing this because they think it is immoral to walk away from their obligation. Others hope that real estate values will rebound. Still others are concerned about the ramifications of a damaged credit rating or the hassle of finding a new residence. If the American dream becomes a nightmare, this could change—rapidly.

There are two areas that could induce a nightmare and trigger a second residential real estate tsunami: the ire toward "fat-cat" lenders, and a strategic default lemming effect. Negative feedback loops have already started in both.

There is national outrage towards Wall Street and bankers. The term "fat-cat" used by President Obama was most descriptive and has broad public support. The outrage is especially acute on fat-cats who become rich lending and trading American mortgages while receiving US government bailout money. Bankers and institutional lending fat-cats seem to be unrepentant despite national outrage. Reports of mega-bonuses appear daily in the media.

The vast majority of lenders are not fat cats. They are patriotic Americans who are very concerned about the financially distressed and the economic recovery. There are 8,000 banks in the US that are doing a great job keeping the US economic engine running. Unfortunately, the greedy few get attention. Bernie Madoff captured headlines for months and raised the American ire by an order of magnitude.

Washingtonians, who have the largest culpability in the mortgage industry, are politically motivated to place blame on financial institutions. Left-wing television is motivated by rating boosts generated by fat-cat sound-bites. Right-wing radio benefits by bashing the left and defending the capitalist way. None of this rhetoric is productive. Moreover, it is corrosive, and is accelerating the likelihood of strategic defaults, especially if housing values continue to fall. As of May 2010, the Case-Shiller home price index indicated that prices of single-family homes continue to slide—the sixth consecutive month-over-month decline. To complicate matters, the federal government's first-time home buyer program ended in April 2010. Due to this program, many homes that normally would have sold in the summer of 2010 were forward-sold, which means that the market is likely to be soft for a period of time.

The asymmetry between homeowners and lenders is close to the breaking point. While struggling homeowners are honoring their mortgage obligations, it is widely reported that lenders are more interested in maximizing bonuses than helping the downtrodden. At some point, underwater homeowners may realize that it is no longer in their financial interests to honor their mortgage obligation. Underwater homeowners with nonrecourse loans would be the first to walk away. Nonrecourse loans means the mortgages are secured by the property as opposed to the individual, which makes walking away relatively easy. Strategic defaults in nonrecourse mortgages could easily trigger a lemming effect for other mortgages.

Lemmings are small creatures that reside in underground burrows. When their species undergoes a population explosion, they collectively swarm in search of better accommodations and food. This behavior often results in mass suicide for the lemmings. The analogy is that underwater homeowners could grow to such a population that it could eventually trigger a widespread exodus, resulting in a second mortgage crisis.

14 million homes are underwater across the US. If this number continues to rise due to a weak economic recovery and increased unemployment, financially distressed homeowners could reach a point that they strategically default en masse. This point will occur if the American homeowner dream collapses.

The seeds for a mass default have already been planted in the homeowner psyche. Almost every day, TV reporters, newspaper editorials, and internet bloggers sensationalize the plight of longsuffering homeowners vis-à-vis fat-cat lenders. Sensationalism causes a negative market outlook. National indignation could trigger a wave of strategic defaults starting in a few major cities, like Las Vegas and Phoenix, where underwater mortgages already exceed 50%, and quickly spreading across the country.

Today, most underwater homeowners remain hopeful and committed to their financial obligations. It is important that opinion-leaders and decision-makers keep this hope alive.

You Break It, You Fix It. Thus far this chapter has focused on government intervention and manipulation of the housing market. They broke it, and now it is up to them to fix it. They are.

While US government homeowner rescue efforts are slow going, there have been successes. More importantly, recovery efforts have successfully stemmed the decline and are showing embryonic signs of movement. These successes are critical to the recovery in the housing market, as well as the overall recovery.

Government residential real estate efforts began in earnest in the Bush Administration, and are increasing in the Obama Administration to forestall a second residential real estate crisis. Their efforts have not been without fault or political motive, but, overall, their efforts are authentic and commendable. Some of the major programs and efforts include:

- $Ts worth of bank bailouts, GSE infusion, and Fed acquisition of toxic MBS
- Various federal and state foreclosure moratoriums
- Hope Now Alliance Program
- Hope for Homeowners Program
- Home Affordable Modification Program (HAMP)
- First Time Home Buyer Tax Credit and Move-Up/Repeat Home Buyer ARRA credits

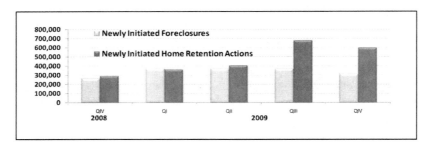

Figure 96: Foreclosures versus New Home Retention Actions[180]

These efforts are beginning to show signs of progress. As shown in Figure 96, the number of newly initiated foreclosures peaked in mid-2009 and started to recede towards the end of the year. Newly initiated home retention actions were largely responsible and doubled over the course of the year to 600,000 actions in the last quarter of 2009. Hopefully, these new retention actions will result in mortgage modifications. If they don't, they may have helped break the dam, due to an excessive buildup of inventory.

---

180 US Treasury, Office of the Comptroller of the Currency and Office of Thrift Supervision, OCC and OTS Mortgage Metrics Report, Fourth Quarter 2009, Table 5, Newly Initiated Home Retention Actions Compared with Foreclosure Actions, 25 March 2010, http://www.occ.treas.gov/ftp/release/2010-36a.pdf

Action	2008	2009			
	QIV	QI	QII	QIII	QIV
Loan Modifications	116,345	189,193	142,362	131,427	102,102
HAMP Trial Period Plans	0	0	80,411	269,436	259,410
HAMP Modifications	0	0	0	781	21,316
Other Trial Period Plans	0	52,015	63,622	123,558	94,667
Payment Plans	174,993	119,862	119,713	153,499	116,600
Total	291,338	361,070	406,108	678,701	594,095

Figure 97: Number of New Home Retention Actions[181]

According to the Office of the Comptroller of the Currency and Office of Thrift Supervision Mortgage Metrics Report, newly initiated home retention actions consist of loan modifications, the HAMP Program and various bank programs as shown in Figure 97. The Administration's Home Affordable Refinance Program (HAMP, also called Making Homes Affordable)[182] "commits $75 billion to keep up to 3 to 4 million Americans in their homes by preventing avoidable foreclosures."

The good news is that many of the trial programs are delaying the foreclosure process. The bad news is that these trial programs are not becoming permanent fast enough to stem the amount of serious delinquencies. Consequently, the Mortgage Metrics Report predicts an "increase in the upcoming quarters as many of the mortgages that are seriously delinquent may eventually result in foreclosure as alternatives that prevent foreclosure are exhausted." Second mortgages and re-defaults (modified loans that subsequently become delinquent or enter the foreclosure process) are also complicating rescue efforts.

Home Affordable Modification Program (HAMP) Snapshot Through April 2010		
Max Goal (Orginal Goal Was 3 to 4 Million)	4,000,000	100%
Number of Trial Period Plan Offers Extended To Borrowers	1,487,594	37%
All HAMP Trials Started Since Program Inception (Mar 09)	1,214,085	30%
Active Trail Modifications	637,353	16%
Permanent Modifications	295,348	7%

Figure 98: HAMP Snapshot after One Year of Operation

As reported on the government's HAMP monthly report,[183] through March 2010, only 6% (227,922) of the goal of 4 million had loans modified under the program (Figure 98). On the other hand, this refinancing program was only initiated in March 2009. Like any new program, it struggled to gain its footing and now is processing applications at a much greater rate.

The Administration is lowering HAMP expectations from 3 to 4 million to 1.5 to 2.0 million preventable foreclosures over the duration of this 5-year program. Borrowers in permanent

---

181 US Treasury, Office of the Comptroller of the Currency and Office of Thrift Supervision, OCC and OTS Mortgage Metrics Report, Fourth Quarter 2009, Table 1. Number of New Home Retention Actions, http://www.occ. treas.gov/ftp/release/2010-36a.pdf
182 Home Affordable Refinance Program, http://makinghomeaffordable.gov/about.html
183 Making Home Affordable Program, Servicer Performance Report Through March 2010, http://www. makinghomeaffordable.gov/docs/Mar%20MHA%20Public%20041410%20TO%20CLEAR.PDF

modifications are saving a median of 36% of their before-modification payment (median savings is more than $500 each month). That provides a significant incentive to stay in underwater homes and continue to make monthly mortgage payments.

Unfortunately, HAMP is caught in a Catch-22. Permanent HAMP loan modifications have not stemmed the re-default rates. The number of permanent loan modifications that have failed under HAMP has been growing at a faster rate than the permanent modifications. In a way, this makes sense. A homeowner who defaults once is more likely to re-default than someone who always pays on time. HAMP cannot fix someone with ineradicable financial troubles or practices.

The Federal Housing Administration (FHA) was originally created to provide insurance for minority and low-income families who could not afford down payments required by private banks. As a result of the housing crisis, the FHA is changing its low-income high-risk focus, to a more balanced approach to the housing market.

By increasing the maximum loan amount to $729,750, the FHA opened up their insurance program to higher-income, less-risky individuals. The FHA also shifted orientation from low income communities, largely in places like Detroit, to more affluent areas, like San Francisco.

FHA is underwriting loans at quadruple the rate of three years ago, even as its reserves to cover defaults are reaching historically low amounts. The FHA already is facing a rising number of serious problems on its insured mortgages. In November 2009, the FHA reported that its cash reserves dropped to 0.53% of the $685 billion of total loans it insures. This is well below the 2% that federal law requires the FHA to have in reserves. To shore up dwindling reserves, the FHA is reversing course and getting tougher on borrowers, by increasing up-front cash and raising minimum credit scores. Their goal is to increase the amount borrowers invest in homes, making it more difficult to default on loans.

The US government's first-time home buyer program appears to be a success—at least initially. The Worker, Homeownership, and Business Assistance Act of 2009 extended tax credit of up to $8,000 for qualified first-time home buyers purchasing a principal residence priced less than $800,000. A first-time home buyer is someone who has not owned a principal residence during the three-year period prior to the purchase. According to the White House,[184]

> "The $8,000 first-time homebuyer's tax credit enacted in ARRA (American Recovery and Reinvestment Act) has brought many new families into the housing market. Those buyers, in turn, have reduced the inventory of unsold homes and contributed to three months in a row of increases in home prices nationwide. Residential housing investment grew 23 percent in the third quarter, one of the contributors to positive economic growth."

The Act establishes income limits of $125,000 for single taxpayers and $225,000 for married couples filing joint returns. As originally established by the Stimulus II program, the $8,000

---

184 The White House, Office of the Press Secretary, "Fact Sheet: The Worker, Homeownership, and Business Assistance Act of 2009," 6 November 2009, http://www.whitehouse.gov/the-press-office/fact-sheet-worker-homeownership-and-business-assistance-act-2009

refundable tax credit was available only to first-time buyers with individual incomes of less than $75,000 or combined incomes of $150,000. The tax credit does not have to be repaid unless the home is sold or ceases to be used as the buyer's principal residence within three years after purchase.

The Act also extends a $6,500 tax credit to "Move-Up/Repeat Home Buyers." To be eligible to claim the tax credit, repeat homebuyers must have owned and lived in their previous home for five consecutive years out of the last eight years. Single taxpayers with incomes up to $125,000 and married couples with incomes up to $225,000 qualify for the full tax credit.

After initial success on the $8,000 first time homeowner credit, the program appears to stalling as the pool of credit-worthy homeowners is drying up. The peak of the program occurred in November 2009 and has decreased every month throughout the first quarter of 2010. An extremely harsh winter is partly responsible for the decline. The key to success may lie in the $6,500 repeat homebuyer credit, but many realtors feel that this amount is too low to encourage potential up-graders to take the risk. As a result, Fannie Mae has lowered its new home sales estimates by 30% for 2010.

Opponents argue that government housing stimuli like the first-time and move-up/repeat homebuyer programs have artificially inflated the existing and new home sales in 2009 . These "forward" sales will disappear when the stimuli end in 2010 and the market will go negative.

Action	2008	2009			
	QIV	QI	QII	QIII	QIV
New Short Sales	16,809	18,619	25,128	30,766	37,584
New Deed-in-Lieu-of-Foreclosure Actions	1,186	1,298	1,120	1,233	1,054
	17,995	**19,917**	**26,248**	**31,999**	**38,638**

Figure 99: Short Sales and Deeds-in-lieu-of-foreclosure[185]

US government incentives and proprietary actions from lending institutions are also showing much improvement in short sales and deeds-in-lieu-of-foreclosures (transfer of mortgages and ownership to banks to lessen impact on borrowers' credit records) (Figure 99). While the numbers are only 8% of all foreclosures in 2009, they are encouraging alternatives to foreclosure.

As mentioned at the beginning of this chapter, the Administration is launching a new fourfold offensive strategy on the foreclosure crisis, which includes increased financial incentives to:

- Distressed homeowners who keep paying on underwater mortgages via reduced payment (principal and interest) amounts or refinancing.
- Banks that cut the principal balance on underwater mortgages.
- Banks that modify second mortgages.
- Banks that conduct short sales in lieu of foreclosing.

---

185 US Treasury, Office of the Comptroller of the Currency and Office of Thrift Supervision, OCC and OTS Mortgage Metrics Report, Fourth Quarter 2009, Table 6. Completed Foreclosures and Other Home Forfeiture Actions, http://www.occ.treas.gov/ftp/release/2010-36a.pdf

The success of this fourfold strategy will be directly proportional to averting another residential real estate debacle. There are many government homeowner recovery challenges that need be addressed and overcome.

US Government Homeowner Recovery Challenges. Major obstacles for US government homeowner recovery programs include fewer qualified borrowers, more stringent lending requirements, depressed economy and home values, and unemployment. Despite all the government efforts, if the unemployment rate does not improve, a second residential real estate crisis may not be avoidable.

According to the Chief Economist of the Mortgage Banker Association,[186]

"Despite the recession ending in mid-summer, the decline in mortgage performance continues. Job losses continue to increase and drive up delinquencies and foreclosures because mortgages are paid with paychecks, not percentage point increases in GDP. Over the last year, we have seen the ranks of the unemployed increase by about 5.5 million people, increasing the number of seriously delinquent loans by almost 2 million loans and increasing the rate of new foreclosures from 1.07 percent to 1.42 percent."

Underwater mortgages and serious delinquencies are creating a shadow wave leading to increased foreclosures. In addition, banks are hesitant to repossess and foreclose, due to the legal process and plethora of unsold, undervalued homes on the market. Government intervention has added to the glut of homes entering the foreclosure process. Government foreclosure moratoriums are creating greater REO backlogs that could eventually rupture, unleashing a torrent of writedowns and devaluations that would subsequently damage banks, the housing industry and the US economy. This damage could range from mild to catastrophic, depending on the resilience of the banks and the strength of the economic recovery.

Let's pray that this wave of writedowns will not happen, because the US government no longer has the magnitude of resources to combat a second residential real estate crisis, as it did for the first residential real estate crisis. $11.6T worth of bailouts and stimuli for the first crisis and the resulting recovery efforts constituted an all-in bet by the US government (Treasury, Fed and FDIC). It is unlikely that the government could pony up this amount of cash for a second crisis.

---

186 Mortgage Bankers Association, Press Release, "Delinquencies Continue to Climb in Latest Mortgage Bankers Association National Delinquency Survey," 19 November 2009, http://www.mbaa.org/NewsandMedia/PressCenter/70050.htm

Organization	Expires	Committed	Max
Federal Reserve			
Mortgage Purchase Program	3/31/2010	$910B	$1250B
GSE Debt Purchase Facility	3/31/2010	160	200
Treasury			
Preferred Stock Purchase Agreements	12/31/2012	111	No limit
GSE MBS Purchase Facility	12/31/2009	220	Expired
GSE Credit Facility	12/31/2009	0	Expired
Source: SIGTARP Testimony to Congress, Jan 10		**$14.T**	

Figure 100: Federal Government Support to Fannie Mae and Freddie Mac[187]

As shown in Figure 100, government direct support to the housing agencies is beginning to run out after $1.4T worth of expenditures. The buying of toxic mortgage-backed securities from banks and other financial institutions is also ending. It is unlikely that this amount of funding will be made available in the future, but the Treasury will likely continue to keep Fannie and Freddie afloat through increased borrowing (via the sale of Treasuries) and increasing the national debt. Consequently, the America public most likely will not have to wait long to see if the housing industry can operate on its own.

The second half of 2010 will begin to tell the story with the government programs ending. Then it will be up to the private sector, which is gearing up. Hundreds of billions of dollars' worth of global private equity funds and foreign sovereign wealth funds are being accumulated for a potential feeding frenzy when the REO dam breaks. These "dry powder" (cash reserves) funds are especially interested in the distressed US real estate (residential and commercial) market. Banks are cautious of losing control. Today, they are parsing out REOs sparingly to keep prices up as much as possible, by creating competition amongst the speculators and bargain hunters.

The big banks, like Bank of America (BoA), Wells Fargo and Citigroup, have begun implementing principal write-down programs that are different from the US government's HAMP interest reduction or extension programs. Both types of programs are synergistic in breaking the cycle of serious delinquencies, strategic defaults, repossessions and foreclosure of underwater mortgages.

Program	Amount	Type	Year	Rate	Payment
Original loan	$ 800,000	ARM Original	30	3.50%	$ 3,592
	$ 800,000	ARM Reset	30	6.50%	$ 5,056
HAMP	$ 800,000	Conventional Fixed	40	4.00%	$ 3,343
BoA	$ 600,000	Conventional Fixed	40	4.00%	$ 2,507

Figure 101: Synergism between HAMP and
Bank Mortgage Adjustment Programs

---

187 Office of the Special Inspector General for the Troubled Asset Relief Program, Quarterly Report to Congress, 31 January 2010, Table 3.3, Page 123, http://www.sigtarp.gov/reports/congress/2010/January2010_Quarterly_Report_ to_Congress.pdf

Let's work through a hypothetical to see how synergism between the US government and private lending institutions could work for distressed underwater homeowners.

- A homeowner with an $800K mortgage owns a home that is now worth $500K.

- This homeowner is beginning to question if it is worth continuing making payments since it will take many years for the residence to regain its original value. In addition, the homeowner has mounting credit card debt and the loss of income from a spouse.

- As calculated in Figure 101, the homeowner had been paying $3,592 monthly on principal and interest on an option-ARM that has reset to $5,056, which is completely unaffordable. Consequently, the homeowner finds himself three months late making the $5,056 mortgage payment (serious delinquency) and is considering walking away entirely (strategic default) since it is not in the homeowner's financial interest to continue to make payments.

- Obama's HAMP program is designed to make permanent loan modifications. To date, HAMP's average mortgage reduction is 36% for approximately 170,000 homeowners. If the HAMP restructures this homeowner's loan to a 40-year fixed conventional loan at a reasonable rate, the new payment would be $3,343, which is close to the original ARM payment of $3,592.

- However, since the homeowner is down to a single family income due to his spouse's job loss, $3,343 is still too much to pay. If the bank determines that it is in the bank's interest to keep the homeowner in the residence, the bank can lower the principal. If the bank lowered the principal from $800,000 to $600,000 the mortgage payment could be reduced to $2,507, which may be enough to keep the homeowner in the residence and resume payments on the mortgage.

Bank of America (BoA) recently announced a pilot program to reduce principal on 45,000 delinquent homes that BoA obtained via the Countrywide acquisition in 2008. This action by BoA is significant because of its dominant position in the housing industry. BoA is the largest mortgage servicer, collecting loan payments on 20% of all US residential mortgages, is the holder of approximately 1.1 million delinquent (60 days+) residential home mortgages that are underwater, and was a major recipient of $45B TARP funding, which it paid back.

BoA officials said the maximum reduction would be 30% of the value of the loan. In our hypothetical example, if the homeowner's $800,000 mortgage had fallen to $600,000, the principal would be readjusted to $600,000 and the $200,000 that had been underwater would be placed in a separate interest-free BoA account. As long as the owner continued to make payments on the $600,000, $40,000 in the special account would be forgiven each year until either the balance was zero or the housing market had recovered and the borrower once again had positive equity. BoA's program is limited to Countrywide borrowers whose loan balance is at least 120% of the estimated home value, who are at least 60 days overdue, who can prove financial hardship and the eventual ability to repay, and that they have loans with large interest or reset rates that can be appropriately readjusted.

There are a number of critics of the program. Some feel that government and public pressure is forcing banks into a public relations campaign that will not produce meaningful results. Others say it is not coincidence that BoA announced their principal reduction program on the same day that BoA reached a settlement with the state of Massachusetts over claims of predatory lending by Countrywide. Other critics complain that these underwater reduction efforts reward failure and set a bad precedent for the future. In addition, many bankers believe that market psychology has already turned negative.

Consequently, most underwater homeowners aren't willing to make reduced payments, believing they have little hope of ever regaining equity in their homes. Both the government and banks are already having trouble getting seriously delinquent borrowers to even return phone calls about the possibility of trial modifications, regarding either interest or principal reductions. Some say it is simply too late and the process is too slow to make a difference. Others worry that reducing loan balances for some could encourage others to default in hopes of a similar deal.

So what is going to happen in the near future?

Optimists envision a future where underwater homeowners are incentivized to stay in their homes, and the foreclosure crisis is mitigated by an orderly transfer of mortgages and mortgage-backed securities from the government and banks to the secondary market. Housing prices would stabilize and eventually increase. Optimists also envision that a little bit of inflation would aid the process by inflating home values relative to fixed mortgages.

Pessimists envision a disorderly process where REOs (bank-owned homes) flood the market, forcing banks to auction off blocks of REOs at significant discounts, thereby driving home values significantly lower. Lower home values would cause more strategic defaults from homeowners who would elect to rent, rather than pay underwater mortgages that are getting deeper underwater. Serious delinquencies would increase, causing more repossessions and foreclosures. In the end, a second mortgage crisis would ensue, bringing significant distress on the entire US financial system—this time without the financial wherewithal to bailout, buyout, stimulate or incentivize like the government did in the post-Great Recession era.

Whatever one's point of view, 2011 and 2012 will be a crucial period for the US housing market. The US government is beginning a process to determine its proper role in the residential real estate industry. This is sure to cause serious debate. The state of the industry and the overall economy will be the key determinants.

At the policy level, debate will continue about the role of the government in the housing industry.

Despite all the challenges, many still believe that all the government homeowner recovery efforts are very necessary to stabilize the residential real estate market and the overall economy. Others worry about the mounting national debt and unforeseen consequences of government meddling. Real estate, unemployment, consumer spending, GDP growth, and debt are all elements of the economic recovery equation. Intervention in one of these issues impacts all others.

It was the US government sponsored enterprises that created exotic financial instruments for the mortgage industry to generate cash in pursuit of the government's national objectives. While their intentions were honorable, the unanticipated consequences were nearly catastrophic. Now the US government controls the mortgage industry.

Barring future crises and unknown disruptions, our government appears to be better prepared for the future. For those who argue that the US government should not have been involved to the degree that it is, their argument is moot. The US government is the key player and is working the problem. After the housing problem is solved, then we can discuss strategic changes. To do so now makes recovery harder.

To be successful, the US government has to defeat the downward cycle that begins with unemployment, which leads to delinquencies that generate defaults, short-sales and foreclosures, which further depress home values, causing more underwater mortgages that create the conditions for a wave of strategic defaults, and the second residential real estate tsunami.

Chapter 15:

THE MARKETS

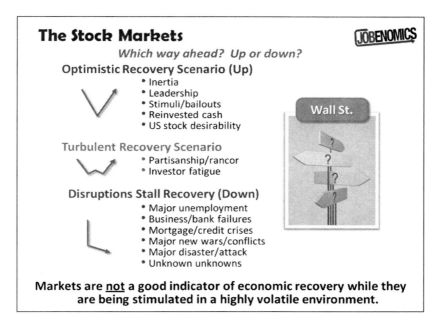

The Stock Markets　　　　JOBENOMICS

Which way ahead? Up or down?

Optimistic Recovery Scenario (Up)
* Inertia
* Leadership
* Stimuli/bailouts
* Reinvested cash
* US stock desirability

Wall St.

Turbulent Recovery Scenario
* Partisanship/rancor
* Investor fatigue

Disruptions Stall Recovery (Down)
* Major unemployment
* Business/bank failures
* Mortgage/credit crises
* Major new wars/conflicts
* Major disaster/attack
* Unknown unknowns

Markets are **not** a good indicator of economic recovery while they
are being stimulated in a highly volatile environment.

Figure 102: Chapter 15 Summary

Stock markets are not good indicators of economic health while they are under the influence of government stimuli in a volatile global political/economic environment. If there were any doubt, 6 May 2010 proved it. On 6 May 2010, a brief panic about Greece's defaults, along with reticence regarding the US economy, and a technical glitch, sent the Dow Jones Industrial Average down over 1,000 points—the biggest intraday point drop ever recorded.

As discussed earlier, plausible cases can be made for each of the three V-, W- and L-shaped recovery scenarios. Consequently, it is almost recklessly optimistic to say that the dramatic rise in the US stock markets is evidence of a V-shaped recovery. The opposite is the case. The upward momentum of the "V", caused by the infusion of historic amounts of liquidity has, in turn, uplifted the markets.

Over $11T worth of government liquidity has been injected in the market to spur recovery. This money is being matched by the private sector, which is reinvesting because of opportunity, as an alternative to low yields offered by banks, or simply getting back into the market to keep from falling behind. It is important to note that all sectors in the stock markets are rising, which indicates that there is so much money available that it floods the entire marketplace in order to be absorbed. As the saying goes, a rising tide raises all boats. In this case, the tide is rising so rapidly that a classic asset bubble may be forming.

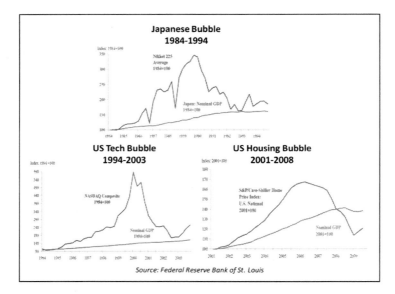

Figure 103: Asset Bubbles[188]

The three most recent and notorious asset bubbles were the Japanese real estate bubble in 1984-1994, the US technology bubble in 1994-2003 and the US housing bubble in 2001-2008, which led to the Great Recession (Figure 103).

In the late 1980s, the value of all the real estate in the Tokyo metro area was reportedly worth as much as the real estate of the rest of the world. When this over-priced bubble burst, it caused a 20-year deflationary cycle that lasts today. Many investors still vividly remember the dot. com and telecom technology eras, where emerging hi-tech companies with little revenue and no profits were highly valued due to the illusion of unlimited scalability, due to the promises of the information age. To the disbelief of many, the tech bubble burst and devastated many investors. The most recent housing bubble burst is well known to investors around the world.

---

188 James Bullard, President and CEO, Federal Reserve Bank of St. Louis, The First Phase of the U.S. Recovery and Beyond, Shanghai, China, 11 January 2010, Various sources: WSJ, IMF, Financial Times, BEA, S&P, Fiserv, MarcoMarkets LLC, http://research.stlouisfed.org/econ/bullard/GIC_ShanghaiJanuary_11_2010.pdf

The major difference between the US housing bubble in 2001-2008 and previous bubbles involved the magnifying effect of derivatives and other asset-backed financial instruments that were tied to the housing market. The catalyst for the burst was $10Ts worth of mortgage-backed securities and credit default swaps that were derived from $1Ts worth of underlying sub-prime mortgages.

$100Ts worth of derivates still exist in the market today.

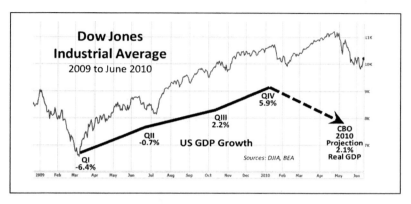

Figure 104: Current Equity Bubble or Not?

The rise in US markets is remarkable. The question is, is this a bubble or not?

Unlike the previous bubbles, Figure 104 shows that the rise in the Dow Jones Industrial Average and the US GDP rise during 2009 have been compatible. This is a good sign. However, the rise in GDP is also directly linked to the infusion of tens of $Ts worth of liquidity. Consequently, if all this "artificial" liquidity were subtracted from GDP growth, the GDP line in Figure 104 would be inverse to the one shown. Let's do some math to prove this point. The CBO's US GDP growth projection for 2010[189] is 2.1%. 2.1% of an annual GDP of $14T is $294B, which means that all of this country's goods and services should grow by this amount. $294B is a relatively small amount compared to the $11.6T worth of liquidity injected into the US financial system by the Fed, FDIC and Treasury to avert an economic crash and spur the recovery. Consequently, if we redrew the GDP line as negative, or flat, the graph in Figure 104 would look very similar to the three asset bubbles in Figure 103.

So is the current run up of the stock markets an asset bubble? No one really knows. The current run up started from a substantially depressed low. Asset bubbles are easy to spot in hindsight, but not so easy with foresight. However, it does not take an expert to know that extremes of anything usually produce very unusual rejoinders. If you believe that the rise in the markets is due to bounce from the crash in association with a real rise in GDP, then there is no bubble. If you believe that the rise of the markets and GDP is largely due to artificial stimulation, then a major bubble may be building. Investors and policymakers will have a much better perspective in 2011 after the stimuli end.

189 Congressional Budget Office, The Budget And Economic Outlook: Fiscal Years 2010 To 2020, CBO's Economic Projections for Calendar Years 2010 To 2020, Table 2, http://www.cbo.gov/ftpdocs/108xx/doc10871/01-26-Outlook.pdf

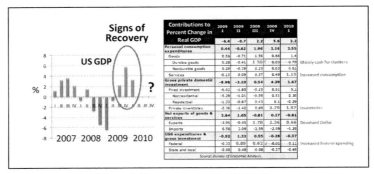

Figure 105: GDP May Not Be a Reliable Indicator in These Times

The good news is that the recovery over the last five quarters has been phenomenal. Figure 105 examines GDP in more detail. According to the Bureau of Economic Analysis (BEA),[190] 2009 QI was one of the worst in US history with a 6.4% decline in GDP. QII rose 5.7% (-6.4% to -0.7%) due to imports and government spending. QIII rose 2.9% (-0.7% to 2.2%) largely due a big jump in durable goods that was caused mainly by the Cash for Clunkers program. After this program ended, durable goods dropped 2% in the next quarter. QIV rose 3.5% (2.2% to 5.6%) mainly due to a large increase in inventories. This increase in inventories was due to companies restocking shelves and warehouses after the economic crisis scare subsided. This restocking has not resulted in many new jobs, as companies are still cautious about the future. 2010 QI dropped from 5.7% to 3.2%, but it still posted a positive gain, largely due to increased consumption and inventories. The 2010 Q1 increase in services consumption is particularly meaningful. This means that more people are shopping, going out to eat, doing delayed repairs, etc.

The massive infusion of public and private sector liquidity certainly has shocked the economy back into a GDP growth mode. Now the true measure of success is at hand. Success depends on continued private sector consumption, and the willingness of private investors to replace the US government as the principal source of capital. Market-watchers are cautiously optimistic, but are uneasy about how the market will react to changes in the Fed's monetary policy and potential economic disruptions, such as eurozone defaults or the US foreclosure quagmire.

	\$T					% average Change from	Change from
	2005	2006	2007	2008	2009	2005 to 2009	2005 to 2009
Personal consumption expenditures	8.8	9.3	9.8	10.1	10.1	70%	14%
Gross private domestic investment	2.2	2.3	2.3	2.1	1.6	15%	-25%
Net U.S. exports of goods and services	(0.7)	(0.8)	(0.7)	(0.7)	(0.4)	-5%	-46%
Government consumption expenditures and gross investment	2.4	2.5	2.7	2.9	2.9	19%	24%
US GDP (\$T)	12.6	13.4	14.1	14.4	14.3		

Figure 106: GDP Growth 2005 to 2009

190 Bureau of Economic Analysis, US Department of Commerce, Table 1.1.2. Contributions to Percent Change in Real Gross Domestic Product, 5 May 2010, http://www.bea.gov/national/nipaweb/TableView.asp?SelectedTable= 2&ViewSeries=NO&Java=no&Request3Place=N&3Place=N&FromView=YES&Freq=Qtr&FirstYear=2009&LastY ear=2010&3Place=N&Update=Update&JavaBox=no

Figure 106 comes from the Federal Reserve Flow of Funds Accounts[191] and shows the change over the last five years in US GDP and its principal components. What is interesting about the data is that US GDP stayed about the same ($14.4T to $14.3T) during the Great Recession. Consumption actually increased 14% from 2005 to 2009. Over the period, consumption averaged about 70% of GDP and is the reason that America is called a consumer based society. As to be expected, government consumption expenditures and gross investment has the biggest jump (24%) over the period. As a percentage of GDP, the government grew 1% per year. It will be interesting to see what happens in 2010 with the government numbers, since state and local government are downsizing, while the federal government is growing.

As discussed in Chapter 9, prognosticators fall into three categories: V-, W-, and L-shaped recovery advocates. The V-shaped recovery advocates point to the tremendous surge in US stocks (Figure 107) as a true sign of recovery and that employment will eventually recover, as well. W- and L-shape proponents do not agree. W-ers theorize a weak recovery besieged with downturns, whether it be unemployment, debt, or reaction to government stimuli. When President Roosevelt tried to withdraw government stimuli in the Great Depression, stocks fell as the economy reentered depression. L-ers are even more pessimistic and worry that another economic event, energy crisis, war, or even a national disaster could plunge an already weak economy into serious trouble.

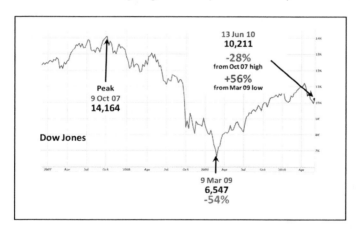

Figure 107: Dow Jones Industrial Average 2007 To 2009

The Dow Jones Industrial Average (Dow) is the best known and most widely followed of the major Wall Street stock market indices. The Dow was created in 1896 by Charles Dow, the editor of the *Wall Street Journal*, and Edward Jones, a statistician. Today, the Dow is comprised of 30 large, publically-owned corporations, including notables like IBM, General Electric, American Express, Caterpillar, DuPont, McDonald's, Procter & Gamble, Home Depot, Microsoft, Wal-Mart, Verizon and Walt Disney. The Dow lost 54% of its value in the Great Recession. Due largely to massive government intervention and investor confidence, the Dow has regained 65%

---

191 Federal Reserve, Flow of Funds Accounts of the United States, 2005-2009, 11 March 2010, F.6 Distribution of Gross Domestic Product, http://www.federalreserve.gov/releases/z1/Current/annuals/a2005-2009.pdf

of its value, but is still 24% off its previous high. To say that there is volatility in this market is an understatement. The major question facing Dow market watchers is, what will happen when the US stimuli are withdrawn and artificially depressed interest rates are allowed to climb? Hopefully, the answer is that the market will be able to operate on its own, without government support.

Date		Points	%	Close
2008	29-Sep	778	7.0	10365
2008	15-Oct	733	7.9	8578
2001	17-Sep	685	7.1	8921
2008	1-Dec	680	7.7	8149
2008	9-Oct	679	7.3	8579
2008	14-Apr	618	5.7	10306
1997	27-Oct	554	7.2	7161
2008	22-Oct	514	5.7	8519
1998	31-Aug	513	6.4	7539
2008	7-Oct	508	5.1	9447
1987	19-Oct	508	22.6	1739

Source: Dow

Figure 108: Top Single Day Drops in Dow Jones History

The biggest drops in Dow Jones history did not happen during the Great Depression. They happened within the last several decades (Figure 108).

The largest single day point drop of 778 points occurred on 29 September 2008. The September 2008 trigger events were all related to a failure of a large US financial institution (Lehman Brothers) caused by over-leveraging derivatives and negative reaction to the initial US government bailout efforts. In the following three week period, four other top ten drops followed, for a stunning total of 3,212 points.

The largest single day percentage drop of 22.6% happened on 19 October 1987, known as Black Monday. Black Monday was caused by a number of relatively minor causes (computer trading, overvaluation and illiquidity) that triggered market hysteria. This hysteria started in Hong Kong and rapidly spread to America, and the world.

The largest intraday drop happened on 6 May 2010 with a drop of 998 points in a period of one hour for a total percentage drop of 9.2%. This historic drop was triggered by the European debt crisis, a trader error, and nervous investors worried about the state of the nascent US recovery. The market rebounded later in the trading day for a net loss of 348 points.

The lesson learned from major trigger events is that global disruptions and government intervention can evoke market hysteria. Today, market volatility has never been higher.

A recent *New York Times* Bestseller book, by Harry Dent, entitled, *The Great Depression Ahead: How to Prosper in the Debt Crisis of 2010-2012* provides significant analyses and a few startling predictions. Dent is a prominent forecaster who is well published on booms and busts. In his book *The Great Boom Ahead*, published in 1992, he accurately forecast the unexpected boom of the 1990s.

According to Dent, the Dow Jones Industrial Average will "fall in between 2,300 and 4,500 by late 2010 with 3,350-3,800 our most likely target."[192]

Dent's forecast supports a W-shaped scenario with the Dow's first peak at 14,164 in October 2007, crashing in March 2007 to 6,547, rising to 10,000+ high in January 2010, crashing to 3,500 in the summer of 2010 and returning to unknown highs thereafter.

Dent believes that the US is at the bottom of an economic lifecycle caused by a multitude of factors, including the debt crisis, demographics, the real estate bubble burst, and emerging world factors. Dent's theory about the power of mini- and macro-economic cycles is a compelling piece of work. Dent theorizes that the US economy functions like economic biorhythms, where, in late 2010, the US will experience the simultaneous bottoming of mini- and macro-economic cycles which will drive the markets to historic lows, as well as drive the US into depression. These mini- and macro-economic cycles will then reverse, and then rebound over time. Dent also provides a number of ways to prosper during this wild ride. Simply stated, cash will be king.

The second best-known stock index is the S&P 500. The Standard & Poor's 500 Index is usually considered the benchmark for US equity performance since it represents performance of the top 500 US publicly traded companies.

-50%	-40%	-30%	-20%	-10%	0	+10%	+20%	+30%	+40%	+50%	+60%
							2009				
						2007	2006	2003			
						2005	2004	1999			
						1994	1988	1998			
						1993	1986	1996			
				2000		1992	1979	1983			
				1990		1987	1972	1982	1997		
				1981		1984	1971	1976	1995		
				1977		1978	1969	1967	1981		
				1968		1970	1965	1963	1989		
				1962		1960	1964	1961	1985		
			2001	1953		1956	1959	1951	1980		
			1973	1946		1948	1952	1943	1975		
			1966	1940		1947	1949	1942	1955		
			1957	1934		1939	1944	1925	1950		
			1941	1932		1923	1926	1924	1945		
		2002	1920	1929		1916	1921	1922	1938	1958	
2008		1974	1917	1914		1912	1919	1915	1936	1935	1954
1931	1937	1930	1910	1913	0	1911	1918	1909	1927	1928	1933

Figure 109: S&P 500 over the Last 100 Years

---

192 *The Great Depression Ahead: How to Prosper in the Debt Crisis of 2010-2012*, Harry S. Dent, Jr., published by Free Press, a division of Simon & Schuster, 2008, 2009 and "completely revised" in January 2010, Page 26.

In 2008, the S&P tied the Great Depression's 1931 low (Figure 109). By the end of 2009, the S&P sky-rocketed and almost doubled its value – one of the most dramatic rises in history. Wall Street pundits argue that the 2008 low was an anomaly, and the Dow made a proper correction. Strategic planners worry that this market volatility is dangerous. What goes up could come crashing down. Historians look at the dramatic S&P rise and fall from 1931 (-50%) to 1933 (+60%) to 1937 (-40%), as well as the volatility in recent history.

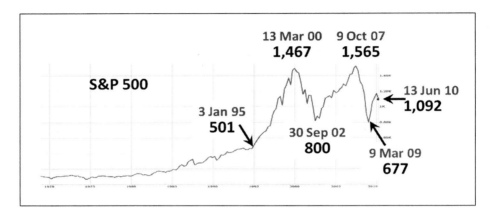

Figure 110: S&P 500 since 1970

As shown in Figure 110, the S&P 500, the bellwether indices of the US economy, experienced slow and steady growth until the year 2000. Then the telecom and dot.com booms and bubble bursts happened. Derivatives and other exotic financial instruments ushered in a new era of artificial prosperity. Wall Streeters pocketed hundreds of billions of dollars in bonuses. Main Street invested heavily in homes. Then, the housing bubble burst, dropping the S&P to 677, followed by the dramatic S&P rise to 1207 in April 2010.

With volatility like this, it is very difficult to predict anything good or bad about the economy or its recovery, based on what's happening in over-stimulated stock markets. For those V-shape advocates who promote the stock market as the leading indicator for economic recovery, caveat emptor (let the buyer beware).

Chapter 16:

INFLATION

Figure 111: Chapter 16 Summary

Inflation is a key economic indicator. Inflation is characterized by a rise in prices and a decrease in the real value of money. Negative inflation is called deflation, which is characterized by a persistent decrease in the price level of goods and services. Deflation leads to lower production, consumption and employment. Positive inflation in the 1% to 2% range is considered normal. Rates above 3% are considered abnormal and trigger government intervention, usually by the Federal Reserve System. Stagflation is an economic condition of both chronic inflation and stagnant business activity, resulting in high unemployment rates. Super-inflation is very high, above 10%, but not out-of-control inflation. Hyperinflation is high, out-of-control inflation that often causes economies to collapse. In the last 20 years, several dozen economies have collapsed due to hyperinflation. With the exception of Russia in the 1990s and Argentina in the 1980s, all other hyperinflation collapses were in small third-world countries or countries ravaged by war.

So where is America in the inflation spectrum, and where are we going? This is a key question on everyone's mind, from Washington to Wall Street to Main Street.

To get a perspective on where the US is going, Figure 112 shows the US inflation landscape over the last two decades.[193]

	Jan	Feb	Mar	Apr	May	Jun	Jul	Aug	Sep	Oct	Nov	Dec
2010	2.63%	2.14%	2.31%	2.24%								
2009	0.03%	0.24%	-0.38%	-0.74%	-1.28%	-1.43%	-2.10%	-1.48%	-1.29%	-1.29%	1.84%	2.72%
2008	4.28%	4.03%	3.98%	3.94%	4.18%	5.02%	5.60%	5.37%	4.94%	3.66%	1.07%	0.09%
2007	2.08%	2.42%	2.78%	2.57%	2.69%	2.69%	2.36%	1.97%	2.76%	3.54%	4.31%	4.08%
2006	3.99%	3.60%	3.36%	3.55%	4.17%	4.32%	4.15%	3.82%	2.06%	1.31%	1.97%	2.54%
2005	2.97%	3.01%	3.15%	3.51%	2.80%	2.53%	3.17%	3.64%	4.69%	4.35%	3.46%	3.42%
2004	1.93%	1.69%	1.74%	2.29%	3.05%	3.27%	2.99%	2.65%	2.54%	3.19%	3.52%	3.26%
2003	2.60%	2.98%	3.02%	2.22%	2.06%	2.11%	2.11%	2.16%	2.32%	2.04%	1.77%	1.88%
2002	1.14%	1.14%	1.48%	1.64%	1.18%	1.07%	1.46%	1.80%	1.51%	2.03%	2.20%	2.38%
2001	3.73%	3.53%	2.92%	3.27%	3.62%	3.25%	2.72%	2.72%	2.65%	2.13%	1.90%	1.55%
2000	2.74%	3.22%	3.76%	3.07%	3.19%	3.73%	3.66%	3.41%	3.45%	3.45%	3.45%	3.39%
1999	1.67%	1.61%	1.73%	2.28%	2.09%	1.96%	2.14%	2.26%	2.63%	2.56%	2.62%	2.68%
1998	1.57%	1.44%	1.37%	1.44%	1.69%	1.68%	1.68%	1.62%	1.49%	1.49%	1.55%	1.61%
1997	3.04%	3.03%	2.76%	2.50%	2.23%	2.30%	2.23%	2.23%	2.15%	2.08%	1.83%	2.34%
1996	2.73%	2.65%	2.84%	2.90%	2.89%	2.75%	2.95%	2.88%	3.00%	2.99%	3.26%	2.93%
1995	2.80%	2.86%	2.85%	3.05%	3.19%	3.04%	2.76%	2.62%	2.54%	2.81%	2.61%	2.81%
1994	2.52%	2.52%	2.51%	2.36%	2.29%	2.49%	2.77%	2.90%	2.96%	2.61%	2.67%	2.61%
1993	3.26%	3.25%	3.09%	3.23%	3.22%	3.00%	2.78%	2.77%	2.69%	2.75%	2.68%	2.96%
1992	2.60%	2.82%	3.19%	3.18%	3.02%	3.09%	3.16%	3.15%	2.99%	3.20%	3.05%	3.03%
1991	5.65%	5.31%	4.90%	4.89%	4.95%	4.70%	4.45%	3.80%	3.39%	2.92%	2.99%	4.25%
1990	5.20%	5.26%	5.23%	4.71%	4.36%	4.67%	4.82%	5.62%	6.16%	6.29%	6.27%	5.39%
Key:	Deflation less than 1%			Normal: 1% to 2.9%			Inflation 3%+					

Figure 112: The US Inflation Landscape over the Last Two Decades

In the last two decades,

- 50% of all recorded months were in the normal 1% to 2% range.
- 46% of all recorded months were inflationary (3%+).
- 4% of all recorded months were deflationary (less than 1%).

Year 2009 was a deflationary year—the first deflationary year since 1955. This statistic is somewhat disconcerting, since it signals that the US is emerging out of very unfamiliar territory. While this can be explained as an anomaly due to the Great Recession, it also could be an indicator that the US could be entering a period as did Japan, after their great asset bubble burst in 1990.

The Japanese rate of deflation chart is reintroduced (Figure 113) as a means of comparison. After the Japanese economy crashed, it took several years before it settled into a period of steady-state deflation. The question facing America is whether the US just flirted with a brief period of deflation, or is America on the brink of a prolonged deflationary period?

193 InflationData.com, Historical US Inflation Rate, 15 April 2010, http://inflationdata.com/inflation/inflation_Rate/historicalinflation.aspx

	Jan	Feb	Mar	Apr	May	Jun	Jul	Aug	Sep	Oct	Nov	Dec
2010	-1.29%	-1.10%	-1.09%	-1.19%								
2009	0.00%	-0.10%	-0.30%	-0.10%	-1.08%	-1.76%	-2.25%	-2.24%	-2.24%	-2.53%	-1.87%	-1.68%
2008	0.70%	1.01%	1.20%	0.80%	1.29%	2.00%	2.30%	2.09%	2.09%	1.68%	0.99%	0.40%
2007	0.00%	-0.20%	-0.10%	0.00%	0.00%	-0.20%	0.00%	-0.20%	-0.20%	0.30%	0.60%	0.70%
2006	-0.10%	-0.10%	-0.20%	-0.10%	0.10%	0.50%	0.30%	0.90%	0.60%	0.40%	0.30%	0.30%
2005	0.20%	-0.10%	0.00%	0.10%	0.10%	-0.50%	-0.30%	-0.30%	-0.30%	-0.79%	-0.99%	-0.40%
2004	-0.30%	0.00%	-0.10%	-0.40%	-0.50%	0.00%	-0.10%	-0.20%	0.00%	0.50%	0.80%	0.20%
2003	-0.40%	-0.20%	-0.10%	-0.10%	-0.20%	-0.40%	-0.20%	-0.30%	-0.20%	0.00%	-0.50%	-0.40%
2002	-1.37%	-1.57%	-1.18%	-1.08%	-0.88%	-0.69%	-0.79%	-0.89%	-0.69%	-0.89%	-0.40%	-0.30%
2001	-0.39%	-0.29%	-0.68%	-0.78%	-0.78%	-0.88%	-0.78%	-0.78%	-0.78%	-0.78%	-0.98%	-1.18%
2000	-0.68%	-0.68%	-0.58%	-0.77%	-0.68%	-0.58%	-0.58%	-0.49%	-0.97%	-1.16%	-0.88%	-0.49%
1999	0.19%	-0.10%	-0.39%	-0.10%	-0.39%	-0.29%	-0.10%	0.29%	-0.19%	-0.67%	-1.15%	-1.06%
1998	1.88%	1.98%	2.28%	0.39%	0.48%	0.10%	-0.10%	-0.29%	-0.19%	0.19%	0.78%	0.58%
1997	0.60%	0.60%	0.50%	1.98%	1.98%	2.28%	1.98%	2.18%	2.47%	2.57%	2.18%	1.88%
1996	-0.50%	-0.40%	-0.10%	0.20%	0.20%	0.00%	0.40%	0.20%	0.00%	0.50%	0.50%	0.60%
1995	0.50%	0.20%	-0.30%	-0.20%	-0.10%	0.20%	0.10%	-0.20%	0.10%	-0.69%	-0.69%	-0.40%
1994	1.31%	1.21%	1.31%	0.80%	0.80%	0.50%	-0.20%	0.00%	0.20%	0.79%	1.00%	0.60%
1993	1.23%	1.43%	1.22%	0.91%	0.91%	0.91%	1.93%	1.82%	1.51%	1.31%	1.01%	1.11%
1992	1.77%	1.98%	1.97%	2.37%	2.05%	2.27%	1.65%	1.75%	2.06%	1.02%	0.61%	1.12%
1991	4.00%	3.56%	3.66%	3.41%	3.40%	3.41%	3.52%	3.29%	2.64%	2.71%	3.03%	2.62%
1990	3.24%	3.70%	3.68%	2.74%	2.50%	2.29%	2.29%	2.84%	2.71%	3.01%	3.80%	3.07%

Key: Deflation less than 1% — Normal: 1% to 2.9% — Inflation 3%+

Figure 113: Deflation in Japan[194]

Deflation. In his now famous November 2002 Deflation Speech to the National Economists Club in Washington DC,[195] Chairman Bernanke (then Federal Reserve Governor Bernanke) told leading economists and policymakers how to handle deflation. Little did he know how prophetic he would be, and how his statements in 2002 would set the framework for the Federal Reserve's handling of the Great Recession and its deflationary aftermath.

Paraphrasing Bernanke's main points, he said:

- Since World War II, inflation has been the bane of central bankers. Most industrial-country central banks were able to cage, if not entirely tame, the inflation dragon. On the other hand, deflation is a much harder dragon to tame.

- Significant deflation in the US in the foreseeable future is extremely small, for two principal reasons: resilience and structural stability of the US economy itself, and strength of the Federal Reserve System. The Congress has given the Fed the responsibility of preserving price stability, which most definitely implies avoiding deflation as well as inflation. The Fed would take whatever means necessary to prevent significant deflation in the US. In cooperation with other parts of the government, the Fed has sufficient policy instruments to ensure that any deflation that might occur would be both mild and brief.

- Deflation is, in almost all cases, a side effect of a collapse of aggregate demand—a drop in spending so severe that producers must cut prices on an ongoing basis in

---

194 Rate Inflation, Japan-Historical Inflation Rates, 15 April 2010, http://www.rateinflation.com/inflation-rate/japan-historical-inflation-rate.php?form=jpnir
195 The Federal Reserve Board, Remarks by Governor Ben S. Bernanke, Before the National Economists Club, Washington DC, 21 November 2002, Deflation: Making Sure 'It' Doesn't Happen Here, http://www.federalreserve.gov/BOARDDOCS/SPEECHES/2002/20021121/default.htm

order to find buyers, and a sharp decline in aggregate spending—recession, rising unemployment, and financial stress.

- Deflation of sufficient magnitude may result in the nominal interest rate declining to zero or very close to zero (called the zero bound). Deflation great enough to bring the nominal interest rate close to zero poses special problems for the economy and for policy. In a period of sufficiently severe deflation, the real cost of borrowing becomes prohibitive. Capital investment, purchases of new homes, and other types of spending decline accordingly, worsening the economic downturn. Although deflation and the zero interest rates create a significant problem for those seeking to borrow, they impose an even greater burden on households and firms that had accumulated substantial debt before deflation. Japan in recent years has faced the problem of debt-deflation—the ever-increasing real value of debts.

- The zero bound limits what central banks can do with conventional monetary policy. When the short-term interest rate hits zero, the central bank can no longer ease policy by lowering its usual interest-rate target, thereby running out of ammunition. This situation is one to be avoided.

- Under the US fiat (that is, paper) money system, the Fed still retains considerable power to expand economic activity, even when the short-term nominal interest rate is at zero. These include:

  o The US government has a technology, called a printing press (or, today, its electronic equivalent), that allows it to produce as many dollars as it wishes at essentially no cost. By increasing the number of dollars in circulation, or even by credibly threatening to do so, the US government can also reduce the value of a dollar in terms of goods and services, which is equivalent to raising the prices in dollars of those goods and services. We conclude that, under a paper-money system, a determined government can always generate higher spending and hence positive inflation.

  o Money is injected into the economy through asset purchases by the Federal Reserve. To stimulate aggregate spending when short-term interest rates have reached zero, the Fed must expand the scale of its asset purchases or, possibly, expand the menu of assets that it buys. Alternatively, the Fed could find other ways of injecting money into the system—for example, by making low-interest-rate loans to banks.

  o One straightforward extension of current procedures would be to try to stimulate spending by lowering rates further out along the Treasury term structure—that is, rates on government bonds of longer maturities.

  o Another option would be for the Fed to use its existing authority to operate in the markets for agency debt (for example, mortgage-backed securities issued by Ginnie Mae, the Government National Mortgage Association).

o If lowering yields on longer-dated Treasury securities proved insufficient to restart spending, the Fed might attempt to influence directly the yields on privately issued securities. While the Fed is restricted in its ability to buy private securities directly, it does have broad powers to lend to the private sector indirectly via banks, through the discount window. The Fed can also offer fixed-term loans to banks at low or zero interest, with a wide range of private assets (including, among others, corporate bonds, commercial paper, bank loans, and mortgages) deemed eligible as collateral.

o In lieu of tax cuts, the government could increase spending on current goods and services, or even acquire existing real or financial assets. If the Treasury issued debt to purchase private assets, and the Fed then purchased an equal amount of Treasury debt with newly created money, the whole operation would be the economic equivalent of direct open-market operations in private assets.

As addressed in Chapter 5 (USG Bailouts, Pledges and Obligations), Bernanke has largely employed most of the actions in his 2002 speech in addressing the economic crisis and its subsequent deflationary cycle. By aggressively and swiftly employing all the tools at its disposal in 2009, the Fed, in association with Treasury and FDIC, powered the US out of deflation.

Unless there are other economic shocks, most economists believe that the current US deflationary cycle is behind us. Dr. Harry Dent,[196] a leading but counterintuitive economic forecaster, disagrees.

"Once credit bubbles go to the extreme they always deflate, and they are followed by deflation in prices, not inflation. Why? Because more assets and credit are destroyed than the government can possibly counteract, without going bankrupt, through a stimulus program."

Dent believes that the massive influx of liquidity into the financial system merely created an eye in the storm that resulted in a rebound which will be followed by a crash in late 2010 or 2011, followed by a prolonged period of deflation.

The manager of one of the biggest inflation-protected bond funds also forecasts deflation, albeit a short deflationary period, followed by a higher than normal period of inflation.

As of April 2010, Dr. Mihir Worah,[197] the Managing Director of the PIMCO Real Return Fund, is telling his clients that as central banks (in particular the US and EU central banks) discontinue their liquidity programs, there is a near-term risk of flipping to deflation. Worah expects deflation to last for several years, followed by a period of "higher and more volatile inflation" than has been experienced in the past. The primary reason he gives for the deflationary period is the inability of the economy to stand on its own after stimuli have been withdrawn,

---

196 *The Great Depression Ahead: How to Prosper in the Debt Crisis of 2010-2012*, Harry S. Dent, Jr., published by Free Press, a division of Simon & Schuster, 2008, 2009 and "completely revised" in January 2010, Page 26.
197 PIMCO, Viewpoints, Mihir Worah Discusses PIMCO's Inflation Outlook and Its Investment Implications, Mihir P. Worah, Managing Director, Portfolio Manager, April 2010, http://www.pimco.com/LeftNav/Viewpoints/2010/Mihir+Worah+Discusses+PIMCOs+Inflation+Outlook+and+Its+Investment+Implications.htm

and the lack of willingness of consumers to resume past consumptive and spending habits. What makes Dr. Worah's deflation forecast so credible is the fact that his job at PIMCO is to protect his investors from inflation, not deflation.

A number of other portfolio managers agree with Dr. Worah, to the extent that they are beginning to advocate US Treasury bonds. Bonds, with fixed interest rates, do well in deflation due to invisible gains generated by falling prices. By recommending bonds, money managers are fundamentally telling clients to hedge their portfolios for deflation, as opposed to inflation. These money managers include the likes of Goldman Sachs, and Blackrock, the world's biggest money manager with over $3T in assets.

Perhaps these money managers understand that many of their clients, like the aging US baby boomer generation, would just prefer the safety and stability of bonds, especially if the 2009 deflationary period returns in 2011. Deflation would be overwhelmingly preferable to inflation to a retiree on fixed income. Deflation acts like a negative tax. For example, 2% money market accounts generate invisible yields of 4% in a -2% deflationary period.

Inflation. Most economists, decision-makers, opinion-leaders and investors believe that inflation is looming as a greater threat to the US economy than deflation.

A growing number of economists, including many on the Board of Governors of the Federal Reserve, believe it is time for Chairman Bernanke to power down the techniques that he used to defeat deflation, since these same techniques exacerbate inflation once the recovery occurs. As of April 2010, this is happening. However, many feel that it is not happening fast enough, and an inflationary ember is likely to be stoked into a bonfire, using government stimulus funds as fuel.

The Fed is cautiously walking a tight rope between deflation and inflation. The Fed is expected to hold interest rates low until the last minute, to keep liquidity flowing to generate a stronger recovery. But, due to the incendiary nature of low interest rates on inflation, the Fed may have to increase rates sooner than later.

Most economists agree that inflation can be caused by increased money supply. While this is true, it is also influenced by the velocity of money. Velocity is how quickly money changes hands. Today, velocity is slow. Many Americans are saving and hoarding, trying to make up for the aftermath of the economic crisis that stripped many portfolios of their value. Since real inflation is generated by people spending new money and borrowing more, it remains to be seen if Americans will return to their spending habits from prior to the recession.

Stagflation. Poor economic performance and inflation were key reasons for President Carter's reelection defeat in 1980. By 1980, the inflation rate rose to 13.5% and unemployment to 7%. Two years later, the unemployment rate peaked at 10.8%. The term stagflation was coined during the Carter era.

Stagflation is a dilemma where inflation and economic stagnation coexist. Stagflation is considered to be worse than either inflation or deflation, since its cure is more resistant to traditional techniques like those employed by the Fed. To spur economic growth, the Fed usually lowers interest rates. But in stagflation, lowering interest rates causes inflation to grow. This causes a dilemma for central banks since it takes away one of their key tools. Consequently, the Fed has to choose which factor is worse and treat that factor.

In today's environment, economic stagnation is considered to be worse than the fears of inflation. Chronic unemployment is a major component of economic stagnation. If unemployment rates continue above 10%, the Fed and the US government will likely take massive measures (especially before the 2010 mid-term and 2012 general elections) to drive the highly emotional unemployment rate down. These massive measures could be explosive on the inflation side of the equation.

Efforts to mitigate the 1970s stagflation caused a price-wage spiral. In a price-wage spiral, businesses raise prices to protect profits from the ravages of inflation. Wage-earners, who are unable to increase pay commensurate with increasing prices, lose purchasing power. Consequently, wages chase prices and prices chase profits. As mentioned in Chapter 19 (Corporate Recovery May Not Increase Jobs), productivity promotes price-wage spirals. As employed workers struggle to maintain their jobs in a stagnant economy, they have less leverage to demand wage increases. Additionally, these workers are working harder and more productively, decreasing the need for new employees. The Great Recession has created even greater toxicity, since corporations have reacted to the economic crisis by downsizing, closing unprofitable operating units, outsourcing, merging and using capital to buy back stock, as opposed to investing in capital improvements. All of these actions favor price-wage spirals.

Hyperinflation. In hyperinflation, prices increase drastically as currency loses value. Hyperinflation is often triggered by economic depressions, wars, and/or loss of confidence in a nation's paper currency. The root cause of hyperinflation is often associated with a massive increase in money supply not supported by growth in the output of goods and services.

The most recent and worst was in Zimbabwe in 2008. It only took a little more than one day for the prices of essential goods to double in price. People made every effort to spend their money before it depreciated in value. Figure 114 shows the Zimbabwe 100 trillion dollar inflation note—the biggest notes in financial history.

Figure 114: Zimbabwe Trillion $ Note

While most hyperinflated economies happened in third-world or war torn countries (Figure 115), there is a remote chance that more developed countries could fall to hyperinflation. A number of developed countries, like Greece, are close to defaulting on their sovereign debt. A recent crisis in affluent Dubai sparked global fears of a domino effect that reverberated in markets and economies around the world. While defaulting on debt does not equate to hyperinflation, collateral damage on the global economy is the same.

Country	Timeframe	Country	Timeframe
Zimbabwe	2008	Georgia	1994
Turkey	2005	Ukraine	1993
Madagascar	2004	Bosnia	1993
Nicaragua	2004	Russia	1992
Angola	1995	Argentina	1991
Belarus	2002	Poland	1991
Zaire	1997	Peru	1990
Brazil	1994	Bolivia	1986

Figure 115: Hyper-Inflated Economies

If there is any positive side to hyperinflation, inflating out of debt could possibly be considered positive in a macabre sort of way. Let's use a hypothetical example to illustrate this point. If a person were able to buy a piece of property for $1M with a $1M loan, that person would be liable for 100% of the debt on the property. If this property hyperinflated to $10M in a short period of time, that person would be liable for the original $1M, that is now only 10% of the value of the hyperinflated property. Bankrupt or corrupt governments, with no other place to turn for debt relief, could use hyperinflation to mitigate the debt. Of course, their economy would be destroyed in the process, but the countries listed in Figure 115 eventually recovered with international assistance. In many of these countries, the rich only became richer in the process.

Chapter 17:
US TREASURIES
AND THE DOLLAR

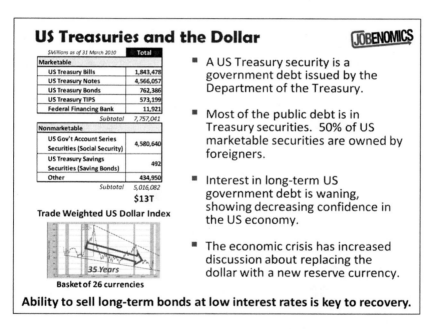

US Treasuries and the Dollar

$Millions as of 31 March 2010	Total
Marketable	
US Treasury Bills	1,843,478
US Treasury Notes	4,566,057
US Treasury Bonds	762,386
US Treasury TIPS	573,199
Federal Financing Bank	11,921
Subtotal	*7,757,041*
Nonmarketable	
US Gov't Account Series Securities (Social Security)	4,580,640
US Treasury Savings Securities (Saving Bonds)	492
Other	434,950
Subtotal	*5,016,082*
	$13T

Trade Weighted US Dollar Index

35 Years

Basket of 26 currencies

- A US Treasury security is a government debt issued by the Department of the Treasury.

- Most of the public debt is in Treasury securities. 50% of US marketable securities are owned by foreigners.

- Interest in long-term US government debt is waning, showing decreasing confidence in the US economy.

- The economic crisis has increased discussion about replacing the dollar with a new reserve currency.

Ability to sell long-term bonds at low interest rates is key to recovery.

Figure 116: Chapter 17 Summary

A United States Treasury security is a government debt issued by the United States Department of the Treasury. US Treasury securities (called Treasuries) are one of the primary indicators of the strength of the American financial system. In comparison to stock market indices, Treasuries are much better indicators that are much less reported and much less understood.

A sovereign nation can pay its expenses in three ways. The first way is to raise taxes. The second is print more money. The third way is to borrow money.

Third-world nations borrow money from larger nations. Since the US economy is the world's largest, the US does not borrow money directly from other nations. Instead, the US sells bonds to other nations and individuals, which is a form of borrowing.

The practice of issuing and selling US Treasuries started in WWI when the US could not borrow from the larger wealthier nations that were also embroiled in war. In order to meet wartime expenses, the US government decided to issue war bonds, which were called Liberty Bonds. These bonds carried a reasonable interest rate and were backed by the full faith and economic power of the US government. Liberty Bonds sold quickly and the US government met its financial obligations. After WWI, when the Liberty Bonds reached maturity, the US government did not have enough surplus funds to pay the bonds, so it issued more bonds at an attractive rate. The Treasury also issued several different types of bonds with varying maturity rates. These bonds also sold quickly and were often traded on the open market at a higher price. In 1929, the US Treasury adopted an auction process that let people and institutions bid on bonds. The highest bidder was awarded the bond. This process is still used today.

Today, the US Treasury Department issues four primary types of securities:

- Treasury Bills (T-Bills) mature in 1 year or less
- Treasury Notes (T-Notes) mature in 1 to 10 years
- Treasury Bonds (T-Bonds or long bonds) mature in 20 to 30 years
- Treasury Inflation-Protected Securities (TIPS) are the inflation-indexed bonds issued by the US Treasury

National debt (also known as government debt or public debt) is debt owed by our federal government via the sale of US Treasuries including T-Bills, T-Notes, T-Bonds, and other securities.

US National Debt

$Millions as of 31 Dec 2009	Debt Held By The Public	Intra-Government Holdings	Total	
Marketable				
US Treasury Bills	1,787,913	5,567	1,793,480	
US Treasury Notes	4,179,412	1,696	4,181,108	
US Treasury Bonds	714,672	3,259	717,931	59%
US Treasury TIPS	567,851	205	568,056	
Federal Financing Bank	0	11,921	11,921	
Subtotal	7,249,848	22,648	7,272,496	
Held by Foreign Governments	3,691,500 48%			
Nonmarketable				
US Gov't Account Series Securities (Social Security)	119,932	4,477,200	4,597,132	
US Treasury Savings Securities (Saving Bonds)	0	493	493	41%
Other	441,229	0	441,229	
Subtotal	561,161	4,477,693	5,038,854	
Source: US Treasury	7,811,009	4,500,341	12,311,350	
	63%	37%	$12.3T	

Figure 117: Composition of the US National (Public) Debt, 31 December 2009

As shown in Figure 117, as of 31 December 2009, the US national (public) debt was $12.3T.[198]

198 US Treasury, Treasury Direct, Monthly Statement Of The Public Debt Of The United States: 31 December 2009, http://www.treasurydirect.gov/govt/reports/pd/mspd/2009/opds122009.prn

US National Debt

$Millions as of 31 May 2010	Debt Held By The Public	Intra-Government Holdings	Total	
Marketable				
US Treasury Bills	1,850,311	5,207	1,855,518	
US Treasury Notes	4,731,332	2,670	4,734,002	
US Treasury Bonds	789,717	4,015	793,732	⎱61%
US Treasury TIPS	563,089	129	563,218	
Federal Financing Bank	0	11,921	11,921	
Subtotal	*7,934,449*	*23,942*	*7,958,391*	
Held by Foreign Governments	*3,884,600 49%*			
Nonmarketable				
US Gov't Account Series Securities (Social Security)	125,057	4,473,685	4,598,742	
US Treasury Savings Securities (Saving Bonds)	0	492	492	⎱39%
Other	434,915	0	434,915	
Subtotal	*559,972*	*4,474,177*	*5,034,149*	
Source: US Treasury	**8,494,421**	**4,498,119**	**12,992,540**	
	65%	35%	$13T	

Figure 118: Composition of the US National (Public) Debt, 31 May 2010

Five months later, as shown in Figure 118, as of 31 May 2010, the national debt grew by almost $637B to $13T.[199] Marketable securities grew by 8.6%. The dollar amount of national debt held by foreign governments grew by $193B[200] in the same period of time. (Note: as of 1 June 2010, the US Treasury's National Debt Clock[201] showed the debt to be $13.05T, a historical high for the US and the world).

National debt can be categorized in three ways:

1.   Marketable versus nonmarketable. Marketable means that these securities can be traded on the open market like stocks. 61% of the US national debt is marketable.

2.   Debt held by the public versus intragovernmental holdings. Intragovernmental holdings consist mainly of Social Security surplus holding accounts (called Government Account Series Treasuries) and Savings Bonds. 65% of the US national debt is held by the public and 35% by the US government.

3.   Internal debt versus foreign debt. Internal debt is owed to lenders within the United States, and external debt is owed to foreign lenders (mainly foreign government surpluses). Foreign governments own $3.75T of US government Treasuries, or about 29% of the total US national debt. More importantly, $3.75T equates to approximately 48% of marketable securities, which provides foreign governments with tremendous financial leverage over the US. China, Russia and a number of Arab oil exporting countries own over a $1T worth of US Treasury securities.

199   US Treasury, Treasury Direct, Monthly Statement Of The Public Debt Of The United States: 29 May 2010, http://www.treasurydirect.gov/govt/reports/pd/mspd/2010/opds032010.pdf
200   US Department of the Treasury/Federal Reserve Board, Major Foreign Holders Of Treasury Securities, 29 May 2010, http://www.ustreas.gov/tic/mfh.txt
201   Treasury Direct, "The Debt to the Penny and Who Holds It," 29 May 2010, http://www.treasurydirect.gov/NP/BPDLogin?application=np

If investors lose confidence in the government's debt (Treasury securities) as a safe haven, the US economy could be damaged permanently. The United Kingdom's national debt is 55% of GDP and the UK is in danger of losing its AAA rating. Global financial markets take this message as much for the US, as the UK.

Date	T-Bills				T-Notes					T-Bonds	
	1 mo	3 mo	6 mo	1 yr	2 yr	3 yr	5 yr	7 yr	10 yr	20 yr	30 yr
1/4/2010	0.05	0.08	0.18	0.45	1.09	1.66	2.65	3.36	3.85	4.60	4.65
1/5/2010	0.03	0.07	0.17	0.41	1.01	1.57	2.56	3.28	3.77	4.54	4.59
1/6/2010	0.03	0.06	0.15	0.40	1.01	1.60	2.60	3.33	3.85	4.63	4.70
1/7/2010	0.02	0.05	0.16	0.40	1.03	1.62	2.62	3.33	3.85	4.62	4.69
1/8/2010	0.02	0.05	0.15	0.37	0.96	1.56	2.57	3.31	3.83	4.61	4.70
1/11/2010	0.01	0.04	0.13	0.35	0.95	1.55	2.58	3.32	3.85	4.64	4.74
1/12/2010	0.02	0.05	0.14	0.34	0.92	1.50	2.49	3.22	3.74	4.52	4.62

Source: US Treasury Department: January 2010

Figure 119: Daily Treasury Yield Curve Rates[202]

Typical daily yield curve rates of T-Bills, T-Notes and T-Bonds are shown in Figure 119. As shown, the yields change daily, and ranged from a low of 0.01% for a 1-month T-bill to a high of 4.74% for a 30-year T-Bond. The reason it is called a rate curve is because the rates fit along a curve, as shown in Figure 120, that shows 3 month, 3 year, 5 year, 10 year and 30 year bond interest rates on 21 April 2010.

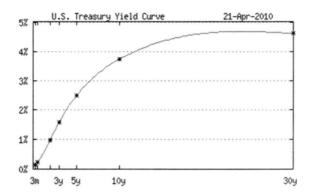

Figure 120: Typical Rate Curve

Economic and international factors are the key drivers to yield rate changes, which signal the desirability of US Treasuries, and, consequently, the strength of the US economy. The strength of Treasuries is directly related to the strength of the US economy, since they are considered safe havens in times of economic stress, since the largest economy in the world guarantees their payment.

When the global economic crisis started in 2007, sales of US Treasuries soared, even though the US was the epicenter of the crisis. This indicated that the rest of the world believed that the

202 US Treasury, Daily Treasury Yield Curve Rates, 12 January 2009, http://www.ustreas.gov/offices/domestic-finance/debt-management/interest-rate/yield.shtml

US was still the safest economy on the planet to invest. If another economic crisis epicenters in the US, the rest of the world may begin to change its mind about the US safe haven, and invest in other countries' bonds.

Treasuries can be indicators of weakness in the US economy. When the US economy weakens, people have less faith in US government guarantees. Consequently, they tend to avoid long-term bond commitments in favor of short-term commitments. T-Bills are short-term (1 year). T-Notes are mid-term (1 to 10 years), and T-Bonds are long-term (20 to 30 years). In common parlance, US Treasuries are referred to as T-bonds, or government bonds. The benchmark bond is usually the 10-year bond, which represents an intermediate bond that gives the government relatively long-term use of a lender's money.

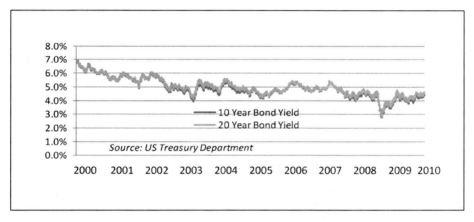

Figure 121: US Long Bond Yield 2000 through 2010 QI[203]

Over the last decade, US long bond yields fell from 7.0% in January 2000, to a low of 2.9% in December 2008 during the global recession (Figure 121). Since all countries around the globe were affected by the recession, US long bonds showed strength as an attractive safe haven.

From December 2008 to March 2010, the 10-year long bond rate has increased from 2.8% to 4.0%, showing a weakening of the US Treasuries. However, 4.0% is a still a positive indicator of US economic health. If for some reason this rate jumped to 6% or higher, it would be a key sign of trouble.

US privately-held Treasury securities are about half foreign owned and half US private holdings (mainly mutual funds, pension funds, state and municipal governments, individual savings bonds, and insurance companies).

Foreign holders of US securities totaled $3.7T. Approximately ¼ was held by China and ½ by the remaining top ten foreign countries (Figure 122).

203 US Treasury, Daily Treasury Long-Term Rates (2000 through 2009), 12 January 2010, http://www.ustreas.gov/offices/domestic-finance/debt-management/interest-rate/ltcompositeindex_historical.shtml

Rank	Foreign Holder of US Treasury Securities	Jan-10 $B	Jan-09 $B	Change	% of Total 2010 Foreign
1	China, Mainland	$889	739.6	20%	24%
2	Japan	$765	634.8	21%	21%
3	Oil Exporters*	$218	186.6	17%	6%
4	United Kingdom	$206	123.9	66%	6%
5	Brazil	$169	133.5	27%	5%
6	Hong Kong	$147	71.7	104%	4%
7	Caribbean Banking Centers **	$144	176.9	-19%	4%
8	Russia	$124	119.6	4%	3%
9	Taiwan	$120	73.3	63%	3%
10	Switzerland	$84	62.1	36%	2%
	Source: US Treasury	**$3,706**	**Total Foreign Holdings**		77%

* Ecuador, Venezuela, Indonesia, Bahrain, Iran, Iraq, Kuwait, Oman, Qatar, Saudi Arabia, UAE, Algeria, Gabon, Libya, Nigeria
**Bahamas, Bermuda, Cayman Islands, Netherlands Antilles, Panama, British Virgin Islands.

Figure 122: Top Ten Foreign Holders of US Treasury Securities, January 2010[204]

The Great Recession and the mounting US national debt have reportedly undermined confidence in US guarantees, especially with foreign governments that hold a sizeable portion of these treasuries. While there has been a lot of rhetoric from countries like China who imply that they might not bid at one of the future auctions, there is evidence to the contrary that they would do so.

As shown in Figure 122, from January 2009 to January 2010, the Chinese increased purchases of US treasuries by 20%. With the exception of the Caribbean, the same is true of other countries that are often considered hostile to the US, but nevertheless buy our treasuries. Russia increased 4% and Oil Exporters 17%, over the same time period. However, these nations are becoming more vocal with their concerns about the US economic and dollar policy and have all openly taken actions in the markets that evidence their seriousness about their concerns.

One method that the Fed uses to keep foreigners interested in Treasury securities auctions is by agreeing to a repurchase agreement. A repurchase agreement (known as a repo) is an agreement to sell a security for a specified price and to buy it back later at another specified price. It is essentially a secured loan. Large portions of the securities are repurchased the day after the formal auctions at a higher price, in order to give the purchasers a higher net yield without having to do it formally. Even so, foreign interest is shifting from long-term to shorter-term securities.

In 2009, China reduced the level of long-term US debt it has bought to the short end of the curve under the 2 year level. Some estimates put this shift to over half of their holdings.

As a consequence, the US government has been raising the long-term bond yields in relation to the short-term notes. Figure 123 shows the difference between the 1-year and 10-year bonds from 30 December 2008 to 5 April 2010. The spread has almost doubled. Equally important, the 10-year bond exceeded 4% for the first time since the end of 2007.

204 US Treasury, Major Foreign Holders Of Treasury Securities, 27 March 2010, http://www.treas.gov/tic/mfh.txt

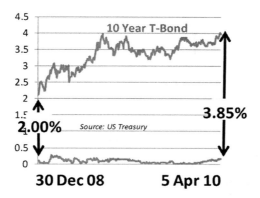

Figure 123: 1-Year and 10-Year Treasury Spreads[205]

The sovereign debt crisis in Europe is likely to enhance the attractiveness of US Treasury yields for the near-term. However, this near-term trend may not be sustainable over the long-term if US deficits and deficit spending continue at current rates.

Many bond-watchers believe that American debt and deficits are causing a loss of appetite for foreign investors, who are beginning to wonder if the US will ever get its fiscal house in order. Inflation fears are also driving away investors who are nervous in locking a relatively long-term, low-rate bond in a potential super-inflationary US economic environment. On the other hand, optimistic bond-watchers say that it makes sense for Treasury yields to rise during a period of economic recovery. Investors are swapping the relative safety of the bond market for the greater potential returns of the stock market.

The Fed is under a lot of pressure to raise interest rates in anticipation of inflation.

- Short-term rates. The Fed is currently holding short-term interest rates near zero, which is helping increase consumer demand and consumption, which is 70% of US GDP. If yields rise too much, the economic recovery may stall as interest rates increase for consumers, and loans and mortgages increase correspondingly. Consumers have evolved from panicked after the Great Recession, to cautious in 2009, to conservatively optimistic in 2010. The Fed is also concerned about corporations and investors, who are currently borrowing cheap dollars to restore inventories, buy assets or invest in various efforts.

- Long-term rates. The Fed is beginning to let long-term rates rise, largely due to declining foreign demand. This could potentially hurt the US housing industry which is still in a precarious situation. 30-year mortgage rates have been hovering around 5% for several years. Low long-term mortgage rates are essential to the housing market recovery and forestalling a second mortgage crisis. The doubling of 10-year bond rates

205 US Treasury, Daily Treasury Yield Curve Rates, 5 April 2010, http://www.ustreas.gov/offices/domestic-finance/debt-management/interest-rate/yield.shtml

from 2% to 4% will start to pressure banks to eventually increase mortgage rates, and that would choke off demand.

Eventually, the Fed will raise interest rates. Everyone is wondering if this will trigger a benign or chaotic change in market psychology. Sometimes small changes create panic. However, if properly managed, large changes can happen with relative calm. The adage about the frog in the pot of water is apropos. If the heat is turned up too fast, the frog will jump out of the pot. If the heat is delicately turned up, the frog will enjoy the warmth until it boils.

The Fed is most worried about a number of issues that could affect market psychology. These issues include consumption, real estate and inflation.

- First, and perhaps the least important, is the psychology of consumption. Over the last two years, $Ts of liquidity have helped heal lending institutions, saved some iconic industrial corporations (e.g., automotive), boosted general consumer spending, and facilitated rebuilding of inventories. If this liquidity shuts off too quickly, consumption could plummet and impact GDP growth. Since the US is only 6 months out of recession, the Fed is sensitive about any action that could be perceived to reverse course in the nascent recovery.

  In addition to keeping interest rates low, the Fed has to determine what to do with the $1.7T worth of long-term assets that it purchased from troubled banks. According to Bernanke, the Fed is open to selling some of the securities as part of its withdrawal from propping up the economy. However, like raising interest rates, the Fed and other policymakers are reluctant to sell assets, since this action could drive up long-term interest rates, stifling consumption and economic recovery.

- Second, and perhaps most important, is the impact on the real-estate market, which is precariously close to another meltdown due to underwater mortgages and foreclosures. Any upward change in interest rates makes it harder for the Administration to implement rescue programs in reducing interest payments on primary and secondary mortgages, as well as motivating banks to renegotiate loans and increase credit to distressed homeowners.

  In addition, the Fed has to determine what to do with the $1.25T worth of mortgage-backed securities on its books. When the time is right, the Fed can sell these derivatives through its open market operations. Some members of the Fed's Federal Open Market Committee want to sell off assets quickly to get the Fed out of the home mortgage subsidy business, which could collapse. On the other hand, when selling these assets in the open market, the money supply becomes more restricted, leaving banks less money to loan.

- Thirdly, and perhaps the most dangerous consideration, involves inflation. As discussed in an earlier chapter, most economists agree that inflation can be caused by increased money supply. Consequently, some members of the Fed's Federal Open Market Committee believe that the sale of assets will dilute the money supply and thereby reduce the threat of inflation.

Financial experts around the world consider super-inflation a real possibility for the US economy in reaction to the infusion of $15T+ worth of liquidity by both the government and private-sector into the US economy. The reason that creditor nations, like China and the oil-rich Arab nations, have large sovereign wealth funds is to keep the immense amount of liquidity generated by profits out of their local economies. They want excess wealth out of the local economy because this wealth is very inflationary and would drive huge asset bubbles. Recently the city-state of Dubai ignored this principle, became inflationary (14% in 2008), grew a real estate bubble that deflated during the Great Recession, defaulted on their sovereign debt obligations, and was bailed out by their sister state, Abu Dhabi. Due to the economic crisis, the US economy was injected with immense amounts of liquidity that could be the catalyst for super-inflationary rates and a future downturn.

The world is worried about a future US downturn. Financially, the US is an oxymoron. It is the largest developed economy in history, but yet it is the largest debtor nation in history. Global analysts are making a good living at predicting which side of this contradiction will eventually dominate. International conspiracists believe that US leadership is secretly planning to inflate the US economy in order to mollify the self-imposed tyranny of $Ts worth of debt. Political pundits debate America's economic resiliency, and wonder if the end of the American era is at hand. While the US is in the economic recovery mode, this intrigue is not likely to abate.

Since the globe is in such uncharted financial territory, nations are beginning to hedge their bets by decreasing their reliance on the US dollar as the world's primary reserve currency.

Key warning signs that often precede decline in the dollar include (1) interest rate cuts by the Federal Reserve, (2) surge in national debt, (3) rising commodity prices, especially gold and oil, and (4) inflation. Today, the first three warning signs are evident.

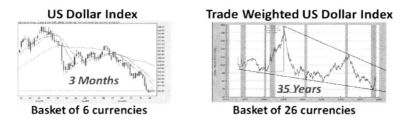

Figure 124: Basket of Currencies

For many years the US dollar has been evaluated against other currencies relative to "a basket of currencies." Figure 124 shows a snapshot of the US Dollar Index (a basket of 6 currencies) and the Trade Weighted Dollar Index (a basket of 26 currencies) during periods of weakening.

A weaker dollar means it is harder to compete for foreign capital. Additionally, if investors perceive inflation and a devalued dollar as inevitable, they could sell off stocks/bonds, and move their capital to other assets and currencies. Both of these trends are happening today.

On the other hand, a weaker dollar means that US workers and products are more competitive in the global marketplace. From a jobs and exports perspective, it is a good thing. From an imports perspective, it is negative. For example, Exxon's CEO reports that the weak dollar is adding $20-$25 to the price of a barrel of oil. A barrel of crude that is currently selling for around $80 should cost around $55.[206]

The dollar currently plays a central role in the world's currency system. The dollar is the main currency in international trade and investment, and it is the linchpin for many countries that link their currencies to the US dollar.

As of the end of 2009, according to the IMF,[207] the dollar is the dominant currency of over 62% of the world's foreign exchange reserves that are denominated in US dollars. The euro comes in second with 28%, the UK pound sterling at 4%, the Japanese yen at 3%, and all the rest at 3%.

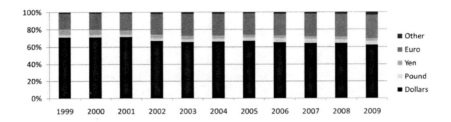

Figure 125: Dollar Denominated Currencies

Largely due to (1) the central role the US played in the current global recession, (2) the shift of the US from being the largest creditor nation to the largest debtor nation, and (3) the growing economic influence of emerging nations like China, the traditional role of the dollar is in question by the international community (Figure 125).

While still dependent on the dollar, the international community is discussing ways to lessen their dependence on the dollar as the dominant international currency. Predictions of the US economic demise are increasingly being advanced by countries hostile to the US, or who have an economic/political motive to advance their own currencies.

Three options are being discussed (1) switch to a new international currency like the euro, (2) switch to a basket of currencies, or (3) switch to a new currency that is tied to commodities.

Switch to the euro. As shown in Figure 125, over the last decade, world currencies denominated in the euro rose from 15% to 21%. In addition, the euro gained strength against the dollar. From October 2008 to November 2009, the US dollar/euro ratio increased from 1.27 to 1.5, a rise of 18% in favor of a stronger euro. It looked like the euro might be a possible replacement for

206 Investor Place, Exxon (XOM) CEO Discusses Impact of Weak Dollar, 13 November 2009, http://www.investorplace.com/experts/douglas_mcintyre/articles/exxon-xom-ceo-weak-dollar-crude-prices.html
207 International Monetary Fund, Currency Composition of Official Foreign Exchange Reserves (COFER), 31 March 2010, http://www.imf.org/external/np/sta/cofer/eng/cofer.pdf

the dollar as the international reserve currency. Then Greece, a eurozone country, threatened to default on its sovereign debt, destabilized the euro, and began a euro slide against the dollar.

The euro no longer looks like as viable a replacement for the US dollar—neither does the Japanese yen or the British pound sterling. However, this has not dissuaded the international financial community from seeking a new reserve currency.

Since no other currency is as powerful as the dollar, it is unlikely that the international community could agree on a single G7 (Canada, France, Germany, Italy, Japan, UK, US) currency replacing the dollar anytime soon. There is also mounting concern about a mounting debt in the US, eurozone, UK and Japan that could shock global financial markets.

Switch to a basket of currencies. One possibility is that the dollar, euro and Chinese renminbi (yuan) form a kind of trilateral system. Each would play a dominant role in their region of influence. The obvious downside of this arrangement would be the perception of economic hegemony.

A broader and more inclusive option would be to use the IMF's basket currency (called the SDR or Special Drawing Right). The SDR is an international reserve asset, created by the IMF in 1969 to supplement its member countries' official reserves. As of April 2010,[208] the SDR's value is based on a basket of four key international currencies (42% US dollar, 36% euro, 13% Japanese yen, and 9% UK pound), but could be modified to include other currencies like the renminbi. SDRs are often exchanged for freely usable currencies.

Switch to a new currency that is tied to commodities. A proposal that is growing in popularity is to create a new currency that is tied to gold, silver, oil or to a basket of commodities. While this option is the most ecumenical, it is the least advanced of all basket options.

The idea of a basket of commodities is not new. It was orginally proposed in the 1940s by John Maynard Keynes, as the chairman of the World Bank Commission that established the Bretton Woods system that was never implemented. Keynes proposed a world currency unit, called the bancor, that would be fixed to a basket of 30 commodities.

In March 2009, the Governor of the People's Bank of China made a speech that China supports a new reserve currency that is based on the bancor, or a bancor-SDR, as a key element of international monetary system reform.[209] The following is an exerpt of his speech:

> "Though the super-sovereign reserve currency has long since been proposed, yet no substantive progress has been achieved to date. Back in the 1940s, Keynes had already proposed to introduce an international currency unit named "Bancor", based on the value of 30 representative commodities. Unfortunately, the proposal was not accepted. The collapse of the Bretton Woods system, which was based on the White approach, indicates that the Keynesian approach may have been more farsighted. The IMF also created the SDR in 1969, when the defects of the Bretton Woods system initially emerged, to mitigate the inherent risks sovereign reserve currencies caused. Yet, the role

---

208 International Monetary Fund, Special Drawing Rights (SDR) Valuation, 2 April 2010, http://www.imf.org/external/np/fin/data/rms_sdrv.aspx
209 The People's Bank of China, Speech by Dr Zhou Xiaochuan, Governor of the People's Bank of China, Reform the International Monetary System, 23 March 2009, http://www.pbc.gov.cn/english/detail.asp?col=6500&id=178

of the SDR has not been put into full play due to limitations on its allocation and the scope of its uses. However, **it serves as the light in the tunnel for the reform of the international monetary system**." (*Emphasis added*)

While Zhou Xiaochuan's comments have generated a lot of buzz on China's economic intentions, seasoned Chinese experts believe that it will be a while before China moves aggressively for a new reserve currency. Unless there is another financial crisis like the one that caused the Great Recession, or an economic crisis centered in the US, the Chinese are likely to stick with the dollar for a number of reasons.

- The foremost reason is the Chinese realize that they are still a developing nation. For all their bravado and hoopla, the Chinese are pragmatists who realize that accepting the reins of superpower status entails a lot of responsibility and expense that the Chinese are yet unwilling to accept.

- Secondly, the Chinese yuan is still tied to the dollar. This has worked to their advantage as the dollar weakened against other currencies, and made the US worker more competitive in currency terms. China purposefully undervalues the Chinese yuan against the US dollar to give its exports a competitive advantage. This undervaluation is the subject of heated discussions between officials on both sides of the Pacific Ocean. It is also the grist for tariffs, trade wars, and protectionism. China's decision to unpeg the yuan from the dollar will most likely occur when Chinese fears of inflation and domestic asset bubbles become greater than the benefits of a ever decreasing labor wage advantage.

- Thirdly, many of the Chinese elite have had their private fortunes and accounts in US dollars, back to the days of the Chinese Civil War between Mao Zedong (Chinese Communist Party) and Chiang Kai-shek (Chinese Nationalist Party or Kuomintang), which has never ended in an armistice or peace treaty. While the world is getting ready to embrace the coming age of the Asian economic dragon, the Chinese elite are keeping one foot firmly planted on each side of the Pacific.

A new reserve currency would have profound repercussions on the US economy. Loss of prestige and investor confidence would undermine US markets. Investors would like to look to other markets as safe havens. US Treasuries would likely lose much of their appeal. The US practice of printing money to cover crises and control economies would be largely lost, further diminishing our global economic and political influence.

In a global economy, the time will come when the dollar eventually gives way to a new international monetary system. The US-based economic crisis has been traumatic for all countries. The "extraordinary" monetary policies exercised by a few central banks, especially the Fed, is viewed by many nations as self-serving at best and hegemonic at worst. The few US policymakers who entertain the idea of a new and more equitable international monetary system have been shouted down as anti-American or pro-World Government. For now, the dollar is king, and this king is good for America. Long live the king.

Chapter 18:
US MANUFACTURING
& EMERGING MARKETS

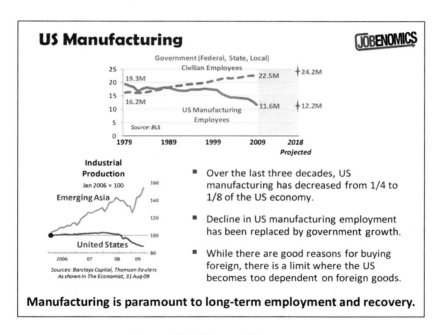

US Manufacturing JOBENOMICS

Government (Federal, State, Local)
Civilian Employees

19.3M ········ 22.5M ‡24.2M

16.2M
US Manufacturing 11.6M ‡12.2M
Employees

Source: BLS

1979 1989 1999 2009 2018
Projected

Industrial
Production
Jan 2006 = 100

Emerging Asia

United States

2006 07 08 09

Sources: Barclays Capital, Thomson Reuters
As shown in The Economist, 31 Aug 09

- Over the last three decades, US manufacturing has decreased from 1/4 to 1/8 of the US economy.

- Decline in US manufacturing employment has been replaced by government growth.

- While there are good reasons for buying foreign, there is a limit where the US becomes too dependent on foreign goods.

Manufacturing is paramount to long-term employment and recovery.

Figure 126: Chapter 18 Summary

While there are many good reasons for buying foreign (free trade, lower costs, etc.), there is a point where the US becomes dependent on foreign made goods and, subsequently, the will of foreign entities.

Small trade deficits are not considered harmful. Large, prolonged trade deficits caused by a loss of manufacturing of tradable goods places the US in a dependent position relative to the international community. In addition, manufacturing is paramount to long-term employment and viable recovery. It is not prudent for any society to rely solely on service-providing industries and government jobs. Only goods-producing industries provide substantive support for the base of a country's economic pyramid.

Over the last three decades, US manufacturing has decreased from 1/4 to 1/8 of the US economy. Correspondingly, American consumption of foreign manufactured products has increased from 1/10 to 1/3. There are both bad and good aspects of these trends. The bad is obvious—loss of US jobs and dependence on foreign goods. The good is that the US helped foster an economic explosion in emerging countries like China and India. Emerging manufacturing opportunities could be a bonanza for US manufacturing. The US is still the world's leader in science and technology, and should leverage this position on next-generation goods and services.

High-technology manufactured goods have been among the most dynamic components of international trade over the last decade. According to the Organisation for Economic Co-operation and Development (OECD), trade in manufacturing was driven by high-technology industries over the last several decades. OECD is an international organization of 30 developed countries committed to democracy and the global market economy. In 2007, high and medium-high technology manufactures accounted for 23% and 39%, respectively, of total manufacturing trade.[210] Despite American manufacturing difficulties, the US still dominates the hi-tech manufacturing sector. It is the mid- and low-technology section that has been largely outsourced offshore.

The US economy has three sectors: government, service-providing industries, and goods-producing industries. The goods-producing sector provides the substantive base of the US economic pyramid. Substantive means being essential, having considerable value and having independent existence. Service-providing industries build upon goods-producing industries. Government exists only because goods-producing and service-providing industries provide the means for the government to function.

In 2009, the goods-producing sector's share of GDP fell to 18.9%, the lowest level since 1947, the first year that statistics were available.[211] Manufacturing is the largest category in the goods-producing sector. Manufacturing's share of GDP has fallen in 9 of the past 10 years.

The US Department of Commerce's Bureau of Economic Analysis (BEA)[212] reports that in 2008 (the latest BEA data available) US manufacturing was the second largest drain on US GDP. Construction was the first, with negative value-added of 5.6%, followed by manufacturing with a -2.7%. Durable-goods manufacturing turned down for the first time since 2001. Nondurable-goods manufacturing has contracted in 5 of the last 10 years.

210 Organisation for Economic Co-Operation and Development, OECD Science, Technology and Industry Scoreboard 2009, http://www.oecd.org/dataoecd/47/16/44212130.pdf
211 US Department of Commerce, Bureau of Economic Analysis, Annual Industry Accounts, Table E. Value Added by Industry Group as a Percentage of Current-Dollar GDP, Page 28, http://www.bea.gov/scb/pdf/2009/05%20 May/0509_indyaccts.pdf
212 US Department of Commerce, Bureau of Economic Analysis, Annual Industry Accounts, Table A. Percent Changes in Real Value Added by Industry Group, Page 24, May 2009, http://www.bea.gov/scb/pdf/2009/05%20 May/0509_indyaccts.pdf

A comparison between the total numbers of US civilian government employees versus the number of manufacturing industries employees provides a vivid example regarding where America is focused, and the direction where the US is headed (Figure 127).

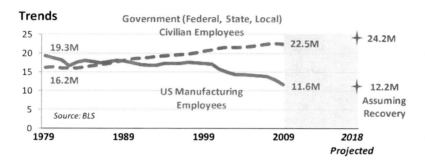

Figure 127: US Government versus US Manufacturing Employees, 1979 to 2018[213] [214]

Over the last three decades, the Department of Labor's Bureau of Labor Statistics (BLS) reports that government (federal, state and local) civilian employees have grown from 16.2 million in 1979 to 22.5 million in 2009, a growth rate of 39%. The total number of US manufacturing employees eroded from 19.3 million in 1979 to 11.6 million in 2009, a decrease of 40%. In percentage terms, the growth of government employees parallels the decline in US manufacturing employees. In real terms, the US has replaced 7.7 million manufacturing jobs with 6.3 million government positions.

Even more shocking than a 39% decrease in manufacturing over this time period is the fact that this decay occurred as the US population soared by 36%, from 228 million in 1980 to 309 million today.

Today, almost twice as many Americans work in government jobs as in US manufacturing. When the military is added, the total number of government employees exceeds twice the number of manufacturing employees in the durable and nondurable goods categories.

The gap is projected to get even wider in the future as US government growth continues to outpace US manufacturing. If the US cannot close this gap, it is unlikely that America will ever be able to close the federal spending/receipts gap that is plunging the US into a quagmire of debt. If the US loses the substantive base of its economic pyramid, the economy will likely be set adrift as the remaining industrial sector (service-providing) will increasingly seek to serve other masters.

Looking to the future, the BLS projects that government civilian (not including military) employees will grow from 22.5 million in 2009 to 24.2 million in 2018, as opposed to US

213 US Department of Labor, Bureau of Labor Statistics, Databases, Table B-1, Employees on nonfarm payrolls by industry sector and selected industry detail, Seasonally adjusted, 5 December 2009, http://www.bls.gov/webapps/legacy/cesbtab1.htm
214 US Department of Labor, Bureau of Labor Statistics, Employment Projections – 2008-18, Table 2. Employment by major industry sector, 1998, 2008, and projected 2018, 10 December 2009, http://www.bls.gov/news.release/pdf/ecopro.pdf

manufacturing employees which will grow slightly from 11.6 million in 2009 to 12.2 million in 2018. This equates to 7.5% government growth rate, compared to 5.0% manufacturing growth rate.

The erosion of the US manufacturing sector over the last three decades is directly related to foreign competition, decay, and outsourcing in manufacturing industries. Lower-tech legacy manufacturers are especially vulnerable. To a large degree, legacy manufacturers that were lost to foreign competition are gone forever. For example, television manufacturing is unlikely to return to the US.

Unfortunately, whether due to nostalgia, compassion for the unemployed, or vote-getting from the masses, legacy industries get the bulk of policymaker time and taxpayer money. In addition to time and money, manufacturing challenges in many legacy industries are largely intractable. Whether one blames management or labor, the fact is that decay is prevalent in many areas. Decay in competitiveness. Decay in skills and education. Decay in capitalization and processes.

Legacy industries that are no longer competitive will go the way of many of the manufacturing companies in the US electronics industry. The last television manufactured in America was a Zenith that was acquired by the South Korean conglomerate LG Electronics in 1995.

America's attention should be on emerging manufacturing opportunities, as opposed to legacy industries. There are two emerging manufacturing markets: the international emerging market and the emerging market defined by innovative solutions to national and consumer needs.

The International Emerging Market. The international emerging market abounds with manufacturing opportunity which is underexploited by the US.

To better understand manufacturing opportunities in emerging markets, one must be aware of industrial production statistics. Industrial production statistical reports are economic reports that measure the total output of factories, mines and utilities. Factories produce manufactured goods. Mines and utilities provide the necessary materials and energy to produce manufactured goods. No country can grow economically without natural resources and power provided by the gas and electric utilities.

While a minor portion of US GDP, industrial production is an important economic indicator, due to its sensitivity to consumer demand, inflation and interest rates. US industrial product forecasts are released monthly by the Federal Reserve.

Figure 128: Industrial Production Comparison of Select Countries

Figure 128 shows industrial production of selected countries around the world. Emerging countries, like China and India, have high industrial production. The US and Europe have much lower rates of industrial production.

These rates present a number of challenges for Western economics which include unemployment, competition for natural resources and power, environmental pollution, unfair trade practices and corruption, protectionism, and conflict. Opportunities include overseas employment opportunities, economic cooperation, increased trade, joint exploration and research, joint ventures, alternative energy and green initiatives, and mutual security agreements.

The majority of Americans view the emerging world as an economic threat. It is. The emerging world growth threatens the status quo. American know-how, manufacturing and technology have been major contributors to the evolution of emerging economies. So why should we be surprised that they are prospering? They have learned from us and improved our inventions. In addition, foreign manufacturers often know and cater to the American consumer better than do domestic manufacturers. If they didn't, our homes wouldn't be full of foreign electronics and our garages full of foreign cars.

Now is the time for Americans to better understand foreign consumers, especially the emerging Chinese and Indian middle classes who have a propensity for things American. American things, from music to movies, from blue jeans to Marlboros, from sports to Christmas, are fashionable. This means opportunity. The best way to exploit this opportunity is by coordinating the diplomatic and business communities. The US has been slow to embrace the emerging world in a coordinated manner. Politicians have one agenda and business another.

Emerging countries like China and India need energy and resources. Emerging oil-rich Arab countries need technology. Demographically declining countries like Japan and Italy need people. War torn countries like Iraq need imports.

It is amazing that the US would be willing to invest its national treasure in Iraq, and then stand idle while the Iraqis grant oil contracts to other countries. Even more shocking is the fact that US oil companies are not even making the finals in the bid process. In addition, most of the initial oil contract awards are going to countries that opposed US involvement and reconstruction efforts. Business needs to be an integral part of the diplomatic process. Joint industrial efforts are key elements of business involvement. Americans spent upward of $T on Iraqi reconstruction and infrastructure development, without provisions for long-term US business involvement. This kind of largess is not warranted or wise. There should be at least some quid pro quo.

America's most glaring challenge to exploit manufacturing opportunities in emerging countries involves reconnecting the US government and US business communities. These communities have been disconnected for six decades. After WWII, the US inherited 50% of the world's GDP. With this amount of wealth, we could afford for government to do its thing and business another. The recent economic and unemployment crises indicate that times have changed.

The US government needs to involve business at the top levels. There are currently no business executives on the Presidential Cabinet. The President's Council of Economic Advisors consists of three academics[215]—one from University of California Berkley, one from University of Chicago, and one from Princeton. All three are talented people, but they have no direct business experience. Congress is not much better. There are more lawyers in both the House of Representatives and Senate than businesspeople.

The US business community needs to be involved in national initiatives. This does not mean run for office. Innovative business leaders can't thrive in Washington. The bureaucratic environment is toxic to the entrepreneurial spirit. On the other hand, business leaders should take the leading role in national-level initiatives starting with manufacturing revitalization.

Most business leaders are waiting to see what is going to happen with the economic recovery before hiring and recapitalizing. Timidity and indecision are an anathema to prosperity. Once upon a time, CEOs used to equally balance national needs, human resources, technology, manufacturing and shareholder value. Today, the emphasis is mainly on shareholder value. The excuse that government is anti-business is no excuse.

Figure 129: Emerging Asia

Emerging Asia is a good place for government and business leaders to reconnect with a common vision and actionable milestones. Closing the industrial production gap between Asia and America (Figure 129) should be a shared goal. The US should strive for a win-win situation that emphasizes mutual manufacturing growth.

As will be discussed in more detail in the following chapters, the US will not be able to stem the flow of manufacturing jobs from the US to developing countries and emerging economies.

---

215 White House, Council of Economic Advisors, 1 January 2010, http://www.whitehouse.gov/administration/eop/cea/about/members

According to *The Economist* special report,[216] "multinationals expect about 70% of the world's growth over the next few years to come from emerging markets, with 40% coming from just two countries, China and India." In addition, foreign multinational corporations quadrupled on the *Financial Times* 500 list over the last five years. With $3,000 cars and ultra-cheap electronics, foreign multinationals are likely to redefine consumerism as the world knows it.

Consequently, it is imperative that collectively US multinational corporations and the American political system anticipate these factors, and become a viable part of the change process. However, this won't be easy since these markets operate under their own rules replete with protectionism, government meddling, intellectual piracy and host of other problems that do not exist in the US. In order to get access to these emerging markets, America may have to play hardball with access to our own market, which is still the largest in the world. Quid pro quo (something for something) can only be achieved if US multinationals and the US federal government are on the same page and working together. There is something very wrong when America's largest toolmaker (Black & Decker) has little presence in the world's largest construction site (China) at the same time US hardware stores are stocked full of Chinese made tools.

Multinational businesses, by their very nature, have to chase the opportunities wherever they may be. Outsourcing will continue, perhaps at an even greater rate than before. This does not necessarily mean that US manufacturing is doomed. We are only doomed if we allow ourselves to be. For example, if US businesses are going to help China, India and Indonesia build their middle class, Americans should be willing to move overseas to make this happen. A coordinated US strategic plan is needed to identify and promote new foreign manufacturing initiatives using American expatriates as the driving force. The British and French have been using their expatriates for centuries to generate business opportunities on foreign soil.

The idea of American expatriates living abroad is not a new concept. American artists and cultural icons have often preferred exotic and foreign places. The American expatriate retirees have swelled in recent years as they have migrated to retirement areas in Latin America. What is new is the idea that the US should exploit its domestic business talent en masse and send waves of expats to create joint business opportunities. If we can do it for the Peace Corps, we surely can do it for a Business Corps. What is needed is a cooperative effort between government and business.

Government is good at promoting goodwill, but poor in maximizing gains. On the other hand, most American business executives are results-oriented, and are often ambivalent towards diplomacy unless or until it impacts their bottom-line. From an employment perspective, America's bottom-line involves manufacturing. While service-providing industries contribute significantly more to the US GDP, it is the goods-producing industries that provide the bedrock.

Can America survive as solely a service-providing country? For a while, yes. However, over the long-term, a country without goods will eventually lose the wherewithal to provide related services.

The Innovative Solutions Emerging Market. The other emerging market is defined by innovative solutions to national and consumer needs.

---

216 The Economist, The world turned upside down, 15 April 2010, http://www.economist.com/specialreports/displayStory.cfm?story_id=15879369

Technology and innovation are the benchmarks for emerging products that are the essential building blocks for manufacturing growth.

The primary issue in pursuing innovative solutions in emerging markets is competitiveness. Is America still competitive, or is the American era over, like many skeptics say? Official US government statistics are not the best source for answering such a question. Perhaps a better source can be found in Paris, France. The French are renowned for their skeptical opinions about America.

The Paris-based L' Organisation De Cooperation Et De Developpement Economiques (or Organisation for Economic Co-operation and Development, OECD) recently released its biennial OECD Science, Technology and Industry Scoreboard for 2009.[217] This Scoreboard considers challenges in five categories: Responding to the Economic Crisis, Targeting New Growth Areas, Competing in the World Economy, Connecting to Global Research, and Investing in the Knowledge Economy. The Scoreboard rates the 30 OECD countries (including the US) in these five categories. OECD member countries include 23 European countries, three North American countries (US, Canada, Mexico), and four Pacific countries (Japan, Korea, Australia and New Zealand). Over 70 other countries are listed as partner countries. Regional initiatives cover Europe, the Caucasus and Central Asia, Asia, Latin America, the Middle East, North Africa and West Africa.

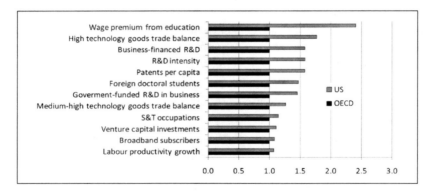

Figure 130: US Competitive Advantages As Seen By the OECD

Figure 130 was derived from OECD Scoreboard data and lists the primary US competitive advantages as seen by the OECD. In the dozen categories listed below, the US is rated 10% to 140% higher than other OECD nations.

Education, research and development, science and technology, high technology manufactured goods and venture capital are considered the primary sources of American competitiveness. The two highest-rated categories were the US wage premium and the high technology goods trades balance. In other words, the US pays well for educated workers and benefits from high-tech manufacturing. Regarding a highly educated US workforce, the OECD Scoreboard states the following:

217 OECD (2009), OECD Science, Technology and Industry Scoreboard 2009, OECD Publishing. DOI:: 10.1787/sti_scoreboard-2009-en, http://dx.doi.org/10.1787/sti_scoreboard-2009-en

"Employment of tertiary-level graduates is an indicator of the innovative potential of an economy and of the capacity of its labour market to allocate human capital to the production process. On average, 35% of persons employed in the OECD area had a tertiary-level degree in 2007. Canada (over 50%), Finland, Japan, New Zealand and the United States (over 40%) ranked far ahead of the European Union, where just over one worker in four holds a tertiary-level degree."

One of the few side benefits of our recent economic crisis is that US manufacturing workers are more competitive for multiple reasons. Unemployment is motivating highly educated personnel to stay in jobs or seek lower paying jobs. Downsizing is forcing more productivity out of the remaining workforce. The devaluation of the dollar makes US goods more competitive internationally. However, these side benefits are transitory. Now is the time to implement new manufacturing initiatives while our competitive advantage lasts.

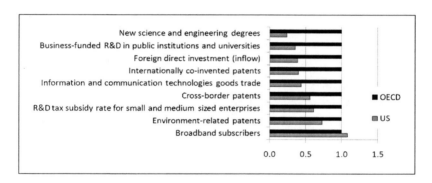

Figure 131: US Competitive Disadvantages As Seen By the OECD

Figure 131 was derived from OECD Scoreboard data and lists the primary US competitive disadvantages, as seen by the OECD. In the nine categories listed below, the US is rated 27% to 76% lower than other OECD nations.

Americans could draw these general conclusions from these statistics:

- Education. As compared to other OECD countries, the US produces only a quarter of the science and engineering graduates. These are the type of graduates that are critical to American manufacturing. US private sector R&D support to universities and other public institutions is only a third of the funding supplied in other nations. US universities rely to a much higher degree on government support and foreign students than other nations. This is changing as state government budgets get leaner and foreign students seek educational opportunities outside the US.

- Foreign Direct Investment. Foreign direct investment in the US is 40% that of other OECD countries, which indicates that the American opportunities are less attractive. Foreigners are investing in emerging countries where they can get a higher return on investment.

- Information and Communications Technology. While the US benefits from trade in high technology goods, there is one critical hi-tech sector that has collapsed in the US. That sector is the information and communications technology (ICT) sector, which includes radio, television, cellular phones, and computer and network hardware and software. Asia now dominates this critical economic sector.

- Patents. While the US has the overall lead in patent filings, cross-border patents are half those of other OECD countries. Even the US environment-related patents are less than other countries. Going "green" is apparently more rhetoric than research. The US-go-it-alone or lone wolf culture may hurt us in the global marketplace. Collaboration is superior to isolation for accessing emerging markets.

- Supporting Small and Medium-Sized Businesses. The R&D tax subsidy rate for small and medium-sized enterprises is 40% less than other OECD countries. As discussed earlier, the US government has invested $11.6T into financial institutions, big business and welfare. A pittance of this money has gone to small and medium-sized businesses that employ the vast majority of Americans. Other OECD countries are making stronger investment in small and medium-sized businesses.

- Broadband Access. Even though the US is slightly ahead of all the OECD nations, the broadband subscriber category was included as a US disadvantage. Americans invented the internet and were the pioneers of the web-based economy. Today, foreigners have closed the gap and are positioned to take the lead. Countries like South Korea are well on their way to implementing 100% broadband capability. The US is still many years away from implementing national broadband access. President Eisenhower implemented our national high-speed, vehicular, transportation system that revolutionized our economy. Can a national high-speed, digital, communication system revolutionize our economy in the same way? Of course, it can. Today, only a quarter of the US workforce has broadband access. Imagine the productivity gains in both the service-providing and goods-producing sectors, if the entire US workforce had high-speed internet access.

In conclusion, America has experienced a thirty-year domestic slide in manufacturing while fostering industrial growth in numerous emerging economies. These emerging economies should be exploited by coordinated government/business initiatives that take advantage of our numerous competitive advantages and adaptable workforce. Manufacturing growth would keep the US top-heavy edifice stabilized by adding substance to the base of our economic pyramid.

Chapter 19:
CORPORATE RECOVERY
MAY NOT INCREASE JOBS

Figure 132: Chapter 19 Summary

While corporations are prospering, the US workforce is not. There is nothing on the horizon that indicates that domestic employment in big corporations will improve in the near future. Notwithstanding the many factors that constrain corporate hiring, there are a number of efforts that could promote business growth, increasing overseas hiring opportunities, and promoting more foreign countries to start businesses in the US.

Corporate stocks have surged from market lows in 2007, but this surge does not equate to hiring. Reasons include layoffs, utilization of part-time workers, demanding more from remaining employees, closing operations, outsourcing, establishing operations offshore, stock repurchasing, mergers and acquisitions, and delayed recapitalization.

The profit motive is the prime consideration. Shareholders invest in corporations to profit. Corporations exist to satisfy shareholders. CEOs are paid big bucks to generate shareholder value. It is the American way of business. It is the international way of business. It is the business version of the law of the jungle. The profitable survive.

Corporations profit by slashing costs. The economic crisis and reduced consumption gave corporate managers ample reason to downsize workforces to increase profitability. In a growing economy, corporations profit via earnings on revenue growth. In a down economy, revenue growth is stagnant and corporations have to slash costs in order to make margin. Multinational corporations seek growing economies over stagnant economies.

One of the largest cost drivers involves worker salaries and benefits. Middle management is first to go. The next to go are administrative and non-core positions, such as research, development, and marketing. Elimination of these positions adds profit to bottom lines. If corporations slash faster than revenues decline, profit margins can be maintained until revenue returns.

Corporations profit by closing marginally profitable operations. Former General Electric CEO, Jack Welch, earned his nickname "Neutron Jack" in reference to the neutron bomb that was designed to annihilate people while leaving facilities intact. Welch's philosophy of being number one, number two, or out, allowed him to aggressively eliminate workers and sell lackluster operations. His ruthlessness towards slashing costs and focusing on the bottom line earned him the "Manager of the Century" award by *Fortune* magazine in 1999.

Today, the Welch slash-and-burn dogma is pervasive amongst US CEOs who focus almost exclusively on shareholder value. While this philosophy has increased US workforce productivity, it has also significantly increased the rolls of the unemployed who often become wards of the government. The financial crisis has only hastened the CEO quest for increased efficiency and leaner operations in the face of mounting global competition.

Number of US Jobs Moving Offshore

Job Category	2000	2005	2010	2015
Management	0	37,477	117,835	288,281
Business	10,787	61,252	161,722	348,028
Computer	27,171	108,991	276,954	472,632
Architecture	3,498	32,302	83,237	184,347
Life Sciences	0	3,677	14,478	36,770
Legal	1,793	14,220	34,673	74,642
Art, design	818	5,576	13,846	29,639
Sales	4,619	29,064	97,321	226,564
Office	53,987	295,034	791,034	1,659,310
Total	**102,674**	**587,592**	**1,591,101**	**3,320,213**

Sources: US Department of Labor and Forrester Research, Inc.

Figure 133: Number of US Jobs Moving Offshore

Corporations profit by outsourcing work and operations. As many Americans have experienced, a significant number of call centers are located in English-speaking foreign cities. Hyderabad, India, has become the IT call center of the world. It also has become a center of excellence for IT-services and entertainment industries.

The exact numbers of outsourcing are hard to ascertain. No official statistics are available. According to US Department of Labor and Forrester Research estimates,[218] outsourcing is expected to expand in numbers and scope. As shown in Figure 133, the number is projected to double between 2010 and 2015. The unusual aspect of the DoL/Forrester analysis is the emphasis on office, sales, legal and management personnel. By 2015, outsourced office positions are projected to increase over 30 times the amount in year 2000. The data suggest that foreign entities that have already developed the goods-producing labor force are now recruiting management and office staffs to augment foreign operations.

Corporations profit by moving operations overseas. Asian growth is projected to be triple that of G7 countries. Many businesses and service firms will look overseas for revenues, profits and employment. In a global economy, multinational corporations with large overseas operations identify themselves globally, as opposed to nationally. This is not only true for US corporations operating overseas, but also foreign companies operating in the US. Foreign nations provide ample incentives for major corporations to move operations overseas. These incentives include free trade zones, limited bureaucracy, tax holidays, low cost labor, and better access to emerging markets. Places like Dubai have grown exponentially in the last decade by offering such incentives to companies.

Corporations profit by delaying recapitalization. Now that corporate profitability has returned and stock values are increasing substantially, many corporations are using this money to improve their financial position, as opposed to investing in new equipment or factories. It is often easier and more lucrative to buy back stock, merge or acquire, than rebuild downsized operations. Many CEOs advocate a wait-and-see approach, which contributes to a slower recovery and higher unemployment. It is easier to make money on money, than it is to make money on goods and services.

As a result of these factors, companies have little reason to rehire workers or to expand US operations in an environment where foreign opportunities are far greater and more lucrative than domestic opportunities. The weight of 26.5 million marginally employed or unemployed workers (U6 rate), coupled with the seductiveness of globalization, could induce considerable change in the US economic landscape. Chronically high US unemployment, weak national growth, increased public indebtedness, exodus of multinational companies, and lofty corporate profits could be the new normal, unless action is taken now.

Yesteryear, most economists believed that corporate profitability was linked to the expansion of national economies. Globalization changed this belief. Companies are now less constrained by the US economy, and corporate success is no longer a sign of US economic health.

As long as American consumers endorse the behavior of multinational businesses, they will continue to ratify their standards. American consumers endorse by buying foreign goods when comparable US brands are available. American consumers endorse when they allow behemoth mega-marts to displace dozens of small, community businesses. Wal-Mart is America's biggest retailer, yet most of Wal-Mart's suppliers are from China. This is the American way, both good and bad. The good is lower prices and convenience. The bad is indebtedness and unemployment. The main point of this book is that the scales have tipped towards the bad, and a proper balance should be restored while we still have time.

In deference to Wal-Mart, the mega-mart is making a major push into China. Wal-Mart[219] now has 146 stores in China, covering 89 cities, including 138 supercenters, 3 Sam's Clubs and 35% interest in 102 Trust-Mart stores. As opposed to sourcing externally like Wal-Mart does in the US, 95% of merchandise sold at Wal-Mart China stores are local Chinese products by which Wal-Mart has established business relations with nearly 20,000 suppliers. China can be as big and successful a market for Wal-Mart as the US. More importantly, it can provide an export channel for US goods. With a little creative thinking, it also could be a conduit for American services. For example, English is the language of business and the Chinese have a voracious appetite for learning English. Wal-Mart superstores in China might be able to capitalize on this need. In addition to China, Wal-Mart is looking at India as a major export destination to source its retail stores for its global operations. These global operations in China and India will be good for America. It is up to us to maximize this global goodness, and Wal-Mart is aggressively doing so. Wal-Mart's international division topped $100B in 2010 for the first time. Wal-Mart's international sales are growing at almost nine times the rate of US sales.[220] If this trend continues, international

219 Walmart, About Us, A Brief Introduction to Wal-Mart in China, http://www.wal-martchina.com/english/walmart/index.htm
220 *New York Times*, As growth in U.S. slows, Wal-Mart puts more emphasis on foreign stores, by Yian Q. Mui, 8 June 2010, http://www.washingtonpost.com/wp-dyn/content/article/2010/06/07/AR2010060704834.html?wpisrc=nl_headline

consumers will soon replace American consumers as the dominant purchasing power on earth. This trend presents a huge opportunity for America—if we can claim it as a nation.

Perhaps the biggest challenges for government policymakers with multinational corporations is to (1) understand the reasons why multinational corporations ship jobs overseas, (2) create an environment where more multinational corporations reshore jobs in America, (3) help US multinationals send more US expatriates overseas to facilitate more collaborative bi-lateral and multi-lateral business relationships, and (4) encourage foreign multinational corporations to come to America.

Why do multinational companies ship US jobs overseas? Multinational companies use the following factors to determine where to locate their manufacturing and services enterprises:

- Good work environment:
  - o National stability, security/crime/corruption, business integrity, attractiveness of growth and business opportunities in the foreign country or region.
  - o Cost of capital, investment capital, government grants, subsidies, and various forms of taxation (federal/state/municipal taxes, excise and custom taxes, tariffs).
  - o Business factors, including amount of bureaucratic overhead, litigation and tort practices and levels, intellectual and property rights, patent protection rules, other government reporting and auditing requirements.
  - o Transportation and communication capabilities.

- Good workforce:
  - o Direct and indirect labor costs.

- Salaries of management, professionals, laborers.
- Benefits including healthcare, vacation time, and government mandated benefits (such as Social Security, Medicare, Medicaid).
  - o Qualified employees and unique skills.
  - o Quality universities, tech schools, research, development, innovation.
  - o Social factors including language, willingness to work and work ethic, unions.

Quite simply, corporations locate businesses based on a good work environment and good workforces. Inherently America is very competitive in both areas, but we have been lackadaisical about maximizing our attributes and fixing our detractors. Americans tend to take business for granted by not appreciating why it exists and what it has to offer. Worse yet, America has turned anti-business. Without a significant change in attitude, businesses will not proper.

In the past, foreign countries' main advantage consisted of cheap labor. Today, this is no longer true. From a business perspective, many foreign countries have closed the gap in providing both good workforces and a good work environment. However, the US workforce is fighting back with higher productivity and lower wages.

Increased US labor productivity has enhanced US workers' ability to compete in the global marketplace. The Bureau of Labor Statistics reports that 2009 was a banner year for US worker productivity. US workers are working harder and longer.

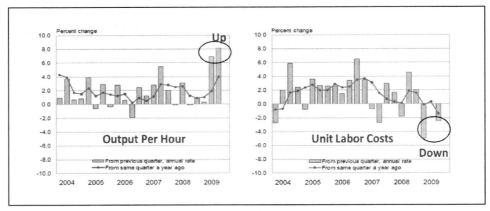

Figure 134: US Labor Productivity[221]

As shown in Figure 134, output per hour is increasing and labor costs are decreasing significantly. Smaller US companies make ideal joint venture partners for foreign corporations. The combination of productivity, market access and modern communication systems allows smaller companies to be competitive in the global marketplace. Smaller companies are often more agile than their larger counterparts.

The recent economic crisis and high domestic unemployment have created a bump-in-the-road for US corporate outsourcing. Citizen anger, government incentives, a weaker dollar, and higher workforce productivity, are causing several of the US major multinational corporations to reconsider on-shoring or reshoring jobs in America. After a decade of globalization, many companies are rethinking the benefits of off-shoring in light of quality issues, logistics costs, intellectual property theft and a host of other issues. However, in the end, corporations will onshore or offshore, depending on their customer base and where they can maximize profits.

The economic crisis has also helped discredit the traditional doctrine of a laissez faire approach to free markets. Economic laissez faire is a doctrine, theory or practice that opposes governmental regulation of, or interference in, commerce beyond the minimum necessary for a free enterprise system to operate. It is a belief that government should intervene as little as possible in the direction of economic affairs. Alan Greenspan, the twenty-year Chairman of the US Federal Reserve and a firm believer in free markets, admitted to a Congressional committee[222] that he had put too much faith in the self-stabilizing attributes of free markets.

---

221 US Department of Labor, Bureau of Labor Statistics, News Release (USDL-09-1778) Productivity And Costs, Third Quarter 2009, Revised, 3 December 2009, http://www.bls.gov/news.release/pdf/prod2.pdf
222 Alan Greenspan, Testimony to Congress, Committee of Government Oversight and Reform, 23 October 2008, http://clipsandcomment.com/wp-content/uploads/2008/10/greenspan-testimony-20081023.pdf

"Free markets" is a thorny issue, with free-traders on one side and protectionists on the other. Increasing unemployment fuels protectionist arguments. Punitive tariffs on Chinese imports have already begun. A 35% tariff was imposed on Chinese tires in September 2009. Over the last three years, Chinese steel producers' share of the US market jumped from 11% to 30% causing a loss of several thousand US jobs. On 30 December 2009, the US International Trade Commission ruled that Chinese steel harms US industry. This ruling allows the US to collect tariffs on Chinese steel imports. The Chinese Ministry of Commerce responded by calling these tariffs "abusive protectionism." It is protectionism, but far from abusive.

International governments are used to US political laissez faire in business affairs. In many ways, they have taken advantage of this, with little objection from Americans who were willing to go deeply in debt to satisfy their consumer cravings. The economic crisis and unemployment may have ended an era of unbridled consumption. Notwithstanding, a balanced position is needed. Protectionists must be careful not to discourage foreign entities from investing in the US in retaliation for tariffs. Free-traders must agree that free trade is not free if the rules of the game favor one side over the other. Both need to accept the principle of tough love—a mixture of hospitality and shrewdness towards our trading partners.

In conclusion, while there is nothing on the horizon that indicates that domestic employment in big corporations will improve in the near future, due to factors that constrain corporate hiring, there are a number of government efforts that could promote business growth, increasing overseas hiring opportunities, and promoting more foreign countries to start businesses in the US. It is time for US federal government leaders to become more pro-business. Governors spend a substantial amount of their time and resources traveling internationally to attract businesses to their states. Our leaders in Washington should spend more time figuring out how to promote US goods and services, and less time spending taxpayer dollars. America represents the world's biggest consumer market with a competitive labor force. Access to this market is the key to increased US job flow. Timing has never been better.

Chapter 20:
SMALL BUSINESS IS THE US ECONOMIC BACKBONE

Small Business: US Economic Backbone

- In comparison to large businesses, small businesses:
    - Generated 64% of all new jobs over the past 15 years.
    - Pay 44% of total American private payroll (non-farm).
    - Hire 40% of hi-tech workers who produce 1300% more patents.
    - Employ more full-time people (60.2M versus 59.7M).
    - Employ more part-time people (21% versus 18%).
    - Are far less likely to outsource jobs overseas.
    - Produce 30.2% of all exports.

- Compared to 18,000 large US businesses, there are 6 million small businesses and 21.7 million non-employee small businesses (self-employed).

The US should focus on job creation in the small business sector since large business and traditional opportunities may be limited.

Figure 135: Chapter 20 Summary

The recession is over. The economy is recovering slowly. Big business is prospering. Small business is still suffering. Since small business is the backbone of the US economy and jobs, if it suffers, America suffers.

The US Small Business Administration (SBA)[223] defines a small business as an independent business having fewer than 500 employees. Compared to 18 thousand large US businesses,

---

223 Small Business Administration, Office of Advocacy, "Frequently Asked Questions," December 2009, http://web.sba.gov/faqs/faqindex.cfm?areaID=24

there are 6 million small businesses, and 21.7 million non-employee (largely self-employed) small businesses.

According to the SBA, in comparison to large businesses, small businesses:

- Generate 64% of all new jobs (average over the past 15 years).
- Employ more full-time people (60.2 million versus 59.7 million).
- Employ more part-time people (21% versus 18%).
- Pay 44% of total American private payroll.
- Create more than half of the nonfarm private gross domestic product.
- Hire 40% of hi-tech workers who produce 13 times more patents.
- Produce 30% of all exports and are far less likely to outsource jobs overseas.

Several common misperceptions about small business are that they do not produce as many jobs, and are more likely to fail relative to big business. Neither is true.

According to a 2008 US Census Bureau study,[224] small businesses generated the most new jobs over the period of 1977 to 2005 (Figure 136). During this period, micro-firms (firms with 1-4 employees) accounted for 20% of new jobs. The study also finds that young firms have a much higher growth rate than older firms.

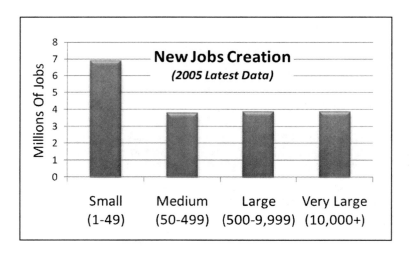

Figure 136: Small Business Generates the Most New Jobs[225]

Regarding small business failure rates, an analysis of Census data[226] shows (Figure 137) that composite exit rates of small firms (below 500 employees) has actually been lower than larger firms (above 500 employees) in 20 out of the last 29 years.

224 Ibid, http://www.ces.census.gov/index.php/
225 US Census Bureau, Business Dynamic Statistics, Longitudinal Business Database 1977-2005, Firm Size, http://www.ces.census.gov/index.php/bds/bds_database_list
226 Ibid

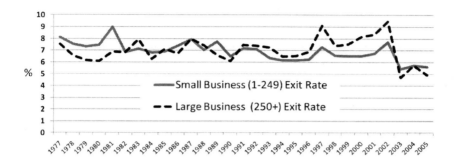

Figure 137: Small Business Exit (Failure) Rate Statistics

This misperception exists because of the high exit rate of micro-firms (1-4 employees), which averaged 18.4% over the last three decades. While this rate is high, their entry rate is even higher at 21.3%, therefore producing a net gain of 2.9% over the period. The entry/exit rate difference for all firms was only 1.9%. Looking at this data from a different perspective, compared to all businesses, micro-firms were 50% more likely to succeed, which is counter-intuitive to common perception.

According to the SBA,[227]

"Seven out of ten new employer firms last at least two years, and about half survive five years. More specifically, according to new Census data, 69 percent of new employer establishments born to new firms in 2000 survived at least two years, and 51 percent survived five or more years. Firms born in 1990 had very similar survival rates. With most firms starting small, 99.8 percent of the new employer establishments were started by small firms. Survival rates were similar across states and major industries."

Due to these misperceptions, small business tends to suffer more in downturns than big business when credit is tight. The Great Recession had a significant impact on small business expansion and the psyche of small business owners.

An Intuit Small Business Owner Survey[228] of 1,004 small business owners in Q3 2009 revealed:

• 81% are pessimistic about the current business climate for small business.

• 86% consider healthcare the most important benefit to attract and retain good employees, followed by workers' compensation (82%) and retirement benefits (65%).

• 60% report that decrease in sales is the biggest impact of the economy on their business, followed by 50% with slower customer payments.

• 56% of small business owners say the recession will last another 2 years or more.

227 SBA Office of Advocacy, Frequently Asked Questions, What is the survival rate for new firms?, http://www.sba. gov/advo/stats/sbfaq.pdf
228 Intuit, Intuit Payroll Survey 2009, http://quickbooks.blogs.com/Intuit%20Payroll%20Survey%20-%20 One%20Sheet.pdf

Much of the small business pessimism stems from difficulty in obtaining credit. Both small and large business policymakers and opinion-leaders agree. According to the Chairwoman of the Small Business and Entrepreneurship Committee, US Senator Mary Landrieu,

"Small businesses are really struggling with skyrocketing health insurance premiums and a tight credit market. Now that we have stabilized Wall Street, it is time to jump-start Main Street."[229]

According to *Forbes* Magazine,[230] a widely recognized big business publication,

"Funding sources for large companies have opened back up in 2009 as big businesses can access both the stock and bond markets for long-term funding needs and the commercial paper market for day-to-day liquidity. Smaller companies aren't so fortunate. For them, the credit crunch is still very real. The big companies with their big dealings are skewing the data that economists look at, which might explain the growing optimism of those taking the 30,000-foot view even as managers on the ground grow wary."

In November 2009, the US lost a total of 169,000 jobs, of which 74% were in small businesses with less than 500 employees. If American is concerned about unemployment, it should focus on where the job losses occur. It is not only in General Motors, it is on Main Street in every community in the US.

The SBA has <u>not</u> been a major player in the US government recovery operations. Of the $787B in the TARP program, only $0.4B[231] has been allocated to the SBA. That equates to ½ of 1%. If compared to the $12T total recovery effort, the number is infinitesimal. Proponents of the US government recovery efforts would point out that stabilizing the financial system directly helps small businesses. This point of view is correct, but it relies on a trickle-down philosophy in an environment where bank lending is tight and small businesses are generally less credit worthy.

Even though it might argue differently, the SBA places a premium on minority and disadvantaged businesses, as well as small businesses in historically underutilized business zones, referred to as HUBZones. This is understandable in normal economic times, but may not be the best approach for achieving economic recovery in today's environment.

When it involves business, especially small business, the US federal government is generally more interested in race, gender and ethnicity than jobs creation. For example, the historically large and comprehensive 2010 US Census is conducting a survey of 2.4 million businesses.[232] These businesses will be asked to provide information about their characteristics and the characteristics of their owners.

---

229 NACS Online, How Much Did Big Banks Lend to Small Business in '09, December 2009, http://www.nacsonline.com/NACS/News/Daily/Pages/ND1230095.aspx
230 *Forbes*, "The Recovery Paradox", Steve Scheafer, 9 November 2009, http://www.forbes.com/2009/11/11/business-volatility-survey-markets-economy-employment.html?partner=weekly_newsletter
231 SBA Funding, www.recovery.gov/Transparency/agency/reporting/agency_reporting1.aspx?agency_code=73
232 US Census Bureau, Survey of Business Owners, 24 April 2010, http://www.census.gov/econ/sbo/about.html

Data Product	Release Date
Preliminary Estimates of Business Ownership by Gender, Ethnicity, Race, and Vet	Jul-10
Hispanic-Owned Businesses	Sep-10
Women-Owned Businesses	Dec-10
Black-Owned Businesses	Feb-11
American Indian- and Alaska Native-Owned Businesses	Mar-11
Asian-Owned Businesses	Apr-11
Native Hawaiian- and Other Pacific Islander-Owned Businesses	Apr-11
Veteran-Owned Businesses	May-11
Company Summary	Jun-11
Characteristics of Businesses	Jun-11
Characteristics of Business Owners	Jun-11

Figure 138: US Census Bureau Survey Of Business Owners

Figure 138 shows the data product and release dates. Considering the historic levels of joblessness, one would think that the Census Bureau would be more interested in jobs creation, rather than diversity and distribution of wealth. To be fair, the US federal government has other surveys that measure employment, but given the tsunami of joblessness and indebtedness, our government needs to better focus all its resources on its top priority, which the Administration claims is jobs.

If funds are made available for small businesses, it should be made available to all, as opposed to race, gender and ethnic set-asides. Priority must be given to key small businesses that possess the technology or services that have the potential to make them big businesses, or having significant value-added for potential jobs creation.

If one believes that (1) small business is the backbone of the US economy, (2) jobs creation is paramount to economic well-being, and (3) small enterprises can grow quickly to a large business, like Microsoft, then American decision-makers and opinion-leaders should establish national initiatives oriented to emerging enterprises, small businesses and the self-employed.

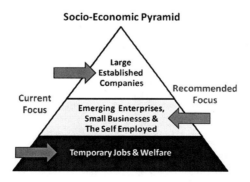

Figure 139: National Small and Emerging Business Initiatives

The current focus of US government recovery efforts is on the top and bottom parts of the socio-economic pyramid (Figure 139). Significantly more attention needs to be placed on the middle in order to spur employment growth.

Large Established Companies. Now is the time for big business to place America's needs on par with shareholder needs. CEOs are perceived to be the greediest and most selfish people on the planet. They are also the most talented.

Shrinking the CEO/worker wage gap would be a good place to start. In the 1960s, CEOs earned 24 times as much as the average worker. In the 2000s, CEOs earned as much as 300[233] times as much as the average worker. The AFL-CIO[234] calculates average compensation of all the S&P 500 CEOs to be in excess of $9.2 million in 2009, which is down significantly due to the Great Recession. It is also down for those companies and financial institutions that took government bailout funds. However, due to historic amounts of liquidity and a meteoric rise in financial stock prices, major financial institutions quickly repaid their bailout funds and awarded themselves a record $145B in compensation.

Thirty years ago, CEOs measured their performance on national needs, technology, workers, integrity, and shareholder value. Unfortunately, only the latter remains. While shareholder value is important, it cannot be the sole justification for companies. Without a new CEO vision, angry masses will eventually tear down the edifices that CEOs built.

Giving back is good for business. Warren Buffett did. Bill Gates does. America is not looking for charity. It is looking for big ideas and national initiatives that come from people with resources. National initiatives pool human and physical resources to solve national problems and needs.

Government is paralyzed by partisanship. Big business has no such constraint. In order for the economic recovery to happen expeditiously, national champions are needed from the big business community.

Welfare & Temporary Jobs. Providing more money to financially downtrodden individuals at the bottom of the pyramid is viewed by many to be the compassionate thing to do. Others would say welfare is merciful, not compassionate. True compassion involves jobs creation, not handouts.

The vast majority of the unemployed do not want handouts. They want opportunity. For all but a very few, welfare stigmatizes. Prolonged welfare becomes bondage. Prolonged welfare rapidly becomes a period (.) as opposed to a comma (,) as originally intended. The long-term unemployed, now at the highest rate in modern US history, lose skills, confidence and face.

Government make-work jobs are at best temporary, and at worst wasteful. If government put the same amount of resources into small business, instead of temporary employment, many more jobs would likely be created as well as avoiding job reductions in the largest segment of the society.

---

233 Economic Policy Institute, CEO-to-worker pay imbalance grows, 21 June 2006, http://www.epi.org/economic_snapshots/entry/webfeatures_snapshots_20060621/
234 AFL-CIO & Institute for Policy Studies, Trends in CEO Pay, http://www.aflcio.org/corporatewatch/paywatch/pay/

As recorded at the beginning of this chapter, 62% of all American jobs are in small business which suffers 74% of all the layoffs. A long-term jobless individual is far more likely to find a job with a small business.

Emerging Enterprises, Small Businesses and the Self-employed. America needs to reorient its focus to the middle of the socio-economic pyramid. National initiatives aimed at emerging enterprises, small businesses and the self-employed provide the highest chance of reemployment for those who want jobs. Focus must be placed on enduring jobs creation, as opposed to just putting people to work.

Super-sizing the SBA will not work. While the SBA has done a reasonable job advocating for small business, its jobs creation focus has been largely on set-asides for minority and disadvantaged businesses. A national initiatives program should be in addition to the SBA and focus on emerging businesses that have a competitive or innovative advantage. Focus would be on the next-generation areas, like energy, information technology, emerging technologies and healthcare. The goal would be to dramatically increase employment in small business goods-producing and service-providing sectors.

The self-employed are the ultimate small business. Web-based enterprises can be global in reach and are ideal for the self-employed. eBay alone employs over 16,000 employees. The top two social networking sites (Facebook, MySpace) receive over 2 billion visits monthly. If the next-generation social networking sites could be wired into the jobs creation arena, the effects could be explosive. A national self-employed business initiative would start with inventorying this labor category by the Bureau of Labor Statistics.

The major points for Section 4: Other Challenges, Issues and Indicators (Chapters 13 through 20) include:

- Closing The Spending/Receipts Gap

    o The federal, state and municipal government spending/receipts gap is not sustainable. If not closed, economic collapse could ensue, most likely starting with cities, and then spreading up the chain to states and, finally, the federal government.

    o Taxes will increase for all levels of society.

    o In today's environment, there is little political will to cut spending. Creating tens of millions of new jobs to raise the revenue line is the best way in the near-term to close the gap.

- Second Residential Real Estate Crisis. A second major residential real estate crisis is a real possibility and the US government is taking major steps to mitigate this issue. The following factors are contributing to the residential real estate challenge:

    o Historical government intervention and manipulation in the housing market.

    o The overuse of financial derivatives by the US government and private sector that created a massive housing bubble.

    o Unemployment and lower housing values have put 25%, or 14 million, of all US mortgages underwater. Most of the homeowners are dutifully paying on their mortgages. However, many homeowners no longer feel that it is in their financial interest to keep paying. 30% of all mortgage payments are seriously delinquent (3+ months overdue). Many homeowners are considering strategically defaulting (walking away) from their homes and mortgages.

    o Foreclosures are on the rise and currently consume 1 out of every 8 homes. The US government and banks are trying to keep the number of repossessions and foreclosures to a minimum due to the already saturated market. Banks may eventually be forced to liquidate their REOs (real estate owned properties due to foreclosure or in lieu of foreclosure) in bulk to speculators, private equity funds and/or sovereign wealth funds, at severely discounted rates that would further reduce housing values and evoke another crisis.

    o The US government has implemented a number of programs to make mortgages more affordable in order to reduce the spate of foreclosures and strategic defaults.

- The stock markets are not a good indicator of economic recovery while they are being stimulated by $Ts worth of government and private sector liquidity.

- There is growing concern that a bubble is forming and the markets could reverse. Optimists feel that there is a little room for growth, while the pessimists feel that a substantial drop could occur.

- The US is emerging from a year of deflation. Most economists fear that inflationary pressures are substantial, due to government policies and over stimulation. Some fear that a major inflationary bounce could occur, leading the US into a period of super-inflation like that of the early 1980s.

- US Treasuries are being sold at great rates, and account for the bulk of the national debt that is approximately $12.9T and growing. Because the dollar is the world's reserve currency, the US is in a unique position to auction Treasuries and print money to subsidize our debt and spending habits. While the world's financial system currently depends on the health of the US, there is movement towards replacing the dollar as the international reserve currency and reducing dependency on US Treasuries.

- US manufacturing employment dropped 40% in the last three decades, while the US population has grown by 40%. Most of the projected growth in manufacturing is expected in emerging and developing countries. Therefore, there is little reason to believe in significant US domestic manufacturing growth, but there are ways to increase the growth of US multinational corporations' business overseas, as well as lure more foreign manufacturing within the US.

- Corporate recovery does not mean increased US employment for many reasons, including growth in emerging markets, outsourcing, downsizing, use of temporary workers, and increased productivity.

- Small business is the US economic backbone and the most significantly neglected segment of the US economy. 21st century technology has facilitated the growth of self-employed, home-based and small businesses which have been underexploited and underutilized.

- The bulk of government and private sector financing is oriented to large and medium-sized businesses. An initiative to provide more funding to the base of the business pyramid would preserve and produce tens of millions of new jobs.

Figure 140: Section 4: Other Challenges, Issues and Indicators Main Points

THE WAY AHEAD: JOBS CREATION

Chapter 21:
THE *20 BY 20* JOBS CREATION PLAN

20 Million New Jobs by 2020   JOBENOMICS

- The goal of *20 by 20* is to produce 20 million new private sector jobs by 2020.

20 by 20 Category	New Jobs (M)
Government	0
Small Business	3
Self-Employed	4
Large Business-Multinational	2
Large & Medium Sized Businesses-Domestic	3
International Corporations and Investors	3
Energy Technology Revolution (ETR) Initiative	5
	20

- Government no-job growth, and private sector support initiatives.
- Small business national initiatives, hiring incentives, loans, support, co-ops.
- Self-employed tax incentives/write offs, broadband access, telecommuting.
- Multinational corporation expatriate use and increased domestic operations.
- Large and medium-sized domestic corporate initiatives and protection.
- Incentives for foreign entities to start business operations in America.
- Directing federal R&D and private capital to major ETR opportunities.

20 by 20 hedges against W- and L-shaped recovery scenarios.

Figure 141: Chapter 21 Summary

The *20 by 20* Jobs Creation Plan. The goal of the *20 by 20* campaign is to assist the private sector in producing 20 million new jobs by 2020. The number 20 million comes from two sources: historical precedent and projected future requirements. Historically, the decades of the 1970s, 1980s and 1990s produced 20 million new private sector jobs. So, the 20 million job goal was achievable in recent history. Regarding the future, new entrants to the workforce require about 130,000 new jobs per month, for 14 million people, if the *20 by 20* campaign is initiated by the end of 2010. Reducing the current unemployment rate to below 6% would require another 6 million jobs. Consequently, a realistic range is somewhere around 20 million jobs.

Where should we start? The initial emphasis should be in the service-providing sector, where the vast majority of Americans are employed. Special emphasis needs to be placed at the base of the economic pyramid.

Goods-Producing	Service-Providing	89.6
Mining and logging	**Trade, transportation and utilities**	
Forestry	Wholesale/Retail/Utilities	
Oil/Gas/Minerals/Coal	Transportation and Warehousing	
Construction	**Information**	
Building (Residential/Nonresidential)	Publishing	
Heavy Construction/Civil Engineering	Motion Picture and Recording	
Manufacturing - Durable Goods	Telecommunications/Broadcasting	
Wood/Minerals/Metals	Data Processing/Internet	
Machinery	**Financial**	
Computer and Electronics	Finance and Insurance	
Transportation/Motor vehicles	Real Estate and Leasing	
Furniture	**Professional and Business Services**	
Manufacturing - Non Durable Goods	**Education and Health Services**	
Food/Beverages/Tobacco	**Other**	
Textile/Leather/Apparel	Leisure and Hospitality	
Paper/Printing	Repair/Maintenance/Personal services	
Petroleum/Chemicals/Plastics	Membership/Association Organizations	
18.0 Million	**89.6 Million**	

18.0

Source: Bureau of Labor Statistics

Figure 142: US Private Sector Civilian Workforce [235]

As of May 2010, 90 million service-providing industry workers outnumber 18 million goods-producing industry workers in the private sector civilian workforce (Figure 142). Over the last three decades, the goods-producing industries shrunk from being the dominant economic segment to a relatively small element in our overall civilian work force. While these goods-producing jobs are critical to a functioning economy, they will be the hardest to recoup, due to international competition and high recapitalization costs. Consequently, the primary focus of a *20 by 20* jobs creation campaign has to be on the service-providing segment of our society, in order to focus on the greatest numbers and strongest element of our civilian work force.

As shown in Figure 143, according to the Bureau of Labor Statistics 2008 to 2018 projection data,[236] the service-providing segment is projected to grow by 14 million people, versus almost no growth in the goods-producing industries. *Jobenomics* agrees.

---

235 US Department of Labor, Bureau of Labor Statistics, Databases, Table B-1, Employees on nonfarm payrolls by industry sector and selected industry detail (seasonally adjusted), 13 May 2010, http://www.bls.gov/webapps/legacy/cesbtab1.htm
236 US Department of Labor, Bureau of Labor Statistics, Occupational Outlook Quarterly, Winter 2009-2010, Vol. R3, Number 3, Industry Employment, http://www.bls.gov/opub/ooq/2009/winter/art4fullp1.htm

Service-Providing Jobs Growth (2008-2018)	
Professional and business services	4,190,000
Health care and social assistance	4,017,000
Educational services	1,683,000
Leisure and hospitality	1,142,000
Retail trade and wholesale trade	910,000
Other services	704,000
State and local government, except education and hospitals	694,000
Financial activities	557,000
Transportation and utilities	387,000
Information	118,000
	14,402,000
Goods-Producing Jobs Growth (2008-2018)	
Construction	1,337,000
Natural resources and mining	(109,000)
Manufacturing	(1,206,000)
Source: BLS 2008-2018 Projections	**22,000**

Figure 143: US Civilian Private Sector Workforce Growth Projections

A *20 by 20* campaign should initially focus on sectors with the highest projected growth. Of the ten service-providing sectors listed in Figure 143, almost 60% of the projected growth is in two sectors—the professional and business services sector, and the health care and social assistance sector. Growth in professional and business services is expected to be led by providers of administrative support services and consulting services. Growth in health care and social assistance is expected to be driven by increased demand from an aging population.

While this growth may happen naturally in a V-shaped recovery, a *20 by 20* campaign would focus on making this happen faster and more robustly. It would also help the small and emerging businesses to gain a stronger foothold in these sectors, which are ideally suited for small business pursuits. However, as discussed earlier, government V-shaped projections are based on optimistic assumptions, such as 6% GDP growth, unemployment decline, and the absence of major crises or economic disruptions. W- or L- shaped economic scenarios would greatly impede jobs creation, thereby making the *20 by 20* campaign even more important.

A *20 by 20* campaign should also initially focus on areas with the highest projected job losses. These areas include retail stores, electronic component manufacturing, motor vehicle parts and auto dealerships, postal service, office supplies and printing services, newspaper publishers and journalists, etc. If these areas cannot be saved, then the *20 by 20* campaign should look at replacement jobs and occupations. Some industries, like newspaper publishing, may not be able to be rescued, due to the introduction of disruptive technologies, like the internet. However, disruptive technologies provide new, and perhaps greater opportunities, but in a much different way.

The transition from the industrial age to the information age was largely caused by the introduction of disruptive technology. Consequently, it has had a dramatic effect on how people are employed. For example, the market cap for Google and General Electric are about the same

($190B versus $166B), but Google has 10,000 employees, compared to 323,000 at General Electric. The information age has also facilitated globalization, and the subsequent flow of US jobs overseas. While these changes pose greater challenges, they provide significant job creation opportunity. A *20 by 20* campaign would use globalization to increase the number of US expatriate jobs overseas, and develop small international businesses to service emerging economies in countries like China, India and Brazil.

20 by 20 is not a public-private partnership in the traditional sense of the term. The private sector must have the lead. A public-private partnership involves funding and operating agreements through a partnership between government and private sector companies, where the private sector performs a public service. Public-private partnerships often do not work, because the parties have different motivations and ideas.

To make *20 by 20* work, not only does the private sector take the lead, but it has to maintain the lead with minimum government manipulation and interference. This does not mean that the government sits idly on the sidelines like fans at a ballgame. The government is responsible for infrastructure development, protection, coaching and marketing. But, the private sector is on the field, calls the plays, and executes the business. The private sector also gets to keep the rewards, albeit if conditions warrant, the government can take temporary equity stakes that can be redeemed by the private sector in the future. The government gets its reward by increased tax revenue on newly created jobs, and reduced welfare costs.

In order to achieve *20 by 20*, policymakers, opinion-leaders and business executives need to divide *20 by 20* into discrete categories, as shown in Figure 144.

20 by 20 Category	New Jobs (M)	Comments
Government	0	No-jobs growth and private sector initiatives.
Small Business	3	Hiring incentives, loans, leasing support, co-ops.
Self-Employed	4	Incentives/write-offs, broadband access, telecommuting.
Large Business-Multinational	2	Expatriate use and increased domestic operations.
Large & Medium Sized Businesses-Domestic	3	Initiatives, support and protection.
International Corporations & Investors	3	Incentives for foreign entities to start US businesses.
Energy Technology Revolution Initiative	5	Federal R&D and private capital to major opportunities.
	20	Million new private sector jobs by 2020

Figure 144: National 20 by 20 Jobs Categories and Goals

20 by 20 jobs categories would include government, small business, large business, international corporations and investors, and a collection of businesses and enterprises engaged in the energy technology revolution (ETR) initiative.

- The goal for government is zero job growth. Considering state budget crises, this goal should be relatively easy, since the bulk of government jobs are in state and local governments. If the federal government imposed a no-growth policy, the total tax burden of government jobs could be reduced.

- The goal for small, emerging and self-employed is 7 million. This sector is currently under-exploited. With government hiring incentives, low cost loans, tax deductions, and other support, this sector should flourish.

- The large business goal is 5 million. The emphasis on large US multinational corporations is on increasing the US expatriate community offshore, as opposed to reshoring jobs back to the US. Business growth is expected to be robust in emerging countries like China and India, and it is important that millions of US expatriate business persons exploit these growth opportunities.

- Likewise, the US should aggressively attract foreign businesses to the US. *Jobenomics* believes that 3 million new US jobs in America is a very reasonable goal. There are ample opportunities in emerging China and India to develop subsidiaries in the US.

- It is imperative that the US take the lead in the energy technology revolution (ETR) that could produce tens of millions of jobs, like the information technology revolution (ITR) and military technology revolution (MTR) did in the 1990s and post-WWII era, respectively. A goal of 5 million new jobs across the ETR spectrum (renewable energy, to fossil fuels, to new technical breakthroughs, such as long-life batteries and algal biofuels) is not only achievable by 2020, but the failure to do so means that America relinquished these opportunities to other countries.

Government: Zero Jobs Growth. Since the objective is to create 20 million private sector jobs, the government would not create any new federal, state or municipal government jobs for this initiative. It is envisioned that the government will freeze government jobs at the current level or, at a minimum, peg the creation of new government jobs to positive GDP growth adjusted for inflation. It does not make sense to create new private sector jobs in order to pay for increased government overhead and services during this critical recovery effort. With the poor financial conditions in the majority of state and local governments, hiring freezes and/or cuts are already in place.

35 million government and shadow-government workers are beginning to overwhelm the 96 million private sector workers who are primarily responsible for paying for government operations.

According to the BLS, the US government workforce has grown by 41% since 1980.[237] Today, a total of 35 million people work for the government, including 22 million civilians, 10 million government contractors (including postal and census workers), and 3 million in the active and reserve armed forces.

25 million work directly for government. The federal government has 2.2 million civilian employees. State government has 5.2 million plus about 3 million in the armed forces (active and reserve). Local government has 14.4 million. The US Postal Service has 600,000 full-time

---

237 US Department of Labor, Bureau of Labor Statistics, Databases, Table B-1, Employees on nonfarm payrolls by industry sector and selected industry detail (seasonally adjusted), 5 December 2009, http://www.bls.gov/webapps/legacy/cesbtab1.htm

employees,[238] which is down from a peak of almost 1 million in 1998. The US Census Bureau is hiring 1 million part-time workers for the 2010 Census.

Zero government growth would also have to include limiting the growth of the "shadow" government, which consists of government contractors who make their livings on taxpayer dollars. It is estimated that the shadow government employs more than 10 million people. The top 200 US government contractors receive approximately $500B annually in contract awards and grants. Contractors make up 53% of DoD's workforce in Iraq and Afghanistan (218,000 contractors versus 195,000 troops).[239]

The federal government's role in a *20 by 20* campaign is to emphasize business development, mentorship, cooperation, education and efficiency for the private sector. There is enough funding within the existing federal budget to accomplish these roles. However, the US government does not have an efficient system for deploying existing funds to meet national objectives.

The US government parcels out R&D amongst various agencies and departments, which manage these funds according to their interests. In order to focus federal R&D resources on emerging technologies and businesses, the federal government should consider establishing a national information management system, that would identify existing sources of funding and tie federal department R&D and the 36 Federally Funded Research and Development Centers (FFRDCs) expenditures to specific national business objectives. The national information management system would focus available finances to critical needs, vet best-of-breed technologies, prioritize the most promising emerging companies and processes, and link these technologies/ companies to private sector investors.

The federal government also needs to increase business exposure in top levels of government. Starting at the White House, a cabinet level position should be considered for business. This position would be in addition to the Department of Commerce, and would require confirmation from the Congress (unlike the various czars appointed by the White House). If the White House is serious about making jobs the "top priority," then it should make room at the top for professionals who can make this happen. These professionals should come from the entrepreneurial sector, as opposed to former CEOs or financial sector officials. The Council of Economic Advisors could be expanded to include business professionals, in addition to the academics who currently occupy all current council positions. The House and Senate could consider Committees for Jobs Creation and a National Council of Entrepreneurship. When President Kennedy challenged the nation to put a man on the moon in ten years, he also helped put in place the leadership team to make it happen. A *20 by 20* campaign will require the same level of commitment and leadership.

Small Business: 3 Million New Jobs. The goal for small business is 3 million new jobs, in addition to the number currently employed.

---

238 US Postal Service, Postal Facts 2010, http://www.usps.com/communications/newsroom/postalfacts.htm
239 Congressional Research Service, Department of Defense Contractors in Iraq and Afghanistan: Background and Analysis, 14 December 2009, http://www.fas.org/sgp/crs/natsec/R40764.pdf

The significance of the small-business sector cannot be overstated. In the industrial age, large businesses were needed to marshal resources and labor. In the information age, small businesses, especially in the service-providing industries, can function as well as large businesses with modern information and telecommunications technology. The challenge for US leadership is that its mentality is still stuck in the industrial age. Major business and government officials are comfortable in managing $1B, $10B and $100B enterprises. They do not know how to govern ten million $1M enterprises, which will be the model for the future. This is why *Jobenomics* suggests that Washington needs to recruit entrepreneurs as opposed to former CEOs. The other alternative is to look at major system-of-systems engineering firms, like SAIC, that are comprised of tens of thousands of small and emerging business units. SAIC[240] is a Fortune 500 science, engineering, and emerging-technology company involved in security, energy, the environment, critical infrastructure, and health. SAIC grew from one guy with a dream in 1969, to 45,000 people today.

The first step for a *20 by 20* small business campaign is to identify proper small business incentives, and develop a small business information system that could collect and feed more complete and detailed data into the Department of Labor's Bureau of Labor Statistics (BLS) Labor Force survey and statistical process. From a *Jobenomics* perspective, a Small Business Survey (SBS) should be an adjunct to the BLS's Current Population Survey (CPS) and Current Employment Statistics (CES). The SBS would survey a representative sample of the 6 million small businesses and 21.7 million non-employee (largely self-employed) small businesses in America. Due to the size of this population, the survey should be an audited online survey that is small business initiated.

Small Business Profile				
Size	Companies	%	Employees	%
1 to 4	2,868,676	51%	6,237,139	10%
5 to 9	1,087,946	19%	7,094,895	12%
10 to 19	665,641	12%	8,581,779	14%
20 to 49	470,524	8%	11,982,902	20%
50 to 99	204,710	4%	8,568,201	14%
100 to 249	200,768	4%	10,256,220	17%
250 to 499	127,654	2%	6,758,792	11%
Source: Census Bureau	**5,625,919**		**59,479,928**	

Figure 145: Small Business Profile[241]

A small business is defined as a corporation with less than 500 people, as shown in the Small Business Profile (Figure 145), as used by the US Census Bureau in the Current Population Survey. This profile could be merged with national priorities (energy, health, information technology, transportation, logistics, etc.) into an SBS matrix that would be very useful to private investors interested in funding base-of-the-pyramid opportunities. The following chapter will discuss this further.

240 SAIC, http://www.saic.com/about/
241 US Census Bureau, Business Dynamic Statistics, Longitudinal Business Database 1977-2005, Firm Size, http://www.ces.census.gov/index.php/bds/bds_database_list

Since these categories are already established by the US Census Bureau, and will be updated in 2010 via the largest and most complete Census survey in US history, the US government should use these categories to establish task forces, actions and milestones to enhance the survivability and growth of each.

Small business success or failure often is measured in thousands of dollars ($K), as opposed to $M, $B or $T. Consequently, a small business opportunity does not necessarily have to cost taxpayers a lot of money. Loans, guarantees and incentives can be conditional and/or short term. If the US government can profit on big business TARP loans, it should be able to do so with small businesses, which collectively are too-big-to-fail.

Positive cash flow is essential to small business health. The main factors to small business cash flow include credit, leases, healthcare, taxes, transportation, and employee benefits. If the federal government wanted to stimulate small business, they should consider the following:

- **Low interest, government-backed loans with early payback incentives**. The US government is doing this for banks and big businesses. Low interest, government-backed loans with early payback incentives would be a boon for small businesses. In this vein, the Administration is considering plans to channel money from the remaining TARP funds to small businesses, as well as starting a Jobs Program (Stimulus III). Administration officials feel the best way is to directly fund banks, and encourage them to boost small business lending. However, banks are often reluctant to take government money due to restrictions, compensation caps and other forms of government control. In order to avoid TARP stigma, the Treasury should consider the creation of a special purpose vehicle, which is a legal entity to fulfill narrow, specific or temporary objectives, while separating the parent company from legal risk. This special purpose vehicle would be to provide several hundred billion dollars worth of low interest loans to emerging enterprises, small businesses and the self-employed. The special purpose vehicle could take equity positions in these businesses until the loans are repaid.

  Another approach is to implement a civil variation on the Department of Defense's Mentor/Protégé Program that is used with major government contractors. Since 1991, the DoD Mentor-Protégé Program[242] has offered substantial assistance to small disadvantaged businesses. Helping them to expand the overall base of their marketplace participation has produced more jobs and increased national income. This program helps small businesses (protégés) compete for business by partnering with large system-of-systems companies, like SAIC, Lockheed Martin, Northrop Grumman, General Dynamics, Booz Allen, Computer Sciences, Verizon, IBM, and Accenture. These companies could be incentivized to partner with groups of small business protégés in the civil sector, much in the way that SAIC manages its internal small business units. This would help small business as well as helping to

---

242 Department of Defense, Office of Small Business Programs, Mentor Protégé Program, http://www.acq.osd.mil/osbp/mentor_protege/

move government contractors off taxpayer dollars to private investors, investment funds, and pension funds. This could also be done on a state-by-state level. Large state pension funds, like the California Public Employees, California State Teachers, New York Common, Florida State Fund, and Texas Teachers, have total assets exceeding $1T. Given the beating that these pension funds took during the Great Recession, they might be motivated to participate with state-level small business protégés if partly underwritten by the US government. A public-private partnership between large business-managed protégés, with federal and state participation, financed by the private sector, could be a major *20 by 20* initiative.

- **Government co-signing or guaranteeing leasing**. A major and highly visible sector of small business is the retail sector. Small retail businesses, and their associated shopping malls, are under severe economic stress. Shuttered shopping malls blight many communities and represent economic failure. Many retail businesses cannot afford, or are not willing to renew their leases (normally 5 years). Additionally, the lease albatross deters many emerging small businesses from incorporating, unless they personally co-sign the lease, thereby piercing the protection of a corporate veil. Government co-signing or lease guarantees could help mitigate this factor. GSEs (Fannie and Freddie) are doing this for homeowners. Small business would welcome similar support.

Almost every community has a bankrupt or vacant strip mall. Vacancy rates for strip malls are at 20 year highs, due to unemployment and lower consumption. Rather than leaving these malls vacant, local communities should consider turning them into business incubators. A strip mall business incubator would be used for small and emerging businesses. The local community could lease office space on a monthly, quarterly or yearly basis, which is significantly preferable to 5-year leases normally required by mall operators. For a nominal fee, the community could also provide back office and administrative services. These services could be provided by part-time telecommuting service providers. The goal of the strip mall business incubators is to give start-up companies easy entry into the marketplace. Once launched, these companies would help provide job, wealth and tax revenue to the local community.

- **Healthcare**. Healthcare costs are a major burden on small businesses. Increased healthcare costs may make many insolvent, and discourage hiring or expansion. The new national healthcare program could run a pilot program, by creating a national small business insurance co-op. This would lighten the healthcare burden on small business, and encourage the unemployed or underemployed to work for small businesses at the lower tier of the wage spectrum. It could also enhance political consensus on the larger issue of healthcare reform.

- **Transportation**. The IRS allows mileage deductions for business travel. Doubling or tripling this mileage deduction for small business would be an economic stimulus that would not require new appropriations. The Administration and Congress could couple a mileage deduction to the low-interest loan program for purchase of American-made vehicles—a version of the Cash for Clunkers program that stimulated the auto industry. A parallel initiative could be devised for small businesses that would promote fuel efficiency, as well as fueling increased productivity.

- **Employee Benefits**. The US government provides benefits for the unemployed, marginally employed, and those on the lower tier of the wage spectrum. Education is a good example, and is one of the top Administration initiatives. The US government provides education benefits to the military (GI Bill) and students (Pell Grants). If the US government provided similar benefits to small businesses, the business could use these as incentives for those entering the work force. Educational benefits are powerful incentives to get people to work, especially for entry level employees, the underemployed and the unemployed. It would also transfer the responsibility from government, to businesses that focus on the bottom line and have the means to hire and fire if productivity goals are not met.

- **Tax breaks**. The US government gives tax breaks for families with children, unemployed workers, new home buyers, people who insulate their homes, and a host of other programs. The TANF program provides Temporary Assistance for Needy Families. A TANSB program could provide Temporary Assistance for Needy Small Businesses. Tax breaks for existing small businesses and new small businesses are equally important, and provide jobs that produce tax revenue. Small business tax breaks can be tied to hiring new people, disadvantaged people, older people, or other socially advantageous categories.

These efforts would help to protect the base of our economic pyramid from further erosion, help emerging business to start, and incentivize small business owners to grow their businesses.

National or state-level small business initiatives are also warranted. Numerous initiatives are possible. For example, the residential real estate industry deserves special mention as an area where small business, government, and the financial sector could cooperate.

As discussed in Chapter 14 (Potential Second Residential Real Estate Crisis), unemployment, foreclosures, underwater mortgages, strategic defaults, and reduced income security of many homeowners are major challenges to recovery of the residential real estate and construction industries. The US government is making a valiant attempt to mitigate this crisis, but it is on a slippery slope offensively. Therefore, a different, more defensive, approach might be considered. In addition to helping homeowners convert unaffordable mortgages, government task forces might help real estate and property management companies acquire blocks of bank-owned real estate (REOs) and convert them into rental properties.

The bulk of the REOs reside in the major banks, so the universe of REOs is relatively small. In addition, a number of investment groups are gathering "dry powder" funds that they plan to deploy when the big banks sell en masse. The bulk transfer of REO assets from the big banks to investment groups will likely provide a windfall to speculators, who will flip the homes for a profit, but will be onerous to those who need shelter. If properly orchestrated, a network of small businesses could help to provide shelter, via rental properties, and provide income to the investment groups until the residential real estate market recovers.

The real estate and property management community is comprised of mostly small businesses that are associated with larger real estate brokerage firms. If the REOs could be converted into rental properties that are managed by local property management firms, a win-win situation could ensue. First, by converting distressed homes into rentals, the residential real estate market would be more stabilized by renters, rather than leaving the homes vacant until they are eventually sold. Second, home values could be stabilized since property aesthetics would be maintained. Third, shelter would be provided to those who need it. Since the number of rental properties would increase, the price of renting is likely to come down. Fourth, current government energy efficiency incentives would help the construction industry upgrade homes to current energy efficiency standards. A fifth possibility could entail ways for current homeowners to convert in-place to renters. Since the US government is having trouble converting mortgages, it might try converting owners to renters. This would keep families in their homes, and give them an opportunity to repurchase the property in the future.

The place to start a pilot program would be in a high foreclosure/underwater mortgage city, like Las Vegas, Phoenix or San Diego. If successful, the program could be expanded across the country. Since the residential real estate market is so large ($T), potentially hundreds of thousands of jobs could be created or maintained. A national effort to upgrade residential real estate to energy efficient and green standards would also help the construction and manufacturing industries, thereby adding potentially hundreds of thousands more jobs to domestic industries. Equally important, stabilization of the housing market would eliminate a major distributive force to our economy.

State and municipal government participation could also be valuable, if they worked with the investment community to create REO Private Equity Funds that could be used to acquire, convert, maintain and upgrade properties to 21st century standards. State and municipal pension funds might be interested, since their investments would be collateralized by property that could be underwritten by government. For example, a $250M fund will be able to acquire approximately 500 properties with the average unit price of $500,000, which is the median single family residence price in 80% of the San Diego metro-area. By buying REOs in bulk from the banks, the REO Private Equity Fund could purchase San Diego homes at a 35% discounted price from current listings, which equates to about 60% off of the peak prices in 2005-06. Bulk acquisition is only half the strategy. The other half deals with 100% leasing and property management. The rentals would provide a stable annual income with reasonable returns on investment.

Jobenomics recently did an analysis on an 8-unit condominium complex REO in San Diego, which was built in 2005 and is currently 100% leased by tenants. At its 2005 peak, the property was worth $3.2 million. Its current list price is $1.7 million. If bought as part of a bulk sale, the bank likely would sell their REO at $1.1 million, which equates to a 65% discount from the 2005 peak price. If the property continued to be 100% leased, the property rental income would be $111,150 (net annual operating income) with an annual CAP rate (capitalization rate is the return on investment on the property) of 7.7% to 10.1%. This would be an attractive investment opportunity for private equity investors, from pension funds to individual investors. First, an acquisition discount of 65% would likely place the property at the bottom of the market, with significant upside potential. Second, the 7.7% to 10.1% CAP rate would provide a much better return on investment than could be achieved in the volatile stock markets, government bonds or bank CDs/money markets. In other words, investors could buy and hold with reasonable IRRs (internal rates of returns) until the market recovers. When the housing market recovers, the investors could then sell and make significant profit on the appreciated value of the property, which has been maintained and even upgraded.

A national or state REO private equity/property management initiative is only one example of a broader *20 by 20* campaign, which would solicit other such ideas from the small business community.

Self-Employed: 4 Million New Jobs. One goal of *20 by 20* would be to add an additional 4 million new jobs to the self-employed category. *Jobenomics* estimates that 4 million is a very conservative number. If the self-employed segment of American society is properly accounted-for, motivated and supported, this number could be much higher.

According to the Small Business Administration, there are 21.7 million non-employee small businesses, which is a euphemistic government term for the self-employed. Before any new jobs can be added to this category, the US has to first quantify, and then understand this greatly undefined category, which could be most lucrative from a jobs creation perspective. An achievable number may be two or three times higher, due to the fact that this segment is the least understood and most underexploited.

While the BLS includes this group in its household survey, it excludes it in its establishment survey and data. According to the BLS,[243] "while the establishment survey excludes the self-employed, the household survey provides monthly estimates of unincorporated self-employment. These estimates have shown no substantial growth in recent years." A BLS[244] data survey shows that self-employment has declined from a peak of 9.4 million in January 1997, to 8.9 million in April 2010. In the information age, it is hard to conceive that the ranks of the self-employed have actually declined, as well as being only 8.9 million out of a total population of 309 million. One reason that the number is so low is that the BLS excludes the incorporated self-employed. Consequently, it is hard to get an accurate picture. As discussed in Chapter 1, the BLS and Census Bureau surveys do not place a high emphasis on this critically important sector.

Jobenomics did a survey of over 50 self-employed and incorporated self-employed businesses, and none has ever been contacted by the BLS. Anecdotally, the fact[245] that 120,000 new websites

---

243 US Department of Labor, Bureau of Labor Statistics, Current Employment Statistics – CES (National), Frequently Asked Questions, Has the establishment survey understated employment growth because it excludes the self-employed?, 5 March 2010, http://www.bls.gov/ces/cesfaq.htm#scope10

244 US Department of Labor, Bureau of Labor Statistics, Data Retrieval: Labor Force Statistics (CPS), Table A-8, Employed persons by class of worker and part-time status, Self-employed workers (nonagricultural industries, seasonally adjusted), 5 February 2010, http://www.bls.gov/webapps/legacy/cpsatab8.htm

245 DomainTools, Domain Counts & Internet Statistics, 2 March 2010, http://www.domaintools.com/internet-statistics/

are created each day belies the BLS's statement that "no substantial growth" has occurred in recent years. The majority of these new websites were formed by the self-employed. The growth in telecommuting also challenges the BLS's assertion. During the January 2010 blizzards that paralyzed Washington DC, the federal government proudly announced that 30% of the US federal workforce was able to telecommute via 14 GSA TeleWork Centers,[246] or from their home computers. If federal government employees can effectively work from home, so can the self-employed.

Equally disturbing is the fact that there are no official government statistics for the underemployed. According to the BLS, it is "difficult to quantify the loss to the economy of such underemployment."[247] In other words, since it is too difficult, why try? 26 million unemployed or underemployed is the reason why. So is 72 million off-the-grid a reason to try. Joblessness is a national curse that is getting worse. Self-employment is a partial answer to providing assistance to those who are willing to work. By ignoring underemployment, the US government has no alternative to providing other forms of welfare. There has to be a better way. The way is workfare, as opposed to welfare.

Generally speaking, a self-employed person may find "underemployed" work satisfactory to maintain their financial independence, or supplement their income. The growing ranks of retiring baby boomers may only need a marginal income to maintain lifestyle or pay essential bills. Many home-bound spouses, disabled or laid-off workers might opt for partial employment to supplement their income. In addition, the long-term unemployed may have to go through the ranks of the underemployed on the way back to full employment.

If aggressively managed and pursued, the self-employed segment potentially could comprise the most significant percentage of the *20 by 20* jobs creation goal. If the US Census Bureau can create a temporary pool of American underemployed workers for the 2010 Census, why can't it create temporary labor pools for businesses that are increasingly relying on part-time workers? The agricultural and farming community is struggling to find such people. So is the healthcare industry.

Women-Owned Micro Businesses. According to the Center for Women's Business Research (CWBR),[248] there are 10.1 million firms owned by women in the US, who directly employ more than 13 million people and generate $1.9T in direct revenue. When one looks at the overall economic impact, the numbers are even more impressive. A recent CWBR economic impact study of US women-owned businesses[249] estimated the overall economic impact at $2.8T with 23 million direct and indirect employees, which is 22% of the US private sector civilian workforce.

The CWBR study data indicated that 87%, or almost 9 million firms, of all women-owned businesses are self-employed businesses without employees. The study also reports that US Census

246 US General Services Administration, GSA-sponsored Telework Centers, 5 March 2010, http://www.gsa.gov/Portal/gsa/ep/channelView.do?pageTypeId=17114&channelId=-24672
247 US Department of Labor, Bureau of Labor Statistics, Labor Force Statistics from the Current Population Survey, Frequently Asked Questions, Is there a measure of underemployment?, 5 March 2010, http://www.bls.gov/cps/faq.htm#Ques1
248 Center for Women's Business Research, Key Facts about Women-Owned Businesses, The Overall Picture: 2008-2009, 16 May 2009, http://www.womensbusinessresearchcenter.org/research/keyfacts/
249 Center for Women's Business Research, The Economic Impact of Women-Owned Businesses in the United States, Underwritten by: Walmart, National Women's Business Council, and Center for Women's Business Research, October 2009, http://www.womensbusinessresearchcenter.org/Data/Research/economicimpactstud/econimpactreport-final.pdf

data showed that nearly all of the growth from 1997 to 2002 came from the self-employed segment. The *Wall Street Journal* reports[250] that over the last three decades, women have been launching new businesses at twice the rate of men. While women-owned business revenues only average about ¼ of men-owned businesses, women often have different goals and objectives than men. In many ways, women-owned businesses should be the model for the 21st century.

From a *Jobenomics* perspective, women are perhaps the greatest untapped asset in America, and should be a key element of the **20 by 20** campaign. The 2010s is likely to be the decade of small business, especially women-owned business for the following reasons:

- The Great Recession has encouraged many women to join the workforce, due to necessity and/or desire,

- There are more women in the labor pool, as well as college-educated women who are entering the workforce,

- Male-dominated industries, like construction, are not likely to return to normal until the end of the decade,

- Social norms are changing, allowing greater participation of women in business,

- Many of the future services related jobs, like elder-care, are likely to dominated by women,

- Women-owned businesses emphasize small, rather than large, businesses that are more likely to grow in the next decade, and

- Most importantly, the rate of employment growth and revenue of women-owned businesses has outpaced the economy and male-dominated businesses for the last three decades.[251]

The *Jobenomics* team intends to help create the conditions that will motivate and incentivize growth of women-owned firms. If each woman-owned business hires one additional person this decade, 10 million new jobs would be produced. This would equate to 10 million direct jobs— half the **20 by 20** goal. Perhaps the best way to motivate and incentivize the growth of women-owned micro-businesses is to highlight the efforts of a successful woman-owned micro-business' owner and coach.

Micro Biz Coach® is a woman-owned small company (www.MicroBizCoach.com) in Columbus, Ohio. Micro Biz Coach teaches people how to start a new business or develop a current business for little or no money. This company was founded and is owned by Nicole Washington who once managed enterprise-wide technology integration for Fortune 100 and Fortune 500 companies. Now, she's developed a passion and a niche for helping small and micro companies develop using internet technology. Micro Biz Coach has added value to hundreds of businesses since its establishment, and its clients have been featured by major media such as CNBC, Fox Business News, TheStreet.com and a host of Clear Channel radio stations.

---

250 Wall Street Journal, What's Holding Back Women Entrepreneurs?, by Sharon G. Hadary, 17 May 2010, http://online.wsj.com/article/SB10001424052748704688604575125543191609632.html
251 Ibid.

Micro Biz Coach teaches businesses how to develop by leveraging internet technology and social media as an inexpensive way to compete with the big businesses. Social networks, like Facebook, Twitter, LinkedIn and MySpace, provide access to hundreds of millions of clients and customers. Almost 23% of Facebook users earn more than $100,000 per year.

On the internet, a small company can have a professional looking brand and reach an international audience for no more than a few dollars a month. For example, Micro Biz Coach created Ten-dollar-tech-tutorials.com to teach computer technology in ten minute segments for under $10 a month. These tutorials not only teach micro business owners new skills, but they show owners how to get paid for the skills they have just acquired. In addition to the tutorials, Nicole works one-on-one with aspiring micro-business clients to motivate and guide them in order to help them fulfill their dreams.

Micro Biz Coach has even taught her elementary school children how to have their own business using information technology and social networks, like Facebook and Twitter. With at least 85% of US households with computers, not to mention their prominence in many US schools, children and young adults these days are "digital natives", according to Don Tapscott, the author of *Grown Up Digital*. Information technology is second nature to the 2020 workforce. The incredible access, ease of use, and the mere pennies it can cost to start up an online business makes it an undeniable vehicle for creating small businesses and jobs in the near future.

Like any business, women-owned businesses need encouragement, networking opportunities, financing and mentoring. With proper support and financing, women-owned businesses could double by 2020. It is therefore important that organizations, like the BLS, measure and track women-owned businesses in order for policymakers to provide appropriate incentives and support.

In today's web-enabled society, and in an environment where six people compete for every job, the self-employed sector may produce the biggest bang-for-the-buck. The internet enables home-based businesses and telecommuting. eBay is an excellent example of how an internet company can facilitate the creation of millions of home-based businesses. Meg Whitman was hired as eBay President and CEO when the company had 30 employees. After ten years under her reign, eBay grew to 15,000 employees, revenues of almost $8B,[252] and hundreds of millions of registered users.

Unfortunately, the last government survey of home-based businesses was conducted in May 2004,[253] which is indicative of the low priority that the federal government places on this sector. eBay is considered to be the first online social network. Today, there are hundreds more that can be used for small and self-employed businesses. By using micro business coaches, like Nicole Washington, who specialize in small business social media, tens of millions of new jobs can be created. Since the US economy has to accommodate approximately 130,000 new job entrants monthly, it seems that micro business creation should be a no-brainer. Since the majority of these entrants are young people who are very comfortable with information technology and social media, it seems that this kind of business initiative is really a no-brainer.

---

252 Meg 2010, Meet Meg Whitman, 6 June 2010, http://www.megwhitman.com/aboutMeg.php
253 Department of Labor, Bureau of Labor Statistics, Labor Force Statistics from the Current Population Survey, Labor Force Statistics, Work at Home, 14 May 2010, http://www.bls.gov/cps/lfcharacteristics.htm#unemp

Direct-Care and Telecommuting. According to the Telework Trendlines 2009 survey,[254] 87% of all telecommuters worked from home. In 2008, 13.5M US adults telecommuted almost every day, 24.2M telecommuted at least once a week, and 33.7M telecommuted at least once per month. The rise in the number of telecommuters represents an increase of 74% since 2005.

If 10 million home-based workers could be provided part-time employment opportunities, via a combination of telecommuting and self-employed businesses, this would equate to a significant contribution to the US civilian labor force. The US government can help make this happen if we get organized. Virtual organizations are the wave of the future.

A national child-care or elder-care system could be a phone call away. There are plenty of facilities available in local communities to get such a system underway. Elderly care is a growing problem associated with an aging population which can be alleviated, in part, by a national elder-care initiative. In-home and community direct-care positions are projected to increase by over 1 million new jobs, due to an aging population and the need for in-home or community-assisted living services. PHI National, a nonprofit organization for caregivers, predicts that direct-care workers will increase from 3.2 million to 4.3 million over the decade.[255]

At 4.3 million, the size of the direct-care occupation would exceed all but one of the 14 largest occupations, as reported by the BLS[256] and shown in Figure 146. Given an aging population and the retirement of the largest and wealthiest segment (i.e., the baby boomers) of American society, the BLS might consider including and tracking an elder direct-care occupational category, as they do for other major categories.

Occupation	Employment	% of US Employment	Hourly Wage	Annual Wage
Retail salespersons	4,426,280	3.27	$9.86	$ 20,510
Cashiers	3,545,610	2.62	$8.49	$ 17,660
Office clerks, general	2,906,600	2.15	$12.17	$ 25,320
Combined food preparation and serving workers, including fast food	2,708,840	2.00	$7.90	$ 16,430
Registered nurses	2,542,760	1.88	$30.03	$ 62,450
Waiters and waitresses	2,371,750	1.75	$8.01	$ 16,660
Laborers and freight, stock, and material movers, hand	2,335,510	1.73	$10.89	$ 22,660
Customer service representatives	2,233,270	1.65	$14.36	$ 29,860
Janitors and cleaners, except maids and housekeeping cleaners	2,145,320	1.59	$10.31	$ 21,450
Stock clerks and order fillers	1,873,390	1.39	$10.00	$ 20,800
Secretaries, except legal, medical, and executive	1,872,070	1.38	$13.96	$ 29,050
Bookkeeping, accounting, and auditing clerks	1,855,010	1.37	$15.63	$ 32,510
General and operations managers	1,697,690	1.26	$44.02	$ 91,570
Truck drivers, heavy and tractor-trailer	1,672,580	1.24	$17.92	$ 37,270
Source: BLS	**34,186,680**	**25.3%**		**$32,390**
				Median Wage

Figure 146: Employment and Mean Wages for the Largest US Occupations, 2008

254 Telework Trendlines 2009, A Survey Brief by WorldatWork, Data collected by The Dieringer Research Group Inc., February 2009, http://www.worldatwork.org/waw/adimLink?id=31115
255 PHI, Press Release, Nearly One-Third of Direct-Care Jobs Will Be Held by Older Women, 17 March 2010, http://phinational.org/archives/press-release-nearly-one-third-of-direct-care-jobs-will-be-held-by-older-women-31710/
256 Bureau of Labor Statistics, Occupational Employment Statistics, Chart Book, May 2008, Occupation Focus, Figure 2, Employment and mean wages for the largest occupations in the United States, http://www.bls.gov/oes/2008/may/chartbook_occupation_focus.htm#figure2

These 14 occupations employ ¼ of the US workforce. Ten of these occupations pay below the US median annual wage of $32,390 in 2008.[257] An elder-care initiative would mean a median annual wage significantly lower because all, or a portion, of the room and board expenses would be provided in lieu of wage.

In-home and community direct-care positions are projected to increase by several million new jobs, due to an aging population, and the need for in-home or community-assisted living services, as well as in-home child-care services.

Today, direct-care jobs are primarily funded through public funds. A national direct-care initiative, designed around a domestic au pair arrangement, could be largely paid by the elderly who need some assistance to retire at home or working families who can't afford child care. Young to middle-aged Americans could be employed to provide direct-care either on a full-time or part-time basis.

The principal role for government (federal, state and/or local) would be to set up the direct-care program, help train potential caregivers, and provide proper oversight and quality control. Even if an elder-care initiative generated only several hundred thousand jobs, it would help several hundred thousand elderly, and people with disabilities, to live independently and with dignity. An elder-care initiative also would help the families of the elderly, who are often faced with the difficult choice of leaving work to care for an elderly parent, or finding an expensive nursing home. An at-home or community child-care program would be especially valuable to part-time workers who want to supplement their income, or build skills to enter the workforce at a later time.

International Small and Self-Employed Business Opportunities. Since the internet is a global communications medium, the self-employed might also find opportunities in the emerging economies, like China and India. The US government could be the catalyst to promote linkage of small US businesses to the international community. Millions of highly talented consultants reside in small businesses that could provide useful services to emerging economies and developing countries. Almost every large and medium-sized city has sister-cities in foreign lands.

Sister Cities International was initiated by President Dwight D. Eisenhower to facilitate "people-to-people" diplomatic exchanges between US and foreign citizens, as a way to foster understanding and tolerance. His idea was that, "you don't go to war with your friends." The original concept developed and evolved into Sister Cities International, an alliance of US communities linked to 2,500 communities in 126 countries around the world.[258] *Jobenomics* recommends that the US government make a major effort to build on the sister-cities concept in the jobs creation area. The idea is that, "you are more likely to get along with people with whom you are doing business."

Take, for example, a medium-sized city like Oklahoma City. Oklahoma City's sister-cities are Ulyanovsk, Russia (population: 700,000), Haikou, China (population: 1.5 million), Puebla, Mexico (population: 4 million), Rio de Janeiro, Brazil (population: 6 million) and Tainan and Taipei, Taiwan (combined population: 3 million).[259] Oklahoma City is noted for its livestock,

---

257   Ibid
258   Sister Cities International, 8 May 2010, http://www.sister-cities.org/about/faqs.cfm
259   Sister Cities International, Oklahoma City, 8 May 2010, http://www.sciokc.org/our_cities.html

energy and light manufacturing industries, which are supported by an array of small and medium-sized businesses. If organized properly, these businesses could offer valuable services to emerging business in Oklahoma City's sister-cities. Oklahoma City is also the capital and largest city in the state of Oklahoma. In addition to a sister-cities economic development initiative, it could lead a state-to-state initiative. China and Brazil are considered some of the best emerging economies in the world. As discussed earlier, these countries are looking for management, consulting and back-office support to help their countries grow.

The US government could also reverse engineer some of the outsourcing that has transpired in the last several decades. It is estimated that over half the outsourced jobs are call-center type jobs that could be better performed by at-home Americans at competitive rates. The average call center employee in India makes between $3,000 and $10,000 a year. While this may not be much to the average worker, it may make the difference to an underemployed or retired worker struggling to make ends meet. The role of the government would be to organize a community at-home-call-center initiative, and let the private sector utilize and pay for it. A number of US industries use call centers, including IT services, direct sales, financial services, technical services, healthcare services, data and document management, customer care, hospitality, retail, utilities, debt collection services, and consumer products. US accounting firms are even outsourcing US tax returns to foreign countries that could be done in the US. States and municipalities have plenty of underutilized facilities that could be used for call center hubs, which can be populated by a combination of full-time, part-time, telecommuting and home-based workers. There are millions of talented self-employed, underemployed, retired, and home-bound workers who could benefit from such an effort. Major companies who outsource jobs to foreign countries could be incentivized to support a domestic effort.

National Broadband System. The Federal Communications Commission's National Broadband Plan[260] to bring broadband internet connections to every American home and business is part of an ambitious attempt to create a new US digital infrastructure that is sorely needed, if the US intends to stay competitive on a global scale. The FCC plans to increase broadband, high-speed internet usage from 65% to 90% over the next decade. The FCC's plan envisions bringing 100-megabit-per-second access to 100 million homes by 2020. South Korea has such capability in-place today.

Unfortunately, to pay for itself, the FCC's National Broadband Plan proposes taxing goods and services sold on the internet, which is a sacred cow to many internet users. Users will also have to pay a fee that will fund a $16B public safety network, as well as fund an effort so that "every American should be able to use broadband to track and manage their real-time energy consumption."[261] These provisions are facing fierce criticism from many powerful interest groups, including privacy groups.

The bottom line is that the National Broadband Plan may not happen. Many perceive this as a government attempt to raise taxes and gain control over a vital element of private sector, under the guise of helping the economy. This is a real shame. The government stands to gain more

---

260 Federal Communications Commission's National Broadband Plan, 7 April 2010, http://www.broadband.gov/
261 FCC National Broadband Plan, Goal 6, 7 April 2010, http://www.broadband.gov/

from taxes off of increased income, than it does on sales taxes. Universal broadband will not only encourage more small businesses to form, but would help all businesses to be more productive. This is yet another example of politics over business. Until government wakes up to the fact that America is undergoing a stealth employment crisis, its laissez-faire attitude towards small business and the self-employed may not change.

Large Business: 5 Million New Jobs. The goal for large business is 5 million new jobs by 2020. 2 million would be generated by multinational corporations, and 3 million by domestic non-multinational corporations with greater than 500 employees. As shown in Figure 147, large businesses employ approximately 56 million people. 5 million new jobs equates to only a 9% improvement over the status quo over the next decade—less than 1% growth per year.

Large Business Profile				
Size	*Companies*	*%*	*Employees*	*%*
500 to 999	107,591	*10%*	5,991,675	*11%*
1,000 to 2,499	125,655	*12%*	8,000,523	*14%*
2,500 to 4,999	112,617	*11%*	6,165,858	*11%*
5,000 to 9,999	116,508	*11%*	6,368,018	*11%*
10,000+	568,110	*55%*	29,848,837	*53%*
Source: Census Bureau	**1,030,481**		**56,374,911**	

Figure 147: Large Business Profile

Multinational Corporations: 2 Million New Jobs. As discussed in earlier chapters, multinational corporations have to follow global trends and opportunities. If the majority of new business opportunities are in emerging economies, these corporations will have to outsource jobs and build facilities in foreign countries to remain competitive.

In the 19th century, British and French colonization created vast expatriate communities that still exist in many parts of the world today. These expats play a very valuable role, especially in the oil-rich Middle East, identifying emerging business opportunities, and developing these opportunities for their home countries. Considering the state of American manufacturing and indebtedness, compared to the financial power of major developing creditor nations, like those in China and the Middle East, American multinational companies should be encouraged to position US expatriate workers in foreign management, administrative and labor operations. OECD data indicates that foreign governments, especially in emerging third-world countries, are willing to accept American expat expertise.

The Obama Administration's excellent initiative to double exports in five years would increase US overseas sales to $3 trillion annually, and create 2 million jobs. The 2 million jobs that the Administration advertizes are probably not achievable if it depends solely on creating domestic jobs. However, if the Administration promotes including critically-needed US expatriate skills to foster bilateral economic development, their plan is much more likely to succeed. To make bilateral economic development happen, it has to be part of the plan, which is presently unilaterally oriented to increasing US exports.

One reason the Administration's export initiative will be difficult is because of foreign offset requirements (jobs tied to sales). According to the US Department of Commerce,[262] offsets are the practice by which the award of contracts by foreign governments or companies is exchanged for commitments to provide industrial compensation, including mandatory co-production, licensed production, subcontractor production, technology transfer, and foreign investment. By making expatriate participation a part of offset agreements, this problem could be largely overcome. Offsets can be either direct or indirect. Direct offsets refer to items directly-related to the system exported. Indirect offsets deal with collateral activities, such as direct investment, purchases of foreign products, tech-transfer, or even tourism.

Expats could be especially valuable in the indirect offsets arena. For example, the sale of an aircraft to a foreign country opens up a host of hospitality industry opportunities. In 2008, US defense contractors had 628 existing offset transactions with 30 countries worth $3.2B, and negotiated 52 new offset agreements with 17 countries valued at $3.5B.[263] These 680 offset agreements were negotiated by individual defense contractors, primarily to sell US weapon systems abroad. If these opportunities were negotiated in a more bi-national business development perspective, rather than a weapon system sales perspective, a lot more jobs could be generated by both countries. The key to sales and marketing starts with a product or service that someone wants. Good marketing professionals try to exploit their entire product line once the initial sale is made. Why should the US fail to do the same? If Lockheed Martin is able to negotiate a sale of fighter aircraft, or Boeing a commercial aircraft, the US Department of Commerce, along with a team of governors and mayors, should try to exploit this sale with other products and services at the national, state and local levels.

Another reason that the Administration's export initiative may not produce the desired number of new US jobs is the reluctance of US manufacturers to hire during a nascent US economic recovery, especially when many foreign countries are recovering much faster. It is much easier for US manufacturers to increase work hours, which averaged 33.1 hours per week for the overall private work force in February 2010,[264] use temporary workers, and accelerate underused production lines, than hire new full-time workers. With a US unemployment rate of 10%, increasing trade tensions, negotiation of more open markets, and increasing protectionism, exports are not likely to grow as fast as the Administration hopes.

Currency exchange rate issues are another matter. As long as countries like China peg their currencies to the dollar, US workers will not enjoy a cost advantage as they do against currencies that are appreciating against the dollar. The use of expatriates overcomes many of these issues.

---

262 US Department of Commerce, Bureau of Industry and Security, Impact of Offsets in Defense Trade: An Annual Report to Congress, 8 May 2010, http://www.bis.doc.gov/defenseindustrialbaseprograms/osies/offsets/default.htm
263 US Department of Commerce, Bureau of Industry and Security, Fourteenth Annual Report To Congress On The Impact Of Offsets In Defense Trade, December 2010, http://www.bis.doc.gov/news/2010/14th_offset_defense_trade_report.pdf
264 Bureau of Labor Statistics, Average weekly hours and overtime of production and nonsupervisory employees on private nonfarm payrolls by industry sector, Seasonally adjusted, Table B-7, http://www.bls.gov/news.release/empsit.t23.htm

One major industry that is often overlooked is agriculture. All too often our "most valued citizens" (a title bestowed by President Thomas Jefferson) are not afforded the attention and respect that they deserve. According to the Department of Agriculture, in the depths of the Great Recession, US farmers and ranchers had a record export year ($114B in 2008[265]). As stated previously, the Department of Labor's BLS does not include agriculture as a measurable industry. Since the BLS employment data focuses on non-farm industries, the agricultural sector is often overlooked in public policymaking from an employment perspective. Given increasing world population and hunger, meeting the needs for renewable energy, and optimizing international trade, US agriculture should be a vibrant export area, as well as for creating new jobs.

Agriculture and manufacturing are essential elements of our economy. Without food and the means to produce it, the American economy will eventually implode. Much more attention needs to be placed on the 1% of Americans employed in agriculture and the 4% of Americans employed in manufacturing, who are the bedrock of our society. Today, government emphasis is overwhelmingly on growing government jobs and providing more handouts to the unemployed, as opposed to growing critical industries such as these.

A quick look at US trade statistics provides a clue on where to focus our international efforts. In 2008, international trade dropped significantly due to the Great Recession. Exports from the US dropped 15%, while imports into the US dropped even steeper (23%). This trend of exports over imports favors US employment. To a large extent, most of the focus is on goods that are dominated by manufacturing. The services sector is often overlooked.

$T	Exports			Imports		
	Total	Goods	Services	Total	Goods	Services
2008	1.8	1.3	0.5	2.5	2.1	0.4
2009	1.6	1.0	0.5	1.9	1.6	0.4
	-15%	-18%	-7%	-23%	-26%	-9%

Figure 148: US Trade Overview 2008-2009[266]

As shown in Figure 148, services are 50% of exports ($0.5T versus $1T) and 25% of imports ($0.4T versus $1.6T). To maximize the services sector, the US could either increase the export of services, or restrict the import of foreign services. It is hard to understand how $400B worth of foreign services was imported into the US in both 2008 and 2009.

Immigration policy is a highly emotional subject in America. The emotion is based largely on the 12 million[267] illegal immigrants that are in the US. There are a number of Congressional proposals that would stiffen immigration requirements and restrict the number of L-1 and H-1B

---

265 US Department of Agriculture, 2008 Performance and Accountability Report, 17 November 2008, http://www.ocfo.usda.gov/usdarpt/par2008/pdf/par2008.pdf

266 US Census Bureau, Foreign Trade, Exhibit 1, U.S. International Trade in Goods and Services, http://www.census.gov/foreign-trade/Press-Release/current_press_release/

267 Secretary Janet Napolitano, Secretary of Homeland Security, Prepared Remarks by Secretary Napolitano on Immigration Reform at the Center for American Progress, 13 November 2009, http://www.dhs.gov/ynews/speeches/sp_1258123461050.shtm

visas for foreign employees. Unfortunately, these restrictions are aimed at a very small percentage of the US workforce. According to the National Foundation for American Policy,[268] a non-profit organization, new H-1B visa holders in the US accounted for less than 100,000 workers in 2009. The availability of work and student visas is critically important to attract talented people to the US, especially top scientists, engineers and professionals who otherwise would be lost to competitors. It is also imperative to keep these people in the country. The current wait for green cards (to allow permanent residency) is 6 to 20 years, which is an unreasonable amount of time to wait for hiring new employees. Until a coherent immigration policy is enacted, the proper course of action would be to increase exports via expats or modern telecommunications technology, as discussed earlier in this chapter.

According to the Secretary of Commerce,[269] the US has 30 million companies, but less than one percent of them export. This percentage is significantly lower than all other developed countries, and of the US companies that do export, 58% export to only one country. By increasing the number of companies that export, and increasing the number of countries that US companies export to, a significant number of jobs can be created. The US service sector generates an estimated 4,000 jobs per $1 billion of exports. Consequently, if the US doubled the amount of exported services from $0.5T/year to $1T/year, approximately 2 million new jobs would be created.

Today, the US federal government is discussing ways to penalize American companies that outsource jobs. The opposite approach might be more productive. US government should look for ways to encourage and support American multinationals to expand overseas, if the net result is more US jobs on a global basis. A goal of 2 million new jobs should not be too difficult, especially if US companies were incentivized to do so by a balanced offshore/onshore approach, coupled with bi-national business development using the expertise of US expats.

Little official or unofficial statistical data is available on outsourcing, or off-shoring. In a global economy, the US government should have a better handle on this data. The US government needs to better balance workforces, in much the same way that it balances trade deficits. The government needs to better understand the size and contribution of the overall US expat community to the same degree that it keeps detailed accounts on overseas US military personnel and civilian contractors—overwhelmingly the largest off-shoring jobs operation in the world. While the US military, and their civilian counterparts, plays an invaluable role in national security and protecting our national interests, they are on the outlay side of the taxpayer equation. US civilian expats already play a valuable role on the revenue side of the equation, but their contribution could be enhanced significantly if there were more visibility and incentives associated with increasing their roles and numbers. Enhanced transparency should be a cooperative effort led by US multinational corporate leaders, with support from the US government. Commercial attachés in US foreign embassies could provide an invaluable service in this regard.

---

268 National Foundation for American Policy, H-1B Visas by the Numbers: 2010 and Beyond, March 2010, http://www.nfap.com/pdf/1003h1b.pdf
269 Secretary of Commerce Gary Locke, Remarks at Trade Promotion Coordinating Committee Meeting Washington, D.C., 23 October 2009, http://www.commerce.gov/NewsRoom/SecretarySpeeches/PROD01_008541

US multinational companies and the US government need to be in global partnership in order to enhance the economy and create jobs. Perhaps one of the most important areas of cooperation is in the energy sector, where the US government and the oil industry are often enemies. The annual outward revenue flow of $0.5T to foreign energy suppliers—most of whom are adversarial to the US—could be better used for jobs creation and other domestic needs. Oil exploration within the domestic US has been a political football for years, with environmentalists at odds with conservatives. For a while in early 2010, offshore oil exploration was viewed as a necessary evil, but the BP oil-spill has reversed direction on this area. Notwithstanding, six in 10 Americans still support more offshore drilling, according to an NBC News/*Wall Street Journal* poll.[270] More than half of the respondents also said they agreed with the statement that "the potential benefits to the economy outweigh the potential harm to the environment." However, the longer the saga of the BP oil spill continues, the worse the public's view regarding offshore drilling will become. Calls for punishing BP have already begun. President Obama vowed a "full and vigorous accounting" of the causes of the spill and approved a criminal investigation by the US Attorney General. The future of one of the largest oil companies in the world is at stake. Within six weeks of the incident, BP has lost $75B, or 40%, of its market value. The future of BP is uncertain. So is the future of other major oil companies, which has major ramifications on US energy prices and economic recovery.

After the US has spent almost 20 years in liberating Iraq, from the 1990 Operation Desert Storm to the ongoing Operation Iraqi Freedom, the Iraqis are now developing major oil fields that have been closed to foreigners for four decades. In December 2009, the Iraqis auctioned ten 20-year service contracts for their major oil fields.[271] The Chinese, Russians and Europeans won the vast majority of these contracts. Of the seven American companies that entered the auctions, only one obtained a meaningful portion of one of the ten contracts. Apparently the $Ts worth of US-funded Iraqi reconstruction, training and nation-building efforts did not count in favor of the US companies. Neither did the tens of thousands of US casualties sustained in Operations Desert Shield, Desert Storm, Northern Watch, Southern Watch, Provide Comfort, Desert Fox, Iraqi Freedom (Phase I, II, III, IV, V), and New Dawn.

Large & Medium-Sized Domestic Corporations: 3 Million New Jobs. The national goal for US non-multinational corporations is 3 million new private sector jobs by 2020.

One place to jump-start US domestic corporations is to reserve taxpayer funded programs for American companies. The $3B "Cash for Clunkers" program was a bonanza for foreign automobile manufacturers—80% of the vehicles bought under this program were foreign brands. One may argue that many of these vehicles were manufactured by Americans in America. On the other hand, the US government then turned around and invested tens of $B of taxpayer money in bailing out General Motors and Chrysler.

---

270 *Wall Street Journal*, NBC/WSJ poll, Public Still Backs Offshore Drilling, 12 May 2010, by Louise Radnofsky and Jean Spenser, http://online.wsj.com/article/SB10001424052748703339304575240513356154980.html
271 *The Washington Post*, U.S. firms lag in bids for Iraqi oil, Russians, Europeans and Chinese win most contracts for developing major fields, by Ernesto Londoño, 13 December 2009, http://www.washingtonpost.com/wp-dyn/content/article/2009/12/12/AR2009121201277_pf.html

Another example involves green energy and the Stimulus program. 90% of the American Recovery and Reinvestment Act 1603[272] Program grants were awarded to wind programs. According to a watchdog group,[273] of the $464M given to develop wind farms, $371M went to companies headquartered overseas.

A third example involves taxpayer funded national security programs where foreign companies play a major role. US defense procurements equate to half of the world's defense market. Since this market is publically funded, more consideration should be given to public priorities, like creating and maintaining high value, enduring jobs in the US – like defense manufacturing jobs.

Free trade is a system of trade policy that allows traders to act and transact without interference from government. *Without interference* are the key words. In today's global economic environment, free trade is somewhat an oxymoron. All governments interfere with trade. There are no level playing fields internationally. To assume so is like saying a broken clock is right two times a day. Prioritization has to be given to what is in America's national interest. It was in China and Russia's national interest to win the 20-year Iraqi oil contracts, after America spent 20 years of its national treasure to make it possible. As America has become economically weaker, major foreign competitors have become more economically aggressive, without the myriad of constraints and regulations imposed by the US government.

The opposite of free trade is protectionism. Protectionism is an economic policy of restraining trade between nations via tariffs and quotas to protect businesses and workers. Protectionism is largely anti-global. Protectionism takes many forms: exchange rate manipulation, bureaucratic barriers, intellectual property piracy, patent restrictions, immigration restriction, export/import quotas, direct and indirect subsidies, tariffs and taxes. Protectionists believe that people should expect governments to protect their economic and national interests.

On a scale of 1 to 10, with 1 being very protectionist and 10 being very free trade oriented, *Jobenomics* would rate the US an 8. Free trade has greatly benefited the US since WWII. Free trade helped make us an economic superpower. Free trade has helped other countries develop economically, which, in turn, helped the US economy.

So what's the answer? It may be time for the US to be less free trade and more protectionist until the US economy fully recovers. Largess belongs to those that can best afford it. Let the major creditor nations, like China and the oil rich Arab states, play a greater role in international affairs. The world's largest debtor nation needs to get its own house in order.

Jobenomics recommends a policy of reciprocity—a policy in commercial dealings between countries that is based on mutual giving and receiving. The relationship between the US and countries like Canada, Britain and Australia would be rooted in free trade. The relationship between countries overly protectionistic would be based on reciprocal measures, until that country amended its arbitrary practices.

---

272 US Department of the Treasury, ARRA Section 1603-Grants For Specified Energy Property In Lieu of Tax Credits Page 19, September 2009, http://www.acore.org/files/Presentation-Ellen%20Neubauer.pdf
273 Alarm: Clock, Wind Farm Companies Big Winners In Latest American Recovery And Reinvestment Act Awards, 22 September 2009, http://www.thealarmclock.com/mt/archives/2009/09/wind_farm_compa.html

When the US economy recovers fully, we can be philanthropic. After WWII, when the US had 50% of the world's GDP, we had a moral obligation to be charitable and help rebuild Europe and Asia. Considering our nascent recovery from the economic crisis, shifting geopolitics, and the magnitude of US debt, Americans can no longer afford to be economically naïve and have a reason to be cautious.

US Manufacturing Industry	NAICS	April 2000 Employment	April 2010 Employment
Food	311	1,560,400	1,462,000
Beverage and Tobacco	312	208,600	185,200
Textile Mills	313	381,700	123,800
Textile Product Mills	314	231,600	121,800
Apparel	315	495,300	165,700
Leather	316	69,800	27,400
Wood	321	622,100	353,600
Paper	322	606,900	399,500
Printing	323	811,100	497,700
Petroleum and Coal	234	124,900	115,300
Chemical	325	984,000	782,000
Plastics and Rubber	326	957,100	630,200
Nonmetallic Mineral	327	554,300	382,200
Primary Metal	331	624,500	367,200
Fabricated Metal	332	1,746,400	1,290,900
Machinery Manufacturing	333	1,454,500	993,100
Computer and Electronics	334	1,787,700	1,092,800
Electrical Equipment, Appliance, Component	335	591,700	368,800
Transportation Equipment	336	2,076,000	1,339,600
Furniture and Related	337	683,900	359,800
Miscellaneous	339	725,900	575,900
Source: BLS	**Total**	**17,298,400**	**11,634,500**
Manufacturing jobs lost in the last decade:			**5,663,900**

Figure 149: US Manufacturing Employment by Industry, April 2000 to April 2010[274]

The logical place for the US government to start with reciprocity is with large and medium-sized manufacturing companies that have declined at a precipitous rate over the last few decades. Figure 149 shows the employment breakdown of major US manufacturing industries, as defined by the BLS. In the last ten years alone, 5.7 million American manufacturing jobs were lost.

---

274 Bureau of Labor Statistics, Industries at a Glance, Manufacturing: NAICS 31-33, 8 May 2010, http://www.bls.gov/iag/tgs/iag31-33.htm

Food, transportation, metal, and computer/electronics are the biggest manufacturing sectors and deserve the greatest amount of attention. These sectors are also subject to the greatest amount of international competition, especially from Asia. Given the fact that Asian nations are recovering from the Great Recession quicker than Western nations, and are projected to have significantly higher rates of growth in the 2010s, it is critical that these manufacturers be protected to the most prudent degree possible. Further decline would be very deleterious to the US.

While four sectors (food, transportation, metal, and computer/electronics) are equally important, transportation may be the best area for the initial *20 by 20* campaign. The transportation sector is comprised of aerospace, motor vehicle, railroad, and ship building manufacturers. Compared to the other three sectors, the transportation sector is perhaps the most taxpayer supported. In addition, the 12.5% unemployment rate within the transportation manufacturing sector is well above the national average.

Taxpayer supported industries should be less subject to free and open competition in the global marketplace (i.e., free trade) than pure-play commercial activities. From a *Jobenomics* point of view, it does not make sense to burden taxpayers to support an industry, and then let that industry outsource jobs to foreign competitors. This is particularly true in the defense transportation sector. For hardcore free-traders, this is a blasphemous point-of-view that smacks of buy-American protectionism. Perhaps it is. However, there is historical precedent. At the onset of the Great Depression, in 1933, the US government passed the Buy American Act to give preference to US manufactured products in government procurements. *Jobenomics* is not suggesting that the US government use the Buy American Act to abrogate other trade agreements, like the General Agreement on Tariffs and Trade (GATT) and World Trade Organization (WTO) standards, but take a much firmer position than it currently does to protect critical manufacturing assets, which have declined by 55% over the last thirty years. Our free-trade policy needs to be changed to a reciprocal-trade policy.

The size of the global defense marketplace is approximately $1.5T, of which the US accounts for approximately half. In 2010, the US Department of Defense procurement and R&D expenditures is approximately $200B—all of which is taxpayer funded. Foreign defense manufacturers, like EADS and BAE, to name a few, have hundreds of thousands of employees in America competing for these dollars. Most of these employees are Americans, but the profits and intellectual capital belong to foreign entities. EADS (European Aeronautic Defence and Space Company) North America boasts of supporting 190,000 American jobs and adding $10B annually to the American economy.[275] BAE Systems, Inc., the US subsidiary of BAE Systems plc, employs 55,000 employees, mainly in the US.[276] In 2009, BAE Systems was the fourth largest DoD contractor with awards of $16.3B.

It has been the Defense Department's policy over the last several decades to be fully open to foreign competition. The primary reason is to encourage foreign countries to buy major US

---

275 EADS North America, Who We Are, Overview, 1 October 2009, http://www.eadsnorthamerica.com/1024/en/organisation/organisation.html
276 BAE Systems Inc., About BAE Systems in the United States, 9 May 2010, http://www.baesystems.com/WorldwideLocations/UnitedStates/AboutBAESystemsUnitedStates/index.htm

weapon systems, like the F-35 fighter aircraft. While this is reasonable, foreign countries are investing less on major weapon systems and shifting domestic spending to other priorities. As a result, the US may have sufficient competitive advantage that may justify a reduction of outsourced jobs in the form of offset programs. "Buy American" is not good policy. However, defense procurement should consider American jobs during the competitive process. If American companies can provide a product that is equal to a foreign product, then the award should go to the American company. Not only does the money stay in America, it provides American jobs and helps maintain our dwindling manufacturing base. If a foreign product is clearly superior, it should be awarded to the foreign entity, assuming that it is manufactured on an equal basis. It makes little sense to use offshore labor when domestic labor is available, in areas like defense manufacturing, which relies solely on US tax dollars as a source of funds. The commercial marketplace is a different story.

Wisconsin's Oshkosh Corporation[277] serves as a good example. Oshkosh Corporation started operations in 1917 and has a long history in the trucking industry. It designs and builds access equipment (vertical mast lifts, stock pickers, drywall lifters, and trailers), fire and emergency vehicles, commercial equipment (cement mixers, garbage trucks, loaders and containers) and defense vehicles and trailers. The downturn in the economy severely impacted the construction sector which impacted Oshkosh to the point that it was approaching ruin after a 70 year history. In August 2009, the company won a $3B contract from the US Army for manufacturing a family of armored vehicles. By most accounts, Oshkosh's was both innovative and competitive. This contract saved the company from potential bankruptcy. Equally important, it provides jobs to a severely depressed community and keeps the company viable until the construction industry recovers. Oshkosh, a midsized company, won against several major foreign firms which are now protesting the award to the US Government Accounting Office (GAO). The GAO upheld the protest and ordered the US Army to re-examine the competition. In February 2010, the GAO sustained some of the foreign competitors' protests, but the US Army chose to award the contract to Oshkosh.

The protest and GAO ruling has spurred a debate regarding how free and open US defense procurements should be. If Oshkosh lost the contract due to a small cost difference, how fair is that to America? First, it is US taxpayer dollars that pay for US Army trucks. Second, more taxpayer dollars will be required for unemployment and welfare benefits if Oshkosh goes under. Third, if US taxpayer dollars are bailing out nearby automobile manufacturers, why not aid truck manufacturers? Lastly, while it may be okay for the private sector to outsource manufacturing jobs, should it be okay for government funded projects to be outsourced in an economic and manufacturing crisis? This debate is not only important for the Oshkosh procurement. It sets a precedent for future procurements. After years of fighting in foreign deserts, the US Army and US Army National Guard inventory of ground vehicles is in dire need of recapitalization. Should this recapitalization be free and open? What would have happened if FDR bought foreign after the Great Depression?

---

277 Oshkosh Corporation, http://oshkoshcorporation.com/about/product_info-access.cfm

On a more positive note, there are examples of international defense cooperation that produces American jobs, as well as reducing taxpayer burden. The F-16 Block 60 Desert Falcon is such an example. The F-16 Block 60 is a sophisticated variation of the popular F-16 fighter aircraft in use by 25 nations. The Desert Falcon was tailored to fit the needs of the United Arab Emirates, which ordered 80 aircraft. In addition to ordering the aircraft, the UAE funded all of the development costs, which were reportedly in excess of $1B. Equally important, is that the US Air Force is helping the UAE Air and Air Defence Forces to build a state-of-the-art self-defense capability. By assisting Middle East coalition partners to defend themselves, it is less likely that US armed forces will have to deploy to the Arab Gulf region. In addition, it helps contain rogue nations, like Iran, from being expansionistic in this critically important region that supplies the world with the bulk of its petroleum products.

International Corporations & Investors: 3 Million New Jobs. Over the last thirty years, foreign companies, especially European companies, have invested and grown significantly in the US. Over the next thirty years, much of the business growth within the US will be from companies in emerging economies in Asia and the Middle East. However, competition for this investment will be significantly higher, due to the fact that the US economy is a much smaller percentage of the global economy, and greater cultural differences between the East and the West, as opposed to trans-Atlantic differences. Consequently, the US needs to market itself in ways that it has never needed to do. As a country, we should market ourselves in much the same way that our states and cities market their community skills and resources to foreign businesses.

One US government program that could be expanded is the EB-5 Immigrant Investor Program.[278] Under the Immigration and Nationality Act, 10,000 immigrant visas per year are available to qualified individuals seeking permanent resident status on the basis of their engagement in a new commercial enterprise. Of the 10,000 investor visas (i.e., EB-5 visas) available annually, 3,000 are reserved for those under a program involving a USCIS-designated "Regional Center." There are over 60 EB-5 Regional Centers in the United States. EB-5 centers are for foreign investors and prominent individuals seeking permanent resident status (Green Cards) based on a minimum investment in the US of $500,000 each, which will create a minimum of ten US jobs, or maintain ten jobs, in a troubled US business. The EB-5 Immigrant Investor Program could be reoriented towards the manufacturing sector.

In the 1980s, the Japanese were motivated to build automotive factories (Toyota, Nissan and Honda) in the southeast US in order to build brand and to mitigate growing "Buy American" sentiment, as a result of the 1982 recession and high American unemployment rates that peaked at 10.8%. The Japanese accomplished these objectives by establishing US assembly, distribution, and warehousing operations, while maintaining R&D and manufacturing operations in their home country. In the 2010s, the Chinese are likely to adopt a similar strategy, and have financial and manufacturing motives to do so. Establishment of assembly, distribution and warehousing operations in economically depressed areas within the US would provide Americans with jobs.

---

278 US Citizenship and Immigration Services, EB-5 Immigrant Investor, 10 December 2009, http://www.uscis. gov/portal/site/uscis/menuitem.b1d4c2a3e5b9ac89243c6a7543f6d1a/?vgnextoid=facb83453d4a3210VgnVCM100 000b92ca60aRCRD&vgnextchannel=facb83453d4a3210VgnVCM100000b92ca60aRC

The EB-5 investment program would provide the initial seed funds to bring foreign nationals responsible for international manufacturing to the US. The role of the US federal, state and local governments is to promote such an initiative, vet potential applicants, and coordinate business-to-business ventures.

Jobenomics is supporting an innovative start-up effort, by the Southbridge Development Group (SBDG) in Southbridge, Massachusetts, to train foreign junior executives in how to start a business in America. The SBDG's International Junior Executive Program is oriented to junior business executives in major foreign manufacturing companies (especially Chinese, Indian, Korean and Japanese) who are responsible for creating new export businesses in the US. SBDG's program provides business education and incubation. Business education will be provided by leading universities, businesses and financial institutions. The program also features an innovative online eDegree program that will assist the junior executives in obtaining advanced degrees in business administration and management.

The International Junior Executive Training program plans to bring Asian junior executives to America to educate them on US business processes. The program will last 12 weeks, with approximately seven weeks in Southbridge for instruction, and five weeks of excursions to:

- Boston, to visit leading US business schools at Harvard and MIT.
- New York City, to visit major financial institutions, media and the entertainment companies.
- Washington DC, to visit the executive, legislative and judicial branches.
- Numerous local trips to cultural events, and meetings with business and government leaders.
- One week of open time, to tour the United States or return home.

It will also expose junior executives to the leading US educational, financial, corporate and political institutions involved with business and international trade. The program will be held several times per year.

The ideal candidate would be a young (25 to 35 years old) professional who would benefit from exposure to corporate, academic and government officials involved in US business decision-making and policymaking circles. Upon completion of training, the Junior Executive will:

- Have a thorough understanding on:
  - o US business environment, business sectors and practices, and the US workforce.
  - o Governmental trade, regulatory and legal requirements.
  - o How to establish a business in the US and obtain investment capital.

- Have high level contacts with business, government and financial leaders, as well as potential joint venture partners.
- Be awarded program graduation certificates, other certificates and documents, and be given a start on advanced eDegrees.
- Be given the opportunity to obtain permanent US entry visas, driver's licenses, bank accounts, and entry into leading US business schools.

The program will feature a school of entrepreneurialism that will introduce these junior executives to American culture and business centers of excellence. The program will also assist junior executives in obtaining resident (EB-5) visas for lifelong access to their US-based business. Senior leaders in government and major conglomerates in China, South Korea and Japan have expressed interest in the Junior Executive Program, as well as in providing funding for the EB-5 visa program. $100M worth of foreign investment capital is expected, which will be used to incubate new  US businesses. SBDG is also working with other private sector investors to raise several hundred million dollars' worth of capital to help start some major manufacturing enterprises with an initial emphasis on assembly, distribution and warehousing operations of electronic, computer and appliance manufacturing that is dominated by Asian manufacturers.

International cultural engagement is another area where the US government could play a major role that would both directly and indirectly promote jobs creation. Over the last decades, the US has been in the transmit mode culturally. The recent economic crisis put Americans in more of a listening mode, which is good for business. The US government has a large role to play in foreign investment in the US. Emerging economies in China, India and Indonesia are recovering from the current economic crisis faster than the US and other Western economies. In addition, countries like China have built a tremendous manufacturing sector on the American appetite for foreign exports, our propensity for debt, and our willingness to outsource. Now that Americans are realizing the short-term nature of these actions, they are importing less and saving more. As a consequence, countries like China are investing more time and money to bolster sagging exports to the US. The time is right to get foreign companies to build more plants in America.

Diplomacy and business go hand in hand. An example illustrates this point. Americans are keenly interested in the Olympics. Chicago's 2016 Olympiad's projected expenditures were $3.3B.[279] At the national level, the US Congress approved a joint resolution of the House and Senate in support of the bid, and the President and First Lady traveled to Europe to lobby for Chicago. Surprisingly, most Americans are unaware of the World Choir Olympics, now called the World Choir Games, which are coming to the US. Since 1988, Europeans and Asians have hosted a total of 81 regional and world choir games, with 5,000 choirs representing 90 countries. Competitions are held in twenty categories defined by age, gender, and genre (sacred, classical, gospel, jazz, pop, barbershop, folklore). In 2010, St. Louis hosts the American International Choral Festival. In 2011, Reno hosts another American International Choral Festival. In 2012, Cincinnati hosts the 7th World Choir Games, with 400 choral groups from 90 nations, and an estimated attendance of 20,000 participants and up to 250,000 spectators—one of the largest international events in US history. The 2006 World Choir Games in Xiamen, China, attracted 600,000 visitors. Americans are keenly interested in musical competition. The successful

279 Chicago 2016, Candidature File – Our Bid Book, Page 24, http://documents.chicago2016.org/pdf/bidbook/ExecSum-ENG.pdf

American Idol show, now in its 10th season, averages 30 million viewers. One would think that World Choir Games would also be well received.

The 2012 Cincinnati 7th World Choir Games could be larger, and exceedingly less expensive, than the 2016 Chicago Olympiad. Unfortunately, federal government support has been tepid and is missing a major opportunity that builds on the St. Louis, Reno and Cincinnati games. Federal and state government officials could help these three local governments maximize the games, from both diplomatic and economic vantage points. Given proper support, the Cincinnati game venue could be increased from 250,000 to 500,000 spectators. In addition, numerous collateral activities could be instituted, including cultural festivals, business leader conferences, side-city tours, documentaries, etc. A US Choral Competition could be conducted at multiple levels (world, multi-national, bi-national, national, inter-state and intra-state games) on a regularly scheduled basis, as opposed to an individual event basis. Potentially, millions of direct and indirect jobs could be created. Cincinnati has a lot to offer to attract international businesses.

EB-5 Regional Centers, the SBDG Junior Executive Training Program, and the World Choir Games are only three examples regarding increased foreign business development in the US. Dozens of other programs could be established in the *20 by 20* campaign.

Energy Technology Revolution Initiative: 5 Million New American Jobs. An Energy Technology Revolution (ETR) initiative would involve government, small business, large business and international joint ventures to develop the next generation of energy products for the world.

The military technology revolution (MTR) was one of the deciding factors in winning the Cold War and creating the largest and most competitive economic superpower on the planet. The information technology revolution (ITR) in the latter part of the 20th century ushered in a new era of prosperity and international commerce. The emerging Energy Technology Revolution (ETR) will become the 21st century's major technology revolution. Like the MTR and ITR, the ETR will likely lead to the creation of tens of millions of new productive jobs, and enhance energy independence and economic security for America. The ETR is a revolution in which America should aggressively strive to be the global leader. A second place finish means the difference of millions of jobs.

America has a plethora of energy technologies in thousands of federal laboratories, corporate research centers, and entrepreneurial "garage shops." An effective ETR strategy would take a system-of-systems approach, and would include:

- Both energy independence and energy assurance.

- A wide spectrum of transportation and electrical power technologies and systems: vehicle fuel economy, alternative fuel vehicles, alternative fuels, exotic technologies, domestic oil/gas production, renewables, and energy infrastructure and efficiency.

- A public-private financial effort using independent organizations and techniques, like the Fed and FDIC are doing with the financial sector.

- Legal and intellectual property protection from special interests and predatory business practices in the face of entrenched, institutional, and other forces that oppose potentially disruptive technologies.

- International alliances and joint ventures.

At a minimum, the US government should establish a US ETR Information Management System that will identify and prioritize promising technologies. The data provided by the US ETR Information Management System would be used to link emerging ETR businesses to private sector funding.

In addition to private sector funding, the US should look to the international community for joint venture and cooperative relationships within the ETR. For example, the Europeans are leaders in nuclear and biofuels. The Arab Gulf states have made tremendous strides in next-generation energy systems and have ample funds for joint development.

A US/GCC ETR joint venture with the oil-rich Arab nations in the Gulf Cooperation Council (GCC) could provide a substantial amount of financing for revolutionary energy technology. Sovereign wealth funds in the United Arab Emirates, Saudi Arabia, Qatar and Kuwait have approximately $3 trillion worth of investment funds. More importantly, these countries are energy-oriented and have strategic plans to build diversified energy economies for the future. A recent bellwether study by the United Arab Emirates called for public-private partnerships with the West to develop corporate enterprises that will last over time. The US government has a unique opportunity to create a US/GCC ETR initiative that couples US technology with Arab financing, via joint ventures across the energy spectrum, with emphasis on fossil fuels technology. GCC governments are currently building a number of "economic cities" and free enterprise zones that could host rapid development of global energy technology solutions. A US/GCC ETR initiative would not only be a win-win for the countries involved, but would help enhance US/Arab relations in these troubled times.

Chapter 22:

ENERGIZING THE PRIVATE SECTOR

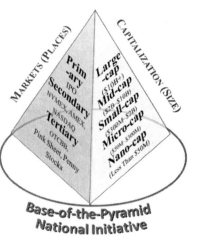

Energizing The Private Sector   JOBENOMICS

- A national public/private initiative is needed to develop new processes to deliver financial capital to the Base-of-the-Pyramid.

- If every major community and state had a base-of-the-pyramid organization, $0.4T worth of US R&D could be leveraged into many new jobs. At $250,000 per job, each $1T would produce 4 million value-added, enduring, new jobs.

- There are numerous other initiatives such as business ministries that could help promote jobs creation and caring for the financially distressed.

MARKETS (PLACES)

CAPITALIZATION (SIZE)

Prim-ary
IPO
Secondary
NYMEX-AMEX
NASDAQ
Tertiary
OTCBB
Pink Sheet, Penny Stocks

Large-cap ($10B+)
Mid-cap ($2B-$10B)
Small-cap ($100M-$2B)
Micro-cap ($50M-$300M)
Nano-cap (Less Than $50M)

Base-of-the-Pyramid National Initiative

The success or failure of America is in the hands of the private sector.

Figure 150: Chapter 22 Summary

Ultimately, the success or failure of America is in the hands of the private sector. There are many things that the private sector can do to achieve *20 by 20*. This has to be a bottom-up process—one led from the private sector, but with support from government at all levels: federal, state and local. Given a place to start, the American private sector will reinvent itself in ways that no book could conceive. For the last 150 years, US government national initiatives have been the catalyst for many remarkable private sector achievements, from the trans-continental railroad that unlocked the commercial potential of the American frontier, to the industrial revolution that made the US a superpower, to the internet that ushered in the information age.

This chapter will offer suggestions on three very diverse subjects for the private sector: launching a Base-of-the-Pyramid National Initiative to create near-term jobs in the small business sector; preparing financially for potential W- and L-shaped recovery scenarios in case the current V-shaped recovery stalls; and creating business ministries to better deploy the underutilized resources of America's 325,000 churches to help people get back to work, and provide better care for the financially disadvantaged. The Base-of-the-Pyramid National Initiative is an example that deals directly with jobs creation. The preparing-financially section deals with protecting household wealth in a changing economy. The business ministry section discusses ways that the private sector can help the increasing rolls of the unemployed and financially distressed. In order for jobenomics—the economics of job, wealth and revenue creation—to be successful, it will require private sector innovation, preparation and community.

Base-of-the-Pyramid National Initiative. The base of the US economic pyramid represents where most of the jobs are. It is replete with small businesses, emerging enterprises and the self-employed.

The most critical element for small business success is matching needs to finances. There are plenty of people with a dream. Whether it is starting a barbershop or developing a life-changing technology, the goal is the same. That goal is the creation of meaningful jobs that enable economic security and the pursuit of happiness.

A national effort is needed to develop new processes to deliver financial capital to the base-of-the-pyramid. American ingenuity and innovation often reside on the bottom of the pyramid, which is starved for capital. For **20 by 20** to work, emerging companies and small businesses need to meet investors, and investors need to meet emerging companies and small businesses.

There are tens of $Ts of private sector capital looking for investment opportunities. A properly executed US public-private Base-of-the-Pyramid National Initiative would exploit this volatility and endeavor to get several $T to next-generation and emerging-technology companies in America.

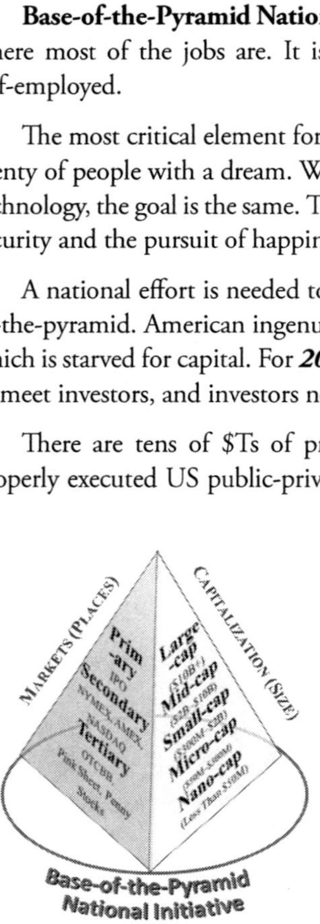

Historically, investors have invested at the top of pyramid, with few dollars trickling down to the base. Due to the recent economic crisis and volatility of the markets, investors are anxious. The May 2010 1,000-point drop in the Dow made investors more nervous. Consequently, now is a good time to launch a national Base-of-the-Pyramid Initiative that identifies, prioritizes and maybe even underwrites next-generation businesses.

Figure 151: Financing the Base-of-the-Pyramid

Figure 151 shows the traditional structure of the capital markets. The two vertical sides of the pyramid consist of markets (places) and capitalization (size). There are three market segments: the primary market deals with the issuance of new stocks (initial public offerings, IPO) and securities (like Treasuries), the secondary market which is known as the aftermarket, where previously-issued financial instruments and securities are bought and sold in exchanges (NYMEX, AMEX,

NASDAQ), and the tertiary market deals with off-exchange trading directly between two parties which is called over-the-counter (OTC) trading. There are five capitalization classifications: large-cap ($10B+), mid-cap ($2B to $10B), small-cap ($300M to $2B), micro-cap ($50M to $300M) and nano-cap (less than $50M). A national Base-of-the-Pyramid initiative would focus on nano-cap and emerging (limited to no cap) businesses.

One thing that the recent economic crisis has taught us is that the "buy and hold" stock market strategy may no longer be a good strategy. Consequently, individual investors, institutional investors and sovereign wealth funds are much more flexible and agile than ever before, presenting opportunity for next-generation products and services. The money is there, but the problem is identifying and qualifying opportunities, which would be the primary goal of a US Base-of-the-Pyramid National Initiative, which would consist of a public/private partnership.

The role of US government at the federal, state and local level is to provide a forum for small and emerging companies to vet their technology, products and services. Historically, it is the private sector's responsibility to provide and fund these opportunities. Today, proactive government support is needed to succeed in the global marketplace, and to advance US economic recovery.

Whether it involves finding a date, a mate, or an investor, getting noticed is the first step. The second step is qualifying the opportunity in a due diligence process. Due diligence involves comprehensive investigations that an investor must make before buying a single share in a business. The third step is validation and prioritization. Third party validation is critical to attracting investors, especially at the base-of-the-pyramid, where investors are dealing with a higher degree of unknowns. Prioritization is equally important. If there are ten inventions in the same area, investors want to know which ones are considered the best, and which ones offer the highest return. The last step is underwriting the opportunity. In regard to the Base-of-the-Pyramid National Initiative, underwriting could involve providing financial guarantees or indemnifying potential investors that the due diligence process was done to the highest standards and that claims are reasonably correct.

($M)	Federal	Industry	University	Non Profit	Total	
Government	27,000	30,826	39,653	3,688	**101,167**	$101B
Private Sector	0	263,310	17,532	31,212	**312,054**	$312B
	27,000	294,136	57,185	34,900	**413,221**	
		Source: National Science Foundation			**$0.4T**	

Figure 152: US 2008 R&D Expenditures

Research and development, whether it pertains to technology or processes, is the grist for business development and jobs creation. The US is an R&D nation. For several centuries, the US has been known for innovation and entrepreneurialism—and it still is. Innovation can be found in our garages, or in labs. Bill Gates and Steve Jobs started Microsoft and Apple in their garages. US R&D expenditure is the highest in the world. Not including garage shop R&D which is privately developed, the National Science Foundation[280] calculated that the 2008 US R&D expenditure totaled $0.4T in federal, industry, university and non-profit R&D centers (Figure

---

280 U.S. R&D expenditures, by performing sector and funding source: 1953–2008, Table 4-3, http://www.nsf.gov/statistics/seind10/appendix.htm

152). These centers would be a good place to start the Base-of-the-Pyramid National Initiative, since most of the information for the due diligence, validation and prioritization processes is already available or easily attainable. Since the federal government funds ¼ of all US R&D across all major sectors (federal, industry, university and non-profit), it has a key role in exposing this technology and spinning off companies in order to attract outside investment. However, ¾ of the US R&D resides in the private sector, which often treats this as proprietary. Consequently, the Base-of-the-Pyramid National Initiative would have to create safeguards to protect proprietary interests, while exposing enough information to attract investors.

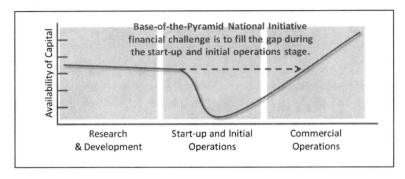

Figure 153: Availability of Capital

The primary challenge of the Base-of-the-Pyramid National Initiative is to ensure consistent availability of capital throughout the entire business lifecycle, from R&D through commercial operations where the bulk of jobs creation occurs. As shown in Figure 153, there is plenty of money already being expended on the R&D phase. There are also plenty of investment, hedge, private equity and sovereign wealth funds that are willing to provide debt or equity funding for the commercial operations phase. The so-called "valley of death" is during the start-up and initial operations phase.

Filling the "valley of death" will be a challenge. While the economic crisis has made investors nervous in the stock market, it also has made them wary of start-ups that may not make it in tough economic times. Credit is still tight. The downturn in the economy has also exhausted many family, friends, angel and individual investors. Start-ups face the disadvantage of being small. Investment funds would rather invest in one $10M opportunity than ten $1M opportunities with the same rate of return. Start-ups also tend to fail after the R&D phase due to the founders' inability to move from innovators to operators. For these reasons, the Base-of-the-Pyramid National Initiative has to mollify these challenges in new creative venture funds for this area. Because Americans innovate, such creative funds are already being developed. One such organization, The University Funds[SM], represents an excellent model.

According to their Managing Director,[281] The University Funds is a new kind of venture capital firm focused on accelerating commercialization of emerging technologies that demonstrate market disruptive potential, which includes alternative energy and related green technologies,

---

281 Jon Nieman, Managing Director, Corporate Relations, The University Funds[SM], 5 April 2010, http://www. theufunds.com/

healthcare/life sciences, and advanced computing/communication technologies. The University Funds uses an unconventional approach by first identifying market needs, then licensing promising technologies from a global network of universities, national research institutions, and corporate technology partners. After licensing, they combine complementary technologies into portfolio companies, commit funding, and provide seasoned executives to manage these companies. Funding is committed in a structured series of investments, which are tied to specific development milestones. By providing centralized administration and shared services resources across portfolio companies, the management teams focus on the most critical product and business development issues.

Will this type of organization work? Apparently, yes. The University Funds management team has signed up twenty leading US universities and national R&D centers, enlisted several dozen corporate partners including a number of Fortune 50 companies, and is well on its way to raising its first $100M emerging technology fund.

By combining an emerging technology fund with a business accelerator, a new species of venture capital firm could become the economic engine for a Base-of-the-Pyramid National Initiative. If every major community and state had a base-of-the-pyramid organization, $0.4T worth of US public and private sector R&D could be leveraged into $Ts worth of new jobs. At a wrap rate (salary, benefits, overhead) of $250,000 per job, each $1T would produce 4 million value-added, enduring, new jobs.

Another way to attract investors is through the internet, which is changing the way investors meet new enterprises. Normally, a new business conducts a "friends and family" round to get the business started, and a prototype built. Next, the business executives need to conduct a "road show" to prospective investors, with a prospectus or private placement memorandum. This road show process can be long and frustrating for most start-up executives. In many ways, it is like the country western song about looking for love in all the wrong places. In order to shorten the process, a number of web-based services, like *Meet the Street*, match management teams with targeted investors. According to their news release,[282] "with *Meet the Street*, portfolio managers are introduced only to senior management teams that they have pre-selected, while corporates are able to schedule non-deal road show meetings with highly-targeted potential investors."

Another way to attract potential investors to a base-of-the-pyramid organization is via penny stocks, over-the-counter (OTC) bulletin board stocks and Pink Sheets. Penny stocks usually trade for pennies through services like the OTC Bulletin Board, or the Pink Sheets. The OTC Bulletin Board, or OTCBB, is a US electronic quotation system that displays real-time quotes, last-sale prices, and volume information for many over-the-counter equity securities that are not listed on a national securities exchange. Pink Sheets are over-the-counter securities that do not meet the listing standards required to trade on the NYSE, NASDAQ, AMEX or other major stock exchanges due to their limited capitalization and/or the limited number of shares outstanding.

---

282 Business Wire, Press Release, Instinet Launches "Meet the Street" Corporate Access Platform, 29 March 2010, http://www.marketwatch.com/story/instinet-launches-meet-the-street-corporate-access-platform-2010-03-29?reflink=MW_news_stmp

The beauty of the Pink Sheets is that they can be listed in a very short period of time (weeks), and since they do not have to meet the listing standards of the major exchanges, the bureaucratic overhead is much less.

Penny stocks are often used by small businesses and start-up companies as an initial source of investment capital. Penny stocks are considered high risk, high return investments. Since these stocks are traded outside the major exchanges, they have had a reputation of being junior variety stocks most suited for day-traders, as opposed to "serious" investors. However, this notion is changing. First of all, the major exchanges are now considered much riskier. Secondly, a number of new websites that offer real-time information on penny stocks are now operational. In addition, newswire services are providing visibility into small stock companies in ways never before available. For example, Newswire.net is a new social network for 13 million independent journalists. According to Newswire's CEO,[283] their social network can be used to write and publish articles or press releases about new companies. Tagged to a Pink Sheet stock symbol, these articles/press releases can then be distributed to 50,000 locations online, including the major stock quote websites for a total cost of about $500, which is very inexpensive for market exposure.

Community-based business incubators are critical to success. Local communities represent that base-of-the-pyramid. As the adage says, all politics are local. So are the economics of job, wealth and revenue creation. Every community in America should have a business incubator that pursues B2B, B2C and B2G opportunities. The focal point of a B2B (business-to-business) incubator is to link emerging businesses with the financial resources of banks, investment funds, private equity funds, and high net-worth individuals. The locus of a B2C (business-to-consumer) incubator is to connect business directly to consumers via the internet, call-centers and telecommuting. The prime focus of a B2G (business-to-government) incubator is to garnish proactive government support for business development and growth. Of the three, B2B is the most important. To make *20 by 20* a success, it has to be led by the private sector. Business to business collaboration is imperative.

CEO Space (www.CEOspace.net) employs a highly effective B2B methodology, which emphasizes collaboration over competition. CEO Space holds five B2B collaborative, instructional, professional credit qualified, trade show "forums" each year and has numerous community-based chapters across North America. At the heart of their methodology is their SNAP process. SNAP—as in snapping your fingers—trains entrepreneur CEOs how to better articulate their vision in a snap, in order to quickly find new customers, markets, joint venture partners capital, or new sources of financing. The typical CEO Space world trade show gathers hundreds of entrepreneurs that cooperatively, versus competitively, network with each other in small groups to develop their business plans. At the end of the one-week forum, all of the entrepreneurs are given an opportunity to articulate their business plan and future needs to the entire forum and potential investors. By the end of the week, thousands of preprinted "See Me" businesses cards are exchanged, critiques given, contacts suggested, venture partnerships formed, and private placement strategies arranged. The bottom line is that the SNAP methodology could

---

283 Chris Ryan, CEO of EXT and Newswire (a subsidiary company), 5 April 2010, http://www.newswire.net/

be a good model for community-based business incubators to copy. Via www.ceospacenation. com, CEO SPACE is bringing its twenty-year proven model for rapid job creation to cities, states and nations. Every community should hold business forums of this nature, to match business ideas to needs, as entrepreneur sector job creation becomes a priority for municipal and state planners joining the jobenomics team. Building intra-community business networks will help grow business and create jobs much faster than the current laissez-faire approach to business incubation. CEO SPACE offers one model, which planners would be well advised to explore and replicate locally.

Since community-based business incubators would provide due diligence and validation services, investors might be attracted to their portfolios in significant quantities, especially if these business incubators provided newswire services, advertizing, outreach and underwriting services to reduce risk and maximize return. The biggest contribution that community-based business incubators could facilitate is connecting small business to hospitable investors. Today, venture capital comes at a very high price. All too often, venture-capitalists want 70% of the equity of an emerging company, which is a major disincentive for many entrepreneurs starting a business. "Vulture" capitalists, who deprive inventors of control over their own innovations, are an anathema to entrepreneurialism and jobs creation.

Properly structured, community-based business incubators would help reduce startup risk, and subsequently could help reduce the cost of capital, as well as limiting the degree of control that an initial investor has over the emerging business. In addition, community-based business incubators could bundle a number of emerging businesses into a portfolio, and use collective bargaining power to attract capital from venture-capitalists, as well as other traditional and non-traditional sources, such as the day-traders in penny stocks.

Community-based business incubators can be structured as either for-profit or not-for-profit entities. The not-for-profit entities could be used for charitable and other tax deductible businesses. The for-profit entities would be used for pure-play commercial pursuits. States and municipalities should consider bonds as a source of startup capital. These bonds could be sold with a guaranteed rate of return to socially-conscious citizens, who believe that jobs creation is a solid investment for their future, as well as the future of their community. State pension funds may be attracted to such an opportunity, which provides a good rate of return, plus potential job opportunities for their pensioners and families.

The jobenomics strategic plan includes community-based business incubators. If the jobenomics concept creates a sufficient groundswell of supporters in the public and private sector, the next logical step is to create a bridging mechanism to link emerging businesses with investment capital at the local level.

In conclusion, the private sector has to take the lead in the jobs creation arena, but they can't do it alone. Government support is needed. Since small businesses are the backbone of the American economy, this is where our focus should be. Consequently, a Base-of-the-Pyramid National Initiative should be launched in every state and every major community across America. The mission of a community base-of-the-pyramid organization is to organize and validate business opportunities, identify or raise funds, and provide business management and acceleration services using modern information technology applications and solutions. The near-term goals would be to generate $1T revenue, and a minimum of 4 million new, high-value, enduring jobs.

Preparing For the W- and L-Shaped Recovery Scenarios. The central question posed by this book involves what scenario (V, W, or L) lies ahead. The answer is that no one really knows. The US, the West, and the rest of the world are in uncharted territory, created by hundreds of $T worth of debt and an interconnected and turbulent world. Depending on one's assumptions, the probability of a V, a W, or an L-shaped future is about equal. A wise person would hope for the best, but would prepare for the worst. Paranoia can be beneficial if the threat is real.

The question that most often arises regarding preparing for the worst, involves the issue of personal investing. This book is about strategy, not investing. However, having an investment strategy based on the V, W, or L scenarios discussed in this book deserves comment.

Other than becoming debt-free, our best advice is to find a financial planning professional who has the expertise to coordinate portfolios, wills, trusts, insurance, taxes, and retirement plans in accordance with your overall objectives. Most modern financial planners have analytical tools and resources that are not available to the average person. Having a balanced and diversified portfolio in these complex and volatile times, which is managed by a professional, is well worth the investment. It is important to agree on a strategic perspective (V, W, L) between you and your financial planner. It is also important to watch for inflationary/deflationary trends, major indicators and signs of collapse.

- **V-shaped recovery investment strategy**. If you and your financial planner are convinced that the President's V-shaped recovery (6% GDP, 5% unemployment) projections are correct, then the stock market is for you. Energy, healthcare, medical and emerging economies stocks are the best place to invest. If a solid V-shaped recovery occurs, the stock markets will probably reach new highs and offer the best bet against inflation, which will most likely result as a market bubble grows. The most dangerous part of a rapid recovery is the creation of asset bubbles. The 1990 Japanese crash, and the US Great Recession, were both caused by real estate asset bubbles. The dot.com and telecom bust in the late 1990s were due to bursting tech-bubbles. After the crash during the Great Recession, the stock markets have staged a remarkable recovery. A deep drop creates a great bounce. This bounce has been amplified by $11T worth of US government liquidity (bank bailouts, corporate incentives and various stimuli), and the purposeful and calculated lowering of interest rates by the Fed to encourage private sector investment. Given one of the deepest drops in history, coupled by the largest injection of liquidity in history, the bounce should be potentially large.

US Stock Market	May 2010	All Time High	Great Recession Low
NASDAQ	May-10	Feb-00	Feb-09
	2395	5132	1378
	Δ	-53%	74%
DOW	May-10	Oct-07	Mar-09
	10831	14164	6547
	Δ	-24%	65%
S&P 500	May-10	Jul-07	Jan-09
	1165	1526	797
	Δ	-24%	46%

Figure 154: US Stock Market Highs and Lows

According to V-shape theorists, the stock markets should soon meet or exceed previous highs. Indeed, the US stock markets are up significantly from the Great Recession lows in Q1 2009 (Figure 154). The NASDAQ is up 74%. The Dow Jones Industrial Average is up 65%. The S&P 500 is up 46%. As measured from all-time highs, the markets still have a long way to go. The NASDAQ is down 53%. The Dow Jones Industrial Average is down 24%. The S&P 500 is down 24%. Consequently, to a V-shape theorist there is still 25% to 50% more money to be made just by reaching previous highs that occurred a few years ago.

Even though 8 out of 9 economists and policymakers are V-shaped recovery advocates, few if any are predicting that the stock markets will exceed or even meet previous highs. So far, the V-shape advocates are cautiously optimistic, but are concerned about the things that dismay W- and L-shaped recovery proponents. Chronic US unemployment, economic contagion in Europe, foreclosure/default problems in the US, and the increasing potential for conflict in Iran are the four issues that worry all economists. V-shape advocates correctly argue that investor anxiety over these issues is limiting the recovery. Stocks waver as investor anxiety rises in proportion to increasing stock market volatility, international tensions, debt issues, natural disasters, and the fear of the unknown.

- **W-shaped recovery investment strategy.** If you and your financial planner are convinced that the W-shaped recovery projections are probable, and the stock markets may drop quicker than you can react, then a more conservative strategy is for you. The foremost strategy is first get out of debt (mortgage, loans and credit cards), and then conservatively invest what you can. Getting out of debt includes refinancing to reduce interest rates and paying down on the principal. While interest payments currently qualify as income tax deductions, these deductions may not be worth much, if one loses a job or a substantial portion of their income. Being debt-free not only reduces anxiety, but gives a person financial security and flexibility in depressed economic times. If you are one of the unfortunate underwater homeowners, your choice will be difficult. Moral responsibility, rebound hope, credit ratings, possessions, family status, and pride are all factors that keep homeowners paying mortgages, when it may not be in their financial interest to do so. A double-dip recession, or a second real estate crisis, will make things worse. If either of these happens, a strategic default is probably warranted. At some point, it does not make sense to continue to deplete one's life savings, if there is little hope of recovery from an underwater mortgage. However, distressed homeowners should make every attempt to work with their lending institution and government rescue programs prior to walking away. Strategic defaults should be done with honor, face-to-face with the lender, with a firm but conciliatory attitude.

The rapid growth in the NASDAQ, DOW and S&P already has the makings of an asset bubble that is susceptible to puncture, if an inauspicious crisis or event transpires. If the US reenters recession, stocks are generally a poor place to invest. Large-cap, high-quality, dividend-paying stocks are largely the exception to this statement. Large-cap, undervalued, blue-chip stocks that pay dividends are superior to other stocks in a recession.

High quality bonds and commodities are usually safer than stocks. Having said this, bonds and commodities are also showing signs of a bubble. There is currently over $2T invested in bonds via mutual funds. In 2009, about $0.5T was invested in bonds, largely as an alternative to a volatile stock market.

Commodities, like gold, are good investments in recessions, but have a high emotional quotient—what goes up emotionally often comes crashing down. Many are investing in commodity-based ETFs (exchange-traded funds) which function largely as mutual funds. Commodity ETFs invest in commodities, like precious metals, energy, agriculture and futures.

Many investors would argue that emerging markets like China are good places to invest, since they are emerging from the global recession and more resistant to a double-dip than their Western counterparts. While this is generally true, emerging economies offer greater unknown-unknowns.

Investors and speculators are also beginning to invest in US real estate that is at historic lows. Unfortunately, a double-dip recession could drive real estate even lower as foreclosures further saturate the market. Over the long haul, real estate could be a relatively safe investment, depending on location and an inflationary environment.

- **L-shaped recovery investment strategy**. If you and your financial planner are convinced that the L-shaped recovery is probable, then a much more conservative strategy is for you.

A growing number of Americans believe that the growing number of potential crises or major events, whether manmade or acts-of-God, makes investing too risky. This attitude tends to be more prevalent with baby-boomers than youthful investors.

For those who hold this view, cash is the answer. As the economy declines, or collapses, cash will be king. In an L- or declining L-scenario, everyone will lose, but some will lose everything. Those who have cash will have opportunities at really bargain basement prices due to widespread bankruptcies, foreclosures and liquidations. Tradable commodities will also be useful in severe circumstances, since bartering will likely be prevalent.

- **Inflationary/deflationary trends.** Inflation and deflation are the wild cards which often surface during volatile V-, W- or L-shaped scenarios.

From an investment perspective, inflation can be worse than recession. Inflation is the worst type of tax for fixed income persons (retirees, unemployed, marginally employed and underemployed) and can last significantly longer than average recessions. The majority of V- and W- economists predict that inflation will be a factor, especially in reaction to US government policies and Federal Reserve interest rate manipulation.

The federal government and the Fed are motivated to infuse a lot of money (printed or borrowed) into the economy, while keeping interest rates low to stimulate the economy and encourage investing. If this intervention is overdone, many fear that super-inflation (like the 20%/year rates during the Carter Administration) will result. A number of foreign governments fear that the US might intentionally super-inflate, or even hyper-inflate, to rid itself of its record high public and private debt. This theory is farfetched, but is a part of the argument for a new reserve currency and devalued dollar. The prospect of Greece defaulting on its sovereign debt has put the euro in a tailspin, and even cast doubt by many Europeans regarding the viability of the European Union.

From an inflation investment perspective, US Treasury Inflation-Protected Securities (or TIPS) are 5-, 10-, 20- and 30-year inflation-indexed bonds that are relatively safe during inflationary times.

2009 was the first deflationary year since 1955 in the United States. Some economists fear that deflation can take hold like it has in Japan for the last several decades, but the majority of economists feel that the current deflationary cycle could create conditions for a bounce with super-inflation rates facilitated by the largely artificial infusion of $Ts into the market.

The exception to the general rule that cash will be king is very high inflation. An increasing number of market watchers believe that super-inflation will occur, because of government policies and intervention. Some even say that many government officials see super-inflation as the only practical means of mitigating debt that we can no longer afford. If super-inflation occurs, then debt will be king over the long-term. Those who can afford to take on debt during super-inflation will see the value of their assets appreciate (inflate) over the fixed-rate period of the loan or mortgage on that asset.

- **Major indicators of change**. While no one really knows what scenario (V, W, or L) lies ahead, there are a number of indicators that will forewarn investors in the short-term. Barring a major unexpected event, the four major indicators to watch are employment, residential real estate, market reaction to the Fed increasing interest rates, and bankruptcies. The EU sovereign debt crisis and conflict with Iran appear to be on the back burner at the time of this writing, but may rapidly return to the forefront. Closing the spending/receipt gap is also a major indicator, but it is more of a long-term issue.

  Employment is the primary indicator. 20 million new private sector jobs by 2020 should be our primary focus. Jobs creation is much more important than jobs losses. Unfortunately, unemployment will have to suffice until a *20 by 20* system is generated. Official unemployment rates above 10% indicate trouble.

  The second major indicator is the residential real estate market. Underwater mortgages, foreclosures, seriously delinquent loans, and strategic defaults are at an all-time high. If a second residential real estate crisis occurs, the federal government will not have the resources it had to fight the first residential real estate crisis. The federal government is currently doing all that it possibly can to mitigate a second crisis.

  The third major indicator is the market reaction to the Fed increasing interest rates. The Fed, who is responsible for US fiscal and monetary policy, lowered short-term interest rates to near zero to stimulate lending and spur a strong economic recovery. While the US is recovering, the recovery has been relatively weak as compared to nations farther from the US economic crisis' epicenter. Major international institutions, like the IMF, are concerned that the Fed will raise rates too soon. Many feel that an early raise will choke recovery, cause a panic, and throw the global community back into recession. Bernanke agrees. The ideal time for the Fed to raise rates is when the public generally perceives that the recovery is well in hand. Low unemployment and high GDP will allow the Fed to safely raise rates. If a strong recovery does not occur soon, the Fed has a real dilemma. They cannot lower interest rates more since they are already near zero. That tool is gone. Their quantitative easing (buying toxic mortgage backed securities) effort is also coming to an end. The Fed's asset sheet is already full of these toxic assets and is terminating a number of these bank stabilization programs, now that banks are in relatively good position. Borrowing and printing more money have reached their limits. Much more borrowing and printing will result in dollar devaluation, a push for a new reserve currency, and public outcry about the tyranny of national debt. In many ways, the Fed, Treasury and FDIC collectively have made all-in bets on relatively weak hands.

  The fourth indicator could be insolvencies and bankruptcies of states, municipalities, businesses and individuals. It is estimated that the spending/receipts gap for the states is around $300B for 2010. Without additional state revenue or bailouts from the federal government, massive state government layoffs and reductions in infrastructure projects are likely. To close the gap with layoffs alone, the states would have to fire 6 million state administrative, police, teachers, utility, healthcare and transportation personnel. Municipalities are also in bad shape. The major indicators to their demise will be degraded bond rating (which will make borrowing money for municipalities much more difficult), as well as Chapter 9 bankruptcies. Businesses face many of the same problems, and will terminate operations and file for Chapter 7 and Chapter 11 bankruptcy protection. The most visible and disheartening sign will be shuttered businesses in affluent malls and strip shopping centers, in upscale communities. The latest guise in these communities to cover this blight is to provide closed business space rent-free to artists to display their wares and project an atmosphere of prosperity and sophistication. There has also been a significant increase in personal bankruptcy filings in the US. The new 2005 bankruptcy law, which required filers to pass a means test, has not slowed down the pace of filing for personal bankruptcies as expected.

The stock markets are not a good indictor until it's too late. The infusion of $Ts of stimuli, $Ts of private sidelined money, and removal of $Ts of toxic assets has drugged the market into false euphoria. Weaning the market off these stimuli will not be easy. As Americans experienced during the 2000 technology and 2008 real estate asset bubble crashes, a stampede usually occurs when someone points out that the emperor has no clothes. The Fed has already been weaning the banks off their drugs by closing a number of crisis lending programs. The Treasury is doing the same. Most of the Treasury's TARP programs are closing, and the remaining money and repayments are being diverted to jobs programs. So far so good, but the recovery is weak. It would not take a major event, real or perceived, to set off a selling panic in the stock market not only by nervous investors, but by a host of computerized programs that are tied to major institutions and pension funds. A 5,000 point drop in the Dow in one week is not inconceivable. On 6 May 2010, the Dow had its largest intraday drop of almost 1,000 points in one hour. In a three-week period between 29 September and 22 October 2009, the Dow had five major one-day drops, ranging from 778 to 508 points, for a total of 3,212 points. The realization of government withdrawal of liquidity has not hit the general investors as yet. When it does, market psychology will be paramount. If someone yells "fire sale," panic could occur and $Ts of private sector liquidity could quickly vanish from the market.

Business Ministries. Today, there are six applicants for every job. This statistic is unlikely to improve in the near-future, and will certainly worsen if a W- or L-shaped recovery ensues. Government and civic organizations cannot meet the growing needs of the jobless and financially oppressed.

The largest social network in America is the one that is perhaps the least responsive. This network is the community of Christian churches. While other religious organizations are also viable, they collectively are much smaller than US Christian institutions. With the possible exception of African-American inner city churches and Catholic Charities, much more can be done by the Christian community, especially if the employment and economic situation worsens. Consequently, churches need to develop business ministries for the financially distressed, in the same way that they have done to respond to other social issues.

According to the US Census Bureau, there are 326,762 American churches[284] with a combined membership of over 161 million, and a leadership team (priests and pastors) of almost 400,000. The largest US Christian congregations are the Southern Baptist Convention with 44,696 churches, United Methodist Church with 34,398 and the Roman Catholic Church with 18,479 parishes within the United States. Since the majority of US churches are small (less than 500 members), it is advisable that they network services and business ministries in their local community or region.

Unfortunately, churches and parishes are unprepared for the tsunami of unemployment that is already upon us (Figure 155). Business ministries are needed to reach within congregations, as well as outside to local communities. While the US church's primary mission is spiritual, it also provides a wide variety of social safety net services, including food pantries, food kitchens and numerous counseling services. For example, the Roman Catholic Church has over 1,700 local Catholic Charities[285] agencies and institutions nationwide that provide support to local agencies to reduce poverty, support families, and empower communities.

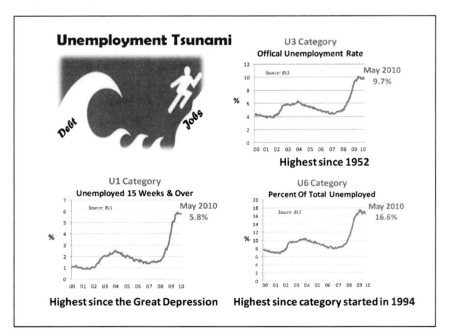

Figure 155: 1st Tsunami Wave of Unemployment

284 US Census Bureau, The 2010 Statistical Abstract, The National Data Book, Religious Bodies, http://www.census.gov/compendia/statab/cats/population/religion.html
285 Catholic Charities USA, http://www.catholiccharitiesusa.org/NetCommunity/Page.aspx?pid=1408

A recent television special[286] on community churches in Portland, Oregon was especially enlightening. According to the reporter, Portland is one of the most secular cities in America. The mayor had a particularly dim view of church, and a dimmer view of Christians. Several of the city's pastors devised a proposal for the mayor and city council. They proposed that their congregations would provide volunteer services to the city, with a promise that they would not proselytize. They would witness only with their actions. Any witnessing would have to be done at church and not during the time of volunteer services. The mayor accepted the offer and assigned church leaders mundane jobs like painting, yard work and housekeeping services for public grounds, buildings and schools. In response, the churches mobilized over 26,000 volunteers to serve the community—not for one day, but for several years running. They have even bought and converted property in drug-infested areas to put these facilities to better use serving the needs of the community. This effort, known as A Season of Service, serves as an illustrious example for potential business ministries.

It is not uncommon for missionaries to foreign countries to engage in community economic development and educational services. This is called the institutional model of missionary work and emphasizes mutual understanding, coexistence, and tolerance, as opposed to conversion. Building hospitals and schools often says more about a person's spiritual values than words. Perhaps it is time to employ these skills at home.

An example of how a group of American missionaries in the Philippines reached out to a distressed group of dissidents serves as an example of how a business ministry should work with people outside the church. Operation Blessing is one of the largest private humanitarian organizations in the world. It is also part of Pat Robertson's conservative, evangelical, and often controversial organization. One would think Operation Blessing would function as bully-pulpit, but it doesn't. A recent cooperative program with the Republic of the Philippines makes the point about the power of business ministry using the institutional model.

According to Gordon Robertson, Pat Robertson's son and heir apparent, Operation Blessing had a team of doctors working in the Philippines. This team found out that a militant group of Islamic terrorists was in desperate need of medical attention. Rather than disregarding the urgent needs of these insurgent fighters from a different religion, the Christian doctors responded, over the initial objections and advice of the Philippine government. In the end, the Philippine government capitulated, and identified the location of the terrorist stronghold of the *Jemaah Islamiyah*. The government also arranged for the Philippine Air Force to transport the doctors and medical team to a nearby town. Without escort, the Christian doctors went into the terrorist stronghold and attended to the sick. They witnessed only by their actions, which was probably advisable given the fact that their patients were radical Islamists with little regard for infidels. The doctors did what they could and left without incident. A short time afterwards, a number of the terrorists contacted local Operation Blessing personnel and stated a desire to lay down their arms. They also stated that they were concerned about the lack of potential job opportunities available

---

286   A Season of Service-A Witness Louder Than Words, CBNTV, by Paul Strand, 10 May 2010, http://www.cbn.com/media/player/index.aspx?s=/vod/PST139_Service_101309_WS&search=%20oregon&p=1&parent=0&subnav=false

to people in their position. An employed terrorist in the jungle is better than an unemployed ex-terrorist starving in a city. To rectify this dilemma, Operation Blessing, with the help of the Philippine government, started a cell phone repair facility that now employs many of these former terrorists. These people reportedly are still Muslim, but they are now Muslims with appreciation and deep respect for the business ministry performed by a group of evangelical Christians.

If unemployment worsens, churches may be compelled to engage in response to increasing despondency. Our instruction manual impels us to do so for all people in need—Christians, non-Christians, and foreigners.

Church leaders need to decide to act proactively or reactively as the unemployment situation dictates. A proactive approach is one where church leaders attempt to anticipate and mitigate expected events or situations. Proactive leaders manage through times of change, and help shape the future. A reactive approach implies that the church should be prepared to be responsive to conditions, if and as they occur. Reactive leaders assess changing realities and amend ideas/actions to fit the circumstance. Whether proactive or reactive, church leaders need to act with the growing community of discouraged, financially distressed, underemployed or unemployed individuals. Given the statistic that hundreds of millions of Americans accept some form of government handout or entitlement program, the need is great.

Many religious leaders feel that business ministries could be in conflict with the church's not-for-profit legal status. These are legitimate concerns that can be easily managed by creating independent non-profit organizations outside the church. Jill's House serves as an example. Jill's House, Inc.,[287] is a 501(c)(3) non-profit organization that is an integrated auxiliary of McLean Bible Church in McLean, Virginia. Jill's House was established to serve children with special needs with short-term overnight care, social activities and a range of therapy activities, providing the opportunity for respite for their families. It is estimated that over 40,000 children with special needs live in the Washington DC metropolitan area. Despite the wealth in Washington and the abundance of government-provided services, reliable respite care is in short supply. McLean Bible Church has stepped in to fill the gap with this unique business ministry.

Starting at the pulpit, priests/pastors need to increase teaching of Biblical financial principles beyond tithing. The principle of caring for widows and orphans applies generally to all downtrodden—both inside the congregation and in the local community. Christians are called to care for their neighbors, including Samaritans (foreigners).

The soaring U1 long-term unemployment rate indicates that the challenges of the financially downtrodden are likely to increase in the near future. Several decades ago, the church took a rather hard-line approach to the subject of divorce. Now that the American divorce rate is 50%, almost every church has multiple ministries to care for the victims of broken families. In much the same way that mounting divorce rates compelled churches into action, families broken by unemployment, poverty and financial hopelessness should compel churches to develop some form of business ministry.

---

287 Jill's House, Description of the organization, our purpose, and persons served, 10 May 2010, http://jillshouse. org/article-about.asp

After accepting the prospect of a church business ministry, the priest, pastor or rector should find a business executive to organize and lead the effort. Business leaders respect hierarchy and success. So to get the right executive, the pastor can choose either a C-level (CEO, COO, CFO, etc.) executive, or the most successful entrepreneur in the congregation. Successful executives attract other successful business executives, who will respond to business opportunities with peers or superiors. Ideally, the business ministry executive will have the drawing power to attract affluent members, and the skills to create a community of interest, focused on the goal of creating opportunities for the financially distressed. If a pastor could attract a well-known and highly-influential business ministry leader, there probably would be little difficulty attracting affluent crowds and starting a number of entrepreneurial activities. This affluent community of interest would eventually operate as any small group ministry—sharing personal experiences, examining spiritual principles, and holding each other accountable.

The next act that the church leader needs to accomplish is to inventory the congregation in terms of financial interests, needs and abilities. This inventory will contain "haves" and "have-nots." Each of these groups has different ministry needs. The haves are already financially secure, so their needs should be more focused on spiritual rewards. The have-nots are not financially secure, and need earthly financial support.

Of the two groups, the haves will most likely be more difficult to recruit and retain. It would be safe to say that most of the successful people in a congregation downplay their resources, skills and connections. Regardless of the reason, these are the attributes that are needed to launch a vibrant business ministry. A strong business leader, along with a strong business ministry team, should be able to actively start and engage businesses, as well as attract sponsors, benefactors and perhaps endowments. Business ministries should attempt to attract retired and former executives and professionals who can be used to educate, train and start businesses.

Regarding the have-nots, church elders need to reach out to people who are reluctant to admit they are in, or are approaching financial crisis. It is much easier to help a person who is currently employed, as opposed to someone who has been unemployed for a long time. The adage of a "stitch in time, saves nine" applies. For the "have-nots," business ministry leaders should first establish strategic and business plans that contain realistic goals and actionable milestones, based on the needs and capabilities of their community and church. These plans and syllabi should be designed by experts, who often reside outside the church. A degree of separation and objectivity are useful, especially considering politics in some churches.

Poor churches often have the greatest need and are the most organized, but have the least access to resources of other churches. In an ideal environment, poor churches would partner with rich ones, and small churches with big ones. If a congregation is too small to generate mass, it should partner with similar churches to gain the appropriate mass and inertia. A network of churches provides an additional benefit of respectful anonymity to those facing financial distress.

For a business ministry to be successful for the have-nots, it has to create jobs and develop critical skills that lead to careers and professions, both of which are vastly superior to work, activity, or toil. It is as critical to keep people employed, as it is to rescue the unemployed. Layoffs can be as emotionally damaging as divorces and deaths. If the business ministry can avoid the trauma of a layoff, reconstructive work is less necessary.

Once a layoff occurs, it is critical to get the jobless engaged in meaningful activity to keep their skills from eroding, prevent loss of self-esteem, and to give them hope—a true spiritual value shared by church-goers and the secular alike. Recently, a New York City social worker stated that different business ministries are needed for those with hope and those without. She said that many of her regular visitors have become so dependent on the welfare system that they adjust their lifestyle to the level of handouts they can receive. Offering them jobs had little appeal. The longer a person is away from meaningful and fulfilling work, the quicker that person becomes a ward of the state. Substance abuse and crime often quickly follow.

There are a number of small group business ministries that can be started almost immediately for those who are at risk. These ministries include small focus groups for those at risk, and their family members; financial, debt, and credit rating services; employment counseling services and mentoring; social networking and job opportunity websites; outside support agencies, services and funding agencies; programs to identify and develop worker skills; and self-employment workshops. While all these efforts are meaningful, they fall short of providing needed jobs.

Jobs have to be delivered by the business ministries. Business ministry successes predominantly will be with service-providing, home-based, self-employed or micro businesses. Consequently, it is imperative that the business ministries:

- Develop communities-of-interest for business leaders and patrons.
- Create employment opportunities, including part-time jobs, self-employment services, consultancies, co-ops, franchises, business incubators, and start-up businesses.
- Create micro-financing programs to help small business start-ups.
- Create an endowment program to fund programs over the long-haul.
- Create a non-profit corporation to disperse these funds in the same way foundations do.
- Provide relocation services to move people to where the jobs are.
- Maximize the use of retired executives and professionals to coach and provide valuable management services for start-ups.
- Utilize experts who are familiar with government jobs programs.

Church technicians are a critical component in jobs creation. It is the techies who know how to maximize social networking systems, develop telecommuting centers, and enable home-based enterprises. Techies and geek-squads would be invaluable in creating low-overhead, church-based businesses to help the self-employed start and maintain home-based business or community cooperatives. If ¼ of the 327,000 churches in America offered a telecommuting capability, these churches would morph into business ministries and community centers, much in the same way as churches that offer pre-school and day-care centers. The majority of churches are largely empty during weekdays. Business ministries could help fill this empty space with meaningful activity for congregations and communities.

A number of national business ministries already exist, which can give churches a jump start. The ProVision Network (PVN)[288] is a sterling example. PVN is a ministry devoted to the concept that "we are all called to do something great but none of us can do it alone." PVN is about uniting those who support the vision of an ethical, successful, profitable business community. PVN communities currently exist in New York, New Jersey, Texas, Minnesota, California, Ohio, Kentucky and Florida.

PVN starts by inventorying individuals according to gifts, abilities and talents, so that a clearinghouse mechanism can be created, which matches opportunities with resources. PVN trains its members to be problem solvers, and forms teams that can bring a multitude of resources to bear on a variety of business projects. As a network of businesspeople, entrepreneurs, professionals, and companies of all levels, PVN is dedicated to establishing excellence and authority in the marketplace, impacting every sphere of influence by using their collective God-given talents and abilities. PVN also arranges micro-loans from area banks in an effort to supply capital to the base of the economic pyramid. The PVN Chapter in New York City is currently working with political, business and religious leaders to establish four community-based business incubators in Harlem, an area of the city especially hard hit by the recession and slow economy recovery.

In conclusion, this chapter discusses three potential initiatives to energize the private sector from three very different directions. Unleashed, the innovative and compassionate nature of the American people will devise hundreds of other ways to create jobs and help the financially distressed recover. This can only be done from the bottom up. Government has a major role to play, but the private sector has the responsibility. If the private sector continues to outsource this responsibility to government, our economic engine will stall, and the quality of life will lessen for all Americans.

---

288 ProVision Network (PVN), Dan Stratton, Founder, www.mypvn.org.

Chapter 23:
SIX IMPERATIVES FOR WASHINGTON

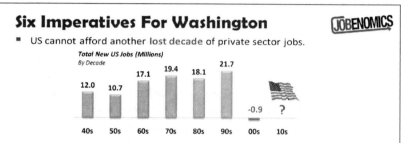

Six Imperatives For Washington ⦗JOBENOMICS⦘

- US cannot afford another lost decade of private sector jobs.

Total New US Jobs (Millions)
By Decade

40s: 12.0 | 50s: 10.7 | 60s: 17.1 | 70s: 19.4 | 80s: 18.1 | 90s: 21.7 | 00s: -0.9 | 10s: ?

- Six Washington imperatives based on **Jobenomics** and a **20 by 20** Champaign.
  1. Close the spending/receipts gap.
  2. Stop the blame-game and focus on job, wealth and revenue creation (i.e., jobenomics).
  3. Create a unified jobenomics vision and goal.
  4. Create a collaborative environment between government and business.
  5. Enable emerging enterprises, small businesses and the self-employed.
  6. Advance jobenomics via a number of bold **20 by 20** national, state, municipal and community-based initiatives and programs.

Create 20 million new private sector jobs by 2020 (*20 by 20*).

Figure 156: Chapter 23 Summary

The US cannot afford another lost decade of private sector jobs. A ***20 by 20*** campaign is necessary, regardless of how the economy recovers. If a robust V-shaped recovery happens, 20 million new jobs will make us even more prosperous. If the US economy hits a bump-in-the-road, a ***20 by 20*** campaign will help weaken downward economic forces.

To lay the framework for a ***20 by 20*** initiative, six necessary actions (imperatives) are needed from Washington. They include:

- Close the spending/receipts gap.
- Stop the blame-game and focus on job, wealth and revenue creation (i.e., jobenomics).

- Create a unified jobenomics vision and goal.
- Create a collaborative environment between government and business.
- Enable emerging enterprises, small businesses and the self-employed.
- Advance jobenomics via a number of bold **20 by 20** national, state, municipal and community-based initiatives and programs.

The first imperative for Washington is to close the spending/receipts gap.

The current spending/receipts gap is not sustainable. Challenges to closing the spending/receipts gap were discussed in Chapter 13. As discussed throughout this book, while cutting expenditures is vitally important, jobs creation is the only meaningful way to close the spending/receipts gap. Creating hundreds of thousands of new jobs is not enough. America needs to create 20 million new jobs by 2020 (**20 by 20**), not only to secure a stable economy, but to add to the tax revenue base to pay our bills.

Upward pressures on outlays far exceed the federal government's ability to cut spending. It seems that Washington is unable or unwilling to accept the seriousness of the $100T+ worth of US debt and obligations, out-of-control spending, and the potential of a no-growth recovery. Even the most ardent fiscal conservatives have not articulated a compelling case for considering W-, L-, or declining L-shaped economic scenarios. For some unapparent reason, the 20-year Japanese declining L experience, the fiscal crisis in Europe, and the economic problems in 48 out of the 50 US states are back-burner issues for US policymakers.

Mandatory spending is also out of control. Several hundred million Americans receive financial aid from the government. The Social Security Administration pays benefits to 56 million people annually.[289] 45 million are Medicare beneficiaries.[290] 100 million accept some form of safety net programs, from Medicaid (59 million[291]), to food stamps (35 million monthly[292]), to assistance to needy families (4 million[293]), to housing and rent subsidies, to mortgage assistance, to tax rebates, to free cash and cell phones. The total mandatory spending has reached the level of all tax revenue. To pay for the running of the government, Washington is borrowing, via the sale of Treasuries and printing money. By 2020 the national debt will be unaffordable, even if the economy recovers nicely.

After subtracting the total unemployed (U6 rate) and 22 million government workers, there are 106 million in the civilian labor force who have to support the 200 million Americans who are not in the labor force. If 10 million government contractors and federal postal workers are subtracted, that leaves 96 million private sector civilians who pay taxes. In other words, 25% of

289 Social Security Administration, Office of Retirement and Disability Policy, Fast Facts & Figures About Social Security, July 2009, Page 1, http://www.ssa.gov/policy/docs/chartbooks/fast_facts/2009/fast_facts09.pdf

290 The Henry J. Kaiser Family Foundation, statehealthfacts.org, Total Number of Medicare Beneficiaries, 2008, http://www.statehealthfacts.org/comparemaptable.jsp?typ=1&ind=290&cat=6&sub=74&sortc=1&o=a

291 The Henry J. Kaiser Family Foundation, statehealthfacts.org, Total Medicaid Enrollment, FY2006, http://www.statehealthfacts.org/comparemaptable.jsp?typ=1&ind=198&cat=4&sub=52&sortc=1&o=a

292 US Department of Agriculture, Food and Nutrition Service, Supplemental Nutrition Assistance Program (SNAP), 26 April 2010, http://www.fns.usda.gov/snap/

293 US Department of Health and Human Services, Administration for Children and Families, Temporary Assistance to Needy Families (TANF), Total Number of Recipients, FY 2009, 15 May 2010, http://www.acf.hhs.gov/programs/ofa/data-reports/caseload/2009/2009_recipient_tan.htm

our labor force works for the government, which is an unsustainable percentage, especially in a troubled economy.

Looking to the future, an aging population, low fertility rates, and anti-immigration policies will further increase the load on a deteriorating private sector workforce. If the US experiences a jobless recovery, the load on taxpayers will grow significantly as millions more join the ranks of the unemployed.

The bottom line is, if Washington can't cut expenses, it should focus on growing our way out of the spending/receipts gap. A minimum of 20 million new private sector (not government) jobs are needed to accommodate 130,000 new job seekers entering the workforce monthly, as well as to put back to work at least half of the 8.4 million Americans who lost jobs during the Great Recession. Cutting the spending/receipts gap has to be Washington's top priority. *20 by 20* would be an excellent initiative, if led by the President and supported by a bipartisan Congress.

The second imperative for Washington is to stop the blame-game and focus on the economics of job, wealth and revenue creation (i.e., jobenomics).

Only one out of four Americans approve of Congressional performance. Presidential approval rates have dropped 20% in the last year. 60% of Americans believe that the country is on the wrong track. These figures are not fictional. They are a composite[294] of respected pollsters like Gallop, Pew, Rasmussen, and a dozen other leading polling organizations. If the Washington blame-game were a reality TV show, it would have been pulled off the air by now.

The latest theme in the Washington blame-game is directed at Wall Street. While Wall Street has earned a significant blame, Washington is equally culpable. Wall Street generally does what it is supposed to do—make a profit. Excessive greed in Wall Street needs to be rectified and criminals punished. Likewise, Washington needs to do what it is supposed to do—represent the will of the people. Washington needs to set its own house in order. The viability of the US economy is the top concern of American people. Americans want enduring, value-added jobs that will, in turn, produce revenue to keep the country running.

As discussed in Chapter 14, Washington intervention and manipulation of the free enterprise system was the primary cause of the housing crisis. A government sponsored enterprise created the first derivates for the mortgage industry. The US federal government also has become the world's leading trader of securities in the secondary financial market. Half of the Fed's assets are in the form of mortgage-backed securities. 59% of the US national debt is in the form of marketable Treasuries securities. An infusion of $12T worth of Washington bailouts, buyouts, incentives and stimuli has distorted the financial system and stock markets.

Washington must stop the blame-game and accept the fact that it is a key participant in the problem. The blame-game leads to anger and bad decision-making. Micro-management, over-regulation, and increased intervention will hamper recovery. Political partisanship limits fiscal expediency, which is essential in a rapidly changing geo-economic environment.

---

294 Real Clear Politics, Poll Averages, 15 May 2010, http://www.realclearpolitics.com/polls/

Notwithstanding the fact that Washington's bank (the Fed), in association with the Treasury, has done a heroic job in preventing a second depression, Washington is over-involved in the free enterprise system. If Washington continues to preempt free enterprise, the economy will be subject to government bureaucrats and political expediency. Free enterprise is the engine for jobs and revenue creation. Washington is responsible for ensuring that this engine operates smoothly. Our economic engine works best on a level playing field, free of barriers and dangerous financial bubbles. Our economic engine works even better when Washington promotes US business and plays a key supporting role.

The third imperative for Washington involves creating a unified jobenomics vision and goal.

History may be the best place to secure the tenets of a common vision. Using the Preamble of the US Constitution as a baseline, government has the lead role in providing justice and security. In the realm of general welfare, the government's role is to promote. The private sector has the lead role in job, wealth and revenue creation. The more the government intervenes in the private sector, the more the nation stands to lose. The US government has to facilitate private sector pursuits by creating conditions where businesses can prosper.

Government intervention in business is hazardous for many reasons, which include:

- A poor track record.
- Little business experience.
- General disdain for business.
- Little accountability or responsibility in starting new businesses that create jobs.
- Orientation towards social welfare, as opposed to overall economic well-being.

Authoritarian governments, like China's, can create corporate states. America cannot. The American economy is based on free enterprise. Government intervention limits enterprise, and government manipulation distorts the economic process. While some intervention and manipulation is warranted, the Washington bureaucracy is currently way over the line. If there is any doubt, just look at the decline of the private sector labor force in relation to the population.

Moreover, a large percentage of Americans will revolt if the government continues on the path of increased intervention. The Tea Party Movement is a potential revolution that models itself after the original Boston Tea Party that rejected excessive British government control and taxation. While the notion of a revolution may be farfetched, paranoia about government control and taxation is not.

An equally large percentage of angry citizens exist within minority communities, especially the African-American community, whose gains have been wiped out by joblessness. According to BLS figures,[295] in August 2007, black unemployment was 7.7% compared to white unemployment of 4.2%—a 3.5% spread. By April 2010, the spread more than doubled to 7.3% (15.9% black versus 8.6% white). Among the 28 US metropolitan areas with the highest joblessness, 15 are located in California and 5 are in Michigan. Discontent is rising in these communities. It does not

---

295 BLS, Data Retrieval: Labor Force Statistics (CPS), Table A-2. Employment status of the civilian population by race, sex, and age, 31 May 2010, http://www.bls.gov/webapps/legacy/cpsatab2.htm

take a genius to see how this discontent will manifest itself. The South Los Angeles Watts Riots in 1965 and the 1992 Los Angeles Riots were products of discontent. In Detroit, Mayor Bing reports[296] that 55% of the children live in poverty and that the unemployment rate is around 30% (some reports indicate that the real unemployment rate in Detroit is as high as 50%). What is happening in Detroit could very well happen in other metropolitan areas.

From a *Jobenomics* perspective, the statistic that 3 out of 4 Detroit school children drop out of high school is completely understandable. Why should they graduate, if there are no jobs to be had? Crime and drug industries often provide a much higher value proposition for kids in severely depressed areas. The flip side is also true for more affluent kids in suburbia. Why should they incur a $200,000 bill for college, when there are six applicants for every job?

Debt and joblessness are the seeds of class warfare. These seeds are germinating. A jobless economic recovery will cause these malevolent seeds to blossom and spread like weeds. Angry minority movements are flourishing on the left. Angry tax payer movements have sprouted on the right. The US government is trying to allay discontent by spending lavishly on financial institutions on the right and welfare programs on the left. Spending might work if a V-shaped recovery occurs, and the private sector picks up the financial mantle—assuming that it will do so in the current anti-business environment. If a W- or L-shaped recovery happens, government money won't last, because need will exceed resources. Class warfare must be avoided. It is a no-win war. The only meaningful way to stop this potential war is through job, wealth and revenue creation. 20 million new private sector jobs by 2020 will provide hope for America. The first step is to establish a *20 by 20* vision—a vision of hope—that is endorsed by both the right and the left.

Jobs creation has now been declared Washington's number one objective. Jobs summits are being held. New national initiatives are being announced. Billions of dollars worth of new stimuli are being proposed for jobs initiatives, programs and incentives. Unfortunately, the path that Washington is pursing is tantamount to a ready-fire-aim approach. Taking proper aim first usually provides a better solution than firing for effect.

To take proper aim on economic well-being and jobs creation, the US government needs to focus on the jobs creation engine. That engine is business—big businesses, small businesses and the self-employed. The role of government is to promote, enable and assist business, especially business owners and employers. Business leaders need to be in the driver's seat. Today, Washington bureaucrats are driving business policy, with little input from the business sector. Washington's closed-door approach to the new healthcare system is one example. The absence of business executives in policymaking positions is another example.

In President Reagan's inaugural address, he stated, "in this present crisis, government is not the solution to our problems; government is the problem." The same is true today. The government can set the overall direction, but it is up to the private sector to execute. Reagan understood this principle and set a course to cut tax rates to spur investment to increase economic

296 The Detroit News, Bing expects Detroit population to drop below 850,000, by David Shepardson / Detroit News Washington Bureau, 16 May 2010, http://detnews.com/article/20100518/METRO01/5180421/Bing-expects-Detroit-population-to-drop-below-850-000

growth, jobs and wages. Critics quickly labeled Reaganomics "trickle-down economics" due to a belief that it benefited the wealthy more than the poor. Notwithstanding, the wealthy are more effective at creating jobs than the poor.

If Washington is serious about jobs creation, it needs to create and promote a common vision and goal. Jobenomics suggests that the *20 by 20* campaign is the place to start. Whatever Washington decides to promote must be done with vigor and commitment. A jobs campaign has to be job number one—not one of many.

The fourth imperative for Washington is to establish a collaborative environment between government and business, focused on jobenomics and a *20 by 20* campaign.

20 by 20 is an ambitious but achievable goal, considering that Americans generated this amount of jobs in the recent past. However, business has to be in charge. They have the talent and resources to create jobs. The more the government postures, pontificates, threatens, blames, regulates and taxes, the more reserved business leaders will become. Washington needs to create an environment that encourages business leaders to take more risk, commit to recapitalization, increase hiring and start new businesses.

To achieve *20 by 20*, government needs to balance the needs of the employed with those of the unemployed. Economic recovery will depend more on jobs created, as opposed to jobs lost.

Today, government is hard-wired to the plight of the unemployed. Given past prosperity, it was natural for the government to focus on social safety nets. Today, America does not have the financial wherewithal that we had a few years ago. To avoid economic collapse in 2008, the US government (both the Bush and Obama Administrations) made an $11.6T all-in wager to save the financial system. While there are signs that this wager is working, our ability to mitigate another financial crisis is severely weakened. If a V-shaped recovery happens and stability returns, we can relax. Until then, there is virtue in pessimism. Adversity, like necessity, can cause a society to reinvent itself. Jobenomics is all about reinvention.

As addressed in Chapter 1 (US Employment), Washington sets the tone for the country. The tone has been largely anti-business and ambivalent towards the employment side of the equation. Government has a huge role to play in motivating, strategic planning, national-level initiatives, goal-setting, reporting, awareness, research and development, oversight, and taxation. These activities require more Washington mentorship than money. *20 by 20* can be achieved by effective Washington leadership in collaboration with business.

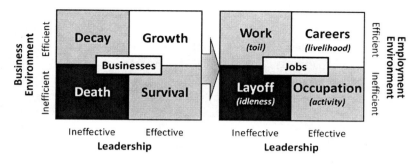

Figure 157: Jobenomics Creation Matrix

As shown in Figure 157, the business environment is directly linked to the employment environment. Ineffective leadership in an inefficient environment produces business death and layoffs. In contrast, effective leadership in an efficient environment produces business growth and careers. Jobenomics focuses on creating careers (livelihood), over occupation (activity), which is superior to work (toil).

If a W- or L-shaped recovery happens, Washington may have to choose between neediness and effectiveness. Neediness concentrates on welfare. Effectiveness targets enduring and value-added jobs. Investing in neediness is short-term oriented, but gets more votes. Effective investment is long-term oriented, and generates more jobs.

Washington's focus is on the very top and very bottom of the socio-economic pyramid, as shown in Figure 158. Government support to large established businesses may have been necessary during the economic crisis, but now they should be able to support themselves. Government support for welfare and temporary work programs continues to be necessary, but does not produce long-term jobs. In order to create the number of jobs needed for a stable recovery, government focus needs to shift to emerging enterprises, small businesses and the self-employed.

Establishing a collaborative environment with the small business community will be difficult for US federal government officials, who feel more comfortable with peer-to-peer relationships, like the CEOs of major corporations. It is easier to have a relationship with the CEO of a billion-dollar corporation, as opposed to 1,000 Presidents of million-dollar companies. It would ideal if the US private sector could create another mega-corporation like General Motors or Microsoft, but it is not likely in the near-term. However, creation of several million emerging enterprises, small businesses and self-employed companies are well within potential in the near-term, given the creativity of the American people empowered by 21st century technology.

The fifth recommendation for Washington is to enable explosive growth in emerging enterprises, small businesses and the self-employed to achieve a *20 by 20* goal.

In order to narrow the US federal spending/receipts gap, which is not sustainable, business vitality is paramount. Given the choice between big business and small business, US government support should be given to small business. To a large extent, the US government is indifferent to small business, emerging enterprises and the self-employed, due to the amorphous nature of this sector that represents 99.7% of all employer firms, and generated 64% of net new jobs over the last 15 years.

Small business employs the vast majority of Americans and is the heart of America's economic engine. Small business productivity is indispensable to recovery and prosperity. Productivity leads to higher employment and profitability, which in turn supports the tax base. The opposite is also true. Unhealthy small businesses reduce productivity, employment and tax revenue. When small businesses fail, the employed join the ranks of the unemployed which increases welfare spending. Greater Washington support for small business has appeal to both the American public and the business community. In addition, small business vitality is common political ground for liberals and conservatives alike.

The Obama Administration is considering a Jobs Stimulus Package (Stimulus III), which is a step in the right direction. On 11 February 2010, the Senate Finance Committee released the first draft of their version of the Jobs Stimulus Package, which is titled, Hiring Incentives to Restore Employment (HIRE) Act. As currently proposed by the Senate, the HIRE Act has more to do with government programs and welfare as opposed to jobs creation. Figure 158 shows the major sections of the HIRE Act. The arrows reflect the opinion of *Jobenomics*, based on the draft legislation that can be found on the US Senate's website.[297] Based on Congressional language, the HIRE Act would cost $125B over ten years, with offsets of approximately $50B for a total availability of $75B, of which only a very small portion would directly benefit small business. To a large extent, the HIRE Act was dead on arrival, even though its sponsors (Chairman Max Baucus, D-Montana, and the Finance Committee's top Republican Chuck Grassley, R-Iowa) were senior members of their parties. The problem is that the bill had little chance to produce meaningful, long-lasting, self-replicating jobs. Government programs and social welfare handouts do not produce the types of jobs that regenerate, multiply and forge businesses.

Hiring Incentives to Restore Employment (HIRE) Act				
	Draft 11 Feb 10	Jobs Creation	Social Welfare	Gov't Program
Title I	Incentives for Hiring and Retraining Unemployed Workers	↗	↗	
Title II	Expensing (of certain depreciable business assets)	↑		
Title III	Qualified Tax Credit Bonds			↑
Title IV	Extension of Current Surface Transportation Programs			↑
Title V	Extension of Current Expiring Programs (energy, education, low income housing, business tax relief, dissaster relief)	↗	↑	↗
Title VI	Unemployment Insurance, Health and Other Provisions		↑	
Title VII	Pension Fund Relief		↑	
Title VIII	Offset Programs			↑

Figure 158: Draft US Senate Finance Committee's HIRE Act, February 2010

---

297 US Senate Committee on Finance, Draft Hiring Incentives to Restore Employment (HIRE) Act, 11 February 2010, http://www.finance.senate.gov/sitepages/legislation.htm

To gain bipartisan support, a miniature version was offered that proposed the elimination of 6.2% FICA (Social Security) taxes for the remainder of 2010 on all new hires who have been out of work for 60 days, and a $1,000 business tax credit for each new worker who stays on the job for at least a year. On 18 March 2010, the President signed the bill into law for a total of $17.6B, a fraction of the original amount. In the end, this bill will probably amount to no new jobs, since the $1,000 tax credit will not come close to offsetting the costs of hiring a new employee.

These types of jobs bills are so trivial that they are almost not worth mentioning. More troubling is the small-mindedness of the legislators who endorse such legislation. The argument that something is better than nothing is vacuous. It is like giving aspirin to a cancer patient. However, to be fair, jobs creation deliberations are just starting in Washington. It is a step, albeit a baby-step.

The typical Washington approach will not work. First, the idea of "stimulating" is inappropriate. To stimulate means to arouse, activate or start. The business community does not need stimulation. It needs the wherewithal to regenerate and revitalize communities and industries. Regeneration is paramount. Jobs that are scalable and repeatable create thousands of direct and indirect opportunities. Business owners will not be incentivized by $3,000 carrots. They will invest their own money and hire heavily, if they can see a way to successfully conduct a profitable business with reasonably steady cash flows.

Generally speaking, businesses do not want to hire the unemployed. Businesses prefer proven personnel with a strong track record. Regardless of the reason, unemployment creates a blank spot on a person's résumé that begs questioning. If the government were really concerned about unemployment, they would launch programs to keep the currently employed from becoming unemployed, and programs for employers to grow their businesses to generate increased hiring. The four most critical skills that employers seek from new employees include professionalism/ work ethic, oral/written communications, teamwork/collaboration, and critical thinking/ problem solving.[298] The longer a person is unemployed, the more these critical skills are brought into question.

For some reason, government is reluctant to rely on the innovation and ingenuity of the private sector, especially emerging businesses, small businesses and the self-employed. Small business has proven that it has the "right stuff" to generate jobs. Washington, however, is reluctant to invest time, energy and money on this amorphous business sector.

The sixth recommendation for Washington is to advance jobenomics via a number of bold *20 by 20* national, state, municipal and community-based initiatives and programs.

President Roosevelt advanced bold initiatives during the Great Depression. President Eisenhower started a massive infrastructure development effort that created the interstate freeway

---

298 The Conference Board, Corporate Voices for Working Families, the Partnership for 21st Century Skills, and the Society for Human Resource Management Study, "Are They Really Ready To Work?, Employers' Perspectives On The Basic Knowledge And Applied Skills Of New Entrants To The 21st Century US Workforce," http://www.conference-board.org/pdf_free/BED-06-workforce.pdf

system. President Kennedy created the impetus to put a man on the moon. President Obama has the oratory skills to promote *20 by 20*, and the expertise to organize communities.

The best way to organize communities is to get them to buy into and get involved in national initiatives that will better their lives, or protect their futures. The *20 by 20* national initiative should contain both proactive and reactive elements. The proactive element of *20 by 20* would develop and implement a Jobs Creation Plan across a number of business sectors. The reactive element of *20 by 20* would develop an Austerity Contingency Plan that would only be implemented as a hedge against W- or L-shaped scenarios. The Jobs Creation Plan would involve wide public participation. The Austerity Contingency Plan would be more discrete and involve a bipartisan commission. If properly executed, the *20 by 20* national initiative could generate public enthusiasm and bipartisan participation, as well as preparing America for unwanted or unanticipated events and crises. The two plans should be synergistic with trigger points for initiating actions and pursuing actionable milestones. The Austerity Contingency Plan would be oriented to mitigating downsides, while the *20 by 20* Jobs Creation Plan would engage in maximizing jobs.

Chapter 24:
THE AUSTERITY CONTINGENCY PLAN

Austerity Contingency Plan

- The Austerity Contingency Plan would be a hedge against W- or L- scenarios with triggers for major actions or reductions.

- A number of European nations have already implemented austerity plans due to economic demise and the possibility of defaulting on sovereign (national) debts.

- The Austerity Contingency Plan would prepare firm limits (cuts) on national debt, entitlements, national security, government growth, as well as significantly increasing taxes if conditions warrant.

20 by 20 and the austerity plan should be synergistic.

Figure 159: Chapter 24 Summary

The Austerity Contingency Plan would be a hedge against W- or L- scenarios with triggers for major actions or reductions. Consequently, it would prepare strict limits (cuts) on national debt, entitlements, national security, and government growth, as well as significantly increasing taxes, if conditions warrant. A number of European nations have already implemented austerity plans, due to economic demise and the possibility of defaulting on sovereign (national) debts.

The time for such a plan is now, while we still have time. According to Ben Bernanke,[299]

---

299 Ben S. Bernanke, Chairman Federal Reserve System, Speech at the National Commission on Fiscal Responsibility and Reform, Washington, D.C., 27 April 2010, http://www.federalreserve.gov/newsevents/speech/bernanke20100427a.htm

"Neither experience nor economic theory clearly indicates the threshold at which government debt begins to endanger prosperity and economic stability. But given the significant costs and risks associated with a rapidly rising federal debt, **our nation should soon put in place a credible plan** for reducing deficits to sustainable levels over time. Doing so earlier rather than later will not only help maintain the US government's credibility in financial markets, thereby holding down interest costs, but it will also ultimately prove less disruptive by avoiding abrupt shifts in policy and by giving those affected by budget changes more time to adapt. The Administration is already beginning to lean in this direction." (*Emphasis added*)

President Obama's Executive Order[300] creating the National Commission on Fiscal Responsibility and Reform would be an ideal bipartisan commission for developing an Austerity Contingency Plan. Their mission already directs the Commission to balance the budget by 2015. As stated in the Executive Order,

"The Commission is charged with identifying policies to improve the fiscal situation in the medium term and to achieve fiscal sustainability over the long run. Specifically, the Commission shall propose recommendations designed to **balance the budget**, excluding interest payments on the debt, by 2015. This result is projected to **stabilize the debt-to-GDP ratio** at an acceptable level once the economy recovers. The magnitude and timing of the policy measures necessary to achieve this goal are subject to considerable uncertainty and will depend on the evolution of the economy. In addition, the Commission shall propose recommendations that meaningfully improve the long-run fiscal outlook, including changes to **address the growth of entitlement spending and the gap between the projected revenues and expenditures** of the Federal Government." (*Emphasis added*)

Hopefully, this commission will be able to get traction, unlike the stalled Congressional commission that was established in July 2009 to investigate the causes of the financial crisis. The Financial Crisis Inquiry Commission,[301] comprised of six Democrat and four Republican commissioners, was supposed to produce, by December 2010, a report modeled after the best-selling 9/11 Commission report. Due to the complexity of the task, resignations, disagreements, and general lack of resources, it appears unlikely that this commission will have much policy impact. It would be wise for President Obama's National Commission on Fiscal Responsibility and Reform to avoid such pitfalls.

The Austerity Contingency Plan may not be politically popular, but would be politically responsible. Americans are keenly aware of the downside of potential events and crises. Hundreds of newspapers, media outlets, internet blogs, and surveys analyze and report daily on international crises and potential worst case economic scenarios. A major theme of *Jobenomics* is preparing for the worst, while planning for the best. Cautious optimism must be balanced with constructive pessimism.

---

300 The White House, Executive Order--National Commission on Fiscal Responsibility and Reform, 18 February 2010, http://www.whitehouse.gov/the-press-office/executive-order-national-commission-fiscal-responsibility-and-reform

301 Financial Crisis Inquiry Commission, http://fcic.gov/

The Austerity Contingency Plan would be based on the premise that pessimism can be a virtue, if it anticipates and eliminates potential problems. A balanced optimistic/pessimistic approach would give Americans a better sense that their government is under control, regardless of circumstance. Any good game plan is comprised of offensive and defensive strategies. The key to success is being able to rapidly respond to changing conditions. The Austerity Contingency Plan would also absorb critics and naysayers whose concerns would be addressed in the plan. Involvement of the critics would be essential in the development of the plan.

Jobenomics addresses many of the potential downsides that could be included in the Austerity Contingency Plan. Therefore only a brief outline of critical areas is offered here. In order of priority, these areas include unemployment, national debt, entitlements, national security, government growth, taxes, and mobility.

Austerity Contingency Plan: Unemployment. Unemployment is a critical issue, but is less critical than the inverse—employment. Unemployment emphasizes welfare. Employment emphasizes jobs creation. By emphasizing unemployment over employment, the US government is in a reactive mode, rather than a proactive mode. Unemployment is a symptom. The lack of productive job opportunities is the disease. The Austerity Contingency Plan needs to include a cost/benefit analysis, weighing the costs of social safety nets versus jobs creation. If the economy does not recover as planned, only essential welfare services may be provided to the unemployed, in exchange for economic growth opportunities for businesses that generate the greatest potential employment opportunities. Today, America has the resources to do both. Tomorrow, our debts force us to choose between the healthy parts of our economy, and the sick.

Austerity Contingency Plan: National debt. The US is now the largest debtor nation in history. While other nations have a larger debt-to-GDP ratio, US debt is dangerously high, and is adding an incredible burden to future generations. By 2020, the interest on the national debt is projected to approach $1T/year—money that could be used productively elsewhere. Consequently, the Austerity Contingency Plan needs to recommend strict and unpopular solutions to narrowing the spending/receipts gap.

Austerity Contingency Plan: Entitlements. By 2011, mandatory entitlement programs (Social Security, Medicare, Medicaid and other mandatory programs) will equal 81% of the total projected receipts taken in by the federal government. If federal tax revenues experience no growth, like they have over the last three years, the cost of entitlements will equal revenues. If this situation is allowed to persist, it will lead to significantly higher national debt or economic collapse. Consequently, the Austerity Contingency Plan needs to set strict limits on entitlements as a percent of GDP.

A number of European austerity plans have recently increased retirement ages. Depending on economic conditions, increased retirement ages may not be enough. If the US Social Security age were raised to 70, and the Medicare age to 67, less than $10B would be saved yearly. The US government could consider amending the law to move entitlements from mandatory to appropriated entitlements. Entitlements, like Medicare Part D (Drugs), could be moved into a discretionary spending account that is indexed to inflation, national debt, and/or GDP.

Austerity Contingency Plan: National security. National security is the largest discretionary account, which currently is 38% of projected 2010 receipts. If the US experiences no-growth revenues, national security will be the likely target for large reductions, since discretionary accounts will receive more scrutiny than mandatory accounts.

The Austerity Contingency Plan would contain provisions for an orderly reorganization of the national security apparatus to obtain maximum security within the constraints of available funding. Without such a plan, in a no-revenue growth environment, the Defense Department will eventually be whittled away, piece by piece, into a hollow and ineffective force. *Jobenomics* believes that most generals and admirals would choose a major national security overhaul, rather than being nickel-and-dimed to death.

Time may be right to consider reorganization from the Department of Defense (DoD) to the Department of National Security (DoNS), via a new national security act in the vein of the National Security Act of 1947. In response to the defeat of fascism and the ascendancy of communism in WWII, the US National Security Act of 1947 significantly realigned and reorganized the armed forces, foreign policy, and intelligence community apparatus.

The National Security Act of 1947 provided a comprehensive program for the future security of the US, and consolidated the Department of War and Department of the Navy into an integrated national security establishment. It created the Department of Defense under the direction, authority, and control of the Secretary of Defense. It also created civilian agencies including the Department of the Treasury, Department of Energy, Coast Guard, Central Intelligence Agency, Federal Bureau of Investigation, National Security Agency, National Security Council, National Reconnaissance Office, Defense Intelligence Agency, and the intelligence elements of the Army, the Navy, the Air Force, and the Marine Corps.

If an austere economic future unfolds, a new national security apparatus may need to be reorganized from a top-down, strategy-driven approach, which better addresses transnational threats that are no longer bound by the traditional lines separating national security, domestic (homeland) security, economic security, cyber security and physical (infrastructure, event and personal) security organizations.

Even with the recent addition of the Department of Homeland Security and Director of National Intelligence, the US national security apparatus still functions largely as it did in the Cold War era. An Austerity Contingency Plan could contain the policy and legislative structure for a National Security Act of 2012 that would be enacted if and when conditions warrant.

Austerity Contingency Plan: Government growth. Government civilian employees (federal, state and local) have grown from 16.2 million in 1979 to a projected 24.2 million in 2018, a growth rate of 49%. According to the White House 2010 budget documents,[302] in 2009, there were 4.4 million federal employees (not including the uniformed Armed Forces) with an annual compensation and benefits of $422B, which equates to $97,580 per person. Subtracting benefits, the average federal worker makes approximately $71,000 per year, compared to $40,000 in the private sector.

---

302 Budget of the US Government, Fiscal Year 2010, Dimensions of the Budget, Pages 368/369, http://www. whitehouse.gov/omb/budget/fy2010/assets/dimensions.pdf

Today, there are approximately 35 million Americans who work for the US government including government civilians, armed forces, government contractors, and postal workers, as compared to approximately 96 million in the private sector workforce. A 1 to 3 ratio is simply unsustainable in an environment where the private sector workforce is decreasing at 13% per decade.

The Austerity Contingency Plan would bring the size and costs of government personnel more in-line with the private sector. State and municipal government personnel are already implementing austerity programs due to declining revenues. If the federal government had not given $140B to the states and municipalities via the American Recovery and Reinvestment Act of 2009, they would have to reduce staffs and services significantly more. It is unlikely that the federal government can continue such largess in the current high debt environment.

The Austerity Contingency Plan would also consider impacts from failing states and other financial crises. The Gross State Product of California is about $1.8T, which is equivalent to the combined GDPs of Spain and Greece. European Union officials fear that economic failures in Greece and Spain could collapse the entire economy of the Eurozone. California's budget crisis could have the same effect on the US. In 2009, California had a $60B budget shortfall and had to reduce state services by approximately 25%. According to Governor Schwarzenegger's 2010-2011 budget,[303]

> "My budget calls for even greater reductions in nearly every aspect of state government than were necessary in 2009....My budget proposal also calls for a far greater engagement than ever before with our counterparts in Washington."

In 2009, the ARRA awarded California over $21B, which significantly helped California avoid a fiscal crisis. Unfortunately, the future still looks bleak for the state that projects an annual $20B deficit in 2010, and beyond.

At some point, the US federal government may no longer be able to provide financial assistance to the states. The Austerity Contingency Plan would plan for the ramifications of insolvency of a number of states and municipalities.

Austerity Contingency Plan: Taxes. Increased taxes are a reality, even if the economy recovers. The US government (federal, state and local) cannot continue to operate in the red without increased taxes.

Without *20 by 20*, taxes will increase significantly for not only the rich, but for the middle class. From 1936 until 1980, the top income tax bracket stayed above the 70% level. Given today's debt crisis and high unemployment, tax rates for the wealthiest Americans could rise significantly from the current level of 35%. The Tax Foundation study[304] finds federal income tax rates would have to roughly triple in order to close the nation's staggering budget deficit in 2010. The Social Security Board of Trustees and the Federal Reserve Board essentially say the same.

---

303 California's Governor's Budget 2010-2011, Governor's Message, http://govbud.dof.ca.gov/pdf/BudgetSummary/GovernorsMessage.pdf
304 Op cit. 142.

Everyone knows that the rich bear the biggest tax burden, but most are unaware of the growing gap between taxpayers and tax consumers. Economists at the Tax Foundation estimate that the top-earning 40% of families will transfer close to $1T to the bottom-earning 60% in 2012. Families earning less than $86,000 will receive more in federal spending than they pay in federal taxes. It is estimated that the bottom 50% of US taxpayers pay no income tax at all. 50% is a seminal number. It means that tax consumers now have the voting power to transfer as much wealth from the rich as their Congressional representatives will concede.

The other endangered taxpayer species is the employer. In 2008, employment taxes were approaching $877B. This tax burden is particularly onerous on small businesses.

Today, the debate in Washington is largely about increased taxes on the rich versus broad-based tax cuts to stimulate business growth. Both arguments have their basis, but fall short in providing a comprehensive solution if the economy falters. Expiring Bush tax cuts, Alternative Minimum Tax exemptions, and ARRA provisioning may not produce enough tax revenue to cover spending shortfalls. Consequently, new forms of direct and indirect taxes will have to be enacted by federal, state and municipal governments to keep running. *Jobenomics* has little doubt that a national sales tax (VAT—value added tax) eventually will have to be established, if a slow growth economic recovery ensues.

The Austerity Contingency Plan would attempt to balance significant tax increases for the rich, moderate tax increases for the middle class, and targeted tax increases for business. It would also evaluate the consequences of increased FICA taxes, state and local taxes, hidden taxes, national sales tax, and the silent tax—inflation.

Austerity Contingency Plan: Mobility. The American work force is unique in its mobility and adaptability. One-fifth of the US work force voluntarily switches jobs every year, many to different cities in different states. Crises and disasters involuntarily move masses of people, like Hurricane Katrina did. The Austerity Contingency Plan would attempt to help federal, state and local governments facilitate movement from depressed to growing areas. Rather than investing in depressed areas, where people are often trapped in a downward economic spiral, the Austerity Contingency Plan could open doors to better opportunity. The Department of Defense facilitates social mobility by recruiting heavily in depressed municipalities. In many ways, the US military functions as a jobs training and relocation service.

In the private sector, movement of large numbers of employees helps downsize organizations that are often resistant to change. The federal government can take a similar approach by establishing public works, healthcare, and international development initiatives, with the goal of breaking the cycle of welfare dependence in economically depressed areas. These initiatives would likely cost less than traditional welfare programs. In addition, they would provide skills and a sense of accomplishment for those suffering the pain of American poverty.

The Austerity Contingency Plan should consider the potential of mass movement. One extreme hypothetical example could involve moving the Pentagon to a city like Detroit. The Pentagon houses 25,000 personnel and employs several hundred thousand contractors in the

Washington metropolitan area. Moving a significant percentage of Pentagon personnel to Detroit would downsize the US military's overhead and provide a vital injection of talent and money into a slowly dying city. Virginia's Fairfax and Arlington counties would suffer economically, but would have a much better chance of recovering than Detroit, since Fairfax and Arlington are two of the wealthiest counties in America with access to numerous other government and corporate opportunities. Movement of government agencies to other cities would have the side benefit of breaking up the Washington bureaucracy, which is highly resistant to change.

Jobenomics is confident that if **20 by 20** is successful, an Austerity Contingency Plan would never have to be implemented. However, there are too many potential malevolent events that could reverse our nascent recovery. Some international events, like a nuclear exchange between Iran and Israel, or an EU meltdown, could be catastrophic to the global economy. Some domestic events, like a second residential real estate crisis, or a sustained investor panic in US stock markets, would cause severe damage to the US economy. If any of these possibilities occur, an Austerity Contingency Plan would be very useful in managing downward economic forces in a rational way.

The major points for Section 5: The Way Ahead: Jobs Creation (Chapters 21 through 24) include:

- After sixty years of economic growth in America, jobs creation has stopped. The American economic engine lost almost a million private sector jobs in the last decade, compared to gains of approximately 20 million new jobs in recent decades.

- Looking to the future, the US government can close the spending/receipts gap by being the key player in a national campaign to generate 20 million new jobs by 2020 (*20 by 20*)—the average number of jobs created during each of the last three decades, and the number of jobs required to accommodate new workers and rehire half of those unemployed by the Great Recession.

- *20 by 20* jobs categories would include government, small business, large business, international corporations and investors, and a collection of businesses and enterprises engaged in the energy technology revolution (ETR) initiative.

- In case economic or other crises interrupt *20 by 20*, an Austerity Contingency Plan is needed. A number of European countries are already implementing such plans.

- An Austerity Contingency Plan would be a hedge against W- or L- scenarios, with triggers for major actions or reductions. Consequently, it would prepare firm limits (cuts) on national debt, entitlements, national security, and government growth, as well as significantly increasing taxes, if conditions warrant.

- Ultimately the success or failure of America is in the hands of the private sector. There are many things that the private sector can do to achieve *20 by 20*. This has to be a bottom-up process—one led from the private sector but with support from government at all levels: federal, state and local. Given a place to start, the American private sector will reinvent itself.

Figure 160: Section 5: The Way Ahead: Jobs Creation Main Points

CONCLUSION

Conclusions

- The tyranny of hundreds of trillions of dollars worth of US debt and obligations will dominate the American way of life for generations.

- This dangerous amount of debt cannot be adequately planned for in current economic models.

  - We are in uncharted territory.

  - V-, W-, or L-shaped recovery scenarios are all possible.

  - All portend to offer long periods of joblessness.

- National debate must focus on the larger issue of getting our economic house in order. Priority must be placed on business health and employment with emphasis on small and self-employed businesses

- A national **20 by 20** Initiative is needed to rally Americans in an unprecedented jobs creation effort focused on enduring and high value jobs.

- A new vision for debt reduction and job creation is needed.

Women-owned business growth is essential to economic recovery.

Figure 161: Conclusion

Planning for the future is more about judgment, intuition and psychology than numbers. Economists and policymakers did not see the 2008 real estate bubble and its subsequent burst. The numbers said this burst was not possible. The advent and use of derivatives were supposed to spread risk. Credit securitization and government underwriting further reduced risk. Not only were they wrong about the numbers, the fundamental philosophy about private sector financial self-governance was a monumental mistake. Unintended consequences of government intervention and manipulation of the private sector were also unforeseen. The Great Recession nearly toppled the US financial system. For a while, many wondered if the US economic crisis heralded the death knell for a debt-ridden, politically-gridlocked, over-consuming, and under-producing American empire. Fortunately, this did not happen. After an extraordinary government effort, the

US economic system was rescued from the economic abyss, and a second Great Depression was avoided. However, the rest of the story is still unfolding. Our future is uncertain.

In the words of Chairman Bernanke,[305] the viceroy of the US financial system, to whom much respect is owed,

> "Today the financial crisis looks to be mostly behind us, and the economy seems to have stabilized and is beginning to grow again. But we are far from being out of the woods. Many Americans are still grappling with unemployment or foreclosure, or both. Cities and states are struggling to maintain essential services. And, although much of the financial system is functioning more or less normally, bank lending remains very weak, threatening the ability of small businesses to finance expansion and new hiring."

Chairman Bernanke believes that economic growth, stimulated by low interest rates, will be sufficient to slowly reduce unemployment over the coming year. With deference to the Chairman, this will not happen for four reasons.

First, the US has gone a decade without generating a net gain in private sector jobs during a vibrant economy with a velocity of money. Why would employment grow in a stagnant economy, with a low velocity of money that has failed to grow significantly, even with the short-term interest rate around zero? Moreover, a decade of zero growth is indicative of a structural problem, especially after six decades of continual growth. The argument that the 2000s began and ended in recession does not wash. The US has had multiple economic shocks in previous decades and still grew.

Second, American culture and politics have become anti-business at worst, or laissez-faire at best. Consequently, business executives have become more risk averse and less willing to build enterprises that may not provide sufficient returns due to an increasingly regulated, taxed and social welfare environment. More and more businesses are viewed as tax generators for social programs, rather than profit centers for those who produce value-added goods and services.

Third, too many are paying for too few. As shown in Figure 162, 96 million working Americans cannot carry 203 non-working Americans, many of whom are on the government dole. Future national trends, like growing debt, deficits, government, entitlements, and welfare cannot be supported by a dwindling private sector workforce.

---

305 Board of Governors of the Federal Reserve System, Chairman Ben S. Bernanke Speech, At the Dallas Regional Chamber, Dallas, Texas, 7 April 2010, "Economic Challenges: Past, Present, and Future," http://www.federalreserve.gov/newsevents/speech/20100407a.htm

(Ms)	Category
96	Civilian Work Force *(excluding 10M government contractors)*
203	Not Working, Retired, Government, Welfare

(Ms)	On The Government Payroll	Source
51	Receive Social Security payments	SSA
45	Medicare beneficiaries	SSA
59	Receive some form of Medicade	Kaiser Foundation
37	Fall below the poverty level	Census Bureau
35	Fed by food stamps (monthly)	USDA
35	Work for the government	BLS
32	Newly added to the healthcare roles	New Legislation
26	Unemployed (U6 rate)	BLS

Figure 162: Too Many Are Paying For Too Few

Fourth, the potential for a jobless recovery is disturbingly real. As shown in Figure 163, two out the last three recoveries from previous recessions (the 1991 Recession that ended in April 1991, and the 2001 Recession that ended in November 2001) did not recover to their previous low U3 unemployment rates, even three years after the end of their recession. Only the 1982 Recession recovered rapidly, within a year, to an unemployment rate lower than the year prior to the end of the recession. The current nascent recovery is staying at the 10% U3 rate, and may go higher for the reasons stated throughout this book.

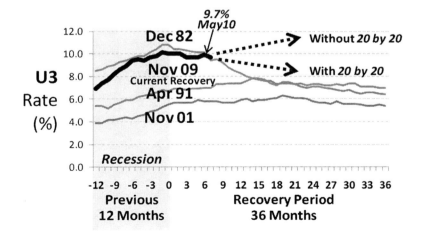

Figure 163: Potential Jobless Recovery[306]

306 Bureau of Labor Statistics, Unemployment Rate, Historical Data, 7 May 2010, http://www.bls.gov/

While higher U3 rates are disconcerting, unemployment is not our chief concern. Employment is the issue. If we do not increase employment, unemployment will continue to grow. The reverse is not true. In the same way that debt begets more debt, unemployment begets more unemployment. Only employment begets employment. That is why **20 by 20** is so critical. The theory behind jobenomics is that jobs create wealth, which generates more tax revenue to run the country.

The bottom line is that the lost decade, coupled with lost motivation, is likely to produce zero jobs growth in the 2010s. Even the most optimistic V-shape economists and policymakers, like the President, are not predicting unemployment rates to return to normal until the 2015 timeframe. So, should Americans resign themselves to an era of joblessness? Absolutely not.

20 million jobs by 2020 is a realistic goal, if American leaders get behind the concept and generate public support for such an initiative.

Jobenomics provides a potential structure for such an initiative, as well as a framework for developing an austerity plan in the event that unwanted or unanticipated crises interfere with the jobs creation process.

Americans will respond to a vision, but not to rhetoric. **20 by 20** bumper stickers will not get the job done. Political leaders will have to prioritize their time and efforts on jobs creation with the same unity and intensity that they did averting financial collapse. More importantly, business champions will need to emerge from the private sector to create the next generation of jobs that will be different from those in the past. Why different? Because, times have changed, we are different, and the world is evolving.

ABOUT THE AUTHOR

Chuck Vollmer is the founder and President of Jobenomics LLC, a company dedicated to developing a national call-to-action campaign to create 20 million new US private sector jobs by 2020. Chuck is also the founder and President of VII Inc., an international strategic planning, systems engineering and investment capital firm specializing in emerging government and business initiatives. Prior to VII, he was an executive in a leading US consulting firm, an executive in the world's second largest aerospace firm, as well as a highly decorated fighter pilot. Over his career, Chuck has started hundreds of new businesses from major multi-billion dollar organizations to small businesses.

9 780984 617005